EVIL IN
AFRICA

EVIL IN AFRICA

ENCOUNTERS WITH THE EVERDAY

EDITED BY
WILLIAM C. OLSEN
& WALTER E. A. VAN BEEK

FOREWORD BY
DAVID PARKIN

INDIANA UNIVERSITY PRESS

Bloomington and Indianapolis

This book is a publication of

INDIANA UNIVERSITY PRESS
Office of Scholarly Publishing
Herman B Wells Library 350
1320 East 10th Street
Bloomington, Indiana 47405 USA

iupress.indiana.edu

Manufactured in the United States of America

Library of Congress Cataloging-in-Publication Data

Evil in Africa : encounters with the everyday / edited by William C.
Olsen and Walter E. A. van Beek ; foreword by David Parkin.
    pages cm
  Includes bibliographical references and index.
  ISBN 978-0-253-01743-7 (cloth : alk. paper) — ISBN 978-0-253-01747-5
(pbk. : alk. paper) — ISBN 978-0-253-01750-5 (ebook) 1. Good and
evil. 2. Good and evil—Social aspects—Africa. I. Olsen, William C.
II. Beek, W. E. A. van.
  BJ1406.E96 2015
  170.96—dc23

                                                    2015017065

1 2 3 4 5 21 20 19 18 17 16

CONTENTS

PART III. EVIL AND MODERNITY

FOREWORD

DAVID PARKIN

The comparative study of moral systems is fundamental to anthropological thinking. This collection of nineteen chapters and the editors' introduction present rich ethnographic cases from sub-Saharan Africa on a topic bearing on the definition of morality that has been at the forefront of anthropological findings drawn from research in the continent. Yet, as the editors point out, anthropologists have been hesitant to use a concept of "evil" to refer to acts and beliefs indigenously regarded as moral inversions or perversions of humanity. The term, *evil*, is indeed an ethnographic imposition drawn from the English and cognate languages and therefore part of so-called Western thinking and moral theology. Yet, notwithstanding this lexical ethnocentricity, people everywhere do treat with horror, utter contempt, or fury those acts, statements, and occurrences (whether human, derived from "nature" or even of "spiritual" provenance) that they see as extreme violations of standard expectations of what it is to be human. The particular cultural expressions of such violations vary considerably: regarded as evil in one society or group but sometimes necessary and even beneficial in another. Not that such cultural relativity is unbounded. The flourishing of human life and perpetuity is surely everywhere respected and cultivated, even at the cost of sacrificing individuals and parts of life itself in defense of that principle against violation. It is this possibility of common human understanding of and response to the violations we may call evil, however they are specifically identified and dealt with, that marks it out as a domain of general and critical enquiry. The book admirably balances a consideration of both general and ethnographically specific questions.

The introduction suggests that, despite its enormous sociocultural diversity and historically inextricable global involvement, perhaps even more so in late modernity, sub-Saharan Africa appears to have broadly distinctive ways of conceptualizing evil. The editors point to what they call the practicality of African religion that defines moral contours and is different from the "other worldliness" of the major Asian religions. Aside from but also intertwined with Islam and Christianity, it is religion less of subservience to a High God but more of negotiation with spirit, ancestor, and perverted human agency, in which moral precepts are accordingly inherently relativized. Islam and Christianity invoke a High God and seek to impose moral absolutes and dissolve the moral ambiguities and ambivalences that arise from the negotiation with evil and its agents. But the world religions have not dissolved the fear of and anger toward, for example, alleged witches, nor the rationality of witchcraft as the most logically acceptable explanation of the otherwise inexplicable suffering that many innocent people endure, sometimes preceded by the blaming of spirits, ancestral and otherwise. As Evans-Pritchard argued long ago (*Witchcraft, Oracles and Magic among the Azande,* Oxford: Clarendon Press, 1937), it makes sense and fills the gap that neither modern science nor other epistemologies have plugged: why me/us and how can I/we reverse the harm and confront its agents? Indeed, if we can point to a strong negotiating tendency in much of Africa, often couched in ritual, as underlying the solution to problems deemed as arising from evil, is this not in fact preferable to absolutist pronouncements of right and wrong and of the inevitable resort to force to settle argument? That said, absolutist moral conflict occurs in Africa, as elsewhere in the world, as nonnegotiable ideologies, beliefs, and prejudices crowd out the possibility of settlement and result in violence. There is the example of antiwitchcraft movements and the killing of witches to eliminate perceived evil, sometimes in the name of a world religion that otherwise condemns such violence. This process of vengeful retribution is, in some form or other, a global phenomenon, whether or not we call it the elimination of witchcraft. But the deprivations and extortionate exploitations of Africa surely make it especially vulnerable to poverty, thwarted aspirations, internecine conflicts, and immense suffering. Reversing such "evils" inevitably often occurs as retaliation against alleged agents who are commonly themselves victims as much as anyone else. There is also the wider context. Perpetrators of violence in the Hutu-Tutsi conflicts face international tribunals, but not so those powerful world leaders who carry out wars and killings in defiance of international condemnation. Is this not a wider, encompassing evil?

As much of the material in this timely volume shows, the problem of evil in sub-Saharan Africa is, ultimately, an expression of powerlessness and of attempts to remedy deprivation through means which themselves may become excessive and regarded as another level of evil. This retaliatory cycle is not exclusive to Africa, which, however, for a long time has had, and has additionally been given, a distinctive vocabulary and set of concepts to identify it.

ACKNOWLEDGMENTS

The idea for a continent-wide book on evil in Africa was born in the aftermath of the volume *Religion in Africa. Experience and Expression* (1994), which van Beek coedited. During the 2006 African Studies Association meeting, the two editors of the present collection decided to pursue the topic of evil in Africa as a sequel to the earlier volume. We appreciate the direction, point-of-view, and guidance offered by David Parkin in this endeavor. Van Beek gratefully acknowledges the preparatory grant from the Dutch Science Foundation (NWO 2004), *The naturalness of evil: towards an evolutionary approach of notions of evil,* which helped sharpen the focus on constructions of evil as an integral part of human existence. His field studies among the Kapsiki/Higi in Cameroon/ Nigeria and the Dogon in Mali have been financed from many sources, including three grants from WOTRO (Scientific Study of the Tropics, now Science for Global Development). Two SANPAD (South African–Netherlands Program for Alternative Developments) research projects, plus the experiences in SANPAD RCI were important in shaping thought about the varieties of witchcraft and accusations. Van Beek is grateful for the broad support of his home institutions, first the Department of Cultural Anthropology at Utrecht University, now the African Studies Centre, Leiden, and Tilburg University. Olsen expresses appreciation to his wife, Vivian, for many years of exchange on culture and African life, and for the conversations and the listening. He also wishes to thank Gyasi Obeng and Kaakyire Gyemfi for overseeing work in Penteng and Mampong and for clarifying details about Asante. Olsen deeply appreciates research funding in Asante (Ghana) for the years 2002–2005 from the David M. Kennedy Center for International Affairs and from Georgetown University's Berkley Center for Religion, Peace, and World Affairs. Appreciation is expressed to Wim van Binsbergen and to Michael Lambek for their critical reading and input on the project and on several chapters. Editorial review was given by Natalie Prado and by Indiana University Press. Both editors express their deep thanks to Karin Berkhout for her work in correcting the manuscript and for drawing up the index, and Ruadhan Hayes for his language editing.

EVIL IN
AFRICA

INTRODUCTION
AFRICAN NOTIONS OF EVIL
The Chimera of Justice

WALTER E. A. VAN BEEK AND WILLIAM C. OLSEN

THE NOTION OF EVIL

In his ethnographic account of the Muslim precept of knowledge in Mayotte, Lambek provides thick descriptive detail regarding the cultural and moral system of behavior, including the imagination of evil. In Mayotte, evil is often personified by a figure that circulates after sunset, dancing on graves in blatant contempt for the memory and space of the departed. Rogue characters of the night go unclothed, walk backward, feast on human waste, disrespect the elderly, mock the living, and are particularly harmful toward children. They disregard human morality, social custom, and relations of kin and society. Such actions form the substance of evil, as "evil is constituted by an inversion or perversion of kinship" (Lambek 1993, 247). In such a setting, the rules of Islam are also laid bare to the pretention of evil as these "grave dancers" are audacious to the point of exposing and defiling the human corpse, thus perverting the capacity of the dead to move along in the afterlife. Sorcerers also have the ability to bring about sudden and traumatic death, a power that sets aside the singular and absolute authority of God. They are known also to bring bodies to life once again, only in its new state the emergent soul must serve the sorcerer and carry out its nefarious designs. These characters are evil because of their mocking dismissal of the moral authority of Islam. Lambek's remarkable account provides a glimpse into African encounters with evil. It demonstrates that the drama of evil in African life serves to disrupt, overturn, spoil, confuse, damage, plunder, and invert that which is common, respectable, and appropriate.

Foundations of how evil is identified and imagined, as well as how people in Mayotte respond to evil, provide a valuable starting point to the subject for the rest of sub-Saharan Africa. Although evil may be "constituted" as an inversion of kinship, it is also clear from Lambek's narrative that evil has effects, and is identified, in many other areas of daily life and existence. Evil appears to be an inversion and corruption of so much more than family and household. In many parts of Africa, kinship and family may experience predatory ramifications of evil in ways unrecognized within the market, or at the business front, or within state houses of parliament. But it is also known that evil may have a presence within the judiciary and legal bodies, corridors of hospitals and the sick bed, the economic, the agricultural, the ecclesiastical, military, and other areas of life. Evil is commonly associated with wildness, deviance, terror, destruction, chaos, unbridled passions and sexual lust, and predatory forces. In Africa, evil effects or substances may be found in the barrel of a gun as well as in pureed vegetables and pulp cereal given to a young child. Evil is associated with inanimate objects, such as an automobile or money, as well among gendered relations of human persons; and evil may be identified with the actions of a head of state or paramount chief as well as those of a cowife. Increasingly, evil has become the recent modus operandi of children and youths in cities and their suburbs. Evil is indeed a foundational component of moral systems. Evil is often a powerful force within relations of a wide range of the material or the supernatural. The importance of this volume is to provide anthropological analysis of the imagination of evil and its insidious and devastating impacts on human life.

This volume explores the cultural meanings and social contexts of evil in everyday life within various African societies. Chapters expand the common themes of evil as a threatening and disruptive force, a force that inverts what is otherwise anticipated and customary within a population. The authors also provide a deeper context of cultural foundations of evil as it is played out within the routines of households, domestic relations, language, markets, extended families, labor and work, the body, gender, money, the life cycle and old age, deity, exchange of goods, Islam, immigration, the home, Christian sects, sexuality and reproduction, tending livestock, theft, state transitions and state murder, and working the farm. Chapters also describe how evil is active in state independence, political corruption, genocide, the encroachment of war, theft and selling of body parts, and the bitterness and aftermath of state terror. In this regard, we seek to understand the meanings of evil; however, we must first comprehend moral precepts in which evil becomes divisive and destructive. As noted by Parkin (1985b), evil is the negative dimension within any moral system (3).

Comprehending evil within a moral order may also shed light on its limitations and boundaries. It also becomes useful to understand the significance of any gray zones where evil may transition into something that is not evil, including its opposite. Mayotte theory of knowledge once again serves as an example. All positive applications of knowledge in Mayotte may be potentially offset by negative ones. Knowledge used for good may be likewise abused or wrongly used, leaving results that are harmful or evil. Evil includes deliberate, malicious, and illegitimate uses of power to injure others. Mayotte themselves view this as an inversion of the moral order of things. Elsewhere, moral systems define evil within an emergence of private and personal manifestations of occult powers. Evil and private uses of earthly powers contradict the same powers exercised for reasons that were public and communal. Such was the case with early twentieth-century Nuer prophets whose use of prophecy and seizures by divinities was recognized as either legitimate or as evil according to "Nilotic notions of the moral community" (Johnson 1994, 328). Cultural dimensions of the moral community thereby provided an adequate framework for Nuer definitions of evil and its private uses. Understanding evil entailed at least a provisional detailing of a moral system and how that system operated within the larger contexts of global influences.

Throughout Africa, evil is a bad idea because people suffer. By evil acts, however defined in a society, people experience terror; they are hurt, persecuted, exiled, murdered, maimed or made disabled, raped, threatened, or robbed; or they become ill or die in an unanticipated or unusual manner. This alarming existential reality is recognized universally. It is then experienced according to personal and cultural variation and historic acumen. Evil disrupts life and initiates power to perpetuate disorder into the human condition. This is the case regardless of how we construct and "theologize" about the ideational systems dealing with evil. There is no escape to actual suffering. There is no negotiation possible with suffering, torture, banishment, or death. When children come in as the suffering other—for instance when they are accused of witchcraft and consequently mistreated and abandoned (ter Haar 2007a; Tonda 2008)—cultural and ethical relativism no longer hold any prerogative. Innocent suffering is the epitome of evil. The dilemma of suffering may easily transform itself into the problem of evil. By itself, suffering is a foundational feature in defining evil, but it is not yet a sufficient cause. What is also necessary is a sense of injustice. Suffering is inexplicable because it is beyond any expectations of "normalcy." Suffering from reasons of evil is sometimes undeserved, destructive, excessive, powerful, offensive, contradicting of daily living, unjust, inescapable, and often deadly. Results of evil are similarly as terrible. Yet, suffering and evil will not always be the same thing, as pointed out by Geertz. Evil may be identified by the inadequacy of symptomatic resources to give meaning to events, persons, and ideas that may transpire beyond the scope of acceptable realms of human existence: "the gap between things as they are and as they ought to be" within a moral compass of right and wrong (Geertz 1973, 106). Evil thus takes on meaning as it becomes "a matter of formulating in world-view terms the actual nature of the destructive forces" (130) that it displays. Parkin explains it this way: "evil refers to various ideas of imperfection and excess seen as destructive; but that these are contestable concepts which, when personified, allow mankind to engage them in dialogue and reflect on the boundaries of humanity" (1985b, 23). Within African communities, Ellis and ter Haar (2004, 65) argue that people are likely to comprehend difficulties and problems of living as due to the existence of evil, which may influence or fashion daily life of individuals or which may reshape the direction of larger communities.

Such negative descriptive conditions may be observable in contemporary and historical circumstances in African lives. They have been recognized within the narratives of some notable ethnographic works. The lives of "camp Hutu" as found in hinterland Tanzania provide one example. As superbly described by Liisa Malkki, Hutu refugee farmers are the survivors of a Tutsi-on-Hutu genocide in Burundi in the early 1970s. Some Hutu remain self-restricted in agricultural encampments awaiting the intervention of the United Nations and the international community to resolve their dilemma of exile in a foreign land and to return to a new nation in Burundi. In the camps, some refugees have retained an agricultural mode of livelihood, while others have become wage earners and educated, and they have turned their backs on the historic features that define the purity of "Hutu-ness." Those residing in camps are "true Hutus." They tell the story of the historic engagement with Tutsi pastoralists, who beguiled them with cattle and eventually displaced them from their land and agricultural livelihood. This encounter and expropriation of property are related within biblical imagery of the seduction of Adam and Eve by the Serpent. Hutu "mythico-historic" narratives recount repeated killings, forced exile, and theft of land at the hands of Tutsi "tricksters," whose historical "manifestations of evil" will one day be punished. Justice for the camp Hutus will thereby prevail through the International Criminal Court, and a new nation will be conceived. Narratives supply descriptive imagery of an "enemy" on all historic and contemporary fronts. The Hutu saw this enemy as aggregate populations who were evil because they presented various modes of destroying traditional modes of Hutu livelihood and history. Personifications found in Hutu mythical narratives create descriptive enemies, and the categories sustain a moral landscape in which evil becomes synonymous with characters and with historic events. A similar description of the evils of 1994 genocide in Rwanda is available in Jennie Burnet's chapter in this book.

Similarly, terror and political oppression were the subjects of accounts of evil within the various Truth and Reconciliation Commissions in South Africa and elsewhere. Truth and Reconciliation Commission testimonials convey a witness of evil while drawing on words, gestures, and conventions to "display meaning" of evil, and the meaning is one of human degradation. Situated within words of testimony are found a core nucleus of evil's horror. This includes the destruction of kinship and home, alienation of the flow of life and space and time, imposition of torture and imprisonment and solitary confinement, the intrusion and extinguishing of livelihood by the state, and disruption of gender and family. The end result of state terror under apartheid was the "penetration of violence into everyday life" (Ross 2003, 48). This assemblage of state power made possible a shaping of daily existence that was subordinate in every way to designs of evil and its dominating manifestations. See also Ashforth in this volume.

The first section of the volume explores relations of evil and power with the contributions of Silva; Whyte, Meinert, and Obika; Jok; Burnet; and MacGaffey. Sources of evil often appear all too self-evident: enemies of the state, opposing forces in wartime or during moments of genocide, destructive mystical beings, external enemies, or enemies among the group and within a population. These immediate manifestations of evil are part of a larger array of malevolent forces and realities that often are beyond empirical reach. They present a total cosmology of evil, and they are identified for both their powerful abilities and for their will to harm, destroy, and kill.

The editors envision this volume as a continuation of the earlier work *Religion in Africa: Experience and Expression,* edited by Blakely, van Beek, and Thompson (1994). We strongly embrace the precepts of African religions and moral systems endorsed in that volume, namely that religion in Africa addresses practical concerns and unresolved problems of the everyday. As such, it is categorically unlike the "otherworldly" posture of most Asian religions. Rather, African religion (17) "means performing or otherwise doing something: consulting a diviner, offering a sacrifice, praying, talking about a problem, enthroning a chief, falling into a trance, making magic, and dancing with masks at a funeral. . . . Religion also often is a means to an end; people are often quite clear about why they do things and what they aim at: health, fertility, rain, protection, or relational harmony. Religion is part of a survival strategy and serves practical ends, either immediate or remote, social or individual."

Within this moral and often mystical framework of practicality, people in Africa are frequently confronted by a scale of evil that ranges from unpleasant and offensive or criminal behaviors to total, unabated evil assaults. Perceptions of evil may include means of addressing and experiencing adversities of everyday living: poverty, corruption, sickness, loss of life, deprivation, homelessness, betrayal, abandonment, starvation, violence. Crime, especially rates of rising violence, brutality, and corruption are particularly notable scenes of evil. This reality is noted in the chapters by Jok for South Sudan, Burnet in Rwanda, and Ashforth for postapartheid South Africa; and it is also identified in works by Donham (2011) and Morris (2006). We also share the perspectives of those writers describing local manifestations of evil as zombies, road warriors, shape-shifters, satanic actors, head hunters, cannibals, vulture or leopard men, and those who steal skin, blood, the penis, or vaginal elements in order to ingratiate their own selves and disrupt natural bodily flows of neighbors and kinsmen (Comaroff and Comaroff 1993). These evil characters are appropriately seen as appearing within global movements of modernity and its flows of things, people, and ideas. Their reality brings into relief the trauma and the peculiar, which are cultural by-products left aside in the wake of the economic and political turmoil and instability of the late twentieth century. These new forms of consumption, the market place, production, and political turmoil have generated "occult economies" (Comaroff and Comaroff 1993) of inversion, power, and evil configuration. In such economies, human body parts become transformed into objects of exchange where reproductive forces may become distorted measures of power and where human fertility consumes rather than regenerates (Moore and Sanders 2001).

Evil and the mystical are present in political events and in wartime Africa as well. African civil wars are waged with global resources and result in mass casualties by way of bullets, machetes, etc. African conflicts are also known to invoke mystical entities that bring about enhanced, more powerful results (Lan 1985). These forces may be used on both sides of the conflict. For example, in Uganda's struggle for nationalism, rebels were characterized as "hyenas, terrorists, and agents of Satan" (Finnstrom 2008, 115). Such descriptions illustrate the despair of living in everyday circumstances of evil and with its violent shambles of wartime. Similar descriptions of the evil of civil war are found in Mozambique where FRELIMO (or Front for Liberation of Mozambique) soldiers campaigned against malicious enemy practices, calling them "sorcery of danger, sorcery of ruin, sorcery of death" (West 2005, 159). It stands to reason with such moral polarities that putting an end to such evil is the only imaginable legitimate outcome. Likewise, national elections and street campaigns in Sierra Leone display politicians who boast openly of their own powerful connections with the occult. The same political crowd makes haunting accusations regarding associations between political rivals and "much worse concealed agencies"

(Ferme 1999, 171). The lesser evil leverages mystical powers for enhancing their public reputation of the political opportunist. This process is regarded in Freetown as an accepted part of any electoral campaign.

A sense of moral judgment is a likely working component of all cultural systems. Moral judgment often includes acts regarded as wrong, reprehensible, hurtful, and occasionally evil. Morality is basic in all cultures and social systems. Its presence may reveal an evolutionary disposition toward empathy, cooperation, and justice (Bekoff and Pierce 2009). In cooperation and empathy individuals relate to each other and build bonds and in justice they redress perceived wrongs; these processes are present in humans as well as in several animal species, such as elephants, cetaceans, wolves, monkeys, and apes. This common source for morality underlines the fact that the basis of human moral agency is rooted in a mixture of intelligence, emotions, and sociality. The fact that we distinguish between good and evil acts or happenings is a given in any culture. Nevertheless, all societies have their own definitions of evil acts, which vary in substance, intensity, as well as interpretation. Societies especially vary in response to evil, in manners of retribution, and how evil issues are resolved. Religion may come in for specific definitions, for the distinction between types of evil, and surely for notions of retribution, through the process Marx called *celestialization,* adding the authority of the "other world" to the social constructs of what constitutes evil. In their more organized forms religions lay claim to being the sources of "morals" and "norms." In this volume, the latter aspect, justice, will be central to the fact that not only do people evaluate the actions of others, but they also act upon these evaluations in an attempt to redress the balance of justice, that is, of their sense of justice. And often the reaction on perceived evil leads to actions that are even more evil, at least in our eyes (see Hinfelaar 2007; Ashforth 1998; Kahn 2011).

ANTHROPOLOGY AND THE OCCULT

Evil is not only bad by definition, but defining evil is not without its problems. Describing evil is problematic. Evil is an adjective, and like many adjectives, it generates problems as a noun. Societies distinguish between evil acts. However, as a noun evil invokes notions of essentialism. It thereby confronts the basic anthropological premise of cultural relativism. Reactions to what "evil" is not have been problematic. Defining "the sacred," for example, has been an academic roadway full of hazards and entrapments. In his introduction of *The Anthropology of Evil* of 1985, Parkin avoids the difficulty by remarking, "From this short paraphrase we see at a glance why the English word 'evil' has been so useful to social anthropologists" (1). Notwithstanding, the term has been considered more problematic than useful as an analytical tool. Thus, most studies on evil have avoided the term until the recent works by van Beek (1994), Clough and Mitchell (2001), and Kapferer (2001).

We see the term more usefully understood in African life as an emic gloss, a word that conveys an experience of great wrongdoing, malevolence, imputed and intended malice, wanton excess, and a desire for destruction and harm from the informant's point of view. As argued, all societies define depraved moral acts, and the notion of evil does some justice to that existential fact. Also, in all societies there are gradations of "things done wrong" and "things gone wrong," gradations in severity, impact, and intent. Evil encompasses comprehending events and circumstances of life at the extreme negative end of existence. This may include experiencing extreme poverty, political repression, corruption, violence, or wartime. Once evil is uncovered, it is impossible to imagine anything worse. For example, Kaguru beliefs in witchcraft form a mode of imagining evil. Some kinds of misfortune and suffering, even death, may be morally justified within a realm of acceptability and expectation. Yet, witchcraft causes misery and suffering that is undeserved and that cannot be reconciled within a normal moral order of things. By definition, Kaguru witches deny this moral code because "witches are what they themselves are not but as recalcitrant kin and neighbours may be" (Beidelman 1986, 9, 139). Witches also introduce into human society aspects of the wild, the bush, and the powers of nature; and these features are remarkably similar to evil beings found in Sierra Leone (Jackson 1989).

Stephen Ellis has drawn attention to the relative stasis in terminology of things of the "occult" in anthropology of religion. He calls for a more detailed terminological instrument, especially for better grounded comparisons—and less easy equation—between European and African witchcraft (Ellis 2007, 47–49; Ellis and ter Haar 2007). We concur by claiming that language, terms, and symbols provide insight into both who we are and how the Other lives. The challenge therein is "o liberate the Other . . . from the chains of a Western intellectual hegemony" (Kapferer 2001, 7; see also Abega 2005). This is done in two ways. The first is done by challenging the "reality aspect" of terms. Their meanings emerge only within dimensions of culture and history that emphasize time, place, and processes of interpretation. The other is a constant referral to the field, to emic terms and distinctions, and to processes of application of the term, as Evans-Pritchard showed to be so productive in his Azande analysis of witchcraft.

As we deal with evil as an academic category, several basic distinctions must be observed. The first is between act and imagination. Theft, murder, torture, rape, persecutions, false accusations, and forced exile are generally presumed as evil within most populations. Other events may be less evident, especially in the occult sphere. Evans-Pritchard's (1937) classic distinction between sorcery and witchcraft is given as one between act and imagination. For him *sorcery* comprises observable acts aiming at a specific effect; a small ritual, words and incantations, or medicines are used in a manipulative way using supernatural or occult means in order to harm, heal, or protect. In sorcery people "say and do" something, and a sorcerer has to learn it as a craft. By contrast, *witchcraft* is the imaginary attribution of specific occult powers to a person: a witch is someone whose shadow or soul is thought to leave his or her body, and to transport itself miraculously, in order to harm a victim. Sorcery is seen as a voluntary act for either good or evil; witchcraft on the other hand is always evil and is thought to be involuntary, as a witch is deemed to be born with such an aberrant soul/ shadow, an inherited, unconscious, and vindictive mystical force. Thus, the two point to different epistemological realities and, as Stroeken calls it, "experiential structures" (Stroeken 2010, 34–35); even if local languages sometimes do not distinguish between the two, the distinction between the intentional power of sorcery and imagined witches is important; moreover, those accused of witchcraft in fact are defenseless victims.

This distinction between sorcerer and witch is relevant in many African cultures, but by no means in all. Still, despite the variability of the notion of witch, it is analytically useful to distinguish between sorcery and witchcraft as two positions along a continuum of occult power. This way, sorcery is one ideal type at the conscious end—overt acts aiming at a goal that is not logically and empirically the result of the act—while witchcraft is at the other end as an imagined travel of the soul/shadow. Many contributions address this framework through the emic distinctions they highlight, each profiling the local distinctions in types of evil. Some zoom in on the sorcery end (van Beek, Dilley), others more on the witchcraft side (Ekoué with Rosenthal), but most give a more comprehensive list of local evils (Larsen, Devisch, Green, Hodgson). Clarity of terms is the first step toward understanding, because using "these terms quite loosely can have unfortunate implications" (Geschiere 2013, 9).

Both sorcery and witchcraft are sometimes thought to be manifest through third parties, such as forest beings, dwarves, familiars, or zombies. In some parts of Africa, this process may also include shape-shifting where the witch departs from his or her body and transforms in the forest into a much more powerful beast. In this case, pythons, elephants, leopards, snakes, or indefinable monsters (*nkala*, Turner 1968, 120) become the vessel for manifestations of occult power. Zombies, like the South African *tokoloshe*, resemble an entity recognized as "undead": people who died and were by sorcery or witchcraft called to this world again, to work as slaves for their sorcerer/owner (Niehaus 2001). They are not considered evil in themselves, but they evoke a haunting image of an afterlife without physical rest where riches are delivered to an undeserving sorcerer. Such manifestations of mystical power also may provide a substantive explanation of extreme differences in local distributions of wealth, as argued by Geschiere (2001). In other cases, as Dilley (this volume) points out for Senegal, familiars generate their own agency, thereby forcing their "owners" into evil acts.

What we as researchers do recognize on this topic are two different things that are empirically solid: the discourse on witches and sorcerers, as well as the actions taken against presumed evil-doers, the accusations, and persecutions: "witchcraft is spoken words" (Favret-Saada 1977, 9, 10). The empirical referent of witchcraft—and most of the time of sorcery as well—is first of all words, discourse. The witchcraft discourse forms the core field of study and, for a large part, also the problem. In fact, modern witchcraft studies take witchcraft as a text, a commentary on and failing explanation of the ills of modernity and globalization (Comaroff and Comaroff 1993; Geschiere 1997, 2001). The second referent is action, since the sad reality is that these "evil words" often are acted upon. People do accuse witches—and witches confess just as naturally—and sometimes purported witches are persecuted, banished, exiled, or—also in the European case—tortured and killed. For anthropologists, just as for most national laws, that is where the heart of the problem lies: individuals suffer because people take action on their notions about evil (Cohan 2011).

Evil is a tricky idea. Imagining, listening, or speaking of evil often gives evil a conveyance or a portal into people's lives. It is then assumed that evil must be acted upon. Listening and understanding can easily lead to strengthening the discourse on evil (ter Haar 2007a). African witchcraft has been perpetually on the anthropological agenda. Its empirical realities have involved belief, discourse, accusation, and confession (Marwick 1970; Douglas 1970; van Beek and Blakely 1994). The evil of witchcraft has been at the core of African anthropology. Accusations and details of evil deeds have induced the exchange of scholars regarding debates of rational versus irrationality or the basis of actual legal proof of criminal conduct. Such arguments serve to test the limits of the Enlightenment Project (Kapferer 2001, 1–2).

For our purposes, the question of the existence of the occult fades into the background. With Geschiere, we believe this to be the correct position of the argument. One cannot really understand, nor correctly study and write about, these discourses on the occult without feeling some empathy toward what it means or would mean to believe in them: "The distinction between what is 'imaginary' and what is 'real' is not so clear in this domain" (Geschiere 1997, 20). However, the suffering through accusations, persecutions, and killings is very real; especially when children are accused, as is increasingly the case (ter Haar 2007b, 16; Adinkrah 2011), the devastating effects of the discourse are glaringly evident, and, as argued, academic distance is not an option. With children accused, convicted, and abandoned because of purported witchcraft, empathy disappears, and the evil of accusations stands out alone; cultural imagination can turn squarely against man.

EVIL AS A COGNITIVE PROBLEM

Evil is a difficult idea. Acts are what we can observe, question, and analyze. Evil is the negative side of any moral system, as Parkin remarked (1985b, 3). In Africa, three fundamental premises have been observed. First, as has been amply testified in numerous studies, the supernatural world in Africa is ambivalent throughout. The mystical world and its agents are never exclusively good *or* evil. Many contributions in this volume stress ambivalence and ambiguity, for example, Devisch on the Yaka, Rosenthal on the Ewe, Dilley on the Haalpulaar of Senegal, Larsen on the Zanzibar, Hodgson on the Maasai, Green on South Tanzania, and van de Kamp for Mozambique.

Second, absent in the African cases are the absolutist supernal realities of omniscient and omnipotent deities. The main relation between man and the African inhabitants of the "other world" is one of mutual dependency and negotiation, even reciprocity. Ancestors often take prime place, and, more than anyone else, they stand in a reciprocal relationship with their progeny: without the first the other would not exist, without the second the first would be insubstantial.

Third, African myths of origin are based on a paradigm that is quite human, immediate, and practical. Good and evil are not so absolute, nor are they overly separated. These three factors—ambivalence, no metaphysical speculation, and no ex nihilo creation—imply that the theodicy problem has little bearing in Africa.

This volume offers a window on the variety of ways in which African Islamic cultures handle this problem of theodicy. Islam recognizes no separation between the sacred and the secular, so in Islam a nonreligious ontology is in principle unthinkable because all creation comes from Allah. The systematic monotheism of Islam provides for no component features separate from that creation, as for a Muslim everything we call good and evil comes from Allah, being just the conditions he deems fit for man to live in. However, Islam in Africa and elsewhere is never singular, and theology does not trump practice. Adversity and suffering must be experienced; injustices and evil must be explained. Local forms of Islam address such predicaments. Our volume offers several perspectives—from Niger, Zanzibar, and Senegal—on how Muslims resolve the problem of the existence of evil within the general framework of Islam. Following the lead of Parkin's analysis on coastal Kenya (Parkin 1985a) several contributions show the intricacies of African thinking within Islam.[1]

Pascal Boyer points out that imagination of the supernatural bears a peculiar and persistent character. He identifies this as "minimally counterintuitive concepts." Concepts of the other world are not entirely strange, but they are different from habitual ones in one important feature. Ideas on the supernatural routinely contradict "some information provided by ontological categories" (Boyer 2002, 74), which means that the supernatural world is populated with beings that are not just different from what we can expect in normal daily life, but different in a specific way. For instance, we know what a human being is—a definite ontological category—and if "something" is human, we can intuitively infer a host of properties: body, shape, movement, speech, mind, etc. If one of these expectations is violated, the concept becomes minimally counterintuitive. Thus a human being without a body is a ghost; he can go through a wall, but for the rest, he acts very much like a human being, and we can understand him, even feel empathy with his plight. Minimally counterintuitive concepts are easy to think, quick to remember, and hard to forget, so these notions of the supernatural stick in the mind. Crucial is that the number of violations of our expectations remains low, one or two seems optimal, which is what "minimally" implies. This means that supernatural beings are usually not alien but quite human, sharing a host of characteristics with their ontological category; so if they are evil, their very evil has a human slant.

African folk tales are replete with dangers coming from the bush, strange people, monsters, or shape-shifters, but these usually are not primarily animal. When animals appear in the folk tales, they are actually more human than any human actors themselves. Notions of animal suffering do not come to the fore in African thought nor in cultural practice. So, all in all, African notions of evil are human in character. Evil acts operate inside human relations and not in nature. Even when evil is incarnate, it is dependent upon a relationship: a witch, a cowife, a mother or mother-in-law, a malevolent son who is only bad if triggered. Otherwise, relations among friends and family are balanced and normal. This continuum is seen in Silva's chapter on Zambia where degrees of "badness" are explored within tense relationships between perpetrator and victim. At the core of this tension is the identification of a victim and his status: the loss of identity.

But of course natural disasters may strike, and are a form of natural evil. Storms, floods, lightening, epidemics, Africa has borne its share of these. What happens, afterward, how do people deal with it? An interesting case is the Lake Nyos disaster.

> On August 21, 1986, the quiet crater lake Nyos exploded, causing instant death for 1,788 people and thousands of cattle. When aid finally arrived in the remote area, they just found the bodies, without a trace of what had happened. At an international conference in 1987, the cause was established as a CO_2 explosion: the deep waters of the lake had been oversaturated with volcanic carbon dioxide, mixed with sulphur, held at bay by a layer of warmer water at the top . . . But that scientific explanation came well after the fact, and well before the conference—and also afterward—people on the spot had constructed their own explanations. First outsiders were blamed: Americans were testing a neutron bomb, French scientists had caused—at least known about—it. Later more endogenous explanations surfaced. At first the idea surfaced that the ancestors had been thwarted, but that was discarded quickly. Ancestors may injure harm or kill, but always selectively, never in these numbers; wiping out their progeny is definitely not a priority for ancestors. What remained as purported cause, for the moment, were disputes over land between "autochthonous" people (an important concept in Cameroon) and newcomers had led to jealousy; local myths tell of drowning newcomers in the lake, of tunnels into the depths as a way into the underground, with pythons and elephants as animal spirit doubles interfering with human life. (Nkwi 1990, 15)

Even this major and spectacular disaster, with its complicated scientific explanation that was accessible for only a few, was quickly brought back to human scale and became the result of defective human intergroup relations. In African thought, morality pertains to humans, and the caprices of the supernatural world are just that, capricious, not evil. Evil is "us." Rasmussen shows in her chapter how moral tests between Touareg precisely define that "us" in times of stress, testing the moral fiber of the kinsman; Hodgson, in her study of Maasai women, points at the gender of evil, and the "other turned evil" appear to be mostly men.

EVIL AS AN EXPERIENTIAL PROBLEM

Evil is everyone's idea. Unjust, sudden, or deliberate death evokes the notion of evil in Africa. In this manner, normality becomes "truncated." Explanations must be developed and disseminated in such cases. Purposes must be revealed; intentions must be stifled and justly curtailed. Otherwise, sudden death may strike another victim. Divination may decipher when death is a natural event or when it is brought about through evil means. Evil is experienced through suffering plus injustice. In the biblical traditions this problem has been voiced eloquently in the book of Job. Job knows his deeds are good; yet he suffers. God, who is just, punishes him without cause. Job has been the subject of a wager between God and Satan, which is never told to him, though the reader knows. Contemplating the injustice of his suffering, Job realizes that evil hits the wrong person: injustice is suffering out of place. Justice is grounded in the word of God, but the two cannot exist apart and are interdependent, for without justice, the conception of God has little meaning. In his final answer to Job, God does not speak about justice at all, not a word, nor does he speak about evil. Instead, he constantly highlights his own power, and in no way is the suffering of Job legitimized.

African concepts of moral personhood focus on a different relationship duality. They are less concerned with the "man-divinity" relationship and more focused on bonds between individual and society. Dependency on the supernatural world is neither absolute, nor unchangeable. African religions bear an inherent relativism. The comparison with Job is enlightening when one recognizes the very impossibility of an African ever saying something like Job does: Job is absolutely certain that he has made no mistakes, done no wrong, committed no sins, offended no deity, and broken no taboo whatsoever. This line of logic is unthinkable in Africa. There is always something in the past that can be unearthed, some people who have taken issue with one's actions, some taboos breached.

The total absence of any third human party in Job is also striking; for an African Job the first question would be one of witchcraft: "Who has done this to me?" Susan Reynolds Whyte remarks about the East African Nyole: "The question I hear Nyole people ask is not 'Why me?' but 'Why you?' Their immediate focus is not on the self, but on the other: who are you behind this affliction and why are you doing it?" (Whyte 1997, 30). African notions of justice are pragmatic and relativistic: the self is never guiltless and the other always has a moral claim, thus retaining moral power (Stroeken 2010). On the other hand, others are never without offense. In her chapter, Judy Rosenthal reports an intriguing dialogue between an African and a Western intellectual on azè, "witchcraft" that well illustrates this focus on relationality and ambivalence, amounting sometimes even to claiming azè for oneself.

African gods are notoriously arbitrary and capricious. They can never be fully trusted. Their powers are meant to be used within society as they constantly intervene in human life. The Dogon honorific title for Ama, the sky god, is: "the God who changes everything," and his long title then lists a number of experiences of this divine capriciousness: he who walks in the bush is put in the village; she who has a bowl full of food suddenly finds it filled with just leaves (van Beek 2010). Human agency is less bound within African theologies. Social relations, particularly kin and family, project ambiguities, tension, and conflict. Maia Green demonstrates how loosening kinship ties make people rely more on achieved performance of these ties than on the belonging to the ascribed kinship network. Jok Madut Jok offers poignant and quite personal examples of the notion of betrayal that is at the core of the combination of adversity and injustice: the core of evil acts is the fact that we cannot trust even our "own" people. This theme is argued cogently in Geschiere (2013).

The mystical world remains fluid according to human experience and less absolute, unlike the duality of Good and Evil in Western culture. Nor is this world overly demanding. The necessity to invoke evil may rise with adversity and with random events. This allows us to speak of African cosmologies as being practical and oriented toward immediate means and ends, rather than as philosophical religions, as may be found in Asia, that are otherworldly or spiritually redemptive. Immediacy also inscribes social relations with sensitivity and with a nod toward action in cases of impropriety. The mystical world is manifest within local power configurations, and it continually relies upon ambiguity and uncertainty in human relations. So in the end, African experiences of evil are part of what Giddens calls the "enabling constraints," the expected happenings within the confines of one's personal history and network of relations. Evil does not come from an absolute and dominant polarity, but from a closer social network. The Christian religions of Africa, especially of the Pentacostalist persuasion, have adopted an external demonology (Meyer 1985, 2001; van de Kamp, this volume). But the devils encountered in these sessions share the relational aspect of all evil influences: they have to be taken seriously, but they can be combated.

PROCESSES OF EVIL

Evil is a powerful idea. Any discourse on the occult applies also to power. Associations are made between political power and occult sources (Ellis and ter Haar 2004). Power and wealth are often part of the same social and religious system. One of the evident features to contributions in this volume is a tremendous increase to both power and wealth in Africa and the world over the past few decades. Wealth and power are best used when they are public, while hidden wealth is suspect and may imply questionable intentions and also danger.

In African communities, things that are hidden interfere with generosity and redistribution (Clough 2001; Mitchell 2001).

Routine motivations such as jealousy, envy, resentment, and greed for material goods are identified as evil. René Devisch analyzes desire as one of the main groundings of witchcraft concepts, in the meantime defining the "witch" not only as one similar to us, but also of one (of us) liable to fall into the same trap (see also Danfulani 2007). Olsen uses killing and dismemberment of thieves to show the odious value theft has in the lives of Asante, and also why thieves must receive exacting and immediate kinds of justice and punishment. Results of theft appear to Asante similar to the results of some kinds of witchcraft, and witches and thieves appear to be driven by similar motivations of unabated greed or a wanton desire to destroy.

Beliefs in witchcraft are difficult to eradicate. Collective memory recalls the nature of evil and who does evil deeds. In the case of witches, memory and vocabulary conspire to imagine a "logical inversion of the stereotype of moral personhood" (Jackson 1989, 96). For this reason, witchcraft discourses cannot be eradicated by combating the discourse or the beliefs consciously. Despite its many differences with the African witchcraft situation, the European example is apt here (Favret-Saada 1977, 2009). The notion of the witch is a meme, easy to learn, hard to forget, indeed minimally counterintuitive. Even when local discourse excludes dialogues of witchcraft, like the Baka of Cameroon, their healers can be consulted by others who do harbor such notions. The Baka healers, in turn, then assume the discourse as their own (Geschiere 2013). The question is whether the notion of "belief" is very apt here. As holds for imagistic religions in general (Whitehouse 2004), not the creed but the rituals are crucial, identity accruing more from participation in the rituals than from creedal orthodoxy. Chapters in our volume on Muslim definitions then make for an interesting internal comparison. In the contributions of Dilley, Larsen, and Rasmussen, we encounter a much more "theologized" system of types of constructed evil, where the more local notions are set off against the doctrinal system of Islam. This process seems to result in a much more elaborated cosmology of evil, set in rather precise terminology, with a general loss of not only ambiguity but also of ambivalence.

So the supernatural world in African religions is diverse and ever present. It serves more as a background for daily life than as a strong guideline dominating individual existence. The stereotype of the all-pervading traditional African religion is probably quite wrong, as Mary Douglas long ago pointed out (1970), as in most traditional religions the bulk of life is lived without any reference to the "other world." Only during rituals, and when confronted with problems, mishaps, misfortune, illness, and other adversity, does the other world become relevant.

Not all evil is witchcraft. But in witchcraft as well as in other instances of evil, there is a definite gap between the views of the victims and the perpetrators. Accused witches usually believe in witchcraft, but not in their own guilt. For the community, evil often justifies extreme actions including violent responses. Olsen well illustrates why the loss of small things hits the victims so hard, rupturing relations to the very core (see also Telle 2001). Revenge on sorcery, in van Beek's chapter, is done with exactly the same occult forces, but involves forms of justice through disasters such as a disease epidemic that threaten to wipe out families who do not redress the situation. The occult arena does not solve the problems, but escalates them. Conversely, juridical systems that do not escalate matters require a closer look at the link between evil and justice. This is the setting for the fascinating forgiveness project in Uganda described by Whyte, Meinert, and Obika (this volume).

A SENSE OF (IN-)JUSTICE

Evil is an inevitable idea. Evil is an inversion of justice. In many tales and myths the avenger easily trumps the original malefactors, simply by being on the side of justice, on the side of the angels. When the revenge is duly performed, the world may continue as it should. All kinds of evil, the occult continuum of sorcery—witchcraft, theft, murder, torture, false accusations, genocide, bodily dismemberment, and acquisition of body parts—share the fact that the act runs counter to a sense of justice. Three elements are needed for a sense of justice: cooperation, empathy, and moral agency. Moral agency is a foundational precept of moral judgment. A sense of justice is the social gut feeling that a particular act is wrong; that people agree on that judgment and, if possible, on the person of the perpetrator; that something should be done about it; and that any punishment meted out is at least proportionate to the evil act.

An evil act, according to Parkin, can infringe on "normalcy" in three ways: excess, imperfection, and incompletion (1985b, 6, 13). Excess is clear in the "new wave" of African witchcraft accusations, targeting those who are extremely wealthy, the powerful, and the ultravisible in society. It is presumed that these persons must have occult forces—politics of the "belly"—in their favor. It is this mystical connection that provides their wealth and power and that differentiates them from all others. In these circumstances, accusations may bear some resemblance to confessions. Powerful Africans may disclose by innuendo their associations with occult powers. Nevertheless, they mostly stop at admitting to have a host of zombies working for them, an idea that is gathering momentum in Africa (Geschiere 2001) as one of the gut reactions against runaway modernization.

Imperfection and incompleteness are useful ways of describing evil, as in the case of dirt, ugliness, and rottenness. In images of evil, the night dominates the day, black trumps white, and dirt is no longer "matter out of place" but a substance of its own. Illness, a constant evil companion in African life, may be regarded in some cases as imperfection. On the one hand, illness results from a breach in one's personal defenses, the normal occult force making a person into an unassailable fortress: the protective magic did not work, was spoilt, lost its power, or has been trumped by a superior one. Illness often is an occult arms race, and then a lost one. On the other hand, illnesses may result from the malevolent will of an evil person who may project a foreign object into the victim's body, send evil forces, or simply bring bad luck through curses or evil invocations. Finally, some illnesses stem from nonhuman origin, either natural causes, such as malaria as it is too common to be explained by "special forces," or spectacular ones, such as epidemics, that are assigned personalized supernatural agents. Small pox and measles are brought by a god in Kapsiki thought, for example (van Beek 2012). Death itself is imperfect in Africa, often depicted as one-legged and one-armed (Schoffeleers 1991), a person yes, but at the same time less and much more than a person, minimally counterintuitive and therefore memorable. Imperfection categorizes people who are structurally different as imperfect and dangerous but also powerful. Albinos, twins, and babies born with the caulk come to mind as examples, as they embody imperfections and thus serve as vehicles for influences of evil (Peek 2011). But then, they also embody ambivalence and point at the constant presence of power as a close companion for African evil.

Incompleteness in the African setting implies a derailing of one's life as it is expected to be lived: the untimely death that has to be avenged, the goods stolen and lifted out of the circulation of goods that characterizes a "whole" society (Olsen's contribution in this volume is compelling in this respect), as well as the most common incidence of evil in Africa, lack of fertility. Divination, medication in all its variety, cleansing of relations, trance, and healing cults address this predicament. Processes like these often identify causes of infertility as evil (Peek and van Beek 2013). A human being is "whole" only as the nexus of a full range of relations, and proper personhood is always relational. When the Touareg gently test their fellowmen on the qualities of their character, they do so in testing the limits of their relationship in order to assess their completeness, even if this leads to counterintuitive claims on one another, or at least counterintuitive for outsiders (Rasmussen, this volume).

In any of these forms, evil demands both active response and justice. As a tool of social relations, "justice" completes an underlying human interaction based on the inherent morality of any social system. Such a moral system always parallels a more official form of justice, which is administered by the political system and includes police and the judiciary. Societies define punishable evil acts—as distinguished from minor "badness" or incivility—and have to address these. For most evil acts, this is most often unambiguous and straightforward, even when formal punishment may not fit the crime. The most difficult issue is occult evil and its aftermath, and this is a problem that challenges the African judiciary even today.[2]

In South Africa, the Northern Province witnessed a flare of witchcraft accusations, as people saw the new freedom as an arena to settle old scores (Niehaus 2001, 2002; Kgatla et al. 2003; Stadler 1993). The many killings (by so-called necklacing) and exiles did not solve the problem either; they just put oil on the fire, or as an older official remarked, "We just got the students in witchcraft. But all the professors are still there!" Witch belief is flexible and foolproof, and is a seductive discourse that seems to explain new kinds of injustices.

Antiwitchcraft movements, or Pentecostal churches rallying against witchcraft and sorcery, often meet with an initial success, freeing people from the influence of witches, shielding them against evil outside influences. But at a later stage, these often impressive measures amount to strengthening the discourse itself; after all, witchcraft appears so important as to warrant a massive war against it. So even when the churches claim that Jesus is stronger, the witches and demons gain in stature as well in the process. Thus, this occult arms race bogs down in an involuted demonology, as Linda van de Kamp shows in this volume and as has been shown by Birgit Meyer in Ghana (Meyer 1985, 2001). The fact that in the Mozambican case van de Kamp presents, the main performers of the rituals come from outside Africa, is highly relevant here: the vicious circle of the discourse on witches and the measures against them has to be broken from the outside. In 2007, van Beek reviewed factors that promote an escalation of accusations. Maia Green also illustrates in her chapter how this process not only operates between cultures, but also within one setting.

THE LURE OF EVIL

Evil is an intriguing idea. Evil stimulates fantasy in any culture and in all ages. We are fascinated by the notion of evil, conjuring horrifying images as we go along, creating a realm in which fantasy holds sway, with dark realms, monstrous figures, unredeemable circumstances, and defiant and destructive powers. We create our evil images along the lines of our own cultures, so the way we think about evil tells us a lot about ourselves (van Beek 1994). As images go, we are presented with devils, demons, monsters, witches, and evil sorcerers. The human imagination embraces the dark side of cosmology as an explanatory tool and as a means for understanding certain lived events and experiences. On the human side, the European images of corpses, skulls, bones, and graves compare with African accounts of severed heads, missing body parts, misplaced genitalia, inverted mouths and fingers, albino skin, and menstrual blood. The discourse on evil runs both fantastic and wild. African images of evil clearly show the human image of the antijustice: the thief, the sorcerer, the menstruating witch who jumps on the scared male, the witch that sucks blood out of sleeping victims, the eye that spoils anything admired, the cannibal witch devouring the living and the dead, with as an apotheosis a host of zombies marching and laboring under the unseen direction of a sorcerer. The images are diverse and terrifying, but they are also ultimately human in form and substance. Devisch shows in his chapter how the most ephemeral of all human images, the dream, forms a creative ground for image formation as well as for the projection of societal values.

The figure of the traitor/trickster is the most iconic form of evil. In the Abrahamic tradition, the figure of Satan has known a similar course: from officer in the heavenly court he became a trickster, then the prince of evil and darkness, and finally the ultimate doom for human evildoers (Kelly 2006). A trickster does not respect boundaries, but crosses borders between god and man, between good and evil, thus forming a splendid example of Mary Douglas's insistence on borders as realms of power. African mythologies contain mythological trickster-like figures, such as Legba or Eshu. But they are more human and more helpful than trickster figures elsewhere, one reason we choose a trickster statue for the cover of this book. In the case of Eshu, they generate bodies of healing knowledge, such as Ifa. African tricksters populate the folk tales in great numbers, playing around with the dumb powers that be. In Africa evil is not the ultimate black of the chaotic rim of the world, but it is at home in man himself, part and parcel of everyone. Jok's portrayal of the state as the traitor—and in his case, the newest one of all, South Sudan—and then a traitor of sky-high expectations, illustrates well the very humanness of evil; the point is not that evil is alien, but that it is eminently understandable for us. And as he is himself a victim, his right to speak out is especially powerful.

Finally, with this notion of betrayal comes in a notion that may subsume most of the way we experience evil: evil is a conspiracy, against me, against us, against humanity. The "other," the "witch," the "sorcerer," the "police," the "state," the "authorities," but also the "demons," *sheitani,* and sometimes "ancestors," all who are "them," conspire against "us." Witchcraft or sorcery is a conspiracy of one, sometimes in witches groups and then clearly conspirational; other cases of "evil" are conspiracies of faceless institutions that surface through all-too real individuals, but still as incorporation of the general conspiracy against "us." Some time ago, Jan van Baal, in his search for the ethics of traditional religions (van Baal 1981), looked for the grounding of ethics in the notion of partnership; later Roy Rappaport would, with different terminology go on a similar quest (Rappaport 1999). Van Baal defined religion as a quest for partnership. As a reflective animal, man is part of his lifeworld, but at the same time transcends it, questioning his situation, his relations with the world, and his own selfhood. Van Baal positions this *condition humaine* at the basis of religion; the human unease with oneself generates a constant existential tension, which we have to deal with. It is this tension that we resolve, temporarily, in ritual, in togetherness, in communion and communitas, but never completely, never finally. From this angle, we would define the experience of evil as a failed partnership with our lifeworld. Our lifeworld is not to be trusted any more, neither at the far away rim, where monsters lurk—as the *hic dracones* at the margins on the medieval maps—nor at its core, our fellow men. The world conspires against us! Job's suffering resulted from a conspiracy on high, but most conspiracies are closer to home: the other ethnic group, the immigrants, our next door neighbors, our kinsmen. Finally, African wisdom predicts that we can never be sure that we ourselves are not only the victims of these conspiracies, but also its perpetrators. Evil, in the end, is our own conspiracy.

BOOK AND CHAPTERS

The nineteen chapters in this book present ethnography from communities in seventeen African countries. All regions of tropical Africa are represented. Ethnographies come from settings reflecting rural, semiurban, and urban areas. As noted, topics focus on forms of unanticipated suffering and personal or communal hardship. As reactions to such problems become routinized, often the cause—or causes—of suffering are identified as evil. Evil influences invade existence at all levels, including personal daily life, communal living, and even the national character. Evil may also spread abroad with an impact on local populations within Europe or the Americas. The reverse is also possible. In this regard, the chapters embrace the argument of Clough and Mitchell (2001), that evil is inseparable from the material and financial excesses of the modern world system. Effects of evil are experienced universally among Muslims and Christians. Evil is known among all economic classes and manifests itself irrespective of gender. At such moments, life becomes too explosive, too disruptive, and too dangerous, even too unrecognizable for normal living to carry on. In this regard, the authors see the value of Parkin's underlying precept that evil and its ensuing engagements "reflect on the boundaries of humanity." Evil is thereby viewed as an explanatory model of that horrific horizon, where words must somehow capture and engage the horrible.

Evil entanglements in the present take into account local, and often, national histories and identities in order to comprehend how the situation(s) arose in their current condition(s). These must also be addressed when any form of remediation to the predicament of evil is deemed to be practical and effective. The authors to the volume indicate that responses to influences of evil in Africa include a host of methods: ritual, the courts, violence, negotiation, sacrifice, police action, divination, and so forth. Essays disclose that evil is never static in the sense that it may encompass a movement of ideas from village to city, and back again.

The chapters encompass three categorical aspects of evil in Africa: the state and war, evil and religious practices, and evil and modernity. Evil is identified as an active ingredient of contemporary African systems of morality. In a moral sense, individuals and populations experience life in measures of what may be embraced and tolerated and what must be rejected or condemned. Populations do not generally equivocate on what must be eradicated, cast out, or abolished. But their ability to carry out such processes is not always effective. The chapters in this volume provide examples of how evil is identified and then how evil becomes a problem that must be resolved. Remedies to evil are generally social events. Resolutions to witchcraft accusations, to theft, to the aftermath of genocide or war or civil strife, to missing body parts, to apartheid's harsh realities, and to responses to gender or to moral character all involve notably community efforts. The individual rarely stands alone in the quest to oppose evil. In other words, evil in Africa is rarely a singular experience.

Finally, many in Africa today consider a great deal of the problems found in the continent, as well as those imported through Western influences, to be an affirmation of the realities of evil. Even so, responses to evil illustrate the abilities to resolve such issues with whatever resources may be at hand. The chapters in this volume teach us that encounters with evil in Africa are not so much uncontrollable and intractable forces. Rather, the essays remind us of the global nature of African life in that everyday African communities often define evil, as well as how to respond to its impact through transnational entities such as commerce, Koranic prayer, mercenary forces, international human rights, the United Nations, missions, nationalism, war and genocide, Christian ethics, migration, hospitals, the Internet, national media, schools, and so forth. Nevertheless, while using such realities, local African populations—like people everywhere—move in directions that give them some degree of assurance in their lives, some measure of continuity, and some level of recognition that acknowledges both the realities of evil and the perceived methods for countering its nefarious and damaging effects in their daily living.

NOTES

1. See also Rasmussen (2004, 2013).
2. See Ashforth (1998); Nantchouang (2005); Niehaus (1993, 2001); and Ellis and ter Haar (1998).

REFERENCES

Abega, Séverin C. 2005. "Approches anthropologiques de la sorcellerie." In *Justice et sorcellerie,* edited by Eric de Rosny, 25–32. Paris: Karthala.
Adinkrah, Mensah, 2011. "Child Witch Hunts in Contemporary Ghana." *Child Abuse and Neglect* 35:741–752.
Ashforth, Adam. 1998. "Witchcraft, Violence and Democracy in the New South Africa." *Cahiers d'Etudes Africaines,* 38, no. 150–152: 505–532.
Beidelman, Thomas. 1986. *Moral Imagination in Kaguru Modes of Thought.* Bloomington: Indiana University Press.
Bekoff, Marc, and Jessica Pierce. 2009. *Wild Justice: The Morals Lives of Animals.* Chicago: University of Chicago Press.
Blakely, Thomas, Walter E. A. van Beek, and Dennis Thompson, eds. 1994. *African Religion: Experience and Expression.* London: James Currey.
Boyer, Pascal. 2002. *Religion Explained; the Human Instincts that fashion Gods, Spirits, and Ancestors.* Boulder, CO: Westview Press.
Clough, Paul. 2001. "The Political Economy behind the Powers of Good and Evil." In *Powers of Good and Evil. Moralities, Commodities and Popular Belief,* edited by Paul Clough and Jon P. Mitchell, 233–252. Oxford: Berghahn.
Clough, Paul, and Jon P. Mitchell, eds. 2001. *Powers of Good and Evil. Moralities, Commodities and Popular Belief.* Oxford: Berghahn.
Cohan, John A. 2011. "The Problem of Witchcraft Violence in Africa." *Suffolk University Law Review* 44, no. 4:803–872.
Comaroff, Jean, and John Comaroff, eds. 1993. *Modernity and Its Malcontents; Ritual and Power in Postcolonial Africa.* London: University of Chicago Press.
Danfulani, Umar D. D. 2007. "Anger as a Metaphor of Witchcraft: The Relation between Magic, Witchcraft and Divination among the Mupun of Nigeria." In *Imagining Evil: Witchcraft Beliefs and Accusations in Contemporary Africa,* edited by Gerrie ter Haar, 185–204. Trenton, NJ: Africa World Press.

Donham, Donald. 2011. *Violence in a Time of Liberation*.Durham, NC: Duke University Press.

Douglas, Mary, ed. 1970. *Witchcraft Confessions and Accusations*. ASA Monograph. London: Tavistock.

Ellis, Stephen. 2007. "Witching-times: A Theme in the Histories of Africa and Europe." In *Imagining Evil: Witchcraft Beliefs and Accusations in Contemporary Africa*, edited by Gerrie ter Haar, 31–52. Trenton, NJ: Africa World Press.

Ellis, Stephen, and Gerrie ter Haar. 1998. "Religion and Politics in Sub-Saharan Africa." *Journal of Modern African Studies* 36, no. 2:175–201.

———. 2004. *Worlds of Power: Religious Thought and Political Practice in Africa*. London: Hurst.

———. 2007. "Religion and Politics: Taking African Epistemologies Seriously." *Journal of Modern African Studies* 45, no. 3:385–401.

Evans-Pritchard, Edward E. 1937. *Witchcraft, Oracles and Magic among the Azande*. Oxford: Clarendon Press.

Favret-Saada, Jeanne. 1977. *Les Mots, la mort, les sorts: La sorcellerie dans le Bocage*. Paris, Gallimard.

———. 2009. *Désorceler*. Paris, Éditions de l'Olivier.Ferme, Marianne. 1999."Staging Politisi." In *Civil Society and the Political Imagination in Africa*, edited by Jean Comaroff and John Comaroff, 120–144. Chicago: University of Chicago Press.

Finnstrom, Sverker.2008. *Living with Bad Surroundings*. Durham, NC: Duke University Press. Geertz, Clifford. 1973. *The Interpretation of Cultures: Selected Essays*. New York: Basic Books.

Geschiere, Peter. 1997. *The Modernity of Witchcraft: Politics and the Occult in Postcolonial Africa*. Charlottesville: University Press of Virginia.

———. 2001. "Witchcraft and New Forms of Wealth: Regional Variations in South and West Cameroon." In *Powers of Good and Evil. Moralities, Commodities and Popular Belief*, edited by Paul Clough and Jon P. Mitchell, 43–76. Oxford: Berghahn.

———. 2005. "The State, Witchcraft and the Limits of the Law—Cameroon and South Africa." In *Justice et sorcellerie*, edited by Eric de Rosny, 87–120. Paris: Karthala.

———. 2013. *Witchcraft, Intimacy and Trust: Africa in Comparison*. Chicago: University of Chicago Press.

Hinfelaar, Hugo F. 2007. "Witch-hunting in Zambia and International Trade." In *Imagining Evil: Witchcraft Beliefs and Accusations in Contemporary Africa*, edited by Gerrie ter Haar, 229–246. Trenton, NJ: Africa World Press.

Jackson, Michael. 1989. *Paths towards a Clearing: Radical Empiricism and Ethnographic Inquiry*. Bloomington: Indiana University Press.

Johnson, Douglas. 1994. *Nuer Prophets*.Oxford: Oxford University Press.

Kahn, Jeffrey S. 2011. "Policing Evil: State Sponsored Witch-hunting in the People's Republic of Benin." *Journal of Religion in Africa* 41, no. 1: 4–34.

Kapferer, Bruce. 2001. "Introduction: Outside All Reason—Magic, Sorcery and Epistemology in Anthropology." In *Beyond Rationalism. Rethinking Magic, Witchcraft and Sorcery*, edited by Bruce Kapferer, 1–30, Oxford: Berghahn.

Kelly, Henry A. 2006. *Satan, a Biography*. Cambridge: Cambridge University Press.

Kgatla, Simon T., Gerrie ter Haar, Walter E. A. van Beek, and Jan J. de Wolf. 2003. *Crossing Witchcraft Barriers in South Africa: Exploring Witchcraft Accusations: Causes and Solutions*. Utrecht, Netherlands: Utrecht University Press.

Lambek, Michael. 1993. *Knowledge and Practice in Mayotte: Local Discourses of Islam, Sorcery and Spirit Possession.* Toronto: University of Toronto Press.

Lan, David. 1985. *Guns and Rain: Guerillas and Spirit Mediums in Zimbabwe.* London: Currey.

Marwick, Max, ed. 1970. *Witchcraft and Sorcery: Selected Readings.* Hammondsworth, United Kingdom: Penguin.

Meyer, Birgit. 1985. "'Delivered from the Power of Darkness': Confessions of Satanic Riches in Christian Ghana." *Africa; Journal of the Royal Anthropological Institute* 65, no. 2:236–255.

———. 2001. "'You Devil, Go Away from Me!' Pentecostalist African Christianity and the Powers of Good and Evil." In *Powers of Good and Evil. Moralities, Commodities and Popular Belief,* edited by Paul Clough and Jon P. Mitchell, 104–134. Oxford: Berghahn.

Mitchell, Jon P. 2001. "Introduction." In *Powers of Good and Evil. Moralities, Commodities and Popular Belief,* edited by Paul Clough and Jon P. Mitchell, 1–16. Oxford: Berghahn.

Moore, Henrietta, and Todd Sanders. 2001. *Magical Interpretations, Material Realities: Modernity, Witchcraft and the Occult in Postcolonial Africa.* London: Routledge.

Morris, Rosalind. 2006. "The Mute and the Unspeakable." In *Law and Disorder in the Postcolony,* edited by Jean Comaroff and John Comaroff, 27–45. Chicago: University of Chicago Press.

Nantchouang, Robert, 2005. "Economie: sorcellerie et externalités économiques." In *Justice et sorcellerie,* edited by Eric de Rosny, 125–152. Paris: Karthala.

Niehaus, Isak. 1993. "Witch-hunting and Political Legitimacy: Continuity and Change in the Green Valley, Lebowa, 1930–91." *Africa; Journal of the Royal Anthropological Institute* 63, no. 4:489–530.

———. 2001. *Witchcraft, Power and Politics: Exploring the Occult in the South African Lowveld.* London: Pluto.

———. 2002. "Perversion of Power: Witchcraft and the Sexuality of Evil in the South African Lowveld." *Journal of Religion in Africa* 32, no. 3:269–299.

Nkwi, Paul. 1990. "The Lake Nyos Explosion: Different Perceptions of the Phenomenon." *Discovery and Innovation* 2, no. 1:1–19.

Parkin, David, ed. 1985a. "Entitling Evil: Muslims and Non-Muslims in Coastal Kenya." In *The Anthropology of Evil,* 224–243. Oxford: Blackwell.

———. 1985b. Introduction to *The Anthropology of Evil,* 1–25. Oxford: Blackwell.

Peek, Philip M., ed. 2011. *Twins in African and Diaspora Cultures: Double Trouble or Twice Blessed.* Bloomington: Indiana University Press.

Peek, Philip M., and Walter E. A. van Beek. 2013. "Reviewing and Revealing Realities in African Divination." In *Reviewing Reality: Dynamics of African Divination,* edited by Walter E. A. van Beek and Philip M. Peek, 1–25. Berlin: LIT Verlag.

Rappaport, Roy A. 1999. *Ritual and Religion in the Making of Humanity.* Cambridge: Cambridge University Press.

Rasmussen, Suzanne. 2004. "Reflections on Witchcraft, Danger, and Modernity among the Tuareg." *Africa; Journal of the Royal Anthropological Institute* 74, no. 3:315–340.

———. 2013. *Neighbors, Strangers, Witches and Culture Heroes: Ritual Powers of Smith/Artisans in Tuareg Society and Beyond.* Lanham, MD: University Press of America.

Ross, Fiona.2003. *Bearing Witness.*London: Pluto Press.

Schoffeleers, Matthieu. 1991. "Twins and Unilateral Figures in Central and Southern Africa: Symmetry and Asymmetry in the Symbolization of the Sacred." *Journal of Religion in Africa* 21, no. 4:345–372.

Stadler, Jonathan. 1993. "Witches and Witchhunters: Witchcraft, Generational Relations and the Life-cycle in a Lowveld Village." *African Studies* 55, no. 1:87–110.

Stroeken, Koen. 2010. *Moral Power: the Magic of Witchcraft*. Oxford, Berghahn.

Telle, Karl G. 2001. "The Smell of Death: Theft, Disgust and Ritual Practice in Central Lombok, Indonesia." In *Beyond Rationalism: Rethinking Magic, Witchcraft and Sorcery,* edited by Bruce Kapferer, 75–104. Oxford: Berghahn.

Ter Haar, Gerrie, ed. 2007a. "The Evil Called Witchcraft." In *Imagining Evil: Witchcraft Beliefs and Accusations in Contemporary Africa,* 1–30. Trenton, NJ: Africa World Press.

———. 2007b. "Ghanaian Witchcraft Beliefs. A View from the Netherlands." In *Imagining Evil: Witchcraft Beliefs and Accusations in Contemporary Africa,* 93–112. Trenton, NJ: Africa World Press.

Tonda, Joseph. 2008. "La violence de l'imaginaire des enfants-sorciers." *Cahiers d'Études Africaines* 48, no. 189/190:325–349.

Turner, Victor W. 1968. *The Drums of Affliction: A Study of Religious Processes among the Ndembu of Zambia*. Oxford: Clarendon Press.

Van Baal, Jan. 1981. *Man's Quest for Partnership: The Anthropological Foundation of Ethics and Religion*. Assen, Netherlands: Van Gorcum.

Van Beek, Walter E. A. 1994. "The Innocent Sorcerer; Coping with Evil in Two African Societies, Kapsiki and Dogon." In *African Religion: Experience and Expression,* edited by Thomas Blakely, Walter E. A. van Beek, and Dennis L. Thomson, 196–228. London: James Currey.

———. 2010. "Tales of Death and Regeneration in West Africa." In *Proceedings for the Second Annual Conference of the International Association for Comparative Mythology,* edited by Wim van Binsbergen and Eric Venbrux, 41–58. Ravenstein: Private Publishing.

———. 2012. *The Dancing Dead: Ritual and Religion among the Kapsiki/Higi of North Cameroon and Northeastern Nigeria*. New York: Oxford University Press.

Van Beek, Walter E. A., and Thomas Blakely. 1994. Introduction to *African Religion: Experience and Expression,* edited by Thomas Blakely, Walter E. A. van Beek, and Dennis L. Thomson, 1–20. London: James Currey.

West, Harry.2005. *Kupilikula*.Chicago: University of Chicago Press.

Whitehouse, Harvey. 2004. *Modes of Religiosity: A Cognitive Theory of Religious Transmission*. Walnut Creek, CA: Altamira Press.

Whyte, Susan Reynolds. 1997. *Questioning Misfortune: The Pragmatics of Uncertainty in Eastern Uganda*. Cambridge: Cambridge University Press.

PART I

EVIL AND THE STATE/WAR

1 POLITICAL EVIL

Witchcraft from the Perspective of the Bewitched

SÓNIA SILVA

"Evil *is* not any*thing*," David Parkin asserts in his introduction to *Anthropology of Evil* (1985b). Evil is an odd-job word, a word with a lot of baggage, but evil is also a word whose analytical value in anthropology is to push researchers beyond conventional categories. Instead of asking what evil is, let us explore where evil takes us.

Depending on route, the concept of evil can take us in two different directions: morality or ontology. In the first direction, evil is part of morality, being oftentimes interchangeable with bad. In Martin Southwold's words (1985, 131), this is evil in the weak sense. In the second direction, ontology, evil is perceived as a form of extreme wrongdoing. Southwold speaks here of radical evil or evil in the strong sense, this being a realm where the moral discourse of wrongness, wickedness, and immorality seems lacking and displaced. Although Southwold does not deny the continuum between weak and strong forms of evil, he believes that it is important "to keep 'evil' in the strong sense, the better to point to the problems that arise" (1985, 132). I concur.

One "problem" that arises when we define evil in the strong sense is that the concepts of good, bad, and evil are no longer equidistant. Neither is the continuum that they define uniform. It is certainly the case that the continuum good-bad-evil is predicated on the setting of boundaries or limits and, therefore, on the possibility of transgression (Clough and Mitchell 2001, 1). To think of good is always to think of bad, which lies on the other side. Evil is no exception. The Old Teutonic form from which the English term *evil* derives, *ubiloz*, means 'to exceed due measure' or 'overstep proper limits' (Pocock 1985, 42). Yet radical evil differs from immoral acts such as stealing, adultery, and crimes of passion. In his reflections on evil, Aristotle captures this difference by relating the idea of excess with *ápeiron,* the inexplicable (Hobart 1985, 166). As inexplicable excess, the concept of evil leads one to reflect not only on the boundaries between morality and immorality but also on the "internal constitution and external boundaries" of humanity (Parkin 1985b, 6).

Further developing this train of thought, both Pocock and Hobart note that the term *evil* has an ontic weight. In contemporary usage, Pocock affirms, the term *evil* has "a distinctive ontological weight" (1985, 46)—"hence also the terms favored by the popular press which do echo those that people [in England] actually use: 'beast,' 'wild animal,' 'savage'" (1985, 52). Agreeing with Pocock, Hobart states, "[Pocock's interviewed] majority are more Aristotelian— although it might surprise them!—in seeing evil as inexplicable excess, to the point that it is no more a moral judgment but an ontological assertion: there are truly evil acts which show the perpetrators to be inhuman. If evil is so extreme, then the dubious doings of ordinary humans pale in comparison with such monsters" (1985, 167).

Building on the work of both Pocock and Hobart, specifically their idea of evil as excess with an ontological weight, I argue that the concept of evil takes us to a ghastly realm of destruction and transfiguration where the discourse of morality feels lacking and out of place. This is an ontological realm where humans metamorphose into wild animals, beasts, even monsters, which are "worse than animals." In addition, now carrying the idea of evil as excess with an ontic weigh in a different direction, I posit that the shift from the moral to the ontic becomes expressed in the form of highly systematic, often ritualized processes of interpersonal predation that lead, if not curbed, to suffering and death.

Atrocities, however, can be committed and endured not only in the visible realm (genocide, serial killings, witch hunts) but also, as I will show momentarily, in the invisible realm (zombification, bewitching). Some scholars may favor visibility over invisibility, reality over belief. But from the standpoint of those who inhabit cultural and cosmological worlds in which interpersonal encounters are likely to occur in both visible and invisible planes of existence, such dualisms as reality versus belief stand in the way of understanding.

Similarly, interpersonal violence can take place not only in what anthropologists and other thinkers, following Max Weber (1948), often designate as the public domain of politics but also in the more intimate domain of one's home or village. Anthropologists have shown that power in Africa is oftentimes embedded in religion, a point persuasively argued by Arens and Karp in *Creativity of Power* (1989, xvii). But power in Africa, and elsewhere, also undercuts the conceptual differentiation between politics and society. We are as likely to find "brotherliness" (Weber 1948, 155) in politics as to experience enmity at

home. The social is political through and through. Consequently, and returning now to that ghastly region of absolute violence where the concept of evil has
taken us, I reserve the concept of political evil for those interpersonal processes
in which one or more individuals mercilessly prey upon others, dehumanizing
and depleting them of their vitality, if not their life. Humans are as capable of
empathy, identification, love, and solidarity as they are of indifference, condemnation, hate, and discord. In this field of intersubjectivity (Jackson 1998,
1–36), the concept of political evil signals the point in which the interpersonal
process of intrusion and predation, unfettered by moral concerns, advances
coldly and systematically toward annihilation.

There is something sacred in political evil. Although bad and evil are equally
political in the sense of corresponding to interpersonal acts of encroaching and
coercion, as suggested, bad morphs when it becomes political evil. In the movement from bad to evil, the process of systematic, ritualized objectification of
one by another is unleashed, reducing humans to the conditions of predators
and prey (Silva 2013). The movement from morality to ontology is also a movement from morality to absolute violence.

FROM WITCHCRAFT TO BEWITCHING

I now turn to the world of witchcraft in northwest Zambia, witchcraft being
often described, to borrow from Parkin, as the "prototype of all evil" in Africa
(1985b, 15). It hardly matters, as mentioned, whether you and I see witchcraft
as reality or belief, for witchcraft in Africa is experientially real, being widely
considered a major cause of lethargy, illness, and death. For many Africans,
witchcraft is a "matter-of-life-and-death reality," writes Gerrie ter Haar (2007,
19). Similarly, it hardly matters that most of us have never, to the best of our
knowledge, experienced the dangerous world of witchcraft firsthand. In two
years of fieldwork in the Chavuma district of northwest Zambia, I never ap-
prenticed myself to a male or female witch (the term in the Luvale language
spoken in Chavuma is *mukandumba*, or person-with-lions), attempted to join
a coven, or selected a *mukandumba* as an informant. In fact, except for those
witchcraft healers and basket diviners who openly claim to be witches as a way
to bolster and broadcast their powers of healing and clairvoyance (Silva 2011),
I never knew of anyone, man or woman, who publicly admitted to practicing
witchcraft or engaging in acts of bewitchment. My sources of information were
therefore of two kinds: those peculiar, self-proclaimed male witches of sorts
who nevertheless, being highly respected public figures, do not engage, or admit to engage, in acts of bewitching, and those laymen and women with whom

I struck up conversations that led to the sensitive topic of witchcraft. Notoriously, these laymen and women did not describe themselves as witches; instead, they saw themselves as the potential or actual victims of bewitching.

In what follows, paraphrasing the words of these men and women, I attempt to convey their experience of witchcraft as a form of political evil. Four experiential themes recur in their discourse: dehumanization, intrusion, depletion, and consumption. All my interlocutors dwelled to some degree on the same experiential themes even though the content and tenor of our conversations on the topic of witchcraft changed according to focus. Because their discourse—all discourse—simultaneously reflects and culturally molds the experiences narrated (van Beek 2007, 298), it offers a privileged glimpse into the world of witchcraft and bewitching in northwest Zambia from an experiential perspective.

I start with "witchcraft in general," a type of account in which the evildoers are typically female. These accounts describe the methods employed for recruiting new members into the society of witches, the social dynamics of the coven, and the witches' dealings and doings—their witch*craft*. I was told that recruiting starts with the giving or receiving of food, often salt. A witch will walk through the villages asking for salt, *Nguhaneko mungwa! Nguhaneko mungwa!* Suspicious of the intention behind such a request, particularly if voiced by an elderly woman, the potential giver may opt to excuse herself, saying that she is very poor and has no salt to offer. By refusing to reciprocate she hopes to escape the cycle of indebtedness among witches. But the witch will persevere. Under the cover of darkness, the witch will invade that poor woman in her sleep, "causing her to dream" (*kulotesa*), and then proceed to accuse her of being selfish and greedy: "How dared you refuse a bit of salt to a fellow woman in need?" As punishment for her heartless and ungenerous behavior, the victim will be told to join the society of witches, or else die and be eaten.

Witches may also adopt the opposite strategy to multiply their numbers and fill their bellies with human meat. Instead of asking for salt, they will donate salt to women in need. Later, the witches will invade the receivers in their sleep, causing them to dream, and asking for the salt back. Every receiver of salt will likely respond, apologetically, that she has already used the salt in her stew (*ifwo*). But the witch will riposte in a cold, threatening tone: "That salt that you used in your stew belonged to my fellow witches. Now, you must join the coven and pay back your debt in the form of one of your relatives." The most malicious among the witches will demand an infant.

These gifts of human meat that create and sustain the society of witches through ties of mutual indebtedness are known as *jifuka*. To seal her promise of murder, the new witch will be asked to tie a knot in a rope while saying these words: "I will tie up so-and-so." There will be no return now. The new witch will attack at night, invading her victim in his or her sleep and causing him or her to dream. The witch will force the victim to work for her every night, tilling the fields, fetching water, collecting firewood, and going on errands. I was once told that some witches force their prey to carry them on their shoulders from Chavuma to Zambezi, a distance of eighty-four kilometers on the gravel road. Having worked like a slave all night, the bewitched will wake up in the morning feeling pains in the legs, arms, and shoulders. Over time, he or she will feel exhausted and depleted. In particularly malicious cases of bewitchment, the victim will see witchcraft familiars such as hyenas and lions during sleep. The witch may also force sexual intercourse or the ingestion of raw meat, clear signs that death is imminent. The victim is said to die twice: to his or her relatives, who will bury the corpse at the cemetery; and to the gluttonous witches, who will butcher and devour their prey at the cemetery.

The process of bewitching is not random and chaotic. Bewitching is a highly systematic and ritualized process in which the four experiential themes of political evil recur each time: dehumanization of the victim as prey, intrusion into his or her sleep as well as body in the form of forced sexual intercourse and ingestion of raw meat, depletion of the victim's vitality through nocturnal forced labor, and finally, the cannibalistic consumption of the victim's body at the cemetery.

Listening to these stories at night around a bonfire or maybe a small *mbaula* fire—minuscule circles of light surrounded by a thick wall of darkness—can be an uncanny experience. Significantly more perturbing though is listening to accounts that involve relatives, friends, and neighbors who have been bewitched. I refer to these accounts as "witchcraft in particular." As Koen Stroeken (2010, 125) also noticed during her research among the Sukumaof northwest Tanzania, these accounts, being more personal, offer a glimpse into the world of witchcraft from the perspective of the bewitched. From this perspective, bewitching acquires an experiential weight in the form of pain, weariness, illness, and fear. I begin with two cases of witchcraft in particular that I vividly remember.

Konde

In April 1996, the village headman who had welcomed me to his village suddenly died. He had been an important regional cadre of UNIP (The United National Independence Party of Zambia), a faithful supporter of President Kenneth Kaunda, and a wise Luvale elder, respected and loved by all. Over seven hundred people attended his funeral. Some of the attendees drove all the way from the cities of the Copperbelt and the capital of Zambia, Lusaka, and others flew in from Zimbabwe and Ireland. Konde's funeral was a beautiful and peaceful ceremony. Christians sang church hymns and read passages from the Bible. Respected elders offered memorable eulogies that described in great detail Konde's contributions to UNIP during the liberation struggle and after independence.

During the three nights of vigil that preceded the burial at the cemetery, however, the atmosphere was very different. For the smaller group of relatives and friends who attended the vigil held at Konde's village, the confirmation that Konde had been bewitched, as many suspected, arrived on the first night. Many were napping on woven mats around two large bonfires. Suddenly, one of Konde's daughters, Musami, a well-spoken young woman who attended the regional high school, stood up from her mat and readied herself to report what she had heard and seen on the night prior to her father's death.

Musami started by informing her audience that Konde had felt an excruciating pain on his right hip in the morning prior to his death (vakandumba are sometimes said to manipulate substances and injure from afar, much like sorcerers, or vakakupanda, typically do). Konde had fallen to the ground, crying and screaming, "I'm dying! I'm dying!" Then, he had returned to bed, leaving his relatives suspended in a state of apprehension and deep concern. But the situation became clearer that night, Musami added. She had woken up in the middle of the night feeling a heavy weight on her legs below the knees. She had heard "the spirits" (her words) urging, "go, go outside and look," so she had jumped to her feet and run outside as fast she could. "I will never forget what I saw that night," she told her audience at the vigil: three vakandumba standing in the village plaza and holding large chunks of raw, blood-dripping meat; her father's body on top of the large anthill; and a hyena. She had screamed, waking her relatives. Having identified the witches as their neighbors, she had started off in the direction where they lived. Had her mother and half-sister failed to stop her, she would have hit them.

By dawn, Konde lay moribund in bed. He told his relatives that one of his three predators, a man, was troubling him too much (in accounts of witchcraft in particular, vakandumba are not always women). Musami asked her relatives to summon Kazuzu, a renowned expert in witchcraft-related conditions, but Kazuzu was away. Around 9 AM, Konde said to Musami: "They are really troubling me now. I'm leaving, my daughter. Be a good girl." He lifted his hand in her direction. Then he folded his arms over his chest, letting out the sound of a hyena from his mouth.

I have no words to describe the growing tension on the vigil grounds as Musami told her story. Had a group of devout Christians not started to fervently sing church hymns, effectively muffling Musami's hateful words, Musami and others would have likely chased the alleged predators who had chosen not to join the wake. However, not even the Christian hymns erased the grisly images of witches holding chunks of raw meat and Konde lying on his bed, his arms crossed on his chest and his mouth open to let out the sound of the hyena.

On the second day of the vigil, Musami and I sat next to each other. After we chatted a little about this and that, politely avoiding the topic of witchcraft, I asked her about the "spirits" that she had heard. Those spirits, she said, first visited her in dreams during her time in the Western Province of Zambia. The spirits wanted her to become a healer like Kazuzu, but first she wanted to finish her studies and become an engineer. She was only seventeen. Now that her father had passed away, she worried about her future. Who was going to support her studies? Then she steered the conversation in a different direction. Her father and she had been laughing and singing together two nights before he died. They loved to sing Christian songs even though they were not strong believers; they were sort of Christians with no congregation. Herself, she never went to church.

Mary

In July 1996, I accompanied healer Kazuzu to a village in Chavuma where he was to conduct a Kanenga ritual. Kanenga are nightlong rituals performed to free the bewitched from the grip of their predators. In this case, the one bewitched was Mary, a Chewa woman from eastern Zambia.

Mary and her husband, a Luvale man named Kayombo, lived many years in Lusaka and the Copperbelt. Kayombo worked as a driver (a "land-pilot") for the Zambian army. When he retired in 1995, they decided to move to Chavuma, Kayombo's homeland, and settle in the village of his matrilineal relatives.

In Chavuma, it took Kayombo less than a year to build a big house, furnish all five rooms, acquire several goats and chickens, and start a small local business selling groceries. Then, the trouble started. In the span of what seemed only a few weeks, Mary became very thin. Kayombo took her to the regional hospital, but the doctor offered no conclusive diagnosis; all he did, Kayombo said, was to prescribe a handful of aspirin pills. As Mary became ever more emaciated, weary, and thin, Kayombo began to wonder whether she had been attacked by malicious witches who were causing his wife to dream and forcing her to work for them every night. This would explain her rapid loss of weight and vitality. He also reasoned that the witches were likely among his older relatives living in the village, some of whom were envious of his accomplishments. "How could I, such a young chap, own so many things? They wanted me to have a small little house like theirs, and suffer like they do." Their envy (*lwiso*) had hardened their hearts and driven them to attack Mary. Kayombo told me that basket diviner Sakutemba, whose basket they had recently consulted, had reached the same conclusion. And so had healer Kazuzu. On his first examination of Mary prior to the Kanenga ritual, Kazuzu had told Kayombo, "Yes, this thinness and inactivity of hers are the work of witches living among you. We must hurry."

In the late morning following Kanenga, Kayombo invited healer Kazuzu, my research assistant Cedric, and I for lunch in the comfort of his living room. Mary joined us later. She sat on the larger couch in the room and placed her baby boy beside her. Her boy, however, was not a baby, as I had surmised; he was instead a two-year-old boy. Mary explained that her illness had dried up her milk. Her boy had not grown and could not walk because they had no means to purchase nutritious food. We also chattered about her older children who lived in the Copperbelt and Lusaka.

I asked Mary how she felt now that she had been through Kanenga. "I feel lighter and healthier," she said, "even though it wasn't easy to stay awake all night and be splashed with medicinal water on my naked torso in the cold of the night. Now, yes, I feel lighter and healthier." In the weeks to follow, Mary would on occasion walk the long sandy path on the way to my house in Chavuma, her son tied to her back, for a chat with me over a cup of tea. Behind the image of a sick woman with warm eyes, beautifully braided hair, and impeccable clothing, I could see glimpses of her past self. Her son died in October 1996. Mary died one month later.

A missionary nurse at the mission hospital informed me that Mary and her son had died of AIDS. Her husband as well as diviner Sakalwiji and healer Kazuzu reported that Mary had been bewitched. Others agreed with the latter but combined interpretations and diagnoses. In their opinion, Mary had definitely been bewitched, but the witches had hidden behind AIDS to protect themselves from future accusations.

I heard many accounts of bewitching in which the experiential themes of dehumanization, intrusion, and depletion surfaced. Cedric, my research assistant, for example, once explained the general feeling of frailty that he had recently experienced thus: "I was waking up in the morning with an overwhelming feeling of weakness, as if I had not slept all night. I could not understand what was causing these pains in my legs, arms and shoulders. One day my wife asked me, 'Are you feeling tired every morning?' I said, 'Yes, you're right.' Then, she told me what was happening. 'No wonder,' she said, 'you're being overworked by those two women [meaning two elderly women who lived in an adjacent village]."' In these accounts of witchcraft in particular, the main theme is not the witches' recruiting strategies and their shady dealings; instead, it is the gradual, systematic depletion of the victim's vitality by the ruthless evildoers. In extreme cases, as mentioned, the bewitched see hyenas and other witchcraft familiars in their sleep and are forced to eat raw meat and engage in sexual intercourse. These are horrific experiences. Quick to identify the signs of be-witching, others in the community will encapsulate the victim's sheer power-lessness and sense of doom in one dreaded statement: *vanamukase lyehi* (he or she has been tied up). Understandably, the bewitched being alive, no mention is made of the last form that political evil takes on in witchcraft: cannibalism.

Should the relatives of the bewitched act quickly by taking the case of their dying relative to a basket diviner, there might be room for hope. The diviner will identify witchcraft as the cause of suffering and prescribe the conduction of a Kanenga ritual. I attended three of these rituals in 1996, including Mary's. Much like happens in ancestor-related healing rituals (*mahamba*), the objective in Kanenga is to release the patient from the grip of the aggressor, here the *mu-kandumba*. In addition to copiously splashing medicated water on the patient's torso to the sound of singing and drumming, the Kanenga doctor will identify the perpetrator by name and encourage the ritual participants to discuss the reasons that led to bewitching (typically, feelings of envy or personal grudges about things said or done). Finally, he will walk into the darkness surrounding the bonfire carrying a container of blood from the sacrificed goat. He hopes to persuade the *mukandumba* to release the patient (untie the knot) and take the animal blood in his or her stead.

HUMANITY AND ANIMALITY

According to Parkin, not only is witchcraft the prototype of all evil, but the "archetype of evil is ambivalent power" (1985b, 14). The idea of ambivalent power is familiar to anthropologists working in Africa, bringing to mind such exemplary public figures as healers and political leaders. In northwest Zambia, basket diviners and other renowned male healers are often referred to by a term that evokes the very idea of ambivalent power: *vanganga*. Some *vanganga* go so far as boasting their knowledge of the occult, describing themselves in public as *vakandumba* (witches) or, more broadly, *vakauloji* (occult specialists), though not without a grin (Silva 2011, 79). Luvale male and female chiefs (*myangana*) are sometimes described as *vakandumba* (witches) and *vakauhole* (abductors who turn their victims into zombies). In the end, because people need their chiefs, healers, and diviners, they see covert doings and dealings of the chiefs, healers, and diviners as both evil and necessary. Parkin (1985a, 229) drew the same conclusion for his work on the Vaya, the secret society of elders of the Mijikenda of coastal Kenya, and so did countless other anthropologists for their subjects of study elsewhere in Africa (e.g., Jackson and Karp 1990, 20; and Geschiere 1997, 219).

This said, let us not crystallize witchcraft in Africa as an ambivalent power, and the powerful in Africa as semiotic icons of ambivalence, as if their only role and purpose in office or as professionals were to embody and reveal to their subjects and to themselves the true nature of power. The powerful will do or attempt to do all manner of good and evil things, particularly from the viewpoint of their subjects. Consequently, without implying that "politics" is essentially a realm of violence and domination, and much less dismissing or minimizing the good deeds of particular officeholders, the concept of evil in the strong sense of political evil serves as a reminder that rulers can, and sometimes will, unleash their might on their subjects. In those situations in which chiefs—any rulers—prey on their subjects, ambivalence temporarily dissipates, leaving in its wake a stark environment of suffering and destruction. Absolute violence is definite and crystal clear.

In northwest Zambia, the relatives of the bewitched may opt to consult a basket diviner who is willing to identify the witch by name. However, should the witch be a chief, male or female, it will not be possible to halt, undo, divert, or avenge an attack. This sense of powerlessness at the hands of a chief who acts with impunity is reflected in the divinatory speech and procedure. Should the diviner look inside his basket and see that a chief is to be blame for the death, he will lower his oracle and utter a formulaic expression: *Ngombo yinayi mwilu* (the oracle has gone into the air). That will be all. The consulters will understand the diviner's words and ready themselves to leave.

And yet chiefs have no monopoly over violence. In theory if not in practice, anyone can be a witch. As Parkin shows in his work on the Vaya elders, "[the Vaya are] merely what other Mijikenda are but to a greater degree" (1985a, 229). Witches are everywhere, and everyone is or can become a witch. The world of witchcraft is predicated on the recognition of a sociopolitical continuum that extends across what scholars often distinguish as the social and the political, a continuum along which the possibility of being dehumanized, violated, depleted, and consumed by another, ruler or relative, is real. You only need to be human in order to dehumanize others as prey, invade them in their sleep, force them to eat raw meat and engage in sexual intercourse, put them to work like slaves and rob them of their vitality, and eat them up. Witches reduce their victims to the condition of prey whose sole purpose or function in life is to be drained and eaten. In the process of bewitching others, witches also reduce themselves to callous predators whose immediate goal is to drain and eat, to diminish and destroy (Akrong 2007, 59).

Although trespassing and intrusion are ubiquitous in human interaction— think not only of stealing, adultery, and crimes of passion, but also of love, friendship, and the workplace—only political evil takes us to absolute violence. Evil is not an extreme form of bad or, together with bad, the opposite of good. When bad mutates into political evil, losing its moral resonance, evil becomes the opposite of the virtuous. Interestingly, though, virtue and vice have a lot in common besides the well-known truism that virtues are usually vices in disguise. In both cases, the ordinary changes into the extraordinary not by falling into chaos or disorder but by ascending to an eerie plane where everything is ordered, perfect, methodical, and predictable. In this sense, saints and witches resemble one another.

It is also noticeable that, outside the realm of Christianity and Islam, Africa south of the Sahara boasts no saints or other fully virtuous personae. The African High God is a creator and maker—not the final yardstick of morality. Not coincidentally, I think, many Africans associate the unambiguously positive with colors, substances, and material objects, instead of humans, whom they often see as inescapably ambivalent.

What then is it to be human? Where do we place political evil—within humanity or beyond its external boundaries? Where do we place bewitchment? Witches are most certainly human. What is more, they are seen as persons who are known by name, gender, kinship group, and other social attributes. Yet witches are also described as animals that prey on their own kin. In Pocock's words, witches "are and are not human beings" (1985, 48). But do witches ever cross over from humanity to animality?

Several ethnographic facts suggest that witches never exit the human: first, the lions mentioned in "person with lions" (the literal translation of *mukandumba,* meaning witch) consist of witchcraft familiars. They are "people lions" (*vandumba javatu*), as any Luvale speaker will tell you. Second, the witches' predatory attacks as well as their collective feastings are strangely human-like. The savanna lions and hyenas do not force their prey to work for them or eat human meat with bodkins, as witches are said to do. Lastly, witches live in a social world bound by the laws of contract and reciprocity; they do not live in nature. Among the Amba of western Uganda, witches may stand on their heads, rest hanging upside down, quench their thirst with salt, be active at night, go naked, turn into leopards, and eat people; yet they live in villages and are fully human (Winter 1963). In a nutshell, witches are best perceived not as the absolute other but as humans in reverse. Witches are not the enemy out there; they are the enemy within.

We know from Durkheim that the moral is social; but is the social coterminous with the moral? Witchcraft shows us that it is possible to have a social world where morality has no place. Rather than being "at once within and beyond the limits of humanity" (Pocock 1985, 48), witches are at once within and beyond the limits of morality. Witches are persons who have exited morality and become human predators. Hence the shock and perplexity that political evil always generates. Try as we may to distinguish and distance ourselves from predators by continually patching and reinforcing a thick wall of morality all around us, predators are never far away. Predators, however, do not come from the wilderness far out; they come from the social within. Those animals are human.

Faced with atrocities that defy understanding, people will respond differently. Adopting an extremist position, some people will claim that the perpetrators, being beastly, should be treated accordingly. This is most certainly the view of Pocock's English interviewees, according to whom "hanging is too good for them" (Pocock 1985, 52). Other people, more moderate, will attempt to salvage the human by making sense of animality in human terms. They will, for example, invoke brooding negative emotions (the envy and greed of the witch) or the inscrutable depths of psychopathology (the distorted psyches of dictators and serial killers). Or they might justify the evildoer's complicity and participation in predatory regimes by invoking, as did the Nazi Lieutenant Colonel Eichmann during his trial in Jerusalem, the need to fulfill one's duty and follow orders and directives from above—the "man on the job" rational. In Chavuma, I had a memorable conversation with a middle-aged man who made it a point to underscore what he considered a universal truth: no person on the face of the earth will willingly become a witch. People are forced into the coven by the witches' treachery and wickedness, and, as novices, they have no choice but to sacrifice their own relatives lest they will be killed and eaten instead. It could happen to anyone. Although, during our conversation, this man never advocated for the unconditional forgiveness of all acts of bewitching, he showed the willingness to recognize, if only momentarily, that witches are persons (see Silva 2009).

I wondered what this man had done decades before when an agitated group of individuals accused a local elderly woman of being a witch. Had he joined in when the others chased the woman trying to escape? Had he participate in the killing? I did not ask. I knew that moderation in discourse does not preclude animality in practice—much in the same way that extremism in discourse does not necessarily reflect readiness to kill. Many moderates around the world seem satisfied with the idea that the animals, being human, be ostracized, sent into exile, prosecuted in court, cleansed, or saved. Some extremists defend that the perpetrators should be sent to the death row—a compromise that enables them to achieve what they want without exiting the human.

Extremist or moderate, no one is left untouched by what Parkin calls "the unthinkable that nevertheless happens" (1985a, 241). Try as we may to come up with a reasonable explanation, even a scientific explanation, evil in the strong sense of political evil remains what it has always been—inexplicable excess, a true mystery.

REFERENCES

Akrong, Abraham. 2007. "A Phenomenology of Witchcraft in Ghana." In *Imagining Evil: Witchcraft Beliefs and Accusations in Contemporary Africa*, edited by Gerrie ter Haar, 53–66. Trenton, NJ: Africa World Press.

Arens, W., and Ivan Karp. 1989. Introduction to *Creativity of Power*, xi–xxix. Washington, DC: Smithsonian Institution.

Clough, Paul, and Jon O. Mitchell, eds. 2001. *Powers of God and Evil: Moralities, Commodities and Popular Belief*. New York: Berghahn Books.

Geschiere, Peter. 1997. *The Modernity of Witchcraft: Politics and the Occult in Postcolonial Africa*. Charlottesville: University of Virginia Press.

Hobart, Mark. 1985. "Is God Evil?" In *The Anthropology of Evil*, edited by David Parkin, 165–193. Oxford: Basil Blackwell.Jackson, Michael. 1998. *Minima Ethnographica: Intersubjectivity and the Anthropological Project*. Chicago: University of Chicago Press.

Jackson, Michael, and Ivan Karp. 1990. Introduction to *Personhood and Agency: The Experience of Self and Other in African Cultures*. Uppsala: Uppsala University.

Parkin, David, ed. 1985a. "Entitling Evil: Muslims and Non-Muslims in Coastal Kenya." In *The Anthropology of Evil*, 224–243. Oxford: Basil Blackwell.

———. 1985b. Introduction to *The Anthropology of Evil*, 1–25. Oxford: Basil Blackwell.

Pocock, David. 1985. "Unruly Evil." In *The Anthropology of Evil*, edited by David Parkin, 42–56. Oxford: Basil Blackwell.

Silva, Sónia. 2009. "Mothers of Solitude: Childlessness and Intersubjectivity in the Upper Zambezi." *Anthropology and Humanism* 34, no. 2: 179–202.

———. 2011. *Along an African Border: Angolan Refugees and Their Divination Baskets*. Philadelphia: University of Pennsylvania Press.

———. 2013. "Reification and Fetishism: Processes of Transformation." *Theory, Culture & Society* 30, no. 1: 79–98.

Southwold, Martin. 1985. "Buddhism and Evil." In *The Anthropology of Evil*, edited by David Parkin, 110–127. Oxford: Basil Blackwell.

Stroeken, Koen. 2010. *Moral Power: The Magic of Witchcraft*. New York: Berghahn Books.

Ter Haar, Gerrie. 2007. "Introduction: The Evil Called Witchcraft." In *Imagining Evil: Witchcraft Beliefs and Accusations in Contemporary Africa*, edited by Gerrie ter Haar, 1–30. Trenton, NJ: Africa World Press.

Van Beek, Walter E. A. 2007. "The Escalation of Witchcraft Accusations." In *Imagining Evil: Witchcraft Beliefs and Accusations in Contemporary Africa,* edited by Gerrie ter Haar, 293–316. Trenton, NJ: Africa World Press.

Weber, Max. 1948. "Science as a Vocation." In *From Max Weber: Essays in Sociology,* edited by Hans H. Gerth and C. Wright Mills, 129–156. London: Routledge and Kegan Paul.

Winter, E. H. 1963. "The Enemy Within: Amba Witchcraft and Sociological Theory." In *Witchcraft and Sorcery in East Africa,* edited by John Middleton and E. H. Winter, 277–299. London: Routledge and Kegan Paul.

2 UNTYING WRONGS IN NORTHERN UGANDA

SUSAN REYNOLDS WHYTE, LOTTE MEINERT,
JULAINA OBIKA

Evil in northern Uganda is notorious. The film *Kony 2012*, depicting the Lord's Resistance Army (LRA) rebel leader Joseph Kony as the incarnation of brutality, went viral in social media soon after it appeared. More than 120 million people, mostly young Americans, have clicked in to watch a video about a war and a part of Africa about which they had known very little. It described Kony's guerrilla tactics of abducting children for the LRA. In the video, we meet Jacob, from Acholiland, who was seized and made to watch his brother being killed by the rebels. The American narrator explains this to his four-year-old son and shows him two photos: one of Kony as "the bad guy" and one of Jacob as "the good guy" and victim. The evil of Kony and the LRA is brought home through footage of people whose lips have been cut off and children who had to leave their rural homes every night to sleep more safely in town. The film depicts Kony as *the* reason for the war and for the displacement of the entire population of Acholiland to "protected camps" where they lived in dire circumstances for many years. It was made by a nongovernmental organization, Invisible Children, to mobilize a global campaign, including U.S. military action, against Kony, who has been indicted by the International Criminal Court. Despite its success in bringing attention to the LRA war, it was heavily criticized as manipulative, naïve, and potentially dangerous (de Waal 2012; Dreibert 2012; Curtis and McCarthy 2012). The film did not mention the part played by the Ugandan government and the national army, the Uganda People's Defense Force (UPDF), in the horrors of the war or the efforts made to end it by Ugandan politicians and organizations. Neither did the film engage with the ambiguities arising from the overlap between perpetrators and victims in this war. Cynics said it led to a form of "slacktivism" that allowed watchers to feel good and engaged just by clicking a computer key.

While Kony became globally infamous as an icon of evil, the people of Acholiland were dealing with a myriad of ills, not electronically but through direct action. Everyday acts of forgiveness are in many ways the opposite of military action against radical evil. In this chapter we examine how people pardon wrongs in the aftermath of so much maleficence.

THE SEMANTICS AND POLITICS OF EVIL

The heated debate that *Kony 2012* evoked points to larger questions about how identifying evil opens the way for certain kinds of action, and closes off other perceptions and possibilities. Even before the viral video, scholars had argued that both government and humanitarian actors focused exclusively on the barbaric, irrational, radically evil character of the LRA to the exclusion of other sources of suffering. Finnström (2008, 2010) reviews the media coverage of LRA child abduction, mutilation of victims, and spiritual inspiration, arguing that this representation denied any political dimension of the Acholi conflict. Dolan (2009) asserts that the Ugandan government and its army, the UPDF, who forced everyone into camps, together with the donors who provided humanitarian aid, were complicit in the "social torture" that characterized life in encampment. Atkinson (2010, 307) and Branch (2011, 19ff) likewise criticize the moralized portrayal that locates all evil in the demonic madman Joseph Kony and by implication places the government, the UPDF, and the international donors on the side of the angels. All of these researchers bring evidence of "demonization"; Finnström (2010, 74) cites President Museveni's epithet for the LRA—"Satan's Resistance Army."[1] They do not deny that the LRA committed atrocities, but call for recognition of the broader political context and the need for a more comprehensive agenda than eliminating or bringing to justice the LRA commanders. This wider view is increasingly necessary because of the cessation of hostilities in 2006, the return of most displaced people to their rural homes, and their continuing efforts to create some kind of normality as they get on with their lives.

Taking this approach further, we can consider the wider spectrum of evil, wrongdoing, and suffering in Acholiland, and the kinds of responses that are possible when malignancy is construed one way or another. Or perhaps better, we can examine the ways in which a response frames the bad in a particular way and justifies a course of action. Our assumption is that cosmologies can be inferred from practice and ways of telling about experience, and that the pragmatic and semantic dimensions are closely intertwined.

Common to most dealings with evil and wrong in Acholiland are attempts to restore order, to make something right or clean or connected again. To do wrong, *bal*, is translated as "to spoil"; what is spoiled is a pattern that is good, harmonious, whole, or normal. The many ways of trying to put things right portray spoiling or disorder in different guises. Broadly speaking, there are rituals that relate suffering to cosmological powers with their own force, only partly linked to human intentions and actions. And there are less formalized practices of recognizing disorder and setting things right that directly concern human agency and the quality of relations between people, without explicitly involving cosmological forces.

Rituals enact cleansing and the reestablishment of order in many different ways. To undertake such rituals is to construe suffering in terms of the powers of *jok*, a cosmological force that can take the impersonal character of pollution or the more agentic form of spirits working on or through persons (p'Bitek 1971). Often it is in attempts to deal with suffering that people call to mind events that have spoiled order and set the powers of *jok* in motion. Preeminent examples are the birth of anomalous children (twins or those born with unusual features such as an extra finger) and actions that set off pollution (adultery).

But it is another type of ritual and another concern with pernicious power that has preoccupied local people, spokesmen for Acholi tradition, donors, and scholars in the postwar period. These address the disorder of war by cleansing those who committed atrocities and cooling (*kweyo*) the heat of the vengeful ghosts (*cen*) of those who died violently, unjustly, or without proper burial. Scholars and aid workers from the global North have worked with spokesmen for Acholi tradition to catalog rituals that might be used to promote healing in a culturally sensitive way (Pain 1997; Baines 2010; Harlacher et al. 2006; Ochola II 2009). The name of one of these reports, "Roco Wat i Acholi: Restoring Relationships in Acholiland," points to the understanding of evil as spoiled relationships that can be repaired. Like the other reports, "Roco Wat" discusses rituals as ways of expunging evil and allowing people to get on with their lives.

Rituals require resources, often an animal for sacrifice, and always some food or drink for the participants to share. Several donors have stepped in with funding, especially for two kinds of cleansing rituals. The USAID (United States Agency for International Development)–funded Northern Uganda Transition Initiative has supported rituals to cleanse (*ryemo cen*) areas of the *cen* spirits that afflict people as they move back to their rural homes. Especially in the first years of resettlement, there were reports of people coming across remains of unknown and unburied dead, or seeing strange figures, or hearing voices as they began to clear the bush for farming again. Other donors have funded a more politically loaded ritual, *mato oput,* as a way of purifying fighters who have been polluted by the atrocities they committed, so they can be reintegrated in local communities. A simpler cleansing ritual, *nyono tonggweno,* stepping on eggs, was also performed on a large collective scale with the same intent of reintegrating returnees (Harlacher et al. 2006, 69; Finnegan 2010, 431–432).

Scholars have criticized these endeavors to codify Acholi traditions for resolving disorder and to fund rituals marked as "traditional." They note the reification of practices that have been more fluid (Allen 2010) and the inevitable distortions that accompany the channeling of donor funding to traditional authorities (Branch 2011, 171). Both Allen and Branch are concerned with the political implications of fixing ritual responses to malignant disorder. Allen finds the project problematic because it is not national; it assumes that Acholi people are different from other citizens of the state (Allen 2010, 258). Branch stresses the reaffirmation of authority structures within Acholi society that is inherent within what he calls "the turn to culture" (Branch 2011, 154–178). For both, modes of dealing with evil have significant consequences for power relationships and can be seen as part of a political agenda. They are less concerned with the concepts of cleansing inherent in the rituals than in the notions of restorative justice that are so important for politicians and donors.

Yet whether we see rituals as attempts to wash away pollution or to reintegrate evildoers, they have certain fundamental characteristics as rituals. They are framed events with a beginning and an end. They are public and collective to some degree. And they address, and therefore assert the existence of, forces beyond human agents. Baines (2010), for example, describes efforts to set right relations with "intimate enemies" who had committed wrongs during the war and shows how spirit possession and ritual cleansing facilitate social reconstruction in local settings. In their public nature and orientation toward nonhuman sources of malignancy, such responses differ from the unmarked forgiveness processes that also are ways of dealing with malignant disorder and attempting to restore relationships.

While rituals of cleansing are events, ordinary forgiveness as we came to understand it is a development that unfolds over time within a relationship. It is a matter of untangling in Parkin's (1985, 240) sense of the straightening out of human relations. Indeed, the Acholi word for forgiving (*gonynyo*) means untying,[2] releasing, or letting go that which was knotting up a relationship. The heart is like a bag that can be filled with anger and must be released. People said that "keeping someone (or something) in the heart" blocks the flow between people and the stream of life for the bitter person. They made a link between emotional and social well-being (Ovuga et al. 2012). Untying requires no spilling of blood and refers to no spiritual forces. Unlike Parkin's examples of disentangling, it may not even be articulated in words. But it must be enacted between people; it must be demonstrated in practice.

THE FORGIVENESS PROJECT

Our study of forgiveness in Acholiland was part of a collaboration between researchers at Gulu University and at two Danish universities. We initially employed an experimental combination of art, anthropology, and action. A Danish artist, Tove Nyholm, came to work with us in Gulu District to collect accounts of forgiveness and construct an installation where others could come to listen to "voices from within." She had been inspired by the works of Hannah Arendt and had already made sound installations on the theme of forgiveness in Denmark. The intention of her project was to encourage reflection on letting go of wrongs. It was hoped that this would have a positive ripple effect in the community, whereby those who heard the voices of forgiveness would be moved to either forgive those who had wronged them or ask for forgiveness from those whom they had offended.

At the outset, then, the endeavor had a moral potential that resonated with the Christian message of forgiveness that is familiar throughout Acholiland where the Roman Catholic and Anglican churches have been important for more than a century. Moreover, it seemed to harmonize with the many political efforts to promote reconciliation in the aftermath of the long war, including the cleansing of fighters that drew on elements of Acholi culture (Finnegan 2010). However in analyzing the accounts, and in conversations with others not connected with the artistic project, we came to see it as something more as well: a window onto the untangling of everyday wrongs in the shadow of much larger maleficence.

Through networking, the Gulu University researchers found several adults who were willing to share a personal experience of forgiveness. We explained the purpose of the study to each participant and sought their consent to share their stories with the public on condition of anonymity. Ten accounts, in either English or Acholi, were initially recorded, each lasting between fifteen minutes and one hour. They were carefully edited to clips of three to six minutes, capturing details about the situation, the wrong committed, the decision to forgive, the process, and the impact of the act of forgiveness (Meinert et al. 2014). In one of the huts in the former camp for Internally Displaced People in Awach sub-County, we installed a sound system so that people could sit together in the dim interior and listen to the voices from within telling their stories. In a nearby hut, those who were inspired to record their own accounts could do so.

To reach more people, the researchers broadcast three radio programs on local FM stations (one in English and two in Acholi). Listeners were able to call in and give their views about the study and about the subject of forgiveness. Also, a mobile outreach program was developed; the sound system with the voice accounts was taken to eight villages of Awach sub-County, where people were given a chance to listen and comment on the idea of forgiveness and "letting go" as a tool for the attainment of peace in northern Uganda. More than seven hundred people came to listen to the accounts.

Parallel with the artistic action project, we began to analyze the accounts and gather more material on forgiveness. We did a thematic analysis of thirty-five transcribed accounts. In addition, we carried out interviews with key informants and selected members of the community known for their experience in peace building. They included local leaders, elders, religious clerics, and non-governmental organization representatives. Two focus group discussions were held with groups of elders in Awach trading center and Gulu municipality. The interviews and discussions focused on definitions, perceptions, and notions of forgiveness and reconciliation in northern Uganda.

THE WRONGS OF WAR AND EVERYDAY LIFE

Not surprisingly, all of the accounts were about forgiving rather than asking for forgiveness. Given the value ascribed to "untying" and "letting go," the narrators seemed to be taking the moral high ground in pardoning those who had hurt them. But whom did they forgive and for what? In contrast to the scholarly and political debates about general amnesty for LRA fighters, the International Criminal Court, and public rituals of cleansing as culturally appropriate alternatives to retributive justice, our narrators told personal stories about forgiving people they knew. Many of these wrongs happened during the war, some as a direct result of it. But what we find particularly interesting is the fact that when the participants were asked to share their experiences of wrong and forgiveness, none of them made direct reference to Kony and no one spoke of forgiving the LRA and the UPDF. Neither anonymous government soldiers nor nameless rebels were forgiven, even though some of those who spoke their accounts had suffered terribly at their hands. People forgave those with whom they had existing relationships. The majority of alleged wrongdoers were relatives by blood or marriage; a few were neighbors. Even when the offense was committed by an LRA fighter, it became a matter for forgiveness only when the offender and victim had to resume living together. "Untying" was for intimate enemies, not for abstract or distant evildoers. In telling their stories, people described the injuries inflicted by strangers during the war, but they counted as most hurtful and needing pardon, the failures and betrayals of those close to them. You forgive a face you know.

The wrongs themselves were of two kinds. A minority were directly related to the war: abduction by the LRA, abuse while in captivity, and mistreatment of those who escaped or returned from the LRA. The great majority were "ordinary" transgressions of the kind that happen everywhere in Uganda: neglect by stepmothers, infringements by cowives, disregard by parents, failure to pay school fees, physical assaults. A recurrent theme was betrayal by those upon whom you should be able to depend. Sometimes, the sufferings of war were linked to betrayal by family or neighbors. One girl told us that she blamed her father for her abduction because if he had believed in educating his daughters and not only his sons, then she would have been in school instead of on her way to a shop to buy salt when she was abducted.

Because the offender was someone with a relationship to the forgiver, there were others involved too. The dyad was part of a set of relationships; both resentment and the eventual release of the wrongdoer were part of a wider sociality. When the wives of two brothers quarreled, the brothers were also set at odds. A quarrel between relatives put the whole family in a bad light. Correspondingly, others took an interest in promoting forgiveness and many accounts mentioned family meetings or the intercession of a relative to encourage the wronged person to release the offender.

Hannah Arendt sees forgiveness as a necessary element in social life, where people constantly transgress against one another. "But trespassing is an everyday occurrence which . . . needs forgiving, dismissing, in order to make it possible for life to go on by constantly releasing men from what they have done unknowingly" (Arendt 1998, 240). She distinguishes radical evil, which can neither be forgiven nor punished, from the common wrongdoings that are not intentional. For her, forgiving is an essentially human and social disposition arising "directly out of the will to live together with others in the mode of acting and speaking" (ibid., 246). People forgive because of a determination to go on living with the person who offended them: "Forgiving and the relationship it establishes is always an eminently personal . . . affair in which *what* was done is forgiven for the sake of *who* did it" (ibid., 241).

For Arendt, new beginnings, what she calls "natality," are made possible through forgiveness because the constant mutual release makes human beings free to start over. This view resonates with the accounts of our narrators, who often spoke of the liberating consequences of forgiveness. "Holding someone in your heart," that is thinking of him with bitterness, constrains both the offended person and social interaction. But untying or letting it go allows things to flow again. Our narrators used phrases such as "Now we are free with each other."

The foundational myth of the spear and the bead told in Acholiland, and in other parts of East Africa as well, instructs about the consequences of refusing to forgive. Gipir speared a marauding elephant with the weapon of his brother Gifol (in other versions, the brother was Nyabongo or Labongo). The beast fled with the spear in its hide and Gifol would accept no other as a replacement. He insisted that Gipir find the elephant and return the very same spear, no matter how dangerous and difficult it might be. Later there came a day when Gifol's child swallowed a bead belonging to Gipir. In bitter revenge, Gipir required that the child's belly be slit open so that he could recover the very same bead. As Okot p'Bitek (1971, 20) closes the telling, "The two brothers could live together no more." Gipir left with his people to settle on the west bank of the Nile. Lack of forgiveness made continuing proximate relationships impossible.

"IT IS USELESS TO KEEP A RECORD OF WRONGS"

A young woman we call Santa was twenty-three years old when she volunteered her story of forgiveness. The wrongdoer was her cowife (her "co"), who fought with her and knocked loose her tooth. She was taken to hospital and from there to police where the case was reported and then back to hospital to have her tooth wired up. Her uncle in Kampala rang to her father, asking him to drop the charges and put a stop to the quarrel. A family meeting was convened.

> They warned us not to behave like that because it spoils the name of the home. So we left that behavior and right now we are living in peace with my co and no one jeers at the other. . . . And me, from my heart, I threw the wronged one from my heart, and put the good one. And that's why I'm staying together with my co. . . . I thought in my heart that it is useless to keep a record of wrongs. It spoils the relationship among people and makes them not live in peace with each other. I thought of the harm she had caused me and felt that there was no use holding on to the past and I decided to forget about it.

The ostensible cause of the quarrel was that Santa had been allowed to sell some bananas, but she and her husband suspected that her cowife "was holding something in her heart from earlier, different from the issue of bananas."

Exactly what that was she did not say, but when asked about her background, she told the story of how she had been abducted by the LRA when she was ten years old.

She was so small that the abductors had to carry her when fording rivers. Although some commanders wanted to release her because she was too young, others said that no one from Awach should be set free because people from Awach had killed one of the top commanders. They took her to Sudan, where she lived for years, fleeing with her captors when the Ugandan army pursued them into the mountains. She had a baby when she was sixteen. "It is hard—you run if the helicopters are coming. Thorns tear the head of the child, but you run, thinking about what is going to shoot you—you don't think of thorns." In July 2005, the child's father was killed and she managed to escape with her baby. After some months in a rehabilitation center for returnees, she returned to her parents' home, but reintegration was difficult. "I was not used to the life at home, and it was not easy. I thought of staying in the bush, perhaps I shouldn't have returned."

At the time she told of forgiving her co, Santa had been back home for seven and a half years. Although she emphasized the virtue in untying and said she was now free with her co, she also remarked that she was currently living at her father's home, suggesting that she and her co were not exactly best friends. We could not help but think that the underlying problem was that her cowife disdained her as *alum,* a woman from the bush, who returned with an LRA baby. But Santa's account of wrong and forgiveness was not about the "big wrong" of the war or her abduction or the robbery of her childhood or being attacked by the Ugandan army. It was a story of releasing from her heart someone with whom she had to go on living.

Arendt's point that forgiveness allows people to go on living together draws our attention to the consequences of releasing the wrongdoer, something that our accounts always emphasized. Forgiveness permits people to maintain relationships of civility with those who had offended them. In situations of mutual interdependence, such civility can prove useful; even someone who has hurt you may help you when you need her. One narrator put it bluntly: "Someone can kill your dear ones and you still talk to them. Water can also kill and you still use the water. Fire can also burn your child, and you use fire. What about human beings like you? You should talk to them and forgive them." Several spoke of how they could share things with the offender once they had forgiven. Peter, whose wife was bitten by his brother's wife, explained that now they were on good terms again, they could ask anything from his brother and sister-in-law and not be refused. That people considered the practicalities of forgiving in contrast to holding a grudge was clear from the way so many spoke of it being "useless" to hold bad things in the heart, implying that it was useful to forgive.

The profound value of social harmony, clearly evident in Santa's family, is emphasized by Holly Porter (2012) in her study of justice and rape in the Acholi subregion. Whether the offense of rape was dealt with by swift punishment or, as was more common, by forgiveness on the part of the victim, the ideal was to maintain harmonious relations within the moral community. Congruent with our own findings, Porter showed that women were more likely to forgive perpetrators they knew, even though they felt betrayed. They wanted harsh punishment for men with whom they had no relationship, or only a distant one. "How women who have survived rape are oriented toward punishment of the aggressor is deeply impacted by whether he is a vital part of the future moral community" (Porter 2012, 94). The idea of a future moral community corresponds well with our impression, and Arendt's argument, that a basic concern is the continuation of social relationships. In some cases, however, the tone may better be described as civility than deep harmony.

MITIGATION AND THE MUTABILITY OF EVIL

When people told how they had forgiven, they sometimes explained why someone could be released. They mentioned mitigating factors that induced them to leniency. Having felt wronged, bitter, and resentful, they commented on how they came to change their minds (or their hearts). That is to say, they saw the wrong in another light, or as Parkin puts it, they treated evil as negotiable: "In other words, the blame for any evil act can be shifted, or its severity reduced, to the extent even of excusing the original perpetrator" (Parkin 1985, 227). In this sense, evil is mutable.

The most common mitigating factor was simply time. Our narrators said that it took time for them to begin to let go. Time was almost always passed in close enough proximity so that they saw the wrongdoer and interacted with others who were connected to them both. Janet told how she finally began to talk to the man who had betrayed her to the rebels: "We started because people are in the group, . . . I found it really bad not to greet him, since they come there to our place and we also go to their place." Brian began to forgive the teacher who had beaten him unjustly because the teacher married his aunt and used to come with her to visit in his home. For some people, a month passed before they began to relent; others mentioned ten years in which they could not forgive an injustice done to them.

A wrong can be excused if the wrongdoer was in some way not responsible for his or her actions. The most dramatic accounts of this type were those of cruel acts performed by rebels and those they had abducted. Stories that had to do with actions carried out in the rebel army emphasized that the moralities of rebel life belonged to "the bush"—*lum,* meaning tall grass, bush, and by extension rebel (Verma 2012). It was "another world" and "another time," which excused actions that would otherwise be considered immoral. Being *alum,* in the bush, in the power of others, and under the influence of "evil," the offender was not responsible for what he was doing. Many of those who fought for the LRA were abducted and forced to loot and kill. "It was not their intention," was an oft-repeated phrase. In the reception centers, the returnees were told that they were not at fault for being with the LRA (Mergelsberg 2010, 165).

These aspects of unintentionality and being absorbed in "another moral world" were considered significant mitigating circumstances in the account of an abductee who, years later, found himself sharing a room in a school hostel with his abductor. Moses was about fifteen years old when he was seized by the LRA. He was forced to carry a very heavy bag with items looted from his home. It was an extremely tough and frightening time, especially in the beginning. Moses was with the rebel group for three to four months and explained how he gradually got acclimatized to their ways and moralities and learned the practices of looting, abducting, killing, punishing escapers, walking bare-chested, and drinking urine, when there was no water: "So while in the bush, in captivity . . . because you know when you get acclimatized with the condition, you will now develop that behavior. Because, you know, behavior is learned. It is not inborn. So now, I started also catching up. I started also catching up with them. Life was so hard. I went even bare-chested. So imagine moving in the bush."

Moses got injured twice; both times he was shot by the UPDF. The second time, the wound was so serious that he could not walk but had to be carried by the other rebels, and on those grounds he managed to negotiate release from the LRA. Together with two escorts, Moses got to a reception center in Kitgum (KICWA, the Kitgum Concerned Women's Association) where his wounds were treated. His family was very happy and relieved that he managed to escape, and they wanted him to come straight home. But the staff at the center advised the family to first send him to World Vision to be properly rehabilitated before he joined the family and went back to school. Returnees (children and young people who had been with the rebels) were often considered semidangerous, wild, unruly, and in need of reeducation. After about two months at the rehabilitation center, Moses was allowed to return to his family and from there went back to a boarding school.

Years later when Moses met his abductor at school, Moses had a wish that the abductor would admit his wrongs against Moses and ask for forgiveness, but this did not happen.

> [The Abductor] said that it wasn't his intention to do [what he did]. Because for him, he was also working on instructions given by *Lapony* (the teacher/leader of the rebel group) . . . I wasn't interested in hearing that. I was expecting him to have said: "Okay look here. We are sorry for what has happened. But can we now, you know, begin, you know, a meaningful life." But he didn't say that. What he said was that it was not his intention. So there is no way he [could] say that maybe I forgive him. Uhhm. So now, my advice to him was that since we now know each other and we have recognized each other, can we keep it to ourselves? That at one time, we served ahhh, in the rebel activities, but that was not our wish. We were on a force to do so. And he had to understand. Because we were in the same room. We could take breakfast together. Go to school together . . . , we stayed together. And we promised each other to let go of those memories. Whether bad or good. Because in the bush, if you were enjoying life, maybe you went here and there, you looted things, you enjoyed, beating up people who tried to escape from the group. You enjoyed. So that is why I was advising him to let go of whatever good or bad things we have done. Because if from the hostel, we again met the roommates, and other members from the hostel, and they knew that we were once, you know, abductees, then they would fear us, or start discriminating us.

Moses explains how he decided to forgive himself for the bad actions he carried out while in the bush, including the fact that he also enjoyed some of them.[3] His explanation of how he became used to the (im)morality of the bush world, how it became normal for him, seems to fit with Arendt's (1963) point about the banality of evil. He simply did what the others were doing and what was ordinary in that situation. He did not intend to do harm, but one thing led to another and actions evolved in that way. Arendt pointed out that evil seldom comes in radical forms, but it often comes with a kind of banality that blinds us. All human beings may experience losing their sense of judgment and getting involved in evil actions. That is why we need the faculty of forgiving, according to Arendt.

In retrospect, Moses recognized the evil aspects of his actions. Yet he could not convince his abductor to make the same confessions and beg for forgiveness. Moses explained that his roommate was still involved in some business activities using capital he had obtained from looting. He was not yet ready to condemn the actions of the past, because he was still benefitting from them economically. The abductor would merely agree to keeping their secret.

Like Moses, others drew a sharp line between the (im)moralities of the bush and the ordinary world of the postcamp period. George told of an LRA fighter who abused him with particular malice when he was abducted. Two years after George escaped, his tormentor turned up in the same place where he was working and came to greet him. At first George still felt angry, but gradually he saw that his bitterness was "useless."

> I started to see . . . maybe he didn't know what he was doing. . . . Me, what I saw, you know . . . Kony was abducting people when they were still young. Even me, I was abducted when I was young, so when you reach there, sometimes you see that that life is maybe the only life—the life of killing people, the life of mistreating people. . . . Let's forgive people who were doing things from the darkness. He was in the darkness. . . . He came and found me in light. . . . If he comes back into the light and he is still continuing with his [bad] action, then it is unforgiveable. But when he was still there, he was still in darkness. He was following what he was in because when someone is in the bush, he is in darkness, not seeing anything. He only thinks of things in the bush. The things that come into his mind are killing—violent things only.

Arendt wrote of "releasing men from what they have done unknowingly" (1998, 240) and discussed the Christian message that people should be forgiven "for they know not what they do." Construing the *lum* as a world of darkness, another place and time, is one way of excusing people for doing evil unknowingly. But there were many other more ordinary excuses that people mentioned in telling how they forgave. Michael forgave his father's sister's son (his nephew in Acholi terminology) for fighting him, because the nephew was drunk: "Had it been that he didn't drink, nothing would've happened. So as alcohol had taken him, himself he is begging for forgiveness."

Sam's father refused to pay his school fees, using his money instead on the children of his new wife. Sam was angry at his stepmother, but even more so at his father. When he finally forgave him, it was because he realized that his father was not able to see what was important. "I think he was living a life of those of his friends who don't think of the future, so that's why I used to see him with those who don't have a plan. They couldn't give him a plan, that's why he was lost [and did] all those things. . . . He was lost, not knowing what he was doing. You know people, even if they are matured, sometimes they get lost, sometimes they do not know what they are doing. Then they may understand it later—that those things he was doing were wrong."

Ignorance was also a mitigating element in a serious land conflict, where a youth claimed the land of his father, who had been killed by the rebels. He threatened his brothers with whom he should have shared it and refused to talk to his elders. After police involvement, arrests, and a hate-filled period where "we could not see each other as human," his father's wife decided to forgive him and sit him down with clan elders who would bring him to his senses. As she recounted: "We were even wishing that boy should die, because he was just laughing at their father's death. Then we thought of it later and said, 'Heee! This boy is our blood, he is the son of our husband. It is just ignorance disturbing him.'"

PRACTICING AND TELLING FORGIVENESS

In Parkin's analysis of concepts of evil among Giriama and Swahili people on the Kenya coast, he differentiates between rituals that cleanse pollution and those in which relations are untangled. The former worked through sacrifice alone, while the latter needed words to confirm relationships and assert the nature of wrongs, intentions, and restoration. In Acholiland, there are rituals of cleansing, as we have noted, that have been attributed new importance in the aftermath of the war. It seems that the ritual acts themselves are considered effective in purifying the affected persons and places. However, the forgiveness accounts we have heard and the conversations we have had about Acholi ideas of forgiveness suggest another idea of efficacy. Words are usually spoken, as in the ceremonies Parkin (1985) describes for disentangling,[4] but this was not always the case. What was important was to show forgiveness in practice, not simply to speak words. Steven said he forgave the bully who used to beat him up regularly on the way to school. But no words were ever said: "You know with forgiveness, sometimes it doesn't have to come from the mouth, but from how you relate with the person who once hurt you. If you are free with each other, holding no grudges, you just know that forgiveness has already taken place." Others said that you could tell if someone had forgiven "by heart" and not only "by tongue" by watching their actions: did they share food, spend time together, converse? Daniel had quarreled with his brother, who moved into his house while Daniel was away at school. When Daniel came home for holiday, his brother refused to vacate the house. With the help of senior relatives, he forced his brother out, and they were so annoyed with one another that they refused to eat together or greet one another. Their father, aunts, and uncles tried to reconcile them and reminded them of the brothers Labongo and Gipir, who could not forgive one another over a spear and a bead. They were forced to shake hands, but "real happiness was not there." They still did not speak for several days, until finally Daniel went to his brother's home and sat and talked to his wife. Step by step they began to visit one another, to enter each other's houses, and to share things. It was not the words, but their actions, that made the forgiveness efficacious.

CONCLUSION

If we approach evil as something that is construed through means of control or management, then we are able to inquire about the interests in formulating it in a particular way and the consequences of different ways of dealing with it. This is prominent in the case of the *Kony 2012* film, which mobilized Americans for political and military action by personifying radical evil. Also the use of Acholi rituals of forgiveness had a collective political purpose, including, as Finnegan (2010) points out, the forging of a common Acholi identity.[5]

The forgiveness accounts we have presented work differently. They are less about collectivities than about relations between particular individuals embedded in specific social situations. When evil is formulated as a wrong committed by someone who can be forgiven, it is domesticated and personalized. The forgiver can show virtue on an immediate scale, in a way that is meaningful in everyday life. The larger context that causes suffering may be a drawn out violent insurgency or the AIDS epidemic or the political economy that ensures poverty or the institutionalization of gender inequality or fate that deals a bad hand. But making maleficence and wrongs forgivable brings them to a proximate level that is both graspable and practical. The evil of the war was construed in ways that required releasing relatives and neighbors, just as did the recurring trespasses of ordinary life. War wrongs, at least those in our accounts, were thus assimilated to the same category of transgressions as common ordinary wrongs and dealt with in the same way.

Arendt valued the faculty of forgiving because it allows us to undo what we have done and thereby to break the irreversibility of vengeance. Forgiving, according to Arendt is the only action that is not a reaction but a new action that makes new beginnings possible. That revenge is the real danger is captured in the Acholi saying: *alunya loyo lakwong*—"revenge is more painful than the first crime" (Ochola II 2009, 14). As our interlocutors put it, revenge or the resentment that spurs it is useless. In contrast, they explicitly celebrated forgiveness as the means to go on living together, in civility if not in true amity.

There can be no doubt that forgiveness carries a heavy ideological weight in Acholiland; its value has been overdetermined by Christianity and by the concerted effort to find in Acholi heritage principles and practices that can be deployed for reconciliation after the war. We know that forgiveness is not as final as the accounts imply and that it is being idealized. But we appreciate the ideals that the accounts convey and the declared intentions of trying to get along and move along.

When we undertook the forgiveness project, we expected that people would tell stories about the wrongs of the war, in line with the massive attention to the brutalities of the conflict and the need for reconciliation. The fact that they told of "ordinary" transgressions and that even the evils of war were personalized suggests to us that a more experiential approach to understanding evil is necessary. This does not mean depoliticizing evil and wrongdoing. Rather it means that we must expand our delineation of the political arena to include everyday relationships and how they are affected by larger maleficent forces.

NOTES

1. Interestingly, the LRA likewise demonized the Ugandan army: "according to Kony, the whole UPDF is controlled by Satan . . ." (Titeca 2010, 66).

2. Forgiveness can be translated as *timo kica,* "to do mercy or kindness," and this was the name of our project. *Timo kica* can also mean amnesty (Allen 2010, 251) as in *timo kica lumuku,* "showing mercy for everyone." Reverend William Onyango, chaplain of Gulu University, prefers *gonynyo* because it is more specific, referring to the untying that makes people free. While the Church of Uganda uses the phrase *iwek balwa,* "leave aside our wrongs/sins," in the Lord's Prayer, the Roman Catholics pray *gonya balwa,* "untie the wrongs." Also, evangelical Christians use *gonya* rather than *timo kica.*

3. See Verma (2012) for an excellent analysis of alternative stories of life in the bush.

4. Like other groups in Uganda, Acholi are reported to respect the ability of certain relatives to curse and to have a ritual in which words must be spoken to remove the curse (Whyte 1997, 155–177, p'Bitek 1971, 145–153) in line with Giriama ritual practices of disentanglement.

5. There is an important contrast between the politics of ritual change reported in the civil war in southern Sudan and that in northern Uganda. Hutchinson (1996, 137–141) describes how a military leader promoted the removal of gun deaths from the sacred category of *col wic,* thus deritualizing the consequences of war. The politicians and donors in Acholiland reinforced the ritual management of war effects by strengthening rituals such as *mato oput.*

REFERENCES

Allen, Tim. 2010. "Bitter Roots: The 'Invention' of Acholi Traditional Justice." In *The Lord's Resistance Army: Myth and Reality,* edited by T. Allen and K. Vlassenroot. 242–261. London: Zed Books.

Arendt, Hannah. 1963. *Eichmann in Jerusalem: A Report on the Banality of Evil.* New York: Viking Press.

———. 1998. *The Human Condition.* 2nd ed. Chicago: University of Chicago Press.

Atkinson, Ronald R. 2010. *The Roots of Ethnicity: The Origins of the Acholi of Uganda.* 2nd ed. Kampala, Uganda: Fountain Publishers.

Baines, Erin. 2010. "Spirits and Social Reconstruction after Mass Violence: Rethinking Transitional Justice." *African Affairs* 109: 409–430.

Branch, Adam. 2011. *Displacing Human Rights: War and Intervention in Northern Uganda.* Oxford: Oxford University Press.

Curtis, Polly, and Tom McCarthy. 2012. "Kony2012: What is the Real Story?" *The Guardian.* March 8, 2012.

De Waal, Alex. 2012. "Don't elevate Kony." http://sites.tufts.edu/reinventingpeace/2012/03/10/dont-elevate-kony/

Dolan, Chris. 2009. *Social Torture: The Case of Northern Uganda, 1986–2006.* New York: Berghahn Books.

Dreibert, Michael. 2012. "The Problem with Invisible Children's Kony 2012." http://africanarguments.org/2012/03/08/the-problem-with-invisible-childrens-kony-2012-by-michael-deibert/

Finnegan, Amy C. 2010. "Forging Forgiveness: Collective Efforts amidst War in Northern Uganda." *Sociological Inquiry* 80: 424–447.

Finnström, Sverker. 2008. *Living with Bad Surroundings: War, History and Everyday Moments in Northern Uganda.* Durham, NC: Duke University Press.

———. 2010. "An African Hell of Colonial Imagination? The Lord's Resistance Army in Uganda, another Story." In *The Lord's Resistance Army: Myth and Reality,* edited by T. Allen and K. Vlassenroot, 74–89. London: Zed Books.

Harlacher, Thomas, Francis Xavier Okot, Caroline Aloyo Obonyo, Mychelle Balthazard, and Ronald Atkinson. 2006. *Traditional Ways of Coping in Acholi: Cultural Provisions for Reconciliation and Healing from War.* Gulu, Uganda: Caritas Gulu Archdiocese.

Hutchinson, Sharon. 1996. *Nuer Dilemmas: Coping with Money, War, and the State.* Berkeley: University of California Press.

Meinert, Lotte, Julaina Obika, and Susan Reynolds Whyte. 2014. "Crafting Forgiveness Accounts after War in Northern Uganda: Editing for Effect." *Anthropology Today* 30, no. 4:10–14.

Mergelsberg, Ben. 2010. "Between Two Worlds: Former LRA Soldiers in Northern Uganda." In *The Lord's Resistance Army: Myth and Reality,* edited by T. Allen and K. Vlassenroot, 156–176. London: Zed Books.

Ochola II, MacBaker. 2009. "Spirtuality of Reconciliation: A Case Study of Mato Oput within the Context of the Cultural and Traditional Justice System of the Nilotic Acholi/Central Luo People of Northern Uganda." www.usask.ca/stu/emmanuel/docs/spirituality-of-reconciliation.doc

Ovuga, Emilio, Julaina Obika, S. R. Whyte, and Lotte Meinert. 2012. "Attainment of Positive Mental Health through Forgiveness in Northern Uganda." *African Journal of Traumatic Stress* 2: 73–81.

Pain, Dennis. 1997. *"The Bending of Spears": Producing Consensus for Peace and Development in Northern Uganda.* London: International Alert/Kacoke Madit.

Parkin, David, ed. 1985. "Entitling Evil: Muslims and Non-Muslims in Coastal Kenya." In *The Anthropology of Evil,* 224–243. Oxford: Basil Blackwell.

p'Bitek, Okot. 1971. *Religion of the Central Luo.* Nairobi, Kenya: East African Literature Bureau.

Porter, Holly E. 2012. "Justice and Rape on the periphery: The Supremacy of Social Harmony in the Space between Local Solutions and Formal Judicial Systems in Northern Uganda." *Journal of Eastern African Studies* 6, no. 1:81–97.

Titeca, Kristof. 2010. "The Spiritual Order of the LRA." In *The Lord's Resistance Army: Myth and Reality,* edited by T. Allen and K. Vlassenroot, 59–73. London: Zed Books.

Verma, Cecilie Lanken. 2012. "Truths out of Place: Homecoming, Intervention, and Story-making in War-torn Northern Uganda." *Children's Geographies* 10: 441–455.

Whyte, Susan Reynolds. 1997. *Questioning Misfortune: The Pragmatics of Uncertainty in Eastern Uganda.* Cambridge: Cambridge University Press.

3 THE EVIL OF INSECURITY IN SOUTH SUDAN

Violence and Impunity in Africa's Newest State

JOK MADUT JOK

When South Sudan finally gained independence in July 2011, after long and bitter wars with North Sudan, the event came to mark such a hopeful moment for the millions of its citizens who expected the advent of new era of peace, security, and prosperity. But while it has only been a year since independence and all of these aspirations might still be realized in the future, the new country has now quickly found itself confronted with really daunting challenges, which have since began to dampen the popular celebrated sense of freedom. The most critical of these challenges was insecurity, especially the threats posed by violent ethnic divisions and antigovernment militias. Among the most highly expected rewards of independence among ordinary South Sudanese have been security, a functioning judicial system, and accountability for acts of violence that had been rampant throughout the years of the struggle for liberation. Since the signing of the Comprehensive Peace Agreement that ended two decades of war with the north in 2005, the eyes of the citizens were set on two important future dates—the referendum on independence to be held in January 2011 and the declaration of independence in July 2011—and they hoped that these would bring relief to that violence that had characterized the history of the united Sudan since independence from British Colonialism in 1956. Wartime violence had been squarely blamed on the Sudanese state, and rightly so, either because it had perpetrated it or because it had failed to uphold its responsibility to protect the citizens against it. South Sudanese, therefore, hung their hopes for safety, equality before the law, and state responsibility upon the attainment of the independence of South Sudan. However, since independence, the young state has found itself unable to immediately shoulder the burden of what it means to be sovereign, free, peaceful, accountable, and responsible for the protection of its citizens against violence and poverty, as well as the burden of building institutions of state. The result of being thus weighed down is that every day South Sudanese have carried the brunt of violent armed forces and an unresponsive and weak legal and judicial system; therefore, serious disappointment has set in among the majority of the populace. This chapter will describe these disappointments, how they manifest themselves, and how the everyday people of South Sudan live with rampant violence, abusive armed forces, and a confused and unresponsive justice system. The chapter describes three types of violence that the citizens of the world's newest nation are forced to live with: (1) the cases of targeted abuse that are characterized by impunity, (2) random violence between various ethnic groups, and (3) some of the institutional problems that lead to failure of the state to protect or seek redress.

HISTORY AND VIOLENCE

One of the most common characteristics of African civil wars is that they are often multilayered, with the conflict between the biggest parties overshadowing the many smaller-scale communal conflicts that, though equally deadly, rage on somewhat unclearly and too complexly to the outside world's understanding. The main result of such complexity is that the peace agreements that usually end these larger protracted and destructive civil wars also try to sweep the smaller wars under the rug in the interest of a quick reconciliation between the bigger warring parties. Unaddressed, with no mechanism for restitution, reconciliation, and postwar reconstruction, as well as a long history of strained ethnic relations, these communal conflicts continue to take their toll on these communities, even long after the world community has heard of or participated in and financed a peace agreement. Nowhere was this scenario more evident than in what used to be the Republic of Sudan, which is now two countries.

During the liberation wars waged by South Sudan to secede from North Sudan, the several approaches to the war that were pursued by both sides, such as the Sudan government's counterinsurgency tactics and the South Sudan opposition's methods of recruiting for its army, had made Sudan's war Africa's longest war (1983–2005) and the world's deadliest since World War II. When it ended in the so-called Comprehensive Peace Agreement, it left behind such massive upheaval that a formal agreement like the Comprehensive Peace Agreement could not have resolved all the related consequences. Some particular impacts that are most relevant to the aspirations of the war-affected populations include various armed groups that did not participate in the peace agreements and leftover firearms that remain in the hands of civilians, which are extremely deadly in light of the strained ethnic relations throughout both sides of the country.

One of the issues that was highlighted very clearly in the peace agreement was the need for all to agree that specific programs would be built into the deal to mitigate the upheavals of the war to help society restore any of its conflict mitigation values and to build a justice system that encourages people to seek legal avenues to restitution. Also built-in were efforts by the state to ensure respect and protection for the citizens' basic rights, including living a decent life, equality before the law, and freedom from abuse from both state authorities and other citizens. The postwar societies were also looking forward to an environment in which they might be able to offload the tragic past of death and destruction, through a kind of reconciliation effort, security sector reform, and the institution of a justice system that puts an end to that violence. However, to date, wartime atrocities that the Sudan government had inflicted on many communities remain at the margins of postwar programs of reconciliation and reconstruction. For example, one of Khartoum's methods of war was to set up proxy armies, selected from different ethnic groups in South Sudan, and to pit them against one another, leading to a widespread intercommunal conflicts and bitter interethnic relations that have now continued to tear apart the social fabric of the two countries, especially the new country of South Sudan. This means that much of the violence that continues to happen in South Sudan today, despite the peace agreement and independence, is intrinsically linked to unresolved past episodes of army-sponsored militia violence.

Other sources of insecurity resulting from the history of the war include the availability of huge quantities of firearms left over from the war, which are now illegally in the hands of civilian youth. Due to the unsettled wartime disputes between communities or individuals, it is now possible for civilians to seek their own justice through violence or take out their anger on the members of an ethnic group deemed to have aggressed in the past. There is also the large national army of South Sudan, made up of former freedom fighters, known as the SPLA (Sudan People's Liberation Army), the former soldiers of the Sudan Armed Forces, and the militias that had fought against the SPLA at the behest of the Sudan government. The latter two were absorbed into the SPLA in an attempt to create a diverse national army as part of the conflict-mitigation endeavor. By accommodating all former foes, it was hoped that this would start a new era of nation-building, by creating the only institution that will ever be as vast and diverse. That was well-intentioned but made for an army that lacks a shared institutional culture about the responsibilities of a soldier, a well-understood command structure, or a unified philosophy that binds the forces together. Instead, the country has created a wieldy army with a haphazard history that is difficult to control and to pay regularly. When unpaid in a given month, the soldiers quickly become a serious liability to the state, sometimes taking their unhappiness out on ordinary civilians in many vulgar ways such as robberies and sexual assaults. This also allows for many soldiers to rebel, desert, or simply to go absent without leave, usually with their guns, becoming a security liability for the communities in which they end up residing. Corruption and mismanagement of army resources has also meant that the requisite training, purchase of equipment, and creation of military productive projects have all been jeopardized, leading to widespread grumbling throughout the armed forces (Rands 2010).

Violence is also linked to poor security sector reforms and South Sudan's weak postindependence justice system. For example, I have observed and received many reports that many acts of violence committed by members of the armed forces have gone unpunished, even when the culprits are known, making it appear that soldiers are beyond the reach of the law, perhaps even protected by the institution to avoid being held accountable for their actions. It is the unpunished actions by soldiers, the lack of consequences for their behaviors, that seem to give more of them the impression that impunity prevails in the new republic. It has become common practice, for example, that the police do not even respond to citizens' reports of assaults, robberies, or rapes by army individuals, as many police responses to such incidents have resulted in fights that pit the police against the army and escalate the situation far beyond what the police would agree to get involved in. In these types of incidents, the army officers often claim that they have their own military police to arrest any culprits, but this rarely happens. Arrest may be made in some cases, but the individuals often end up in military courts that exclude the civilian cases and the accused almost always get off with no consequences for their involvement in criminal acts. That these situations continue to happen in a country whose recent past is characterized by a popular resentment of the Sudanese state for similar behavior by the Khartoum government has been seen as following a pattern of political hypocrisy and a double standard of many African leaders. Coming into existence at this stage in human history and with a sense of moral high ground that South Sudanese seceded from Sudan due to exclusionary policies and mistreatment of Southern citizens, it was hoped that South Sudan's political class would learn from the mistakes made by other countries and reward their citizens with a well-deserved sense of freedom. So what went wrong? Why should a new, hopeful nation, one that enjoys so much international goodwill, not live up to the expectations of its long-suffering population?

INDEPENDENT STATEHOOD AND CITIZENS' SECURITY EXPECTATIONS

When independence was finally attained, after over half century of struggle, the most immediate expected peace dividend for the citizens of the new country, unsurprisingly, was security and an efficient justice system. Without a doubt, economic prosperity, efficient service delivery in the areas of education, health, food security, and infrastructure were all anticipated, but security and justice topped the list of immediate expectations. According to a number of opinion surveys, insecurity for the individual and inability to get justice have been reported among the major disappointments felt throughout the country, especially within the first year since independence in 2011 (NDI 2012). "We have to be alive first before we ask to be fed, to attend school, or to work on development" one informant starkly stated the problem.

It is not surprising that insecurity topped the list of issues that concerned the citizens of independent South Sudan because of the history of destruction, death, and the postwar "scary statistics" about the living standards of the population. Here was a country that had known very little besides war and destruction of property and human life, an experience that was unparalleled in any other region of the world since World War II. For a long time between the mid-1980s and the 2005 peace agreement between south and north, South Sudan was home to the world's largest number of internally displaced persons who lived under extreme state violence in the slums of Khartoum and in the garrison towns in the south. The United Nations Population Fund listed South Sudan as the world's worst place to become a mother, and as having the world's lowest literacy rate, highest infant mortality rate, and Africa's highest youth unemployment rate, with most of these statistics intrinsically linked to insecurity. To date, the new country remains a place where the United Nations says a fourteen-year-old girl is more likely to die in childbirth than attend high school. The citizens had, therefore, hung their hopes and aspirations on independence, though it was hardly realistic to imagine independence alone becoming a panacea for fifty years of destruction and an antidote for the deeply rooted subculture of violence. But why does violence have to add to the already dire situation in terms of services? The challenges we have listed either are the cause of insecurity or happen due to insecurity. Analysts seem to suggest a chicken-or-egg-first situation.

ARMED FORCES AND ENTITLEMENTS

Two things are at the heart of soldiers' violent actions against one another and against the civilians. The first is a sense of entitlement that is widely expressed by the members of the SPLA who take every opportunity to state the fact that "we liberated this country" and to demand "respect and recognition of the sacrifices we have made," as one officer once stated in response to my question about why they were beating a man, an incident I happened to witness in a busy market in Juba, the capital of the new republic. The second are the claims to nationalism among the different units, commanders, and the rank and file, based on whether one was an SPLA "proper" or was absorbed into the national army from the various militias that had been recruited either by Khartoum against the "mother" SPLA or by some revolting officers who disagreed with the SPLA's vision and wanted a different approach to liberation. These units had often fought bitter wars against one another, some of those wars continuing to the present. Those coming from a militia background are often taunted by members of the "mainstream" SPLA as unpatriotic and as people who are just reaping the fruits of other peoples' labors. The result is the mistreatment of some members of the armed forces by others and both groups taking out their unease on the civilians who are either accused by members of the SPLA mainstream of being ungrateful for the struggles the SPLA has made or by those with militia background for what they see as disrespect due to their history. In either situation, it is the unarmed civilians, the very ones that were supposed to have been liberated by these armed men, who suffer. It has become a near-daily reality to hear of beating, shooting, raping, or robbing being done by members of the armed forces throughout the country.

To cite an example closer to home, I was myself a victim of these contested claims to nationalism, that the people who bore arms during the liberation struggle are more nationalistic and are entitled to any actions against those who "did not fight." I was attacked in Wau, the capital of the western state of Western Bahr el-Ghazal and this demonstrates how rampant the violence was. Part of a letter I wrote to the commanding officer shortly after the incident, which to this day has never been replied to nor has any action been taken, follows. I include it to show the degree of impunity involved.

> I was brutally attacked by an SPLA unit at Wau airport on December 31st, 2011. I had arrived when the president of the republic was expected to arrive at the same airport on that same day, and so the security was beefed up. But with no apparent reason when I exited from the airport I found my younger brothers who had come to pick me up being tortured by this unit and when I went over

in hope of finding out what had happened, the soldiers turned on me and beat me so mercilessly and without being asked any questions or given any chance to speak to anyone. I tried to show them my government identification card and it was knocked from my hand. About 8 soldiers plunged on me with punches, gun butts, kicks and they threw me onto the ground, all under the watch of the commanding officer, a 1st Lt by name Haider Kon Deng. He stood there watching the beating for nearly 18 minutes, after which he came over and told the soldiers "enough." And then he took me over to the under-the-tree office and interrogated me for 2 hours, asking me such questions as "are you a spy from Khartoum?"

The beating was so hard and so humiliating that I kept asking them what I had done to deserve such an attack in my own country, by an army that I have always supported and respected. I did not even lift my hands to protect my head and my face, out of respect for their uniform, something I consider to be an emblem of our hard won national sovereignty. But the result was that I sustained injuries so severe that some of them will have permanent impact on my eyesight, my elbow and my nose.

After I was let go and left the airport, I had to go to the police to get a report and headed straight to hospital emergency unit. A few days later, I went to Nairobi for treatment and was admitted for a few days. I have since been back there twice and the doctors say that these people nearly rendered me blind and that I will face future problems with my eyesight. When I inquired if anything was going to be done in this case, the National Security informed me that these soldiers were released and no further investigation will be done with them. Is that what I deserve as a citizen working for the same government that these soldiers purport to protect? Does my government think that I am so insignificant that I don't even deserve an official apology from either the army or the executive that I serve in? Should these soldiers' behavior have no consequences for them?

In the end, after much talk about my incident, nothing was done and the soldiers who assaulted me have gotten away with their crime. That is the kind of impunity that has made it possible for the members of South Sudan's Defense Force to go on committing these kinds of acts without consequences, giving the rest of them the green light to do the same.

The national security group is most commonly referenced by the public as the primary abuser of citizen's basic rights. For example, its members have a rather bizarre practice of driving cars that do not bear license numbers, enabling them to terrorize the residents of big towns who do not have any mechanism of complaint about these individuals and who cannot identify the vehicles. This has been made worse by ordinary criminals who are now copying the security forces by stripping their cars of license plates so as to roam under the cover of the night masquerading as national security agents, taking advantage of the chaos created by the supposed law enforcement agents, and terrorizing the public in a like manner. The sense of paralysis that the army's command and the country's justice system seem to exhibit in the face of these actions is shocking. It is common for senior officers to shrug their shoulders when they receive complaints about the soldiers' transgressions, sometimes admitting that "there is nothing we can do, as that is the nature of SPLA." In fact, the scale of violence and the inaction of the state are so ubiquitous that many citizens have begun to question the value of independent statehood, where the liberators have turned into thugs. "Independence to what end?" inquired one citizen who fell victim to these types of attitude. "Was I expected to pay them for their role in the liberation struggle . . . where is the freedom we are supposed to have fought for and got in July 2011?" the same man continued.

HOW SOUTH SUDANESE COPE WITH EVERYDAY VIOLENCE

In addition to episodes of violence that target individuals, whether deliberately or by mere chance of one finding herself in the wrong place at the wrong time, there are many incidents that result from having a large undisciplined army being put in charge of everyday security, disarmament of civilians, and protection of the nation from any external aggression. For example, after the newspapers reported on the case of my beating, many people came to congratulate me for my speaking out about this, as this has been the experience of so many people, usually without any media attention. One woman told me that she was beaten by five policemen without any cause whatsoever. The only reason they stated was that she crossed the street during the time the president was about to leave his office to travel on the road the woman was trying to cross. "I did not know the president was coming and after all he is my president too . . . and the soldiers could have just told me to not cross instead of plunging on me with clubs," the woman remarked. She said that she could not believe that five policemen ganged up on her and beat her with clubs while she was empty-handed and nonthreatening. She said, "Just one of them could have arrested me by simply ordering me to put my hands together for handcuffs . . . but no, they all accused me of some crime, they tried me, they found me guilty, and they sentenced me to clubbing."

Reports abound about nighttime robberies, sexual assaults, domestic abuse, and murders, especially in major urban centers such as Juba, the capital of the republic. Granted, these are part of the price urban societies have to pay in exchange for the conveniences of urban life and are somewhat unsurprising in a rapidly growing metropolitan area. But in relation to South Sudan's urban centers, the most shocking thing about these incidents is not just their frequency, but also the scale of brutality. However, most of them go uninvestigated and most never make it to court, even when culprits have been identified and apprehended. This is due to a variety of cultural and social values that blur the lines between the moral and the legal. For example, when a woman reports a case of domestic abuse to the police, the incident is often examined from the point of view of certain social norms about the station of women in the society. Even though the law is very clear about punishing domestic battery, the police, the medical officers in charge of examining such cases, and the judges are often far too prejudiced by the sociocultural norms to allow the law to take its course. There was once a famous case of young girl who was gang-raped in Juba and left for the dead. When passersby came upon her and took her to the emergency department, the hospital required that they obtain a police report before the doctor could even take a look at her, as the law requires. When these rescuers took her to the police station to obtain that report, the on-duty officer nearly rolled over in laughter, saying something to the effect, "Why did these rapists have to go for a little girl, could they not find an older woman?," as if age alone is the issue here and not the act of rape itself. Other similar cases where the police have adopted such an attitude do not stand a chance of holding up in court, especially because such attitudes pervade the investigation, leading to the blaming of the victim (Jok 2012a).

Furthermore, issues of jurisdiction between customary practices and the country's constitution make it hard for the judges to hear the cases while some members of the communities are calling for the cases to be heard by the chiefs at the tribal courts (Leonardi et al. 2010). It is sometimes even more difficult to punish rape, as the women are often hesitant to bring forth a case against their attackers in a society that is quick to judge the woman more harshly, saying that she may have provoked the attack either by putting herself in a particular place or by supposedly dressing provocatively. But even when a woman is courageous enough to report the incident, the investigating police are often dismissive of a woman's claim of rape, often downplaying the role of the man in the act. Furthermore, the doctors who examine the victims are not always thorough, often using such phrases as "alleged rape" as a medical conclusion. Because civil authorities act perfunctorily about the application of the law, the cases are left with no foundation.

It must be stated, however, that the scale of violence and weakness of the justice system may be widespread but the cases presented here are not always formally state-driven, in other words, this situation does not always necessarily reflect a form of state violence condoned by the political leadership or the top military command. Where the government institutions fall short in this regard is the lack of visible programs to mitigate this situation, suggesting that security is not being accorded the priority position that the citizens need it to be as the major expected peace and independence dividend (Harragin 2012). In other words, the level of violence that the people of South Sudan are forced to live with is a kind of institutional violence that requires the political leadership of the country to act quickly in the area of security sector reform, an effort that can only yield desired results if it is a concerted transinstitutional endeavor. Such reform needs to be coordinated between the military, the police, the courts, the public health system, and the civil society. If the nation's top leadership is to avoid being seen as either complicit in these acts or behind them, the most important, though obvious, messages to convey in the reform programs are that the actions of the men and women in uniform are guided by the law of the land and not the whims of the individual and that the soldier's main role is to apprehend the would-be law breakers, not to punish them outside the due process of law. For example, given the haphazard composition of the nation's army, a training regime that emphasizes the development of a unified culture of clear understanding of the responsibilities of a person in uniform toward the civilian population is key to stabilizing the nation and protecting the citizens, the *raison d'être* of the security forces (Rands 2010).

The police forces have also been frequently mentioned by the respondents to the research questions of this project as being among the primary rights abusers and part of the violence that pervades postwar South Sudan. The force has been the subject of much criticism, both for failure in its obligations "to serve and to protect" and for its direct involvement in crime perpetration. The people we have interviewed for this piece, including members of the force, have all pointed out the need for major reforms in the South Sudan Police Service. The recommend reforms are instituting basic requirements for qualification by which one joins the police force such as the level of education and careful checking of criminal record, raising the level of literacy among its rank and file, teaching the law books, and issuing identification cards that officers have to present when making arrests or when conducting interrogations. Above all, the police force is as good as its ability to liaise with other institutions on cross-cutting issues of justice, rights, and obligations. The same goes for the justice system, for the constitution to be clear on jurisdictions, and the health system, for sensitization of medical students to pay attention to cultural beliefs and behaviors that affect the delivery of care, as health is never just a matter of biology. These are all undoubtedly long-term programs that might take a generation before South Sudan can be seen to do justice. So the question of how to stem the evil of everyday violence, whether that violence is driven by the state itself or by its failure to protect, remains difficult to answer. A collaborative process needs to be developed across government institutions, civic associations, the citizens themselves, and international development partners. The following section addresses this challenge.

VIOLENCE AND A DISAPPOINTED NATION

In 2008 and 2009, just before independence, the time when South Sudanese had hung their entire aspirations on the referendum and independence, the level of ethnic violence looked as if it could not get worse, but now many citizens of South Sudan believe that violence has been escalating throughout the country (Harragin 2012). There is the increasing urban crime partly stoked by increasing poverty and youth unemployment, violence by uniformed forces, and violence driven by ethnic squabbles in the rural areas and fueled by widespread of firearms that were left over from the north-south protracted civil war. Before independence, all this used to be linked to the counterinsurgency policies of the Sudan government, destabilizing communities as a way to weaken South Sudan's opposition forces by attempting to remove from the SPLA the support base perceived to be coming from the civilian population. So clearly, independence was viewed as the single most popularly desired antidote to localized violence and as a logical conclusion to one of the world's most deadly wars. "We thought that having our own country, liberated by our blood, sweat and tears, run according to our own laws, having our peace, stability, justice and prosperity, having our own institutions that are run by a mix of South Sudanese citizens, and having a nation that is built upon our shared history of struggle and our shared cultural values, conscious of how and why we got here, we would be much better off than what generations of our people before us have experienced at the hands foreign rulers since 1821," remarked one political leader who resigned from government in protest of what she thought was the wrong direction for this country.

Instead, however, many South Sudanese say what they got was increased violence, made worse by three factors, all of them related to the weakness or failure of institutions. The first one is the actions of the armed forces, the "liberators" who are currently acting like mercenaries in their treatment of the people on whose behalf they claim to have gone to war. By all accounts, uniformed men have done more violence against civilians in the postwar era than any other sector of the population of the new state, doing so both in the course of their duties and on their own individual account. Some critics of the armed forces have even suggested that "our national defense forces and the local militias that fight with them" have done more violence to the citizens of South Sudan than the "big enemy in the north." That is probably slightly exaggerated in view of the millions of South Sudanese that perished in the war of liberation at the hands of the state in the old Sudan, but the current armed forces have been emboldened by the impunity with which so many of them seem to get away with heinous actions. Few citizens would point out any case in which the law has dealt sufficiently with uniformed men who abuse citizens.

The second factor is the history of strained ethnic relations that continues to wreak havoc for rural communities in most of the states of the union. The history of the Sudan government's counterinsurgency, which operated on the basis of pitting South Sudan's ethnic groups against one another, and the SPLA's reactions to South Sudanese who had sided with "the enemy" had sowed the seeds of discord that have now continued to color interethnic relations. This history now defines how South Sudanese seek political office, distribute national resources, and assign government jobs; it also defines how the armed forces interact with certain ethnic groups. Some of the ethnic relations are now influenced by stereotypes that write off entire ethnic groups as "enemies of state" or "traitors" or "unpatriotic" based on generalizations that derive from histories of militias or certain political figures with checkered histories.

The third factor is the inability of the citizens to receive legal redress regarding these episodes of violence. As explained earlier, a combination of a sense of entitlement by the armed forces, the lackluster reactions of the police to reports of crime, the incoherence of the courts over their jurisdictions, and the influence of the sociocultural biases against certain sectors of the population have connived against the ordinary civilian by dulling the ability of the state to uphold the rule of law, provide protection for all, and convince the citizens that attempts to take all matters into one's hands is tantamount to lawlessness and increased violence. These issues are as real in the lives of the citizens as they are part of growing pains of a young country and challenges of state-building. But there is no denying the achievements that have been made, nor is it possible to fail to appreciate the difficulties of state-building in a country that has inherited a level of destruction almost unprecedented anywhere since World War II (Jok 2012b).

This chapter attempted to describe how South Sudanese live with everyday violence, whether it is violence perpetrated by the state's armed forces or the inaction of the justice system, both as a deterrent and as a mechanism to ensure restitution. The chapter described three types of violence, mainly done by the armed forces. The first of these is the targeting of individuals, whether by accident or by premeditated criminal action. The second is the generalized acts of violence caused by the history of ethnic relations during the liberation struggle in which the Republic of Sudan pitted South Sudan's ethnic groups against one another as a way to weaken the opposition SPLA, a practice that has now left strained ethnic relations throughout the country, leading to recurrence of ethnic clashes, long after the peace agreement and independence were achieved. The third is the failure of the justice system to curb the scale of violence by punishing crime and creating a deterrent. The result of this situation is that the people of South Sudan continue to live with violence they had hoped would end with the coming of independence in 2011. The chapter makes the case that the way forward is a three-pronged approach, of reforming the military, taking measures to reconcile the ethnic groups that were locked into violence through the actions of North Sudan's government, and rebuilding the justice system, including a clear delineation of jurisdictions of customary and statutory law, to give everyone their day in court and punish the perpetrators of violent crime, soldier or not. This would have to be a long-term program that cannot be achieved through the piecemeal programs that are currently in place, which only emphasize disarmament. Whatever approach the country will embark upon, the one that succeeds in the long run will have to be an approach that coordinates reconciliation and security sector reform, including efforts to imbue the soldiers with an institutional culture that delineates the rights and responsibilities of a soldier vis-à-vis the civilians. Such a program would also have to include emphasis on coordination between all the institutions of government, such that programs on youth, education, new military recruitments, reintegration of former combatants into civilian lives, commemoration of the history of South Sudan's journey to independence, service delivery, and celebration of the country's cultural diversity all have to be geared toward the concept of nation-building, an endeavor that creates symbols that rally the citizens around the concept of belonging primarily to a nation versus belonging to a tribe.

REFERENCES

Harragin, Simon. 2012. "Background Paper for Bor, Twic, Ghol and Nyaraweng Dinka of Jonglei State." Paper presented at Conference on Strengthening Conflict Mitigation and Peace-Building, Nairobi, March 19–21, 2012.

Jok, Jok Madut. 2012a. *Insecurity and Ethnic Violence in South Sudan: Existential Threat to the State?* Issue paper no. 1. Juba, South Sudan: The Sudd Institute.

———. 2012b. "Negotiating Security: Gender, Violence, and the Rule of Law in Post-war South Sudan." In *Gendered Insecurities, Health and Development in Africa,* edited by Howard Stein and Amal Fadlalla Hassan, 84–107. New York: Routledge.

Leonardi, Cherry, Leben Moro, M. Santchi, and D. Isser. 2010. "Local Justice in Southern Sudan." *A Joint Project of Rift Valley Institute and United States Institute of Peace.* London and Washington: Rift Valley Institute and USIP.

Leonardi, Cherry. 2013. *Dealing with Government in South Sudan: Histories of Chiefship, Community and State*. London: Boydell and Brewer.

National Democratic Institute. 2012. *Governing South Sudan: Opinions of South Sudanese on a Government that Can Meet Citizen Expectations*. Washington, DC: NDI.

Rands, Richard. 2010. *In Need of Review: SPLA Transformation in 2006–10 and Beyond*. Geneva: Small Arms Survey.

Sommers, Mark, and Stephanie Schwartz. 2011. *Dowry and Division: Youth and State Building in South Sudan*. Washington, DC: United States Institute of Peace.

4 GENOCIDE, EVIL, AND HUMAN AGENCY

The Concept of Evil in Rwandan Explanations of the 1994 Genocide

JENNIE E. BURNET

While few cultural anthropologists practicing today would be willing to label culturally bound human behaviors as "evil," many apply this label to the gruesome individual and collective acts that constituted the 1994 genocide of Tutsis, politically moderate Hutus, and others defined as an "enemy of the state." Because evil, conceived of as the opposite of good, is defined by a moral system, its application in a particular context involves moral judgment and violates the principle of cultural relativism, which lies at the heart of anthropology. Furthermore, on the continent of Africa, the concept of evil is inextricably tied up in missionary imperialism and its judgments of indigenous African cultural practices, in particular spiritual and religious beliefs and practices. Because evil is bound to a moral system, it cannot be abstracted as a portable theoretical concept to be applied cross-culturally. David Parkin solved this problem by assuming a "common awareness of evil acts" and then raising "the question of how and to what extent certain kinds of behavior and phenomenon come to be identified by this or a comparable term" (1985, 224). Following this same methodology, this chapter explores the ways Rwandans made sense of their experiences of violence during the civil war (1990–1994) and genocide (April–June 1994) by mobilizing the concept of evil. This chapter is based on several years of ethnographic research in urban and rural Rwanda between 1997 and 2014.[1]

Contemporary Rwandan conceptions of evil have emerged from the unpredictable entanglement of competing indigenous religious beliefs and practices with imported colonial religions (predominantly Roman Catholicism, but also including several Protestant denominations such as Lutheran, Anglican, Seventh Day Adventist, Presbyterian, Jehovah's Witnesses, and Pentacostalism).[2] From its first entry into Rwanda in 1900, the Roman Catholic Church, "stifled the development of syncretic religious sects" by adopting an exclusiv-ist stance vis-à-vis indigenous religious beliefs and practices (Taylor 1992, 62): these heterogeneous beliefs and practices were universally labeled as "evil" and "pagan." As a result, Rwandans followed "either a mission religion or a 'tra-ditional religion' or both," but they did not combine them (Taylor 1992, 62). Even up until the present, many Rwandans participate in several religious cults simultaneously although often secretly so as to avoid punishment by the local parish priest or bishop by being excluded from Holy Communion or other rites of the church.[3] Rwandan moral understandings of the world are simultane-ously shaped by these different, sometimes contradictory belief systems.

Between April 6 and July 4, 1994, at least 500,000 Rwandans,[4] primarily Tutsi as well as politically moderate Hutu and others defined as "enemies of Rwanda," lost their lives in a state-sponsored genocide. The genocide occurred in the context of a civil war that had begun on October 1, 1990, when the Rwan-dan Patriotic Front (RPF) rebel group attacked Rwanda with the intention of liberating the country from President Habyarimana's dictatorship. The civil war continued throughout the early 1990s until Habyarimana's government was forced to the negotiating table. The 1993 Arusha Peace Accords brought an official end to hostilities and outlined a transition plan to move the country to multiparty politics and democratic elections. The transition, which had been limping along, was brought to a dramatic and violent halt on April 6, 1994, when President Habyarimana's plane was shot down by unknown assailants. Hutu extremists took control of the government and perpetrated a genocide against Tutsi and others defined as enemies of the state.

The massacres and other atrocities committed by soldiers, militiamen, and civilians against their neighbors and kinsmen were beyond the social imagina-tion of most ordinary Rwandans. These acts constituted an abrupt departure from the social contract. Whether people were hunted like quarry and killed by the Interahamwe militias, mobilized to participate in the killing, or witnesses to the horrors around them, Rwandans struggled to make sense of these ter-rible events in their aftermath. While their explanations and methods of coping were as heterogeneous as their experiences of violence, they mobilized three competing conceptions of evil to understand genocidal violence: the personi-fied presence of Satan who inspired humans to perpetrate evil; genocide per-petrators as possessed by Satan, demons, or evil spirits; and humans exercising their free will and being led astray by greed, jealousy, or other human weak-nesses. These understandings emerge from the imbricated systems of religious belief and spiritual practices, including competing indigenous spiritual beliefs and practices, Roman Catholicism, Protestantism, and *abarokore* (born-again

Christian) movements, that form the cosmological systems that frame good and evil for Rwandans. The Roman Catholic Church, on the one hand, counters these understandings of evil and asserts that the evil acts of the genocide were a result of humans' free will, greed, and their rejection of Christian values. Protestant denominations take a variety of positions, but the growing *abarokore* movement tends to privilege the idea of possession, whether by Satan himself or by evil spirits. Efforts to explain the genocide as extraordinary and having spiritual, as opposed to human, origins may make it easier for genocide survivors to live and worship alongside those responsible for killing their loved ones.

THE CONCEPT OF EVIL IN INDIGENOUS RELIGIOUS BELIEFS AND PRACTICES

Indigenous religious beliefs and practices in Rwanda consisted of a heterogeneous mix of ancestor worship, spirit possession, witchcraft, and sorcery that varied by region.[5] As Iris Berger noted "spirits, myth, and ritual" did not form a "unified system" that flowed together through time and space" (1981, 66). All Rwandans recognized a supreme creator called "Imana" who was the origin of all things in the universe but who did not interfere directly in human lives (Arnoux 1912, 1913; d'Hertefelt 1962).[6] While Rwandans believed Imana was everywhere and in all things because he created them, believers performed no rites to honor him. Imana was perceived as essentially good, and misfortune or evil were never attributed to him but were rather thought to be caused by spirits of the dead, known as *abazimu* (d'Hertefelt 1962, 79).

According to Rwandan mythology, Imana created a universe of three "countries": the terrestrial world inhabited by humans, the superior country (or the sky), and the underworld inhabited by the spirits of the dead (d'Hertefelt 1962). While the *abazimu* inhabited the underworld, they often visited the living on earth. Like Imana, the *abazimu* were invisible and immaterial. Rwandans conceived of humans (and animals) as being composed of a visible part, the body, and an invisible part, the shadow. It was the union of the body and shadow that constituted life. When this union was broken, the shadow was transformed into an *umuzimu*, "spirit." According to d'Hertefelt who was writing about the late colonial period, "the living constantly worry about the spirits, almost obsessively. They have the power to make men sick or to disrupt the smooth function of their affairs" (d'Hertefelt 1962, 81).[7] In Rwanda today, practicing Christians and Muslims continue to worry about spirits, especially the spirits of loved ones who died in unknown circumstances during the civil war or genocide and who never received a proper burial.

According to indigenous beliefs, there were several different kinds of *aba-zimu*, both good and bad. The most important were the ancestor spirits called *abakurambere* (the ones who came first) that protected every Rwandan lineage and household. Rwandans viewed the ancestor spirits as enmeshed in the daily lives of the living. Thus, they took care of them by providing shelter in small ancestor shrines built inside the compound walls and giving food and drink in the form of offerings left in the shrines. Although ancestor spirits might cause periodic difficulties in the lives of the living to express their displeasure, they could not be the source of evil. They were easily placated once the living divined their displeasure through a ritual known as *guterekera,* which involved the manipulation of objects passed down through the family (Taylor 1992, 122), and then took the ancestor spirits' desired action. Beyond their spiritual aspects, the ancestor cults and *guterekera* practices served to reinforce fealty to the lineage.

Parallel, but distinct, religious practices created a secondary community of support for the individual, thus they often attracted people marginalized from their lineage or community (d'Hertefelt 1962). Bizarre misfortunes or persistent symptoms were usually attributed to *abazimu* from outside the lineage who were honored through distinct religious cults called *kubandwa.* The *kubandwa* were particularly strong *abazimu* understood to be the heroes in Rwandan myths (d'Hertefelt 1962). Participation in *kubandwa* cults was widespread across Rwanda; however, as Iris Berger notes, *kubandwa* referred generally to heterogeneous ritual practices that were not always analogous (Berger 1981, 66). In all regions, the legends about *kubandwa* were closely related to "the formation and expansion of new states and class systems" (Berger 1981, 58). For example, David Newbury (1991) documents the importance of a specific set of rituals on Ijwi Island and their dialectical relationship to state power—rites that were historically produced and in turn produced history. Similarly, the Nyabingi cult, which venerated the female spirit, Nyabingi, became popular in northeastern Rwanda and emerged as a millenarian movement resisting against the imposition of the central court's authority over formerly autonomous regions (Des Forges and Newbury 2011, 103). Beyond veneration of Nyabingi, the "dogma of the cult" varied by region, and "anyone who had been moved by the spirit could serve her; anyone who could convince others that he had been so moved could intercede with her on their behalf" (Des Forges and Newbury 2011, 103) Another cult venerating the male spirit, Ryangombe, had become widespread in Rwanda in the eighteenth century (Des Forges and Newbury 2011, xxxiv). While it likely became popular "as a focus for alternative loyalties to the state," Mwami Rujugira and other leaders appointed "a resident 'leader' of this cult at the Court" to integrate it with the supernatural powers of the *mwami* and the *abiru,* ritual specialists responsible for maintaining the spiritual integrity of the *mwami* and Rwanda (Des Forges and Newbury 2011, xxxiv).

The rites of the ancestor worship cults, *kubandwa,* Nyabingi, and Ryangombe converged with Rwandan healing practices and witchcraft beliefs. The ancestor spirits or numerous other *abazimu* might afflict certain individuals, households, or lineages with particular illnesses. As Christopher Taylor described of Rwanda in the 1980s, "bizarre, persistent symptoms or serial misfortunes lead sufferers to suspect a spiritual origin to their illness. Often they consult an *umupfumu*[8] to affirm or deny this suspicion" (1992, 141). The *abapfumu* along with many other ritual and healing specialists with particular names, such as the *abacunyi* ("healers") who knew various herbal medicines and forms of healing, divined or diagnosed spiritual illnesses, helped to cure them, and made charms to protect patients from further trouble (d'Hertefelt 1962). As in many other African regions, certain ritual and healing specialists could also provide the poison (*uburozi*) necessary to cause trouble for an adversary. Rwandan beliefs about and fears of poison, which can administered through material and spiritual forms, persist into the present and strongly shape their habits. For example, family members suspect poisoning in deaths easily explained by modern medicine, such as a stroke, evoking Evans-Pritchard's classic question related to Azande witchcraft beliefs, "Why should these particular people have been sitting under this particular granary at the particular moment when it collapsed?" (1937, 69). In any home, celebration, restaurant, or bar in Rwanda, the server will only open a bottle (whether beer, soda, or water) in the presence of its drinker as proof that it has not been poisoned.

CHRISTIANITY IN EARLY COLONIAL RWANDA

Christianity entered Rwanda in the early years of the twentieth century along with European colonizers. Rwanda became part of the protectorate of German East Africa during the Berlin Conference of 1884–1885, but there was very little contact between Europeans and the territory, except for a few explorers who passed through, until 1899 when the Germans decided to establish their authority over the country (van 't Spijker 1990, 12). With the backing of the German colonial administration, the Society of the Missionaries of Our Lady of Africa (popularly known as the White Fathers) established the first Roman Catholic mission in Rwanda in 1900 at Save, which was located twenty kilometers from the seat of the royal court at Nyanza (Des Forges and Newbury 2011, 27–28). The French cardinal Lavigerie had founded the White Father order in

1868 in Algiers exclusively to work in Africa (Des Forges and Newbury 2011, 27; Linden 1977, 29). Its central African missions were an expansion of its work in Islamic northern Africa, and thus its evangelization was adapted to converting Muslims rather than the so-called pagans, as the European priests referred to Africans who practiced indigenous religions.

Even before its founding, the Save mission played an important role in Rwandan politics. Policy makers in Rwanda's central court, comprising the Queen Mother, Kanjogera, and her brothers who ruled in the stead of Mwami Musinga who was still a child, decided that the missionaries' religious teaching should be limited to the Hutu and Twa (Des Forges and Newbury 2011, 29; Linden 1977, 33). The official policy of the White Fathers was to "convert from above" (Taylor 1992, 53) so this decision initially thwarted the White Fathers' preferred methods of conversion (Des Forges and Newbury 2011, 29). Although the missionaries rejected the central court's first two proposed sites, which were far from central Rwanda where the court's influence was the strongest, they eventually agreed on a location twenty kilometers from Nyanza (Taylor 1992, 53, Linden 1977).

The first Protestant missionaries arrived in Rwanda in 1907. They were German Lutherans from the Bethel Society (van 't Spijker 1990, 27). They established the Betheler Mission in the region of Kirinda in 1907. Although the Protestant mission at Betheler would prove to be successful, Rwanda was to be dominated by the Roman Catholic mission and eventually the Roman Catholic Church. Over the course of its history in the region, the Roman Catholic Church alternately sided with the masses and with the elite of Rwandan society. At times, institutions within the church were in conflict with each other over where to stand.

The *mwami* and central court recognized the Christian missionaries as important emissaries of the colonial state and appreciated their potential value as a means of influencing the German colonial administrators. Nonetheless, they worried about the potential nefarious effects of Christian religious practices on the ritual responsible for maintaining the health of the *mwami* as well as the health of the kingdom (Des Forges and Newbury 2011). The health of these two bodies—of the *mwami* and of the state—was intricately linked in the Rwandan worldview (Taylor 1992). As virtually all ritual attached to the *mwami* or the kingdom was secret, the *abiru*, ritual specialists of the central court, assumed the Christian missionaries had their own secret rituals and potentially evil magic that they kept secret.

The Roman Catholic and Protestant churches forbid participation in any so-called pagan practices, including the *kubandwa*, Nyabingi, and Ryangombe cults as well as the important familial obligations to honor the ancestors through the rites of *guterekera*. Christian converts faced sanctions by the church if they "were caught" participating in pagan rites (Linden 1977, 102). These sanctions could include public beatings, temporary detention in the church tower, or expulsion from the church community (van 't Spijker 1990). When early converts to Christianity refused to participate in the *guterekera* practices, they found themselves under attack by non-Christian members of their families (van 't Spijker 1990, 168). The converts were often accused of being the cause of difficulties, sicknesses, unhappiness/bad luck/evil, and even of being bewitched by the Europeans (van 't Spijker 1990, 168).

Most Christian converts continued to attend *kubandwa*, Ryangombe, and Nyabingi ceremonies and practice the ancestor worship cults in secret at home (Linden 1977, 101–102). For example, some catechumens attended animal sacrifices of the *kubandwa* cults as an antidote "to avert any evil consequences of baptism" (Linden 1977, 102). Nonetheless, Roman Catholic priests and Protestant missionaries characterized virtually the entire panoply of indigenous religious practices as "evil" along with many aspects of Rwandan culture, such as polygyny. According to Linden, the White Fathers understood Imana as "a High God, and therefore 'good,' so Ryangombe and Kiranga, it followed were 'bad'" (Linden 1977, 44). An 1897 entry in the White Fathers' journal, *Chroniques Trimestrielles*, described Ryangombe as "the evil spirit, the Ahriman of the Rundi, compared with the Ormudz, the principal of Good" (cited in Linden 1977, 49). In Burundi, the White Fathers described the *kubandwa* cults as the "Devil's Sabbath" (Linden 1977, 44). Priests frequently spoke at length with recently baptized converts about the spiritual dangers of the *kubandwa* cults as consorting with Satan and "Satan's henchmen" (Linden 1977, 45). In 1903, the diary of the Save mission of the White Fathers, the priest described women dancers as "Satan's henchmen" (cited in Linden 1977, 49).

RELIGIOUS PRACTICES IN POST-COLONIAL RWANDA

By the late colonial period, a generation of male youth, including the Tutsi cadre groomed for government administration along with a small group of Hutu intellectuals, had been educated almost entirely in Roman Catholic schools. This generation had been groomed to view the indigenous Rwandan religious beliefs and practices as so-called pagan superstitions, uncivilized, and evil. This generation strived to distinguish themselves from the uneducated masses by attending church weekly and marrying Christian women in religious weddings in churches among other practices. They officially avoided polygyny by only marrying a single woman although many also kept additional women "on the side" in extralegal, unofficial marriages. Despite these efforts to maintain a public image of Christian piety, many of these educated men continued to participate secretly in traditional cults.

Among the uneducated masses, ordinary Rwandans did not hesitate to observe indigenous spiritual practices and imported colonial religions simultaneously. During his fieldwork in 1985, Gerard van 't Spijker, a Presbyterian missionary, found that the great majority of Christians and non-Christians still practiced the traditional burial and mourning rites (van 't Spijker 1990, 246). Although the Christian mission had consistently and throughout prohibited the traditional, "pagan" rituals, the majority of Rwandans chose to participate in at least some of them. Van 't Spijker reported the reactions of some Rwandan church members: "Many [Rwandan] Christians were convinced that the missionaries followed their own rituals of mourning, (*kwera*) without explaining their secrets to Rwandan Christians. For example, in 1982, the missionary E. Johanssen wore special clothing after the death of his mother, and then after a certain period of time, he again wore his regular clothes. We had concluded that the Johanssen family had finished their rites of *kwera*" (van 't Spijker 1990, 169). Thus, many Rwandans held onto their indigenous practices secretly because they perceived that the Europeans also observed their own secret practices.

CONCEPT OF EVIL IN RACIST PROPAGANDA AND EXTREMIST MEDIA IN THE EARLY 1990S

In the early 1990s, racist propaganda and the Hutu extremist media helped create a social context where genocide appeared to be a rational solution by many Rwandans. Propaganda targeted the RPF rebels and their supporters, moderate Hutu politicians who advocated for democratization and an end to the state party's monopoly on power, and Rwandans of Tutsi ethnicity. The concept of evil played a significant role in demonizing the RPF, members of the opposition political parties regardless of their ethnicity, and Tutsis as a group.

Propagandists and supporters of President Habyarimana, his MRND (*Mouvement Révolutionnaire Nationale pour le Dévelopment,* National Revolutionary Movement for Development) political party and Hutu extremist political portrayed the RPF's mission as restoring monarchy to Rwanda, bringing back feudalism, and reinstituting the servitude of Hutu people. In a popular song played frequently on an extremist radio station, singer Simon Bikindi sang, "the servitude, the whip, the lash, the forced work that exhausted the people, that has disappeared forever. You, the great majority [*rubanda nyamwinshi*], pay attention and, descendants of Sebahinzi, remember this evil that should be driven as far away as possible, so that it never returns to Rwanda" (cited in Des Forges 1999, 77). In these lyrics, Bikindi characterizes Tutsi feudalism as evil, but listeners understood that he also meant to characterize the RPF rebels as evil. During my fieldwork in Rwanda in 1997 and 1998, several Rwandans recently returned from the refugee camps in the eastern Democratic Republic of the Congo recounted stories of elderly Rwandans who marveled that RPF soldiers did not, in fact, have pointy ears or tails as they were led to believe by extremist propaganda and rumors circulating in the refugee camps. Hutu extremists also portrayed Hutus in political parties opposed to the MRND and extremist political parties aligned with the MRND as evil or as the devil. In an infamous speech in late 1992, Leon Mugesera equated Prime Minister Dismas Nsengiyaremye, a member of the MDR political party and a Hutu, with the devil (Des Forges 1999, 84, 111).

In the years leading up to the genocide and during the genocide itself, the extremist media referred to Tutsis as snakes. This metaphor evoked both indigenous Rwandan aversion to snakes and biblical representations of Satan as the snake who led Eve astray in the Book of Genesis. In the same speech, Mugesera evoked biblical imagery of the snake when justifying the need to "massacre this gang of bastards," referring to the RPF rebels: "It is written in the Gospel, you know it, if the snake comes to bite you and you leave it to slip among you, it's you who will perish" (Chrétien 1995, 56). These representations of the RPF rebels as snakes continued up until the genocide began in April 1994. During the genocide, these metaphors were also applied to so-called RPF accomplices, meaning all ethnic Tutsis and those Hutus and Twas who supported political parties opposed to the MRND and Coalition for the Defense of the Republic parties.

During the genocide, the Hutu extremists used this snake metaphor as well as the concept of evil to frame the genocide as a civil war where the use of force against the RPF rebels, Tutsis, and others opposed to the genocide constituted a legitimate self-defense against both a spiritual and material enemy rather than as a crime against humanity. On April 21, 1994, on the eve of massacres in one community, witnesses said the burgomaster (mayor) used a Rwandan proverb to explain the danger posed by the RPF and their "accomplices" (Des Forges 1999, 468): *Iyo inzoka yizilitse ku gisabo ugomba kikimena ukabona uko uyica.* Literally, "If a snake is curled around a gourd, you do everything necessary to kill it." In other words, you even break the gourd and incur the misfortune that comes with breaking a gourd to eliminate evil. Listeners understood that he was giving orders to kill Tutsis. On June 1, 1994, a subprefect in Butare prefecture wrote to the burgomasters, "Search everywhere in the commune for the enemy because he is clever and can sneak in like a snake" (Des Forges 1999, 419). During an attack in Nyakizu commune on April 22, 1994, a genocide perpetrator threatened, "You are snakes. Your god does not exist. We will exterminate you" (Des Forges 1999, 401). These metaphors identified RPF soldiers and their accomplices as Satan himself or at least as the embodiment of evil in its most obvious animal form. This use of the concept of evil framed the genocide as legitimate self-defense rather than as a crime against humanity.

The Hutu extremist media portrayed the civil war as a biblical battle between Good and Evil with President Habyarimana serving as a Christ-like savior (Chrétien 1995, 326). During the genocide, the extremist media continued to demonize the RPF and Tutsis. In an RTLM broadcast on June 12, 1994, announcer Kantano Habimana said, "And you have heard that, since the *Inkotanyi* [RPF rebels] assassinated the bishops, the priests and the nuns . . . all people of the Church have cursed them beginning with the Pope . . . and God himself has abandoned them . . . and even Satan is no longer willing to welcome the *Inkotanyi*" (Chrétien 1995, 197). Because leaders of the Roman Catholic Church in Rwanda did not make any public statements opposed to the genocide or any statements to counter the extremist media, many Catholics at the grassroots-level interpreted the church's silence as tacit approval of statements like these and of the genocide as a whole.

EVIL AND HUMAN ACTIONS DURING THE 1994 GENOCIDE

As mentioned at the start of this essay, Rwandans made sense of the obscene violence of the 1994 genocide drawing on this cultural repertoire of entangled religious practices and beliefs, in terms of three different evocations of evil: (1) Satan himself walking among men and directing the violence, (2) genocide perpetrators as possessed by Satan, satanic spirits, or evil spirits, and (3) humans falling prey to the dark side of free will where they were led astray by human weakness. Each of these interpretations relies on different combinations of indigenous Rwandan and imported Christian belief systems.

The first interpretation of genocidal violence emerges from an understanding of Satan in a human form walking among men and directing the violence. In my fieldwork in Rwanda, I first heard this evocation of evil in 1997 from a male (Tutsi) genocide survivor who was a devout Catholic. In the midst of recounting his story of survival, he characterized genocide perpetrators and their actions: "It was as if everyone had lost his mind, and Satan walked among them leading their attacks. People you thought were your friends, your allies, suddenly turned on you. *You can never know what is in the heart of a man.*"[9]

This interpretation of evil as the personification of Satan can be tied to Roman Catholic and Protestant perceptions of the Ryangombe cult. Most common in northern Rwanda, the Ryanbombe cult attributed great power to the spirit Ryangombe who helped cult practitioners by protecting them from evil spirits sent by their enemies to attack them. During the colonial period and afterward, the Roman Catholic and Protestant missionaries taught that Ryangombe was Satan who was leading people astray. Timothy Longman documented a similar explanation from a man in Gisovu: "What we saw in this country surprised us. These were things commanded by the devil. There were people who were good, who stayed calm. But there were others who were Interahamwe. These were everywhere in the country. Everywhere they went, they sowed disorder, killed people, stole cattle, pillaged" (cited in Longman 2009, 322). In this passage, the man describes the Interahamwe militiamen as Satan's army who overran the country. A European priest evoked an almost identical explanation of the genocide when he told me, "These things are beyond comprehension. It was the work of demons."[10]

Some genocide perpetrators also make sense of their own actions in terms of being visited by Satan. One perpetrator repeatedly said no one had been killed in his community and insisted that neither he nor his neighbors had participated in killing. During the long interview, I kept coming back to the issue as he had disclosed at the beginning of the interview that he had been released from prison for time served after confessing to his crimes. Finally, on the fourth attempt, he began to answer my questions.

AUTHOR: What did you confess to?

MAN: I confessed that I participated in an attack that killed a person. There is no use trying to hide what happened.

AUTHOR: How did this attack unfold?

MAN: This attack happened when we were going to loot a cow and then we killed a person from there.

AUTHOR: Why did you participate in this attack?

MAN: There are times when the enemy, Satan, comes to visit you and you follow him like that.

AUTHOR: How did Satan come to visit you that day?

MAN: At that time, I sold meat, I had a butcher shop. Someone told me he had a cow he could sell me cheaply. I went with him and some others. The cow was outside a house. We took it and then the people who stayed behind began to beat the cow's owner, and then they killed him. There you have it, that is why they say I'm among the killers.[11]

When this man stated, "the enemy, Satan, comes to visit you and you follow him like that," he formulates his actions in a Pentecostal idiom. Pentecostal pastors in Rwanda portray Satan as a presence among humans who constantly tempts and tests true believers. Born to parents who practiced only indigenous spiritual practices, this man had a conversion experience at the age of sixteen years (twenty years before the genocide) when white, Pentecostal missionaries came to his community. During the interview, he mentioned numerous times that his religious beliefs kept him from going to join the Interahamwe groups who were leading the genocide in the region. In the quoted passage, he underlines the contingency of his choice when he begins, "There are times when." Later in the interview he again characterizes his participation as a momentary lapse in judgment, "There are moments when you fall into a trap and then after you notice and you can't continue in this path." From this Pentecostal cosmology, Christians must maintain constant vigilance as Satan can appear on your doorstep as a friend or neighbor with a cow to sell and the next thing you know you are participating in a man's killing.

The second interpretation of genocidal violence perceives genocide perpetrators as possessed by Satan, satanic spirits, demons, or evil spirits. I first heard this interpretation evoked in 1999 when I was speaking with two widows in their sixties whose husbands had died in the refugee camps in Zaire (now Democratic Republic of the Congo). Both women were devout Catholics and well educated for their ages, fluent in French and holding secondary school degrees. In the midst of explaining to me the ways the genocide had eroded sexual morality in Rwanda, one of them said, "During the genocide, men ran around doing whatever they wanted. They took [unmarried] girls and did what they wanted with them. They killed. They did other terrible things. It was like they were possessed by Satan. If you looked in their eyes, you could see something evil there."

From a moral standpoint, this understanding of the evil acts committed during the genocide appears to erase human responsibility. How can a man be responsible for his actions if he is possessed by Satan? Given that these women's husbands had held important positions in the MRND political party and Habyarimana government, the men had occupied, at best, morally ambiguous positions during the genocide. The interim, genocidal government required government officials to enact its policy of genocide. While a few, courageous people simply refused, such as the prefect (governor) of the Butare prefecture who was killed for his refusal, the majority found themselves in a position where they could no longer remain on the sidelines or, whereby remaining on the sideline, implicated in the deaths of civilians at the hands of the Interahamwe militias or government soldiers. In this context, it would have been difficult for these women's husbands to avoid participating in the genocide in some way.

In an interview in 2014, the same European priest invoked this second interpretation of evil when recounting what he had witnessed during the genocide.

> Three men came to the gate after nightfall. [He pauses, shivers, and then shakes his head as if to erase an image from it, then continues.] They were the personification of the Devil. Their eyes were empty. They were sweating profusely and covered in blood. Their clothes were hanging from them in tatters. In their hands, they carried machetes, hammers, nail-studded clubs, chains. [He pauses again, removes his glasses and wipes his eyes, and then continues.] Their weapons were also covered in blood and had shreds of flesh hanging from them. To see them was to become insane. This image haunts me.[12]

The third interpretation of genocidal violence perceives genocide perpetrators' evil actions as a result of the free will God granted humans. Roman Catholic priests, nuns, and lay ministers frequently explained the genocide from this perspective in the years after the genocide. They employed this explanation when speaking to their congregations as well as to foreign researchers. From this point of view, Rwandans who participated in the genocide chose to do evil instead of remaining on the "righteous path." Within Christian theology, this explanation is one of the few that can be used to explain why terrible things happen to good people if God is good. As a Rwandan priest and (Tutsi) genocide survivor explained to me in 2001, "You see my uncle there [pointing at his intoxicated uncle]. When I see him, I sometimes wonder what God was thinking sparing him and then allowing my Uncle [name deleted] to perish in the genocide. Uncle [name deleted] was the head of the family. He did everything for me when I was a child. Paid for my school, paid for my uniforms, helped me get a place at the junior seminary. But, that's how things happened in the genocide: the good ones were killed and we were left with the others." At another time, the same priest explained that the many evil acts that made up the genocide could be understood as humans choosing to deviate from the Christian path.

Occasionally, ordinary Rwandans evoked a similar explanation of the genocide drawing on indigenous understandings of human agency. A Rwandan proverb, "You never know what is in a man's heart," used by the genocide survivor quoted at the beginning of this section, explains the fundamental problem of human agency and Rwandan secrecy practices. You can never truly know what another person thinks as he may be hiding his real thoughts and feelings from you. A genocide perpetrator called on the same proverb when explaining to me why he participated in the genocide. This man had confessed to killing numerous men, women, and children, and was said by others to have killed hundreds, had also hidden and protected some Tutsi women and children at his home. When I asked him why he decided to save some and kill others, he replied: "There was no decision. We were in a group of evildoers. They trained us [morally] to kill. We were together in a group. We watched what was happening, what others were doing. We don't all have the same heart. It's like the bus on the highway coming from Kigali going to Huye [motioning with his hands]. The bus comes and stops for you, you get on, and off you go."[13]

This man's response makes it clear that he did not feel as if he made a decision. Elsewhere in the interview, he explained that his mind was blank when he was killing. He compares the genocide to a bus that comes to town and carries people away. His description of his state of mind coincides with those documented by scholars who have found that mobs have an emergent agency that overrides individual will (see for example, Brass 1997; Tambiah 1996). His was the most chilling explanation of evil I have heard in Rwanda. If perpetrators did not make a choice to participate but instead killed without even thinking, then there is no way to prevent mob violence or to intervene to stop it.

A common element of these explanations of genocide's evil is explaining the unexplainable. The many violent acts that made up the genocide—and that Rwandans witnessed with their very own eyes or experienced with their bodies—were so far beyond the scope of the imaginable that they are inexplicable. While explaining genocidal violence as free will run amuck fits best with Roman Catholic theology, many Rwandans prefer explanations that point to Satan, Satan's influence, demons, and evil spirits because they relieve, at least partially, human responsibility for evil. This perspective positions evil as a thing that can be excised from a person's body, which fits with indigenous healing practices where healers remove abscesses, growths, or objects, understood to be poison implanted by a poisoner, from the bodies of the ill.

NOTES

1. The ethnographic data analyzed and presented in this essay was gathered during fieldwork conducted in Rwanda between 1997 and the present with different research questions in mind. These data consisted of participant observation conducted in a middle-class neighborhood in Kigali, Rwanda (9 months), and a rural community in southern Rwanda (12 months). The author visited many other communities across the country and interviewed ordinary Rwandans, civil society organization members and leaders, religious leaders, and local government officials. For a more detailed explanation of the research methods, see Burnet (2012), 23–33.

2. The impact of these Protestant churches has often been localized to regions where large missionary outposts were established (for example, around the Adventist missions at Rwankeri in the North, Ngoma in the West, and Gitwe in central Rwanda, many inhabitants practice Seventh-Day Adventism [Ngabo 2008, 57]).

3. In some parishes in Rwanda, excommunication is a common practice. During fieldwork in a rural community in southern Rwanda, approximately thirty Catholics were excommunicated by the parish priest for attending the traditional wedding ceremony of two practicing Catholics who did not also marry immediately in the church. They were told that in order to receive Communion again, they would need to attend adult catechism and renew their membership in the church by undergoing the rite of confirmation again.

4. Estimates of how many people died in the 1994 genocide vary widely. While how many died is irrelevant to whether or not the killings in Rwanda in 1994 were genocide, the issue is highly politicized so it is necessary to indicate the sources. The number I use here comes from Alison Des Forges (1999), *Leave None to Tell the Story: Genocide in Rwanda*, 15. For more on the numbers of dead, see Scott Straus's (2006) analysis in *The Order of Genocide: Race, Power, and War in Rwanda*, 41–64.

5. As the scholarship of Alison Des Forges (1986; with D. S. Newbury 2011), Catharine Newbury (1978, 1988, 1998), and David Newbury (1991, 1997, 2001, 2004) has demonstrated, representations of precolonial Rwanda as a centralized state with a homogenous culture obscure the great diversity of beliefs and practices across the region known today as Rwanda.

6. In Rwanda today, Christian churches of all sects and Muslims in Rwanda use *Imana* to refer to God in Kinyarwanda. In the early twentieth century, however, the first Roman Catholic mission in Rwanda instead used the Swahili word *Mungu*, for God (Linden 1977). The German Lutheran mission established in 1907 began to use the word *Imana* for the Christian God (Linden 1977).

7. All translations, unless otherwise noted, are by the author.

8. *Umupfumu* (*abapfumu*, pl.) is a ritual specialist ("diviner") who detects which spirit (or spirits) are causing the problems. Some *abapfumu* also practice rites to calm the spirits.

9. Author's interview, Kigali, Rwanda, July 1997.

10. Interview by the author, March 2014, Kigali, Rwanda. Author's translation from the original French.

11. Author's interview, October 2013, Rutsiro District, Rwanda. Author's translation from the original Kinyarwanda and French.

12. Interview by the author, March 2014, Kigali, Rwanda. Author's translation from the original French.

13. Author's interview, Nyanza District, Rwanda, July 2013. Author's translation from the original Kinyarwanda and French.

REFERENCES

Arnoux, A. 1912. "Le culte de la société sécrète des imandwa au Ruanda." *Anthropos* 7: 273–295, 529–558, 840–874.

———. 1913. "Le culte de la société sécrète des imandwa au Ruanda." *Anthropos* 8: 110–134, 754–774.

Berger, Iris. 1981. *Religion and Resistance: East African Kingdoms in the Precolonial Period*. Tervuren, Belgium: Musée Royale de l'Afrique Centrale.

Brass, Paul R. 1997. *Theft of an Idol: Text and Context in the Representation of Collective Violence*. Princeton, NJ: Princeton University Press.

Burnet, Jennie E. 2012. *Genocide Lives in Us: Women, Memory, and Silence in Rwanda.* Madison: University of Wisconsin Press.

Chrétien, Jean-Pierre. 1995. *Rwanda: Les médias du génocide.* Paris: Editions Karthala.

Des Forges, Alison. 1986. "The Drum Is Greater than the Shout: The 1912 Rebellion in Northern Rwanda." In *Banditry, Rebellion and Social Protest in Africa,* edited by Donald Crummey, 311–331. London: James Currey Ltd.

———. 1999. *Leave None to Tell the Story: Genocide in Rwanda.* New York: Human Rights Watch.

Des Forges, Alison Liebhafsky, and David S. Newbury. 2011. *Defeat Is the Only Bad News: Rwanda under Musinga, 1896–1931.* Madison: University of Wisconsin Press.

d'Hertefelt, Marcel. 1962. *Les anciens royaumes de la zone interlacutrine méridionale.* London: International African Institute.

Evans-Pritchard, E. E. 1937. *Witchcraft Oracles and Magic among the Azande.* Oxford: Clarendon Press.

Linden, Ian. 1977. *Church and Revolution in Rwanda.* New York: Africana Publishing Company.

Longman, Timothy Paul. 2009. *Christianity and Genocide in Rwanda.* Cambridge: Cambridge University Press.

Newbury, Catharine. 1978. "Ethnicity in Rwanda: The Case of Kinyaga." *Africa* 48, no. 1: 17–29.

———. 1988. *The Cohesion of Oppression.* New York: Columbia University Press.

———. 1998. "Ethnicity and the Politics of History in Rwanda." *Africa Today* 45, no. 1: 7–24.

Newbury, David. 1991. *Kings and Clans: Ijwi Island and the Lake Kivu Rift, 1780–1840.* Madison: University of Wisconsin Press.

———. 1997. "Irredentist Rwanda: Ethnic and Territorial Frontiers in Central Africa." *Africa Today* 44, no. 2: 211–222.

———. 2001. "Precolonial Burundi and Rwanda: Local Loyalties, Regional Royalties." *International Journal of African Historical Studies* 34, no. 2: 255–314.

———. 2004. "Engaging with the Past to Engage with the Future: Two Visions of History." *Cahiers d'Études Africaines* 44, nos. 173/174: 430–431.

Ngabo, Jerome Birikunzira. 2008. "Implantation and Growth of the Seventh-Day Adventist Church in Rwanda (1919–2000)." MA thesis, University of South Africa, Pretoria.

Parkin, David J., ed. 1985. *The Anthropology of Evil.* New York: Blackwell.

Straus, Scott. 2006. *The Order of Genocide: Race, Power, and War in Rwanda.* Ithaca, NY: Cornell University Press.

Tambiah, Stanley J. 1996. *Leveling Crowds: Ethnonationalist Conflicts and Collective Violence in South Asia.* Berkeley: University of California Press.

Taylor, Christopher C. 1992. *Milk, Honey, and Money: Changing Concepts in Rwandan Healing.* Washington, DC: Smithsonian Institution Press.

Van' t Spijker, Gerard. 1990. *Les usages funéraires et la mission de l'Église: Une étude anthropologique et théologique des rites funéraires au Rwanda.* Kampen: Kok.

5 POLITICS AND COSMOGRAPHIC ANXIETY

Kongo and Dagbon Compared

WYATT MACGAFFEY

This essay explores the possibility that there may be an inverse causal relationship, in a given historical period, between political stability and the degree of definition of worldview. Evil is not only a moral and ethical problem, but also a political one, in that evildoers real or imaginary must be legitimately dealt with.[1] Because political institutions and activities are intrinsically historical, ideas about evil and the means to deal with it can be expected to change. Indeed, "dealing with" evil by consulting a diviner, healer, or shrine; following through on the recommendations; and mustering economic and social support for remedial action, is itself political activity and may redistribute power and authority in the community (Bohannan 1958). A diviner must know the culturally established repertoire of potential causes of good and evil but also which course of action is likely to be endorsed not only by his client, but also by others whom it may adversely affect.

Although the traditional anthropological tendency has been to describe both the sociopolitical organization of a given society and the "beliefs" of its members as handed down in more or less immutable and characteristic form from time immemorial, I suggest that when political institutions are chronically weak, the sense of helplessness in the face of evil will give rise to anxiety accompanied by increasing intellectual speculation as to the moral organization of the world. This speculation may be carried on literally in private conversation but more practically in rituals developed to deal with current social disorders. This suggestion is itself highly speculative, an effort not only to compare my experience of the "moral imagination" (Beidelman 1986) in two different societies but to integrate politics and "religion" and to approach both historically. In speaking of "political stability," I do not imply that stability is necessarily realized in hierarchical form, as in "kingdoms."

Based on several periods of extended residence in Kongo communities in the Democratic Republic of Congo between 1964 and 1980, most of my professional work has concerned the history, culture, and social organization of the Kikongo speaking peoples of the West Atlantic coast of Central Africa. In 1996, however, I began to spend two months every year in northern Ghana, in the modern metropolis of Tamale and the traditional kingdom of Dagbon. This, I found, was a very different Africa, although the people of both areas speak distantly related languages of the same Niger-Congo family, and although there are odd little cultural correspondences, such as the idea that a newborn child and his placenta are analogous to a chief and the mat on which he sits. Whereas in Kongo, chiefs had faded to a memory, in Dagbon, they parade on horseback, surrounded by retainers, volleys of gunsmoke, and the strident chant of praise-singers. Public meetings in Kongo were enriched by subtle wordplay and the counterpoint of call and response, and in Dagbon, by the discriminating etiquette of title and precedence. Although most people in Dagbon are at least nominally Muslim or Christian, they speak respectfully of traditional shrines and their keepers, consult diviners in case of need, often keep protective charms in doorways and on their persons, and argue about the proper treatment of witches. There is a difference, to be sure, between villagers and educated city folk who consider themselves enlightened and speak condescendingly of "traditionalists" (pagans), but in practice the difference is not clearly marked. The worldview that might make sense of all this seems quite vague. David Tait, noting the same vagueness among the neighboring Konkomba, attributed it to their lack of a central political organization, but that Durkheimian argument can not apply to Dagbon. In Kongo, on the other hand, though political institutions were uncertainly established, cosmological ideas were relatively clearly defined.

In Kongo, space and time were organized as the opposed and complementary worlds of the living and the dead, separated by boundaries such as the edge of the forest, the bank of a stream, nightfall and dawn, the succession of fathers and sons. Everything exceptional among the living was explained by interventions from the land of the dead, some of them direct but most of them mediated by "experts," by witches, chiefs, prophets, or healers. People recognized as such experts held "religious commissions," that is, definite but contingent roles, not regular offices. These roles, which were as much economic and political as religious, were differentiated by moral and political judgments: not by what anyone in fact could do but by what others assumed he did. A witch (*ndoki*) was a man or woman thought to use power derived from the land of the dead for harmful and selfish purposes. This power, called *kindoki,* was not in itself evil; it was also necessary to chiefs and healers, though they were supposed to use it for good, that is, with approved results.

In the Congo basin, and probably in Africa generally, the popular assumption is that life should be humdrum, without notable fortune good or bad. Because the same, limited technologies of production and reproduction are generally available to everybody, unusual success or misfortune is attributable to extranormal techniques. As a Kongo writer put it, "Although witches recognize one another, no witch can ever know himself to be a witch. Non-witches just use their eyes. If they see a woman who always seems to have money, they know she operates a money-*kundu.* If they see a hunter who always hits his quarry they know he operates a gluttony-*kundu*" (Janzen and MacGaffey 1974, 16).

Kundu was thought to be a sort of gland in the intestines, obtained by traffic with the inhabitants of the land of the dead, which equipped the owner with exceptional powers. Because life was supposedly a zero-sum game, good fortune was believed to accrue to one person only at the expense of someone else. To fight witchcraft and remedy its effects, people turned (in the 1960s) to prophets (*ngunza*) and healers (*nganga*); these experts differed in that the prophet said he or she had been chosen by God for this work for the benefit of the community at large, and therefore charged no money (though gifts were expected), whereas the healer justified his fee by saying that what you get for nothing is worth nothing. On the other hand, because to charge money for a service suggested selfishness, the healer invited comparison with the witch, and might himself be accused of witchcraft. The last of the experts was the invested chief, who in the nineteenth century had been expected to defend the community "at night" against the combined onslaught of witches; under colonial rule, however, chieftaincy had been abolished, leaving the people defenseless, as many of them thought.

Because witches seem imaginary to outsiders, devices to counter "witchcraft" are readily interpreted as psychologically or religiously motivated, but *kindoki* is a way of talking about the uses and abuses of power. When disorder seems to prevail, counter-*kindoki* measures are called for. The principal protection against witchcraft was provided by fetishes (*minkisi*), of which there was a constantly proliferating variety, including both individual objects and group initiations, forming a continuum from private to public. Initiates, singly or in groups, went into seclusion, often in the bush, there to learn the meanings and uses of medicines, with the associated songs, full of coded cosmological references. Initiation itself was represented as a visit to the land of the dead and a rebirth of the candidate among the living, often strangely garbed, uttering cryptic formulae, and equipped with new powers. The micropolitics of such a development included the requirement that supporters provide for the initiand's needs during the ritual process; greatly increased prestige for the graduate; behavioral rules and restrictions imposed on those associated with him, including clients in search of remedies; a flow of foodstuffs and fees toward the new healer and his entourage; and the power to direct accusations and prescribe remedial routines. The success of a new *nkisi* could produce a local political reconfiguration or might start a regional movement.[2] In any case, its procedures and the stress of the problem it was supposed to correct prompted in the minds of participants new reflections on and representations of the universe of human experience.

Victor Turner did not think of rituals as projects for social change; he argued that they channeled collective action to restore peace and harmony in the face of corporate bodies that by their structure differentiated among persons instead of uniting them. That is a different function altogether, but it is not my intention to adjudicate among competing functions. Contrasting his approach with that of Lévi-Strauss, he pointed out that although the Ndembu construct a complex of symbolic oppositions, they do so not intellectually but by arranging the contraposition of "sensorily perceptible objects, such as a hen and a cock of different ages and colors." (Turner 1975, 16). This is not in fact all that different from Lévi-Strauss's idea of *la pensée concrète,* but the point is that the values so expressed remain verbally inarticulate, no matter how powerful the emotions they channel. In a literate civilization, cosmological models are proposed and recorded for further reference and discussion; eventually some become authoritative. Turner found no cosmology among the Ndembu, but he was looking for "myths," explicit narratives resembling those familiar to Europeans, that would define such a cosmology. Yet his sketch of the spatial construction of the Isoma ritual, a circular site in which the patients pass underground through a tunnel from "death" to "life," is obviously a cosmographic diagram, as nearly explicitly as one could hope to find in preliterate Central Africa. As an account of their world, it was made real and powerful for the participants by their physical and emotional experience of the ritual process (Turner 1969, 30).

In the Kongo of the 1960s, the use of *minkisi* had been repressed, though not discontinued, and witchcraft was a constant preoccupation, while the political and moral distinctions (who was a healer; who appeared to be a healer but was "really" a witch; who said he had been sent by God but was "really" in it for the money) were frequent topics of debate and accusation. The land of the dead was a constant presence, reported in dreams and in strange experiences in the forest; the daily distribution of fortune and misfortune also suggested that many of one's neighbors had dealings of one sort or another with the dead.

Although Bakongo thought of the land of the dead as a place to which one could go and come, it was also a conceptual space in which they could inscribe models of their society and contingent explanations (offered, for example, by a diviner) of particular experiences and problems (MacGaffey 1968, 2000, 206–208). The models, and the particular explanations that emerged from reflection on ritual performances and strange experiences, were always *products of a hesitant process of inquiry, not excerpts from an anterior body of doctrine.* Cosmology generated questions rather than answers.[3] Field notes from 1965, like Kikongo texts from 1915, record individuals disputing details of the cosmology: Are *simbi* spirits ancestors who have died the second death, or not? How do they relate to *bankita*? Moreover, the political histories of the various Kikongo-speaking areas before and after colonial occupation have been very different. It is not surprising therefore that ethnographers have recorded variant elaborations of the basic postulate of two worlds, visible and invisible (Hersak 2004). No one could say for sure how the moral universe was organized as a total system, or felt the need to do so, but arguments about it, motivated by anxiety over daily concerns of life, death, and the pursuit of elusive well-being, revealed a certain structure of opposed values: public versus private benefit, power of death versus power of life. These values are salient not only in Kongo, but also throughout the Congo basin and in the forested areas of West Africa.[4]

One widespread form of politico-ritual reform movement that has attracted much scholarly attention is the cult or "drum" of affliction, in which a sufferer is advised by a diviner to undergo initiation to a particular ritual, which he or she is then qualified to administer to others. After World War II, when wage labor in gold mines was introduced to the Nzabi, a northern Kongo-speaking group, young men were enabled to challenge their elders' hold on wealth. The resulting social confusion produced widespread fear of rampant witchcraft, to which the Njobi cult provided a response. Suspects were ritually tested; those found guilty were cleared of their witchcraft and became adepts of the cult. Myths of the cult's origin build a palimpsest superimposing three stories: (1) of the actual journey of a candidate to seek out the healer; (2) of a visit to the land of the dead, signposted in the manner of countless West African folktales by crossroads, twins, talking apes, and so on, from which the secrets of the cult are obtained (MacGaffey 1977); and (3) of a return to the country from which the Nzabi originally migrated, and from which they hoped to recover moral integrity and political renewal. Once again, ritual (in the context of social distress) was simultaneously (attempted) practical reform and cosmological reaffirmation; only a social scientist would want to disentangle them and systematize them separately (Dupré 1982, 360–361).

In Dagbon, there is no concept, comparable to *kindoki*, of a single yet morally divisible occult force operated for different purposes by different kinds of experts. There seems to be no generally known folklore concerning the journey to the beyond, or about coming and going there, although it is said that, in the invisible vicinity of dynastic shrines, drumming may be heard when no village among the living is celebrating anything. In the forest, one may encounter strange creatures who cause possession or confer magical charms, but the land of the dead appears not to be well thought out. The exceptional knowledge of healers is inherited, or occasionally learned, rather than the result of a visitation or a journey. There is no pervasive debate about the authenticity of this or that healer, no political or moral rivalry among them, though some are considered "better" than others. The repressive presence of Islam, Christianity, and modernity are factors to be considered, though their influence remained superficial until the 1980s.

After some time in Dagbon, I concluded that the same four fields of occult action (chieftaincy, public healing, private healing, and witchcraft) do exist, as in Kongo, but they are differently weighted and expressed. The difference is that Dagbon has a clearly defined political establishment. Chieftaincy is not a commission but a presumptively perpetual office, meaning that, when a chief moves on, the vacancy has to be filled by regular procedures. The counterpart of the chief is the tindana, a shrine-keeper responsible for the maintenance of good weather and abundant crops; this also is an office—one does not argue about whether someone is or is not a chief or tindana (although succession to chieftaincy may be fiercely contested). Individuals may be advised to take their problems to a shrine, but the principal activity at a shrine is its annual festival of "washing" or renewal. High-ranking chiefs, men or women, are inherently dangerous to those around them; the most dangerous of all is the Ya Na, the king of Dagbon. In 2005, the highest-ranking female chief, the Gundo Na, gave her colleague the Zo-Simli Na a staff fortified with protective talismans specially commissioned from a prominent Muslim cleric in the capital, warning her that if, when in public, she should strike anyone's foot with it, that person would surely die. Tindanas, men and women, are also sufficiently dangerous that they should be treated with respect. It is not supposed that these powers protect the community or are directed specifically against witches.

From time to time people, usually but not always elderly women, become "witches" by accusation (*sonya*, witch; *sogo*, witchcraft); they are dealt with by violence or banishment, not ritual means, although the accusation may be tested by consulting a shrine. Other commissions are those of assorted healers, diviners, and Islamic malams serving individual clients, who are frequently consulted and provide protective amulets (*gurima*), worn secretly by many people, but also medicines (*tima*) that can do both good and harm. Pagan households protect their front doors by means of a medicated "trap." The sources of evil thus fended off are not well defined, but they are mostly to be feared in large gatherings. Men, in general, think that women are always plotting against them and need to be controlled; men, on the other hand, are entitled to use even harmful medicines in their competition with other men (Bierlich 2007, 27–29). The striking feature of the whole moral system is its formal regularity: annual festivals, local and family shrines, and perpetual offices; there is no history of recurrent religious movements. Ambivalent occult power clusters around the key features of the political structure, including male authority over women.[5]

At the domestic level, Kongo differs from Dagbon mainly in that relatively little attention was paid to lineal ancestors. Kongo social organization was "matrilineal," in the limited sense that there were exogamous, landholding, matrilineal descent groups, whereas Dagbon has been conventionally described as "patrilineal." In fact, the family in Dagbon is a bilateral descending kindred with a patrifilial bias. Access to land is obtained through the local chief, and competition within the family is focused on titles to which the family may have claims. The dead are buried in the family compound; prayers are addressed to family shrines by the head of household, both on behalf of individuals in need and collectively at annual festivals. A man hoping for advancement may have a better chance by associating with his mother's family: it is better to be *pagabia* ("woman's child") than *dobia* (man's child), but one does not offer gifts to maternal ancestors. Family organization and ancestor cult are thus in harmony. As Bierlich reports, there is no division between the living and the dead, the bush, and the ancestors; they are not in separate spheres (Bierlich 2007, 42).

In Kongo, the local matriclan section was the primary site of competition over productive and reproductive resources; individuals turned to their respective fathers and patrilateral relatives for support against matrilateral rivals, and in need might address prayers to a father's grave, located in the village cemetery in the forest. The ancestor cult was thus disharmonic, a cult of one's fathers, not the founders of the matrilineage, and it was occasional rather than regular. Perhaps for this reason, though the dead are intimately influential in everybody's life, there was a certain sense that they are elsewhere. As another Kongo text says, "We say they are in the forest, but they say it is we who live in the forest, they who are in the village." At night, the dead lead a life that mirrors that of the village during the day; game animals in the forest were thought to be their domestic livestock.

To explore the difference further I need to adopt a perspective that is both historical and regional. In northern Ghana and neighboring Burkina Faso, an area including Dagbon and several other kingdoms but mostly populated by so-called acephalous societies, or "tribes without rulers," the chief/tindana pair is universal, even in societies that have no "chiefs" but only elders (Liberski-Bagnoud 2002; Tait 1961). Where there is a political hierarchy, tindanas are responsible not only for shrines related to general welfare but for the induction procedures that confer on chiefs the exceptional and essentially violent power, called *nam,* that makes them chiefs. In Dagbon, as in Central Africa, traditions say that chieftaincy was introduced by alien conquerors, a story historians have been all too ready to accept. Reviewing the issue with respect to the Mosse kingdoms of Burkina Faso, where similar stories are told, Michel Izard concedes that conquests may have happened, but he argues that the distinction between chief and tindana, authority and terrain, "invader" and "autochthon," is structural, testifying above all to "the inescapable divide in the ideological task of representing the relations of men to nature and of men among themselves" (Izard 2003, 148). Izard proposes, instead of a fixed relation between conquerors and autochthons created by a single act of conquest, a complex dynamic of constant adjustment and reallocation of opportunities and responsibilities ("endoconquest"), carried on not only in this or that kingdom but throughout the area of the Oti-Volta (Mole-Dagbani) languages.

The acephalous societies of this area should be thought of not as having being unable to develop central governments but as having "refused" to do so, at least for the time being (Skalník 1987; Scott 2009; MacGaffey 2013). Even in these societies, the chief/tindana functions and the associated offices persist, though the chief may be no more than a lineage headman. The kingdoms, on the other hand, especially Dagbon and Gonja, built chiefly hierarchies from the proceeds of looting and tolls on international trade from about 1700 onward. As compared with Kongo, where Belgian rule had abolished even such chiefs as survived the end of the slave trade, the political system in Dagbon in the twentieth century was substantial, sweeping everybody up in a romance of the kingdom as a regulated space and leaving less room for anxiety.[6] The only major witch hunt occurred in 1955, on the eve of Ghanaian independence, when northerners were worried that they might become subject to the neocolonial rule of the south (Tait 1963). The shrine that was the focus of this activity was of southern origin.

A relationship similar to the chief/tindana couple existed in Kongo in the sixteenth century between the chief and the *kitome* (Thornton 1983, 59; Hilton 1985, 25). By the nineteenth century, it appears that this pairing, and the role of a ritual figure and shrine-keeper (*nthomi,* a cognate term) in installing chiefs, persisted most clearly in parts of Kongo closer to the coast, where relative wealth derived from the Atlantic trade supported traditional hierarchies, better than the inland economy did (Hagenbucher-Sacripanti 1973, 33–34, 64). Even at the coast, the rush of international commerce had destroyed the Loango kingdom by 1870; there is evidence that the political vacuum was filled by a great increase in the number of magical configurations or charms (*minkisi*) expected to sanction treaties, punish thieves, and protect houses and villages. The Kongo kingdom remained as no more than a memory.

In Belgian Congo in the twentieth century, the role of defender of the common good was filled for a time by followers of the prophet Simon Kimbangu, but by then not only had chieftaincy faded, but also entirely new political forces were taking over the country, accompanied by new movements and agencies attempting to cope with evil. On the eve of national independence in 1959, the indigenous Kongo press was full of explicit efforts to understand history, independence, and international relations in local terms: at independence, they asserted, the world would turn upside down, black would become white, and the ancestors would return (MacGaffey 1968). These efforts, however, merely elaborated similar cosmological speculations that had been put forward since the beginning of the century. Hypothetically, in sixteenth- or eighteenth-century Kongo, when chiefs and shrine-keepers were in place, cosmology would have been as vague as it is now in Dagbon.

John Janzen, reviewing the distribution of cults of affliction among the speakers of Bantu languages, finds that they are most likely to emerge (from an ancient cultural base) in societies without central organization and in situations of distress for at least some part of the population. He notes their political potential: they may provide impetus for the emergence of centralized polities but have also channeled opposition to them (Janzen 1994). He urges us to trace the life cycle of particular rituals as they emerge, change, dissolve, or perhaps become institutionalized. As ancestor cults weaken with the decline of hierarchical authority, cults of "nature" spirits corresponding to the common environmental concerns of the community may take over. Janzen's survey tends to confirm the hypothesis that political reform in conditions of political instability, when evil appears to run unchecked, is an important function of emergent rituals such as cults of affliction or *minkisi*. It may be that participation in rituals that arise from, or are revitalized by, an apparent need to deal with political instability leads to a more definite sense of the organization of the moral universe than is necessary in conditions of political stability.

NOTES

1. The distinction between real and imaginary is one that only outsiders need to make (MacGaffey 2000a).

2. My thinking here has been influenced by Graeber (2006).

3. On the contingent nature of cosmological ideas, see Beidelman (1986, 26–27 passim) and Brenner (1989).

4. The first published ethnographic summary of the Kongo worldview, treated in some quarters as a sacred scripture, is that of Fukiau (1969). For religious commissions in Kongo, see MacGaffey (1970, 1986, 6–8). For commissions elsewhere, see MacGaffey (2000b).

5. For an excellent impression of the political instability of Kongo, "oscillating between anarchy and tyranny," see Doutreloux (1967, 196–202).

6. Staniland describes "untarnished devotion to the status and authority of chieftaincy, the pursuit of which still seemed to be the consuming preoccupation of all Dagombas of appropriate age and rank" (1975, 168).

REFERENCES

Beidelman, Thomas O. 1986. *Moral Imagination in Kaguru Modes of Thought.* Bloomington: Indiana University Press.

Bierlich, Bernhard. 2007. *The Problem of Money: African Agency and Western Medicine in Northern Ghana.* New York: Berghahn.

Bohannan, Paul. 1958. "Extra-processual events in Tiv political institutions." *American Anthropologist* 60, no. 1:1–12.

Brenner, Louis. 1989. "'Religious' Discourse in and about Africa." In *Discourse and Its Disguises,* edited by Karen Barber and Paolo F. de Moraes Farias, 87–105. Birmingham, UK: Birmingham University, Center of West African Studies.

Doutreloux, Albert. 1967. *L'Ombre des fétiches.* Louvain: Nauwelaerts.

Dupré, Georges. 1982. *Un ordre et sa destruction.* Paris: Office de la Recherche Scientifique et Technique Outre-Mer.

Fukiau, André. 1969. *N'kongo ye nza yakun'zungidila.* Kinshasa: Office National de la Recherche et du Développement.

Graeber, David. 2006. "Fetishism as Social Creativity, or Fetishes Are Gods in the Process of Construction." *Anthropological Theory* 5, no. 4:405–436.

Hagenbucher-Sacripanti, Frank. 1973. *Les Fondements spirituelles du pouvoir au royaume de Loango.* Paris: ORSTOM.

Hersak, Dunya. 2004. "There Are Many Kongo Worlds: Particularities of Magico-Religious Beliefs among the Vili and Yombe of Congo-Brazzaville." *Africa* 71, no. 1:614–640.

Hilton, Anne. 1985. *The Kingdom of Kongo.* Oxford: Clarendon.

Izard, Michel. 2003. *Moogo.* Paris: Karthala.

Janzen, John M. 1994. "Drums of Affliction: Real Phenomena or Scholarly Chimaera?" In *Religion in Africa,* edited by Thomas D. Blakely, Walter E. A. van Beek, and Dennis L. Thomson, 160–181. Portsmouth, NH: Heinemann.

Janzen, John M., and W. MacGaffey. 1974. *An Anthology of Kongo Religion.* Publications in Anthropology 5. Lawrence: University Press of Kansas.

Liberski-Bagnoud, Danouta. 2002. *Les dieux du territoire*. Paris: Centre National de Recherche Scientifique.

MacGaffey, Wyatt. 1968. "Kongo and the King of the Americans." *Journal of Modern African Studies* 6, no. 2:171–181.

———. 1970. "The Religious Commissions of the BaKongo." *Man* 5:27–38.

———. 1977. "The Black Loincloth and the Son of Nzambi Mpungu." In *Forms of Folklore in Africa,* edited by Bernth Lindfors, 144–151. Austin: University of Texas Press.

———. 1986. *Religion and Society in Central Africa*. Chicago: University of Chicago Press.

———. 2000a. "Aesthetics and Politics of Violence in Central Africa." *Journal of African Cultural Studies* 13, no. 1:63–75.

———. 2000b. "The Cultural Tradition of the African Rain Forests." In *Insight and Artistry in African Divination,* edited by John Pemberton III, 13–24. Washington, DC: Smithsonian.

———. 2000c. *Kongo Political Culture*. Bloomington: Indiana University Press.

———. 2013. *Chiefs, Priests and Praise-singers: History, Politics and Land Ownership in Northern Ghana*. Charlotte: University of Virginia Press.

Scott, James C. 2009. *The Art of Not Being Governed*. New Haven: Yale University Press.

Skalník, Peter. 1987. "On the Inadequacy of the Concept of the 'Traditional State': Illustrated with Ethnographic Material on Nanun, Ghana." *Journal of Legal Pluralism* 25/26:301–325.

Staniland, Martin. 1975. *The Lions of Dagbon*. Cambridge: Cambridge University Press.

Tait, David. 1961. *The Konkomba of Northern Ghana*. London: Oxford University Press.

———. 1963. "A Sorcery Hunt in Dagbon." *Africa* 33, no. 2:136–146.

Thornton, John K. 1983. *The Kingdom of Kongo*. Madison: University of Wisconsin Press.

Turner, Victor. W. 1969. *The Ritual Process*. London: Routledge and Kegan Paul.

———. 1975. *Revelation and Divination in Ndembu Ritual*. Ithaca, NY: Cornell University Press.

PART II

EVIL AND RELIGION

6 AMBIVALENCE AND THE WORK OF THE NEGATIVE AMONG THE YAKA

RENÉ DEVISCH

Intercorporeality and the ethic of desire and evildoing, stripped of their Western modernist thought patterns and view of the person, are among the foci of anthropological and psychoanalytical efforts[1] that I have been undertaking for the last decade.[2] These were led by the following research questions: How may desire, which unknowingly takes hold of interrelated subjects, make someone either compassionate or madly envious and even maleficent? How much does desire inhabit intercorporeality and inspire close family members to either intensely share life and a communal mode of inhabiting the life world or deflate and undermine the physical and communal life in the kin group? Moreover, how does desire, which is either amiable and comforting or toxic and thus fundamentally ambivalent in its insatiable search or passion, entrap the subject in the "work of the negative" (Green 1963). The meaning of this phrase is that the subject becomes engaged in the snares of "the real"—a Lacanian notion that refers to the undisclosable strangeness or destabilizing void at stake in each of us and our midst.[3] Is bewitchment or ensorcellment, as disclosed in one's dream work or unmasked by way of a divinatory oracle, thereby not a mode of overthrowing the victimized or accused subject ensnared in her wicked plot, fatal anxiety or death-drive?

In her host group, the Africanist ethnographer may be a witness to the awe, doubt, or fear in people's ritual, oneiric, mediumistic, "magical," or manipulative contact with cult spirits, the ancestral shrine, witchcraft, and the power objects of sorcery. Witchcraft draws on some ambivalent *innate* capacity or "forces" of the body-self for invisibly undermining or protecting a blood relative; the yiYaka notion of forces[4] (*kikesa*[5]) and daring (*ngaandzi*) is evocative of the sheer affect and passion that generates attraction or repulsion, trance, horror, and cruelty in and between bodies. Sorcery refers mainly to a *learned* occult and manipulative use of specific power objects meant to bundle forces from the spirits to either cast bad luck and evil on another or offer her vigor, protection, and good luck.

These topics inevitably challenge the researcher to extend the investigation beyond the domain of the observable, touchable, and explicable. She may thereby feel compelled to revise her ontological and epistemological frameworks molded by the secularized Western-derived human sciences. Such revision proves unavoidable in view of an in-depth comprehension of the host group's relation with the invisible realm of the divine, ancestors, spirits, bewitching, or ensorcelling forces. Indeed, for the anthropologist, the intercultural encounter may act as a revealing screen, through which the unsettling otherness at the very core of both the other and the anthropologist herself, coresonates yet resists to disclose in its full, greatly unspeakable dimension of reality. My own work started only a decade after such an intercultural encounter. In the field and subsequent years, the anthropological experience led me to investigate people's interaction with the invisible realm of forces in its unrepresentable and nonverbal dimension. It led me to a scrutiny both of people's dream stories relating to some threat from ancestral wrath, witchcraft, or sorcery, and in line with the divinatory etiological unraveling of wicked forces that ensnare the client in an intergenerational and intercorporeal plot of "nocturnal debts" and revenge, envy, and malevolence. More specifically, this interest prompted an enquiry into the intercorporeal, intersubjective, and interworldly agency and effect in dream work, spirit possession, healing, and witchcraft or sorcery. The notion of interworldliness refers to people's views on the world-to-world echoing and coaffecting, namely among the human, animal, and/or thing-like, as well as the visible and invisible, life-forms.

A major question regards how the group deals in particular with the surreptitious work of the negative that the members detect in the irruptive climatic or ecological forces (rain, river and whirlpool, lightning and thunderstorm, clawed and predatory animals), or in "the realm of the darkish night" haunted by witchcraft and sorcery. In the people's understanding, the work of the negative manifests itself in the intergenerational moral debts and the colonial or family trauma, as well as in local experiences of state-related injustice or abuse. The inquiry is done from the "perspectivism" of the host group (cf. Viveiros de Castro 2004), namely from its primary and dominant concern with fellow people's intercorporeal coresonance and their life-enhancing or life-deflating intersubjective reciprocity in the kin group; it is a concern in view of sustaining, if not deflating, in one another the "uterine life-flow" and the "agnatic life-force" (Devisch and Brodeur 1999, 51–54; see also infra).

This contribution zooms in on a recent case of dream work by Nwasa, a final-year student at the University of Kinshasa, living in harsh conditions (Devisch 2007). The study suggests that an aspectual and culture-sensitive psychoanalytical reading can well contribute to laying bare the culture-specific interpersonal and intersubjective molding of liberating or repressive fantasies among the yiYaka speakers in Kwaango and Kinshasa. It shows that dream work and its culture-sensitive interpretation at the microlevel may shed an intriguing light on some insolvable intercultural confrontation of the family ethos with a Western-derived emancipation ideal. The reading takes into account the intercorporeal play of boundless desire,[6] affective powers and shared imaginary in the client's collaborative or tense relationships with significant others. The culture-genuine and contextual interpretation of Naswa's two consecutive dream episodes of the same night, witnesses to the sphere of "death-angst" engulfing his body-self; the dream implicitly attacks the order of the ethical law of inescapable reciprocity in the kin group. The authoritative dream interpretation that his older neighbor offers forces Nsawa to a drastic change of destiny. This culminates in stopping his university studies, a turnaround that impedes his and his family's modern emancipation.

In the following intercultural approach, I avoid any encompassing psychoanalytical interpretation, especially shunning an ego-psychological approach that focuses primarily on the cognitive-mental apparatus of the modern Western subject. Even if an aspectual psychoanalytical reading may give due credence to an intercorporeal and intersubjective topology and is very cautious not to conflate language with communication or the subject with her message, it so often inadvertently bears the traces of its limited culture-specific provenance.

OMINOUS DREAMING AND FATAL INTERCULTURAL CONTACT

My case study focuses on two consecutive ominous dreams, reported by Nsawa, a yiYakaphone forty-eight-year-old man. For the last ten years he has lived among the predominantly yiYakaphone slum-dwellers in Masina. This shanty town was formed in the 1960s and 1970s by massive immigration from Kwaango land to this swampy area situated between the river Congo and the international airport of Ndjili-Kinshasa. The houses consisting of breeze-block walls and tin roofs are rudimentary abodes of two or three rooms. Around 1986, the major streets of the area were connected to electricity and water, but no paved roads or sewage and sanitary systems have been provided. Only a few homes along these streets have electricity. For the majority, kerosene lamps are the only source of lighting, cooking is done on charcoal fires, and water is drawn either from the river or shallow wells dug near one's dwelling. Masina has shown the poorest indices of educational and employment qualifications for the whole of Kinshasa. In 1976, 46.6 percent of the populace of Masina were described as illiterate and the situation is now worse. Because of its dense settlement, Masina has been nicknamed "the People's Republic of China."

Nsawa's boundless and unwavering fascination with his university diploma forms the subject of his dream narratives: it centers on his fear of failure in his university studies that appear to him under the spell of witchcraft and sorcery. It is a conundrum characteristic of his generation of educated but very poor inhabitants of Kinshasa. With the political independence of the Democratic Republic Congo in 1960, young people came to imagine the university diploma as guaranteeing access to the emerging social and material privileges that thus far had been reserved for colonials. Popular painting, songs, stories, and the first novels by Congolese in the 1950s and 1960s depicted the colonized local heirs to these white power figures. But the dreamed-of privileges of the colonizer, that the school-educated heirs hoped to attain, were shrouded in the paradoxical fantasies of omnipotence, engulfing anxiety and ambivalent *jouissance* or enjoyment (see Lacan 1975).

Nsawa had these dreams in 2002 during his final year of MA studies in educational sciences at the University of Kinshasa. Dream narratives were solicited in my name by a fellow-student of his and coming from the same region; Nsawa knew me only by word of mouth. To show his academic acumen, he recounted his dreams in French, sometimes mingled with his mother's tongue yiYaka. Nsawa, his wife and their two kids, lived with his parents-in-law, together with his wife's three sisters and two brothers; for years, a simple chair had been his place to sleep; his brothers-in-law squatted in the fruit tree to sleep.

The two dream stories may, at first glance and given Nsawa's Christian schooling, appear to us as recognizable Freudian dreams, but an older neighbor, applying a more complex cultural framework of meaning, interprets them in terms of an intercultural conflict. Since his baptism at the age of seven in the first year of primary school, Nsawa had been a practicing Catholic loyal to the Catholic missionaries in his rural birth area of Kasongo Lunda and later in Masina. He defines himself as a "child of the missionaries" (*mwana missioni*), perceiving his adoption into the Catholic missionary church as a pathway for climbing out of his destitute life conditions. He earns a little cash as an occasional vendor of second-hand clothes from some European Relief Service that he obtains through bulk buying at the parish; he moreover sees the parish as a stronghold for fencing off the family obligations from turning to greedy witchcraft or sorcery aggression. In his ward in the Masina shantytown, as a university student he does enjoy some reputation, albeit an ambivalent one.

This status has its bleak side, as he fails the ascent from the state of misery in the overcrowded ward he lives in. Worse, for shelter and daily needs, he remains inexorably dependent on his in-laws. Like Nsawa himself, most school-educated peers in his vicinity remain fascinated by their daydreams, well aware that their families and neighbors might attribute any material progress they might make to occult practices.

That day, Nsawa had been worrying about his destitute state and the uncanny shortfalls that continually hampered any progress on his MA thesis. He had recently managed to earmark some scarce savings for the academic registration with regard to the thesis project. But that very day, he was forced to devote his small amount of savings to medical care and medicines for his children. He could not avoid suspecting his parents-in-law of some stratagem to thwart his diploma. Now follows the report, given a week later, of the two consecutive dream episodes of that night.

DREAMWORK

Dream narrative 1: About 2 AM, in dream I have seen the following: I was sleeping in bed, together with my wife. I saw how we were making love. In the midst of conjugal union, my wife's junior sister came to take place in-between us. She grabbed my penis, took it out of my wife's vagina, while saying: "Papa Nsawa, from now on, you will no longer have sex with my senior sister. From now on, we both are the ones to have sex." [The dream being rendered in French, the sister-in-law's intrusive sexual acts evoke the folk fantasies about the Western-derived hedonist lifestyle of the upper-class Kinois. These fantasies are fed by international TV-programmes and magazines, accessible in the shanty towns, that according to folk Kinois norms portray adulterous sexuality and autoeroticism.] *She then started touching and caressing me all over my body, and undressed herself. Grabbing my penis as if to insert it in her vagina, she said to me: "Before we'll have sex, first present me a report on your studies. How do they progress? How far is your thesis? Upon obtaining your diploma, will you marry me, or will you marry someone else? Please, inform me on your studies at university. Will you soon come out with the title of master in educational sciences, or not? And your thesis, when will you finish it? In case you're already finished it, will you defend it, and when?" She asked me all these questions three times.*

About to answer her questions a first time, under the bed I saw a puddle with eel-like fishes (ngola). I took some and handed them over to her. About to give her my answer a second time, I have seen again the eels in the puddle under my bed, I caught some of them and handed them over to her. While she was repeating the questions a third time, I took the eels and gave [them to] her.

A man [in Western outfit] *then appeared at the bed where we were. My bed was indeed above a puddle with eels. This man standing upright in front of my bed told me:* "Mr. Nsawa, the eels that you are giving to your wife, your second wife, are mine. They belong to me. I am the one who have put them in this puddle. And I also have put an ichthyotoxin which will kill them all. Since you are giving them to your second wife, who indeed is your junior sister-in-law, your semeki, this means that you have given her your thesis work which was on the table and the audiotaped research data from the Saint-Clement lyceum." *I then sprang up in bed: I was thus having a dream. Why did I dream in this way? Generally, dreams about sexual intercourse with one's sister-in-law, one's proper sister or one's proper mother are evil or ominous dreams, dreams of bewitchment. I indeed was doubting if I would report* [as practice demands] *this dream to my wife, fearing that she would suspect me of intimate relations with her sister. I then have immediately returned to sleep.*

Dream narrative 2: Around 5 A M, I was dreaming the same things. But this time my sister-in-law made me read the four lists of words and pseudowords like I had submitted them for reading to the school children at the Saint-Clement lyceum. She was about to tape-record my reading:

List 1: "*bois, vers, sans, temps, coup, plan, gris, vif, mais, long, dos, près, plus, doigts, mains, peu, vain, camps, nous, yeux.*"

List 2: "*nual, bum, terv, barsm, toirn, mea, bron, bul, peiv, gaul, tav, blumi, brabil, viords, tians, muités, biamilos, garbulisi, doum, hurib, priarisus, mialasi, loumina, nounabis.*"

List 3: "*sentier, chemin, chemise, chaussure, neige, teinture, fourmilière, fourmis, ondulation, vaillamment, balayer, balayeur, balaye, veiller, veilleur, pieds, piétiner, sang, sanguin, sanguinaire, consanguin, lézard, bouclier, ouvrier, graisse, naissance, connaissance, connaître, connaissant, chocolat, longtemps, long, langue, langueur.*"

List 4: "*tabriel, tabus, talesh, takepel, peulu, peuleux, peulin, peuline, fleuboie, fleurkel, fluorikis, glodia, fodhaio, fodikarion, fodkayali, fodkayoabios, piassul, passuliis, piassuris, piassulas, emezad, amezadios, emezadiais, emezadiles, emezadilois, guadolit, guadolitias, guadolitius, guadolituisia, guadolituilas, staticop.*"

After I had read these four lists of words and pseudowords, my sister-in-law told me: "It's o.k., let's now go to bed and have sex." *All at a sudden, I saw a puddle under my bed. Instead of having sex, though we were both undressed, I started to give her eels. As in the first dream, when she was addressing me her question a third time, a man appeared, saying that the fishes I was handing over to my sister-in-law were indeed his fishes.* "I am the one who have put the ichthyotoxin [namely the fish poison that the women use to make the intoxicated fish float belly-up, so that they can scoop them up into their baskets]. How do you dare to give them to your sister-in-law? Mr. Nsawa, you yourself *have given everything to your family-in-law. Know that neither she nor me have robbed you of your research documents for your university degree."*

When this man had left, and still while I was dreaming, my junior sister-in-law repeated: "Finally, let's make love." She grabbed my penis to insert it in her vagina. I did not move, she was the one who made the movements in my place, to make me ejaculate it all. [In other words, the sister-in-law simulates a fantasy regarding 'Western' sex, which according to Congolese feeling is obscene.] *To finish, she said: "Papa Nsawa, from now on we are husband and wife. I have just rendered your tape-recording and the other university documents, go and defend your thesis. Yet you should not leave me as you are getting your MA degree and becoming an important guy ('un grand type') to be soon called Minister.* [And then she formulates a curse:] *Even if I myself did not attend school, you are my husband: do not flee away from me. If you would intend to doing so, know that you will not succeed to get your degree. Why then would you flee me? Will you flee me?" As I wanted to give her my answer, she had already left.*

AN EMIC OR ENDOGENOUS INTERPRETATION
OF THE DREAM STORIES

Nsawa, upon waking up, says his morning prayers and plans the work for his thesis; he soon notices that his audiotapes and notebook with research data are missing. Deeply worried, he immediately goes to consult his aged and wise neighbor Lupenzi about the dreams. Breaking into tears, the old man replies:

> If it is true that your in-laws finance your study, you will never get your diploma. This water pool is a sign of your inescapable failure: the puddle which you see in your dreams forebodes the misfortune that is begetting you; your studies [have] drawn you in the water. Your in-laws are after your children whom they intend to kill in compensation for hosting you, your wife, and two children. The eel-like fishes in the water are none other than your sons. They are under your bed because it is on that bed that you have fathered them. By forcing sex on you, your sister-in-law states that your children born from her sister also belong to her. What she does is a curse on you, bewitchingly calling on you a demonical bad luck (*n-syeenina*): your studies are cursed and at the risk of no longer progressing. Your notebook and audiotapes are in the hands of your brothers-in-law, the vicinity's most reputed witches. They put the image of their sister, your wife, at front stage in view of hiding their occult threats and that of your mother-in-law. Do not listen to your mother-in-law's soothing words. At any rate, she will take defense of her children, if needed by betraying and accusing her daughter who is your wife. Consult a diviner and then a healer in view of un-bewitchment and reversing the misfortune prefigured by the eel-like fishes sent by your in-laws. By handing the fishes over to your sister-in-law you acquiesce with the bewitchment that your brothers- and mother-in-law are calling upon you.

Returning home overpowered by anger and worry, Nsawa gathers his children and in-laws. "My brothers-in-law," he explains, "witnessed first to their full innocence. However, they were trembling out of fear, confessing that Madam, my wife, had given them the audiotapes for some tape-recording of music. When playing the tapes they did not hear any music, but just barking dogs. When I asked them to return me the dissertation project and notebook with the research data, they answered: how sad, the notebook has already been used as toilet paper."

The Western-looking man standing next to the bed and who claimed to own the eels, without any doubt may fascinate any Freudian therapist. However, the many other dream images and Lupenzi's emic dream interpretation invite us to further follow the old man's hinting at culture-sensitive pathways for research. According to Lupenzi and Nsawa himself, the dreams and their interpretation seem to chart a multilayered conflict as well as several angles for solution. The red thread that Lupenzi traces concerns Nsawa's social failure, which is embedded both in an unsolvable dissension from the in-laws' expectations and a life-threatening intercultural conflict that is moreover part and parcel of the University of Kinshasa's Western-derived venture.

First, in the eyes of the in-laws, the dreamer fails in the culture-specific patriarchal family ideals at the core of his society's setup. By staying with his wife and children at his in-laws, Nsawa fails as *pater familias*. The yiYakaphone society sees parenthood (*-buta baana*, literally, making children) as a particular modus of weaving (*-kuba*). People allude to marital sexuality in terms of *-biindasana maalu*, literally inciting each other to surrender in interweaving the legs. In the same vein of reciprocity, the individual gains subjecthood (*wuka muutu*) through a never-ending interweaving and border-linking quest. Like the nodes border-linking a tissue with manifold other tissues, a subject's identity is foremost sociocentric, developing between co-constituting subjects in plural fields along a plurality of tasks. Unlike Nsawa, it is in the ward of his father, and by no means in that of his father-in-law, that a man should increasingly profile himself as a patriarchal family head. Such a virilocal residency guarantees, together with patrifiliation, the social identity of his children. In the eyes of his in-laws, Nsawa appears more married to his diploma, which is more than ever uncertain now, than to the mother of his children and the bride-givers.

From the viewpoint of the family ethos, Nsawa fails as an honorable, virile-reproductive husband. In the eyes of his father's family and his in-laws, he is homeless. His inability to ensure a conjugal and parental home, according to customary law, unbinds his exclusive marital rights. In Nsawa's dream, paradoxically, the youngest sister of his wife positions herself as a sexual partner, and as such in line with a fantasized Western-style of eroticized sex, one through which she claims marital rights. Yet this adulterous dream scene is highly ominous as she transgresses local sociomoral codes. According to the usual norms, the conjugal bed is exclusively for conjugal reproduction. That sociomoral code indicates that sexual transgression bereft of ritual purification calls down an ominous pollution onto the young family. It may cause a lethal bleeding (*phalu*) of the partner and the baby. After all, the dream depicts a sexual meeting that inverts the local definition of conjugal conduct and shame. According to the sociomoral codes pertaining to reproductive conjugal sexuality in the yiYaka speaking community, *genitor* and *genitrix* relate to one another as active to passive, bony-hard to soft, cold to warm, above to under, right to left. It is the olfactory exchange and the play of hands, legs and pelvis, more than gaze and word that define, accompany, and stimulate the reproductive conjugal communion.

Second, Lupenzi elucidates a life-threatening intercultural conflict. The second dream story brings forward a Western-looking man who denies Nsawa any right to manage the future of his family. This denial is evoked by the question regarding the ownership of the fish in the pool of water under the bed. According to the dream interpretation by Lupenzi, this authority figure is not the ancestor but the demanding "white or westernized," alien(ating) messenger speaking in the name of Western norms and expectations. He puts the neoliberal division including private property of the means of production on the table. Seen from a rural horizon, the dream scene involving the fish pond under the bed points at a potential source of reproduction and livelihood. However, viewing the so-called dollarization of public institutional life and any form of consumption in Kinshasa (de Boeck and Plissart 2004; Devisch 1995), this Western authority figure denies Nsawa the option to convert these fish into a potential fee for his university studies. The Westernized messenger tells the dreamer that doing university is undoing or literally alienating, poisoning him, after all it is fish/sperm poisoned by the white colonizer, indeed Nsawa's Westernized identification model.

With regard to his university project, the dreamer fails in his attempt to attain Western intellectual ideals and to embody the modern selfhood as idealized at university and in the mass media. The dream equates Nsawa's insatiable fascination with the university diploma with a self-defeating quest for Western-style eroticism and enjoyment. It is undoing him, erasing any symbolic function: the fish halt any desire and bring no solution.

Nsawa fails also in his fantasies on the omnipotence of Western-derived, also called whitened, knowledge. In line with the hedonistic supply of consumables that Kinshasa's shanty towns avidly see portrayed by the French and German international TV channels, Nsawa and his sister-in-law are indeed enthralled by the specter of the university diploma. This serves as the fetish or imaginary source of omnipotence and total satisfaction: this is in the dream reflected in the sister-in-law's phrase: "After you will get your university degree and will be a big man and people will soon call you Minister." Yet Nsawa's latest efforts of saving cash from his petty trade and finishing his studies make him flounder, and they render any university project of his hopeless.

CULTURAL CONTEXT OF THE DREAM AND ITS INTERPRETATION

Let us put these dreams against the background of the social and cultural status that yiYaka speakers allot to dream interpretation as an authoritative source of meaning disclosure. The contextual and culture-sensitive scrutiny that we envisage ties in with people's usual sensing out of any unspoken foreboding or warning sign in their midst. Similar to their neighbors in South-West Congo, Angola, and North Namibia, yiYaka speakers use the bantu root term *ngoongu* to refer not only to the primal source of one's dreams, but also to the ceaselessly regenerative life-flow from the primordial chthonic source of all life at the womb of the world; it is figured by a clump of white kaolin taken from the marshy land near the spring of the river that drains one's home area. In the vision of these cultures, the dreamer meets tangentially with the cosmological spaces and dimensions that are rich in paradoxical energies and intermingled images. Deep ravines, marshy soil, a devouring vortex, the impenetrable forest, the dark moon, ghosts and water spirits, orgiastic ecstasy or death agony during delivery are all evocative of some *border-linking* (see Ettinger 2006) between beginning and end, above and below, consistency and agitation, fervor and anxiety, life and death, light and darkness. Dreaming is seen as a border passing, like the river Styx. I would speculate that these border-linking attributes might be interpreted as a culture-specific idiom for hinting at what Lacan calls the world of the unspeakable "real" beyond the transferentially communicable fantasies or repressed unconscious (in the usual Freudian sense). YiYaka-phone locate the deadly fascination at play in bewitchment or ensorcellment, versus one's wondrous uplifting in ecstatic trance-possession, in the body's border-crossing cavities and capacities. Think of the fontanel through which, during pregnancy, the genitor forms the bony structure of the infant from his sperm as it solidifies. There is also the individual's heart as seat of the emotional coresonance between family members, and the mother's womb in resonance with the original and ceaselessly regenerative source of the life-flow.

Behavioral disorders, physical handicaps, a deteriorating health and insanity are only then acknowledged as a problem when the person is incapacitated to fulfil her duties. If that happens, the elders in council enquire from two related angles into those problematic alliances and lingering conflicts in the extended family's history that could have brought the affliction (Devisch and Brodeur 1999, 105–113). First, the problem is examined on a societal level in as much as it appears to incapacitate the afflicted while blocking vital intercorporeal and intersubjective connections. Second, narrowing down on the loss of health, the council examines what either closes up the afflicted and makes her insensitive, numb, and withdrawn or renders her out of control or incontinent, confused, or intrusive, while either obstructing or untying the fabric of life. In terms of healing (-*buka*), all that drastically and lastingly either hinders life's development or unbinds the fabric of life is attributed, in the last analysis, to a transgression, the casting of a spell or a bewitchment/ensorcellment by a uterine ascendant of the afflicted. After handling these impediments and remobilizing the social fabric, particularly, cult healing aims at regenerating the interweaving (-*kuba*) of body, group, and lifeworld into a life-giving and life-enforcing fabric.

Mediumistic divination (Devisch 2012, 2013) regarding a case of witchcraft or sorcery attack, more secretly consulted in town than in the rural milieus, is grounded in the principle that anything inhibiting or obstructing life may ultimately be attributed to one or another instance of transgression against the order of basal reciprocity. Diviners reckon this transgression as a form of theft (-*yiba*), the *quintessential notion of evil,* as it represents the most fundamental denial of society's foundational basic order of exchange or reciprocity. It is an ill-intentioned life-disabling or life-threatening act or infringement of the basal law of exchange in the family group. This law primarily concerns the uterine line of filiation of the ceaselessly regenerative life-flow, transmitted and recycled through the mothers, from the ceaselessly regenerative womb of the world or primordial chthonic source of all life. An oracle proceeds first to identify in which way the client's fate results from some basic infringement of the law of exchange. It seeks to trace the curse or retaliating bewitching or ensorcellment that sought to vindicate such infringement, as well as the ancestral wrath the transgression may have provoked. In doing so, the oracle transforms a crucial violation of the client's vital weave into a specific and manageable enquiry.

A curse (*n-sasu, -sasa,* literally incantation) primarily addresses the uterine life-flow, embedded in this basic order of reciprocity or law of exchange. A curse consists of invoking the ineluctable sanction if indeed a transgression or wrongdoing has occurred: "If it is true that the one who has committed a theft falls ill, then I may fall ill, too, if I have stolen. But if I have taken nothing from the one who has robbed me, and if I have no debts toward her, may she who has stolen my goods fall ill." The principle or rule underlying the transmission of life along maternal lines is indeed that of exchange. Any act contrary to exchange, such as stealing, witchcraft/sorcery, or sexual abuse, is qualified as theft by both everyday language and ritual discourse. Such an act is naturally associated with a rupture within uterine kin and its subsequent afflictions.

In each maternal line, both the curses and the acts they seek to avenge, like the unfortunate consequences they have, are determined by a cult. Curses constitute the persecutive valence of the prohibition that imposes a sanction whenever it is violently transgressed. A third register of divinatory etiology refers to the question of why the illness or misfortune has afflicted this particular individual rather than another. Retracing the illness and the misfortune with regard to its essential kinship dimensions, the oracle will never attribute the affliction to one sole factor such as a bewitchment or ensorcellment. An ailment could result from the fact that the afflicted has been involved in a confusion of homes, that is, a distortion of the boundaries of the domestic, conjugal, or corporeal space. The afflicted could equally have been the victim of a rupture with avuncular relations and thus be deprived of the vital link with her uterine life-flow. As with the confusion of conjugal limits, the problem is perceived as a perversion of corporeal boundaries: since the body is no longer able simultaneously to be both a confined space and a site of exchange, it becomes either extremely closed or completely incontinent (Vandenbroeck 2009).

The oracle is then followed by a family council whose task it is to negotiate any steps that need to be taken to avert evil and bring healing to the afflicted person and, ultimately, to achieve the renewal of the social and cosmic fabrics. In this investigation, the maternal uncle of the afflicted or deceased is a key figure. His relation is such that he can either protect or harm his niece or nephew by preventing or authorizing some retaliatory life-taking within the uterine kin group. It is the subsequent family council that invites a healer to neutralize, redirect, and enhance life-sustaining forces in the family and initiate healing.

INTERCULTURAL LIFE PROJECT: A LETHAL FASCINATION

With this impression of the culture in which Nsawa grew up and lives, I come back to the story of the two consecutive dream sequences. Nsawa's fascination with the promising horizon of the white diploma appears in the sociocultural context just as hollow and devoid of any symbolic meaning-bearing or realistic reference as the pseudowords put forward in the test for his final thesis. The quest for the diploma has been hollowed out by the fantasies that disown Nsawa and render him, in the eyes of his in-laws, an abject caricature of himself. His cliché-like fantasies regarding the university diploma deny the deadweight of history and his destitute life situation. As I will show, a total impasse results for Nsawa. His academic project can no longer bring him anything worthwhile, nor generate any recovery of self-esteem or social status. After all, in the perspective of his fellow people's imagination, the fatal incontrovertible law of witchcraft lies behind his failure to finish his university studies. In other words, the threat of the abject, surfacing in Lupenzi's interpretive explanations and the in-laws, makes the university project slide down into the chasm of lethal threats and the unimaginable void of "the real." But that is exactly what Nsawa cannot ground his existence on.

Intercultural Impasse

Nsawa's university studies and emancipation project are bogged down in dogs barking and used toilet paper. In the collective imaginary, the dog is the incestuous animal and thus the quintessential horror. In Lacan vocabulary, used toilet paper expresses another figuration of the abject object that eclipses the symbolic order of language and culture. In the fantasies of his brothers-in-law, Nsawa's striving to get a university degree at the expense of his inescapable family duties ultimately means: "You are a man of nothing, mere shit." This view echoes Nsawa's erotic dream fantasy regarding a Western-style sexual affair with his seductive sister-in-law. In the view of the dream, such fantasy is as imaginary as obtaining a university degree and thereby access to fashionable consumption.

The dream sheds light on an imaginary and totally unrealistic dimension of the collective unconscious prominent in Nsawa's school-educated generation of those born around the time of accession to political independence of the Democratic Republic of Congo in 1960. When the Mobutu state turned bankrupt in the late 1980s and 1990s, that dimension was voiced in the sermons and exorcisms of his contemporaries in the neo-Pentecostal churches and healing communes of the Sacred Spirit. As for many of his generation, the clash between local and Western cultures, for example, at the bankrupt University of Kinshasa, bereft since 1991 of any North-South interuniversity cooperation, generated an unmanageable angst and irreconcilable conflict.

According to the autochthonous dream interpretation offered by Lupenzi and enforced by the reactions from Nsawa's in-laws, the dream puts Nsawa in an intractable conflict. He must abandon his fatal project of Westernizing his close family's life project and reinscribe himself and family in the patriarchal order along the agnatic line of descent, and the basal order of the law of exchange primarily at stake in the uterine filiation and alliance relations. But he is in no economic position to do so, unable as he is to create a position as the responsible head of a family and his own virilocal place to live. The *Jenseits des Lustprinzips* figures here as fate. As he cannot inscribe himself in the basal order of the ethical law of inescapable reciprocity in the kin group and become for his close family and in-laws a "big man that people will soon call Minister" and a source of dreamed-of omnipotence and unlimited *jouissance,* the only option open to him is to sacrifice himself or one of his sons on the interfamily altar of the incontrovertible counterlaw of retaliation. This is tacitly haunting Nsawa's self-understanding, which I would render along the following unspoken argument from the in-laws: "We, your wife's family, have helped you throughout these years to pay for your studies and have hosted your family, in the hope that you, once graduated, would recompense for this. But now, just give us, if not yourself, one of your sons (that is, your own progeny, future and descent) as compensation." According to Nsawa's dream and the collective unconscious that is revealed in it, the clash of cultures in his case does not have the emancipation effect, whether imaginary, sociopolitical, or economical, as claimed by the official development rhetoric. Instead the dreamt of encounter of cultures only addresses the level of *jouissance.* According to Lupenzi and Nsawa's in-laws, this *jouissance* leads to a devastating impasse or a self-destructive petrification: Nsawa is stranding in a being-to-nothing, *un dés-être.* The wasting away of the tape recording for his research into barking dogs and of his research notes into toilet paper qualifies his impasse as a destructive or toxic *jouissance* that psychologically cannot be processed or symbolized. The inability to overcome his fascination with the white diploma and relate to a socioculturally meaningful pathway of life figures as an instance of what Kristeva (1980) qualifies as *chora.*

Beyond the Impasse?

Since that time, Nsawa has tried to save his own life and that of his children by renouncing his university diploma. According to our latest information in early 2006, he has tried to escape the fatal bewitchment by joining, together with his wife and children, a healing commune of the Sacred Spirit. After all, this institutionalizes the unceasing pendulum motion, called *bascule,* between inflated *jouissance* and enjoyment of horror in the Janus-like figure Holy Ghost-Satan, beyond any hint of growth or emancipation (Devisch 1996, 2003). In the 1970s and 1980s, President Mobutu issued a call for cultural authenticity exhorting the people to leave the lifestyle of the rural village and cast away the colonial model for man and society. Since that time, prophetic movements have both parodied and echoed this call in a radicalized way, albeit from their own proper perspective. They do not offer a historic project: their celebrations conjure an oneiric and euchronic time frame. They disempower the monopoly on human perfectibility appropriated by the white civilizing and missionary oeuvre, as well as by President Mobutu's authenticity project of the 1970s and 1980s. Seemingly, their anarchistic celebrations criticize the overdependency of the Congolese society on both the Western evolutionist model and the traditional persecution fantasies of witchcraft or sorcery and the ancestral revenge. Or, rather, they devalue this model and these fantasies by an ambiguous parody that blends the various epistemologies, be they imported or local. They tame and theatricalize the experience of a dominating (post)colonial state, by way of the ambivalent Sacred Spirit–Satan figure, their heterodox use of Bible texts, as well as their ostentatious liturgies and healing sessions. Their mimicry criticizes and parodies the use of the book, in particular that of the state bureaucracy before as well as after independence (Devisch 2003).

At the background of his dream work was the haunting question of sorcery or witchcraft. What sorcery enhances or decreases are those forces that mainly come into play—through gaze and words, the sharing of meals and physical intimacy—in and among individuals, beings, and worlds. Witchcraft or sorcery practices can equally dazzle and obfuscate, enrage or madden the perpetrator or the victim, but they can also inspire or heal. The play of forces is very much at the horizon of the collective imaginary and influences people's interpersonal loyalties or their aloofness. According to the terminology introduced by Sir Edward Evans-Pritchard (1937; Devisch 2005), *witchcraft*, similar to the *evil eye*, primarily refers to congenital or innate (most often unconsciously activated), defensive as well as offensive capacities of the body-self. They may be directed at thwarting off evil and guaranteeing good fortune and protection for the family, or they may cast harm onto their aggressor. In the form of so-called white magic, *sorcery* relies on the use of a fabricated object to seek good fortune and protection of the family, but these objects may be reassembled and reoriented as "black magic" to harm or undermine their victim. These objects of power act beyond the discursive or cognitive order embedded in words and paradoxically exploit and pervert society's order of law and reciprocity as internalized in the members' habitus or bodily dispositions. They excite, in their victims and protégés, whirligig fates of cruelty and licentiousness, unbridled energies and affects, beyond any possible rebalancing. Sorcerous objects substantiate a "counterpoint of culture" (Daniel 1996) that resists (re)incorporation into the harmony of a still higher order of balanced connectedness, meaningfulness, or society.

The local folk allusions to witchcraft and sorcery in stories, suspicions, practices, and fetishes refer to the broad field that I call polymorph witchcraft and sorcery (Devisch 2005), the field of the occult. Gossip deals mainly with the forms of feared malefic witchcraft and sorcery within the confines of the kin group. Yet, most folktales also evoke the benign use of objects of power for harnessing untamed forces, in particular in the domain of the hunt (Devisch 1993, 86–91). The encompassing notion of witchcraft and sorcery evokes in the individual experience a knot of unbridled desire and lust, drift for life and death, possibly indeterminate fear and obsessive enjoyment, or of the abject. In this the collective, imagination contrasts any notion of value with the shameless derailment of it. As for the collective representations regarding malefic or predatory witchcraft and sorcery, they speak of the suspected aggressor or the victim only in the third person: to personally admit one's implication in bewitchment, ensorcellment, or use of any malefic fetishes is inconceivable. It is mainly in the divinatory etiology of evil and the hidden dimensions of the dream that the nebulous realm of witchcraft and sorcery fantasies is submitted to some shared critical scrutiny and reflexivity among elderly kinsmen gathered in council.

The collective imaginary and popular discourse of witchcraft and sorcery among yiYaka-speaking Kinois as, for example, evidenced in Nsawa's dream reports appears to be haunted by the life of ease and extravagance displayed in the "downtown" scene. This is situated at the edge of Kinshasa's largest food market that constitutes the preeminent feminine domain of sociability. People's dream-like mirroring moreover reinforces social disparities and functions as a grid that stigmatizes any individual or social space deprived of this life. Yet, witchcraft and sorcery fantasies among the deprived majority are flagrantly at odds with the ontological and rationalist presuppositions and foundations underlying the dominant concerns and discourses from the West of exact sciences, logical positivism, bourgeois moralities, neoliberal economy, and globalizing information flows.

The popular imaginary and discourse regarding *maleficent witchcraft* in rural and Kinois yiYaka-speaking milieus witness people's strong fascination with becoming other in an ungoverned and unbridled elsewhere. Predatory witches are depicted as capable of doubling themselves by leaving behind their sleeping bodily sheath and traveling in the air or under the ground as an invisible bird or insect, particularly at night. In that, they seek to appropriate the victim's life-flow and life force, or to join other witches and similar accomplices among the deceased. The dark night until the first cock's crow, in the collective imaginary, evokes unruliness and the forces of death that overturn the diurnal order, as do the nocturnal predatory animals and witches. Meeting on the witches' market, naked consanguines begin to sing and dance in order to give themselves over to their utter desire. They mix up in frenzied incestuous sexuality or feed on raw human flesh that is butchered and shared. A form of nocturnal witch tribunal (*yifwaandu, pfuundu*) regulates the carving up and distribution (*-laambula*) on the basis of the above-mentioned incontrovertible counterlaw of retaliation.

Eating and intrusive gaze form the double bodily focus upon which the popular imaginary concentrates its fascination regarding witchcraft. One mode of witchcraft is primarily at stake among uterine kin. In this field, it is spoken of as *eating* (*-dya*) the victim. It is the prey allotted at a nightly monstrous tribunal on the witches' market that regulates for those present their nocturnal debts (*kabu dyakun-kolu, pfuka zaphiiba*) vis-à-vis other uterine kin. These debts were left open from similar witches' markets. The collective fantasies hold that the witch "devours" the life-flow of a blood relative, most readily one of these with whom she shares meals and daily physical proximity. The other mode concerns the bewitching through one's *envious gaze* (*-mona yiphala*), evocative of the evil eye notion in the Mediterranean area. It exceeds the circle of uterine consanguines and may hamper, destroy, or pry the life substance and (re)productive potential of a victimized agnatic relative.

Thus, witchcraft and the night are the topos of carryover and transience, that is, of mutability, unboundedness, or infringement and the fulfilment of largely unspecifiable desire. It is a topos celebrating seduction and ardor, greediness and intemperance, as well as the compulsive yet hallucinatory moods of pain, disgust, revenge, impasse, or void.

THE ETHIC OF DESIRE: AN ENDOGENOUS ACCOUNT

We need to establish an endogenous or emic account of the ways in which a given culture contributes to develop a genuine embodied and barely verbalized form of "subjectification" of the individual (Foucault 1984; Deleuze and Guattari 1980, 131–164). This concerns the gradual sociocultural shaping of the individual's physical body (*luutu*), literally, the skin, that is the pulsative-energetic, sensory, and desiring bodily envelope into a "norm-alized" relational embodiment or body-self (*muutu*). The self as an imbrication of physical and relational body, particularly qualifying a respected if not feared elder, is thereby able to interconnect along normalized modes with the lifeworld of visible and invisible beings. Invisible entities include spirits, deities, ancestors and struggles between God and Satan for those converted to Christianity, arcane or sorcery powers, plant and animal life, and things.

The witch draws on an innate and exceptionally powerful flux of affective and desirous *forces* or energies (*kikesa*), daring and compulsion (*ngaandzi*), that make up the very core of her bewitching capacity. This pervades the victim's dreams and fantasy and haunts the fantasy and imaginary of particular fragile family members. Of heuristic value here is, first, Spinoza's concept of *affect* that helps to qualify the yiYaka concept of forces. Second, Merleau-Ponty's (1964) phenomenological notion of *the flesh* (*la chair*) appears close to the yiYaka term of *luutu* or "physical body/embodiment" as source and scene of the affects, desires, and senses. The notion of flesh thus connotes a bodily tissue of desiring and sensory being-in-the-world and of ambivalent desire. The expanding and ambivalent sensuous body tries to indulge itself from time to time, amounting to border crossing and desirous or gluttonous impetuosity and lust, agitation and fierceness, intemperance and (self-)destruction in a frenzy of touch, smell, taste, sight, and hearing. The sensuous body presents itself as an object for these senses and is at the same time itself an actor in touching, tasting, smelling, looking, listening, or speaking, possibly abusively and self-demeaning, either in resonance or dissonance with the affects, feelings and messages of the other. This is why, through the senses and desire at play in and through the body, a person unwillingly and defenselessly exposes herself to, and tunes in with, the greed and attack by the witch or sorcerer.

At play in and through the body is the *ethic of desire* (Lacan 1986, 359) that stirs the subject's and her family's complicit passion toward transmitting and sharing life across its doom and gloom. Desire appears as an imposing and largely opaque inner force that men and women in their proper gendered modes may turn into a driving force of society. Desire originally develops around the nods of intentions and demands that the close kin group and local society interweave around and between the body of the infant and themselves.

In a first and widely accepted understanding in yiYaka-speaking society, desire (*luzolu, -zola*) denotes an essential yearning, will, or want arising from within the body-self, while being expressed in language and thus submitted to its regulation and the other's assent. This yearning or demand is addressed in the presupposition of common values and preferences to a fellow subject, one who may be of the other gender, generation, or group. It is through such desirous demand or will that youngsters may solicit cheerful recognition or mutual sympathy (*-zolakana*), often among those of their own gender and age group. It is this desirous will that makes conduct and things appear to one another as they do. An adult man should express his desire in his vigorous, purposeful, or willful appearance, and through words and deeds that, like the gravity of a senior man, solicit admiration (*-zolana*). Having heart (*kena yembuundu*) is the quintessential attribute of a desired woman, admired for her control over her impulses, wants, and envy and for her generous care for the housemates and, when aging, for her good words in the home. Love turns the desire into a reciprocal and deliberate one. This is one addressed to the other's desire, *-zolasana*, literally, by reciprocally stirring the other's motivation, desire, or passion while being solicited by it. This witnesses to the extimacy at the very core of self: the individual never possesses, masters, nor escapes her desire. Desire decenters the subject, from her mere state of a plurality of wants and physical needs, into recognizing her longing for desirability and valuation from other people, or spontaneously responding to wishes and demands, constraints, or interests of others. Desire is ceaseless; it does not stop one from longing for pleasurable and painful experiences or questioning oneself how one is moving through life.

Second, when desire focuses on an unpleasant awareness of some momentary physical lack and the attraction to satisfy that need so as to attain a mere pleasurable state of satisfaction, a yiYaka idiom describes it as a physical appetite or hunger, termed *ndzala*. Such understanding entwines the enticing aroma of food that stirs one's "hunger for food" and its subconscious urge for satiation, or merges one's tiredness into a "hunger for sleep." It entwines one's material needfulness with a "hunger for money," or the alluring appeal that a woman may have for a man and vice versa with one's sexual "appetite for woman." Here, culture does not so much privilege the subject, but the mere intercorporeality in as much as it senses out *ndzala* in its being caught by some lack and its satiation.

Third, a barely culturally attuned hunger or craving (also *ndzala*) may selfishly turn into a largely imaginary or hallucinatory, yet socially blameworthy, ingression into the other, such as when it clearly develops into envy and jealousy (*yiphala*), lust and passion (*luhweetu*), or greed and rapacity (*kheni*). In the cultural view, such overwhelming or intrusive desire especially occurs when a person enviously or resentfully pursues a type of thing or power that normally she would deny to others and that hinges on bewitchment. This craving contrasts with the sociocultural emphasis in its many linguistic and food prohibitions on attuning oneself to the propensity of and coresonance between life forms. In Kwaango land, the sociocultural shaping side to side with ecology's harsh conditions inspires a mere frugal mode of living, however, without subduing the subject's desire to some all too willful ascetics. Collective representations focus on the ambivalence in the grips of "ethic of desire" at the core of one's extimacy. Compared to the alternation of day and night, the seasons and the lunar cycle, desire alternates between moments of willfulness and those of overwhelming impulses from selfish obscure forces. Desire springs from the desire of the other and molds and orients the subject's sociocultural openness to the enigma of desire, that is, "the real" as ever enigmatic and elusive or haunting.

It thus appears how much yiYaka-speaking society conceptualizes desire (-*zola, ndzala*) regarding various modalities of deficiency. It also considers desire as a longing for relationship, exchange, and recognition from others, hence, for ever more intercorporeal and intersubjective interwovenness. Here lies the core of the ethic of desire in yiYaka socioculture. It is the maternal uncle's role to sustain desire's impetus toward a relation. He appears as the one whose function is to help, through ritualizing, his sister's children and their family. He should help to intertwine the impulses toward physical reproduction and the satisfaction of the body's physical needs with society's expectation. Members are expected to outreach in some loyalty and attunement to others, other beings, and things beyond mere self-perpetuation and the circle of one's own making. The maternal uncle personifies the sociocultural *ethic of desire*. This means the fundamental willing in the individual and her uterine kin that besets life, steers it into sensibility and accordance, adjustment and reciprocity. Desire is meant to respond to and resonate with the sense of existence in the larger society and the lifeworld.

Dream work according to the yiYaka speakers is opening up the dreamer and her local group—perhaps figured in the dream—to a space-time ahead of itself. Dreaming and dream sharing is the golden road to some unexpected *signifiance*—that is, unconsciously emerging meaning production—and to a particular meaning-bearing interpenetration of the individual and collective unconscious. People acknowledge how much dreaming ventures into the subject's unthought-in-thought regarding her past or future fate. It may thereby lay bare some intercorporeal and intersubjective play of ambivalent desire and affective powers. My research in suburban Kinshasa shows how much some dreams, such as Nsawa's, may quite authoritatively come to disclose frustrated but unsatisfiable desires, such as of school-educated Kinois. The reported dreams bring out fantasies and phantasms, as well as expectations and frustrations regarding the university degree seen as a Western-derived source of omnipotence. Such dreams may unloose the subject's toxic or destructive *jouissance* and make it strand in the realm of the abject and horror.

Thus, desire is fundamentally ambivalent, generating the phantasms of assumed Western hedonism, on the one hand, while, on the other hand, morphing into the dark fantasies of ensorcellment, the counterfantasies. In the subconscious domain of affects, the desirous one exposes himself to bewitchment or ensorcellment and, henceforth, undergoes an increasingly grave and complex crisis and with time gradually abdicates his status as a subject. He believes that others are responsible for his misfortune and surrenders his weakened body to the uncontrollable events and overpowering threats surrounding him. The victim who surrenders gradually plunges into fatal anxiety and chaos, disorientation or despondency, or into the void of the unthinkable "real." And he meanwhile exposes himself to the morbid desires unleashed by certain envious and wicked relatives. The fatal desire of others, or their hatred and aggression is incorporated by the weakened individual, for in his bodily disposition and condition he has opened up to images in which the forces of life and death, of love and hatred, of placebo and nocebo intersect and consume his life-resources.

NOTES

1. It is with Ettinger (2006) and the later Lacan (1962–1963, 1975, 1975–1976, 1986, 2001) that I find most clues for some aspectual psychoanalytical reading of my anthropological data. Such a reading results also from our monthly seminar, since 2002, with colleagues and clinical psychoanalysts of the Belgium School for Psychoanalysis and, since 2007, at the Psychoanalytical Study Centre Diest.

2. This inquiry draws on periodical research stays between 1971–1974 and 1986–2000 among the yiYaka-speaking people in the rural northern Kwaango region of Southwestern Democratic Republic of Congo and in some of Kinshasa's shanty towns (Devisch 1993; Devisch and Brodeur 1999). From December 1971 until October 1974, I lived as an anthropologist in the yiYaka-speaking society of northern Kwaango land along the Angolan border, in the Taanda settlement of thirteen villages that had some 120 inhabitants on average, or 6 persons per square kilometer, at 450 kilometers to the south of Kinshasa. From 1986 to 2003, the investigation developed in collaborative ventures with Congolese and Belgian colleagues, during the annual research stays of some three weeks, among emigrants from Kwaango in Kinshasa's shanty towns of Camp Luka-Ngaliema, Kimbanseke, Kingabwa, Masina, and Yolo-Sud. Among the yiYaka-speaking people in Kwaango land and Kinshasa, the realm of witchcraft and sorcery is part and parcel of people's anxieties, concerns, and sense of kinship, particularly in the face of affliction and death. The data I gathered throughout this time on divination, healing, and sorcery confirm in detail the observations of Jesuit Father Leon de Beir (1975), who between 1938 and 1945 observed healing and antisorcery practices in the Taanda region. Those practices show remarkable resemblances with the neighboring Koongo and Luunda traditions (Buakasa 1973; de Boeck and Plissart 2004; Jacobson-Widding 1979; MacGaffey 1977; Turner 1975; Van Wing 1959).

3. Formerly, the real was considered the order of nature. But both the dominant discourse of science and the encompassing solutions that capitalism and modern technocracy claim to deliver undermine the symbolic horizon and interweave of the Western subject's various registers of experience. The exact and applied sciences as well as technocracy repress from the public discourse both the symbolic register and people's bodily experience, as well as contingent events and the sensorial, in as much as they evade integration in a historical reading and categorical representation. Preempting the postmodern mutation, in his post-1970 seminars, Lacan leaves the issue of the (Names of the) Father and focusses on the "presencing of the real" (Lacan 1975–1976, 1986, 2001,

2005 [1962–1963]). At hand is the Borromean knot intertwining the "symbolic, imaginary, and real" in lines with the split subject's particular modality of unrepresentable *jouissance*. The latter escapes the symbolic and the imaginary and ties in with desire's unsayable intercorporeal longing and *jouissance*'s insatiable or fearsome vacuum or *manco*. Yet, the postmodern subject and worldview are in utter contrast with the Bantu focus on coresonance between the visible and invisible, the touchable and nontouchable power fields at play in the human being, society, and the lifeworld. Here coresonance and covibration between fellow humans and the lifeworld are sustained by some keen sense of flair, vivacious dreams, and finely tuned intuition.

4. My pretense here is based on my participatory anthropological experience in the yiYaka-speaking milieus, but also on my privileged knowledge of the turn of things at the University of Kinshasa, first as student (1969–1971), and later during the annual hospitality from 1991 until 2007 (Devisch 2007).

5. Terms in yiYaka language are rendered in italics. Incidentally, the prefix *ku-, wu-* of the infinitives is replaced by the hyphen.

6. In line with Lacan (1986), it is important to see that desire is for each individual articulable in the intercorporeal and intersubjective fields. Desire is specified in the discourse of the other. It tunes in with the demand of the other, namely by what is said—actually, virtually, or in fantasy—among interlocutors. While encompassing the alien or estimate at the core of one's sociocentric self, the ethic of desire calls for at least some minimal reciprocity among kin so as to steadily favor the propitious bearing and transmission of the life-flow. Desire also taints, in culture-specific ways, the subject's suggestible and greatly unconscious, open-ended and unreflecting search to favor life's and existence's unfolding beyond irruptions of crisis, deterioration, or destruction. Desire qualifies the subject's socio- and cosmocentric stance in life. It remains unsatisfiable or even arouses anxiety, as it is unconsciously grounded in a structural lack. Facing the void and not-knowing of the real, it opens up to alterity in ourselves and the other.

REFERENCES

Buakasa, Tulu kia Mpansu. 1973. *L'Impensé du discours:* Kindoki *et* nkisi *en pays kongo du Zaïre.* Kinshasa, Democratic Republic of Congo: Presses Universitaires du Zaïre.
Daniel, Valentine E. 1996. *Charred Lullabies: Chapters in an Anthropology of Violence.* Princeton, NJ: Princeton University Press.
De Beir, Leon. 1975. *Religion et magie des Bayaka.* St. Augustin near Bonn, Germany: Anthropos.
De Boeck, Filip, and Marie-Françoise Plissart. 2004. *Kinshasa: Tales from the Invisible City.* Ghent, Belgium: Ludion.
Deleuze, Gilles, and Guattari, F. 1980. *Mille plateaux: Capitalisme et schizophrénie.* Paris: Minuit.
Devisch, René. 1993 *Weaving the Threads of Life: The* Khita *Gyn-Eco-logical Healing Cult among the Yaka.* Chicago: University of Chicago Press.
———. 1995. "Frenzy, Violence, and Ethical Renewal in Kinshasa." *Public Culture* 7, no. 3:593–629.
———. 1996. "'Pillaging Jesus': Healing Churches and the Villagisation of Kinshasa." *Africa* 66, no. 4:555–586.

——. 2003. "Parody in Matricentred Christian Healing Communes of the Sacred Spirit in Kinshasa." *Contours: a Journal of the African Diaspora* 1:171–198.

——. 2005. "Witchcraft and Sorcery." In *A Companion to Psychological Anthropology,* edited by C. Casey and R. B. Edgerton, 389–416. Oxford: Blackwell.

——. 2007. "The University of Kinshasa: From Lovanium to Unikin." In *Higher Education in Postcolonial Africa: Paradigms of Development, Decline and Dilemmas,* edited by M. Afolayan, 17–38. Trenton, NJ: Africa World Press.

——. 2012. "Divination in Africa." In *The Wiley-Blackwell Companion to African Religions,* edited by E. Bongmba, 79–86. Oxford: Blackwell.

——. 2013. "Of Divinatory Co-naissance among the Yaka of DR Congo." In *Reviewing Reality: Dynamics of African Divination,* edited by Walter E. A. van Beek, and Philip M. Peek, 25–58. Berlin: LIT Verlag.

Devisch, René, and C. Brodeur. 1999. *The Law of the Lifegivers: The Domestication of Desire.* Amsterdam: Harwood.

Ettinger, Bracha. 2006. *The Matrixial Borderspace.* Minneapolis: University of Minnesota press.

Evans-Pritchard, Edward. 1937. *Witchcraft, Oracles and Magic among the Azande.* Oxford: Clarendon.

Foucault, Michel. 1984. *Histoire de la sexualité III: Le souci de soi.* Paris: Gallimard.

Green, André. 1963. *Le Travail du négatif.* Paris, Editions de Minuit.

Jacobson-Widding, Anita. 1979. *Red-White-Black as a Mode of Thought: A Study of Triadic Classification by Colours in the Ritual Symbolism and Cognitive Thought of the People of the Lower Congo.* Stockholm: Almqvist and Wiksell.

Kristeva, Julia. 1980. *Pouvoir de l'horreur.* Paris: Seuil.

Lacan, Jacques. 1962–1963. *L'angoisse: Le Séminaire, livre X.* Paris: Seuil. 2004. Repr., edited by J.-A. Miller.

——. 1975. *Encore: le Séminaire, livre XX,* edited by J.-A. Miller. Paris: Seuil.

——. 1975–1976. *Le Sinthome: Le Séminaire, livre XXIII.* Paris: Seuil. 2005

——. 1986. *L'éthique de la psychanalyse: Le Séminaire, livre VII,* edited by J.-A. Miller. Paris: Seuil.

——. 2001. *Autres écrits,* edited by J.-A. Miller. Paris: Seuil.

MacGaffey, Wyatt. 1977. "Fetishism Revisited: Kongo *nkisi* in Sociological Perspective." *Africa* 47, no. 2:140–152.

Merleau-Ponty, Maurice. 1964. *Le visible et l'invisible.* Paris: Gallimard.

Turner, Victor. 1975. *Revelation and Divination in Ndembu Ritual.* Ithaca, NY: Cornell University Press.

Van Wing, Joseph. 1959. *Etudes Bakongo: Sociologie, religion et magie.* Vols. 1 and 2. Paris: Desclée de Brouwer.

Vandenbroeck, Paul. 2009. "The Energetics of an Unknowable Body." In *Backlit Heaven: Power and Devotion in the Archdiocese Mechelen,* edited by G. Rooijakkers and P. Vandenbroeck, 174–204. Tielt, Belgium: Lannoo.

Viveiros de Castro, Eduardo. 2004. "Exchanging Perspectives: The Transformation of Objects into Subjects in Amerindian Ontologies." *Common Knowledge* 10, no. 3: 463–484.

7 AZE AND THE INCOMMENSURABLE

LÉOCADIE EKOUÉ WITH JUDY ROSENTHAL

Translated by Judy Rosenthal

Aze (usually translated as "witchcraft" in English) was a subject of great concern in Goldcoast (Ghana), Togoland (Togo), and Dahomey (Benin) during the colonial period and is perhaps of even more urgent concern today. Recent research by Douglas Falen (unpublished manuscript 2013) in Benin impresses on us just how thoroughly modern (if not postmodern) preoccupations about *aze* continue to be, not only in rural areas and isolated villages, but also for urbanites, the university-educated, and the middle class.

During my own research on Gorovodu in Togo and Ghana, I heard the word *aze* pronounced daily, and I also found it in the colonial archives in Accra and Lomé. The fear of *aze* is indicated as one of the major motivations for the proliferation of Kunde and Abrewa "antiwitchcraft cults" among Ewe, Asante, and Fante at the turn of the last century. It just so happened that British colonial authorities considered these *vodu* movements to be anticolonial as well as anti-*aze*, and they did their best to wipe them out (Rosenthal 1998). These are precisely the cults that today are called Gorovodu in Togo. All of the priests and practitioners that I have spoken with over the years have told me that Gorovodu was for healing and for protection from every sort of harm, especially that caused by *aze*.

Aze is usually said to be an unintentional sort of evil, one that is especially active in women, for women have the powers of life itself and therefore also of death. (Falen discusses this gender bias at length, and it comes up in Ekoué's story.) Some priests say that all of us possess *aze* in the form of unconscious desires to do harm, especially on account of *n'bia*, that is, our feelings of jealousy, envy, death wish, and what we might call *schadenfreude*. Indeed, the terms *aze* and *n'bia* are almost always linked. *N'bia* is the wish for others to be harmed; *aze* is the practice of carrying out that violence. But Gorovodu priests say that the feelings themselves cause harm; they circulate in the air and reach the minds and bodies of others like an invisible poison.

There are also the usual narratives about cohorts of *azetowo* (see also Falen 2013), witches who meet at night and demand of each other that they "eat" a loved one; that is, they cause someone in the family or in the village to become ill, to miscarry, perhaps to die or to lose a child (the case in the story told by Ekoué). Although it is not clear how many West Africans, including Togolese vodu practitioners, actually believe that such witch covens exist, it is clear that almost everyone believes that the jealousy or death wish of someone in the family can harm others, including causing an infant's death.

Gorovodu prayers beg the spirits to protect everyone from all *aze*, including "our own power for evil that we might not even know about." So there is an interesting distinction in popular discourse between conscious, intentional practices of evil and the "natural," unbidden, and perhaps unconscious wish for others to shine less than we do—their loss is supposedly our gain. In this latter scenario, unless we monitor ourselves carefully and pray to be free of our own *aze,* we all behave as merciless competitors for good fortune—love, beautiful children, wealth, respect, and recognition. Yet another definition of *aze* is simply personal power, knowledge, and energy to do either good or evil. Fishermen, for example, say that they employ their *aze* to ensure a good catch. Falen (2013) provides extended ethnographic examples of "good *aze*."

And now begins this conversation and narrative, a doubly "emic" text where the two anthropologists are also the informants, where "native knowledge" and "etic theory" dance with one another. The two writers are careful not to provide any resolution where none exists in reality, and this extends to their own contradictory feelings and notions.

Ekoué and Rosenthal sit in a café at La Place d'Italie with notepads next to their coffee cups and pens in hand. In the midst of a story about her life Ekoué mentions *aze*. "Shit, Léocadie," Rosenthal growls. "I'm so tired of hearing about *aze.* Why do all of you Togolese women always bring it up to explain practically everything! On this matter I'm a clueless Westerner, even after years and years of working with Vodu, and I don't like all the *aze* talk. It depresses me."

Ekoué smiles. "I'll try to humor you," she says. "I'll try to interpret the reasons why we interpret all of our interpretations and everyone else's interpretations with talk of *aze*." Rosenthal listens. It is indeed about interpretation of interpretation—interpretation all the way down, no "transcendental signified."

What follows is Ekoué's text with a few questions and comments by Rosenthal. After Rosenthal transcribed the conversation and the story, Ekoué reworked much of it so that it said (at least in the original French) what she wanted it to say.

> EKOUÉ: When I am asked to speak about witchcraft with a European or American I am expected to enter into another dimension, a sort of conformity with Western notions. As soon as I do that I begin to cheat (*agir en porte-à-faux*), whereas I cannot cheat in the clinic (in ethno-psychoanalytic practice). Today I can speak honestly about witchcraft because for all of these years I have not been able to cheat in clinical work. In the presence of patients I cannot censure what is not Western. Elsewhere, an African is necessarily in a position of auto-censorship, is always brought to censure her words and her interpretations when it comes to talk about sorcery.
>
> Westerners always have their own notions of sorcery and the way it has functioned in Europe and the U.S., and they use that frame to investigate African sorcery, but that simply does not work. The questions themselves are full of traps so that the answers are pulled into a discourse that has its own agenda and cannot result in an African interpretation. Sorcery [or witchcraft] as interpreted by Westerners is always about trials, the law, judgment, and capitalism. It is as though when we speak of sorcery in terms of sociology [and anthropology], we use a huge fishing net for catching sharks, when we should be using a very fine spider web made of silk.
>
> *Aze* and most other Mina and Ewe words that are translated as *sorcellerie* in French [and "witchcraft" in English] are used to talk about the incommensurable. It's not only about the latest versions of capitalism's invasion of Africa, and the vampire nature of some individuals' exploitation of others, such as we read in the recent ethnographies about witchcraft (e.g., Geschiere 1997). It's also about the untranslatable difference between the West and the rest, and about the unspeakable, the unrepresentable,[1] that which resists all explanation, even in Ewe and Mina worlds. It is especially about *n'bia*—jealousy and death wish—the banal yet destructive rivalry that exists to some extent in the psyche of every person in the world, but that we Togolese have made conscious with our concept of *aze*.
>
> We know that we feel wounded in our narcissism when others succeed precisely there where we ourselves have failed, whatever it is we are

lacking that the other possesses—a good job, beauty or wealth, love, a brilliant child, etc. And we know that our feeling of loss in the face of another's gain, and the strong emotion of resentment or hatred of the other who "has," sometimes the feeling of the unfairness of our own emptiness there where we perceive the other to be full—we know that these negative feelings we harbor against the other can harm us and can harm the other, socially, psychologically, and in Togo and Ghana, magically. That is why there are so many recipes for undoing *n'bia* and the *aze* that it can lead to, for protecting ourselves and our children from it, for punishing those who do not take care to monitor their own negative emotions toward others. We say that some people with *aze* literally (thus spiritually) join *aze* coteries who meet during the night and plan their success at the expense of others' health or even with the sacrifice of others' lives, or their children's lives. We say that they turn into owls and watch and wait in trees to do harm. We say that such people trade on their natural *aze* so as to use it intentionally to destroy others. Other people may be destructive without even realizing it because they are not conscious of their desire to harm. Now I'm going to tell you a typical story of *aze,* one from my childhood.

In my memory it is as though it happened yesterday. I was born in Abidjan of Togolese parents, and we lived in Treichville, the most African outskirt of the capitol city of Côte d'Ivoire. I was seven years old when a strange event took place in the large compound in which we lived. A little boy of four died suddenly, and his death arrived like a thunderbolt, shaking the lives of everyone in the neighborhood. The morning before he died he was quiet, although since he had begun to walk he had filled the compound with his baby talk and later with his singing. Very quickly everyone had recognized the strength of his intelligence, for without even trying he remembered better than the older children who attended school all of the songs and lessons that they recited and practiced at night before going to bed. However, that morning his silence shocked all of us and worried the children who hurried off to school while the adults spoke in low voices. When the children returned home from school they heard the wailing that had already for several hours accompanied the pain and tears of the mother.

During those days burials took place the same day as death. The mortuary cold room had not yet made its appearance in sub-Saharan Africa. Heat reigned, so funeral wakes were forbidden. The child had died that morning and was buried that afternoon. All the members of his extended family and their close friends were there to accompany the little one to his resting place.

Now the courtyard shared by his family, ours, and several others was to become the theater of a strange scene. Facing the lodging of the mourning family was a tiny two-room hut practically in the middle of the large collective courtyard. The hut was occupied by an old woman and her niece. It was adjoined to an enormous baobab tree. It was made of adobe and therefore was cooler than the other dwellings, which were built of concrete blocks. Strangely, the tiny porch just outside the door of the hut, usually curtained off for privacy, was left open that day, so that the little funeral cortege could see the old woman inside, dressed in a simple piece of cloth (*pagne*). It was not like her to sit there visible to others, and only in *pagne*. She sat on a mat, her legs stretched straight out, inside a circle marked on the mat by chicken feathers, with alternating black and white feathers. She stared at the little casket that was carried out of the courtyard by way of the central path, on its way to the cemetery. Alone among all those who could not ignore the sad event, the old woman had thus made her first appearance that day. No one had seen her offer her condolences to the mourning family, or even exchange a single word with the other neighbors of the concession. The adults were stupefied, and the children began to enter a world of disquieting strangeness and fear.

During the months that followed the funeral, the members of the mourning family remained inside their lodging. They finally moved, so they said, because they had other children to protect. That is the way this story of *aze* began among us. Our neighborhood, which had sprung up quite recently, was quite the opposite of the more elegant administrative residential quarters in Abidjan. Ours was inhabited by Africans from other countries—immigrants. The old woman and her niece belonged to an Akan family, expatriates of long date, from the Gold Coast (now Ghana). Her niece was from the border area of the Gold Coast, and the two women kept in close contact with their family and friends on the other side of the border. The other families in our compound came from Dahomey (now Benin), from Upper Volta (now Burkina Faso), and from Togo.

The old woman was still attractive, and her niece adored her. She was the only person of her age in our quarter, and not a single child dared appear on her porch (which was pleasant for its cool shade thanks to the baobab). The niece had already lost her grown son. Since his death, she had remained alone except for her aunt, to whom she was devoted. The unexplained death of her son came back to the surface during this period. The two women were Christian, of a Protestant denomination, and it was therefore permitted for them to not search for the causes of her son's death; above all, they were not to search for a meaning through divination. [All West Africans not of a monotheistic persuasion would have gone to a diviner—an Afa bokono among Ewe and Mina—to find out why the person had died, but Christians considered that practice to be pagan.] Everyone in the concession was either Christian or Muslim, and the moments consecrated for religious practice provided the rhythm of daily life, of the end of the week and rest from work. Like numerous other African citizens, we all thought of "traditional" African practices as backward.

The circumstances surrounding the little boy's death and burial stunned us all and stirred up memories and ideas of obscure origins. The huge baobab that was hanging over the lodging of the two women was so high and so thickly leafed that it had become a kingdom of owls [*azeheviwo*, or "witchbirds"]. From that day on, children no longer tried to stave off the moment they had to go to bed. As soon as they lay down for the night they closed their eyes tightly so as to go to sleep as quickly as possible. The baobab that had become a tree for night-birds was thereby also a tree for *azetowo* (witches). That image fed the children's night terrors. It was good to sleep together, and heaven help the child whose parents thought they were favoring him by giving him a bed of his own.

The days went by. The atmosphere had completely changed in our big courtyard. We all avoided the two women but were careful to show our respect for them in all of the usual ways. We went about our daily business in silence, whereas before that event our activities were full of the banal noise of life, exclamations of pleasure or of anger, laughter and crying of children.

The old woman's niece was troubled by her aunt's behavior the day of the child's death. Without knowing exactly why, she went to consult a diviner. She wanted to know why she herself had remained without a husband and children for so long. The old diviner smiled and gave her some leaves to put in her bath water. She used this whitish *amasi* (mixture of leaves and water) for her daily ablutions. It was as though she was protecting herself from her aunt, whom she silently accused, through her ritual behavior, of having killed her (the niece's) husband as well as the little child who had recently died. Then her aunt's legs began to change form and become cylindrical. The old woman soon returned to Ghana with her niece and stayed there. Later the younger woman came back to our compound in Treichville, spoke of her aunt from time to time, and said that the old woman's limbs had become cylindrical. But she said less and less to us as time went by, and eventually she left the neighborhood.

That is a childhood memory, my own childhood memory, shared with a certain number of children. In it there is the element of the imaginary.[2] On the basis of that story, what happened inside the head of each one of us? It was said that the little boy had "returned home" ("to his own country"). Many questions remained with regard to the cause of that child's death, but also with regard to the physical transformations of the old woman. Such phenomena are interpreted in the same fashion in Ghana, Cote d'Ivoire, and Togo. Obviously, as a little Togolese girl I knew about the physical modifications the old woman was said to have undergone after her niece accused her of having harmed her own family. (The niece did not, however, employ the word *sorcery*.) I had always heard the description in Togo, by people who were speaking of the sorcery of old women. . . . Often what was said about that form of sorcery was that the old women's limbs changed shape. In these stories of sorcery, in the descriptions of the witch, she or he is never someone who will be lynched, for example, but rather someone who will be abandoned, left in some corner. People will come and insult her and say to her, "You are the one who killed so-and-so. You must leave." But she remains a member of a lineage, in which she has harmed one of her own, a family member (close or distant), and one cannot in all decency condemn a member of one's own family [or lineage].

But what is extraordinary, what is often said, is that even before the situation becomes clear (before accusations begin) our *azetowo* (witches, sorcerers) enter into a process of internalizing the representations of sorcery—they have already taken the first step, by feeding the representations of sorcery, by saying, "That child who has died, I killed it." ("*Enye xoe*"—"I'm the one who took it.") They also say, "You are persecuting me," speaking to the child's spirit. And, addressing others, "It's because of you that I took the child." It's a vicious cycle. The witch is speaking both to the spirit of the victim and to the family of the victim. It is an old woman or man speaking to spirits persecuting her [or him] and at the same time saying to the family of the victim, "Leave me alone." "*Enye wu devia—devi hou-an amega degbedo la va nyi eye nti me xoe do.*" ("That child became a powerful person—that's why I took it.") The witch says of a child that is still alive but ill, "I tried everything to have that child, but his soul (*kla*) is too strong." What is interesting is that the person doesn't ever say that she is crazy; she waits for the title of *azeto* to be accorded her. She won't necessarily be harmed.

ROSENTHAL: How does she feel about all of that?

EKOUÉ: Her experience is that of feeling *n'bia,* or jealousy, or something that troubles her sufficiently for her to demand the title of *azeto,* even when she wants to get out of the role of *azeto.* Judeo-Christian thinking makes of sorcery something that can't be remedied, but in Africa the *azeto* is someone with links to other persons. Her deeds have to do with her links with others, her kinship. Individuals who have lost most of their family members might be *azetowo* or victims of *azetowo* or both. Ewe and Mina ideas of *aze* go beyond Judeo-Christian thinking of the good/evil oppositions and beyond the discourse of guilt. A person can actively claim the title of *azeto.* West Africans in rupture with tradition, especially those who became Christian, looked elsewhere for the answers to their disquiet over the existence of unexplainable and unjust death and other misfortune. (The geomancer or *bokono* [diviner] was said by Protestant missionaries and Catholic priests to be the devil.) To avoid grave problems, African Christians fasted, prayed to Mary, gave God gifts, etc., which were the same sorts of solutions that would be resorted to in non-Christian Africa.

My story constitutes an important instance of an endless constellation of stories that nourish and give meaning to the relationship between West Africans and *aze.* One cannot refuse to recognize the influence of Christianity that came to make sorcery into something linked to Satan. So we might draw a parallel between Christian visions of sorcery and Christian interpretations of Legba, for example. Legba was the absolute trap trickster of Christianity, for since the days of the colonial occupation missionaries have translated the word Satan as "Legba," although Legba had nothing whatsoever to do with Satan. (It was as though Legba had indeed tricked the Christians.) Now the *azeto* does in fact have to do with evil, but with a basis in *n'bia.* And that is something basic to human nature, not just to the nature of some transcendent Satan. In Togo and Ghana, we say that human nature has been both good and bad since the beginning, both peaceful and violent, both creative and destructive, like everything else in the world, everything in the entire cosmos itself, according to West African religions.

So the West African discourse on the subject of sorcery is constructed of such stories. We might say that when an anthropologist interviews an informant on issues of sorcery, the stories that are told are the result of this cultural construction carried out over generations around the predicament of sorcery, suffering, and misfortune. Every individual contains within herself positive and negative elements—they are integral to all human beings. They have a power to act on reality (agency), and the result can be violent. Thus one could say that a person is (considered to be) more powerful in Africa than in Europe. That is why there is such a discourse about the danger of keeping jealousy or rivalry in the stomach (*edome*); these negative passions have their own agenda, so one must get rid of them.

Here, I must remind you that the relationship between ethno-psychoanalysis and anthropology is always deeply unstable. The symbolic and practical wealth of the clinic is that in essence it pushes us toward a balance. We have to be watchful. If we lean more toward anthropology or toward psychoanalysis too entirely, we put ourselves or the patient in danger. Devereux (1970) already wrote about that. We need an anthropological reading of psychoanalysis as well as a psychoanalytical reading of anthropology.

The West African community develops a strategy of enculturation and of specific rules of conduct and laws so that the good of all might reign, so that *aze* can be used for the good. *Aze* in its constructive dimension is a motor for a creative imaginary, both in its social sense and in its very personal form.

ROSENTHAL: Several elements of your narrative make me think of René Girard's (2002) writing about how Oedipus and Apollo are both cursed divinities who are accused of bringing on the plague, and whose punishment then stops the plague. They are the ones responsible for the crisis *and* responsible for bringing order back to society. He says that this duality characterizes all forms of the sacred. Women who say they are witches sometimes are the sacrificial lambs or the scapegoats of a crisis. They know that they are not guilty in the strict sense, but they are ready to take upon themselves the weight of guilt or shame so that a ritual may be performed, so that something is done about the crisis and about those who are ill. Then healing can begin. I think that the work of René Girard on sacrifice, mimesis, and ritual violence can be interesting in our study of West African religion, even if we don't agree with his use of the word "primitive" and don't adhere to his almost doctrinal position on mimesis. We can't deny that many origin stories and foundational myths in face-to-face societies include a murder that is situated at the beginning of everything. "Our long-lasting incapacity to perceive the threat that internal violence constitutes for primitive society prevents us from recognizing that ritual provides a relatively effective protection against this threat" (Girard 2002, 249 [Rosenthal's translation]).

While you were describing the "cylindrical shape" of the *azetowos'* arms and legs (a changing of shape, or a shape shifting that is interpreted to be part of the person's wish to harm others), I was thinking about Girard's (252) discussion of Artaud's *Le Theatre et la Peste* (29). "[Artaud] interprets the physiological process as a dissolution of organs, a sort of fusion, a liquefaction of the body, or, on the contrary, a desiccation and pulverization. This loss of organic differentiation is mythical as far as medical science goes, but all powerful with regard to aesthetics in the sense that it models the pathological symptoms on the falling apart of the culture, producing an irresistible impression of disintegration."

EKOUÉ: Yes, the frightening *aze* that we are speaking of is the power for good and evil that is not controlled. It therefore can easily slide into evil consequences. It exists as potential power in everyone. Working with Afa divination helps a person to become conscious of her personal powers and potentials and therefore to not fall into the trap of unconscious acts that would harm herself and others, especially her loved ones, the family and the lineage. Should that happen she becomes an *azeto* and thus a pariah. Initiation in Afa protects a person as well as others. Certain Afa signs include particular forms of violence, and so when the person knows this she can work on herself so as to avoid committing violence against herself or others. The *azeto* develops harmful and destructive power consciously or unconsciously. Her desire is unconscious, but the acts might be conscious. The person can wonder why she is doing harm. That conscious dimension is what brings some people to confess acts of *aze.*

During an Afa ceremony, when it comes to praying to the Na (female forest spirits), one never thinks of a person, but rather of spiritual entities. They are the archetypal mothers of the beginning, myths, and not real women or souls of the dead or ancestral shadows. They are a sort of Vodu substance, the numinous. Twins (*venaviwo*) also are of the same nature—principles of the beginning—a duality necessary for the beginning of the world, the *fetume* (*dzogbese*—the beginning, before conception, where the *kpoli*, or life sign, already exists). Na and *venavi* are in the space where life and nonlife exist together.

ROSENTHAL: That makes me think of Nana Ablewa, the Gorovodu deity among Ewe and Mina, who is a primordial mother vodu (whose color is white) and Nana Wango (whose color is black), the fiercely protective mother and grandmother, the passer, the piroguier or ferryman in her masculine form. Gorovodu worshippers pray to both of these mothers to protect them from *aze* and from *azetowo*.

EKOUÉ: That is full of resonance for what I'm saying. We are truly speaking of the same thing, the same cultures. It is necessary for those of us working clinically to employ these representations, and when we hear these myths we know more about how we ourselves are structured (especially we Africans). You and I validate each other with these examples, this close knowledge; it's like magic.

When you and I speak together, all the experience of the clinic comes into my head as well as the representations woven from the memories of my childhood. Childhood memories give body to theory. We have a creative tension in this work. We confront each other with our knowledge and our theorizations. It is better than supervision in the clinical setting in which a "superior" watches over one's work. Supervision is a sort of maintenance of one's clinical work. But this kind of work delves more deeply.

The notion of *aze* is extremely complex. We have to take into account the universe in which it occurs. People live these stories as pieces of life.

NOTES

1. This would be "the thing," a material/psychic dimension, "abyss," suffering without a name, that no words can describe, that cannot be represented at all, the Lacanian "real," that will appear from time to time in these narratives.

2. Here, rather than simply use the word *imagination*, which would almost have been equal to the task, Ekoué employs a Lacanian term, *l'Imaginaire*, referring to the element of the psyche that is linked to images, the ego, identities, dualities of self and other, "dual relationships," etc. Thus it is a perfect term to refer to a situation of *n'bia*

or rivalry, with its attendant passions of envy and death wish. The other two Lacanian terms that accompany the imaginary are the real and the symbolic, both of which are also useful for ethno-psychologists, anthropologists, and writers of all sorts.

REFERENCES

Devereux, George, ed. 1970. *Psychoanalysis and the Occult.* New York: International Universities Press.

Falen, Douglas. 2013. "African Science: Vodun, Reality, and the Globalization of Witchcraft in Southern Benin." Unpublished manuscript.

Geschiere, Peter. 1997. *The Modernity of Witchcraft: Politics and the Occult in Postcolonial Africa.* Charlottesville: University Press of Virginia.

Girard, Rene. 2002. *La voix méconnue du réel: une théorie des mythes archaïques et modernes.* Paris: Grasset.

Rosenthal, Judy. 1998. *Possession, Ecstasy and Law in Ewe Voodoo.* Charlottesville: University Press of Virginia.

8 EVIL AND THE ART OF REVENGE IN THE MANDARA MOUNTAINS

WALTER E. A. VAN BEEK

THE THREAT OF REVENGE

It is always a dramatic moment during a funeral dance, when the corpse is lifted over the wall and placed on the shoulders of the smith. At the funeral dance of Zra Wuvè, the crowd had been warming up for the dance as usual, the mourning kinsmen brandishing their spears, the women ululating and scraping calabashes over their iron skirts, while inside, the deceased was being clothed and decorated for the dance. When the corpse of Zra Wuvè came in sight and a smith climbed over the wall in order to carry the body, the crowd followed the drummers toward the compound to witness how their dead relative was hoisted on the shoulders of the young smith. Finally, Zra sat high and mighty on the smith's shoulders, in full view of his admiring kinsmen, when suddenly a woman stepped up and shouted: "Such is the taste of death." What then happened I will not quickly forget. When the young smith recognized Masi,[1] the widow of the late Tizhè who was a lineage brother of the deceased, he stopped right in his first steps and put Zra down. Immediately, the drums fell silent, and the people started to ask what happened. Then the word got around what Masi had said, and all participants put down their lances and clubs, spoke to each other in whispers, and quickly went away. After all, everybody already knew what had happened with Masi: she "had gone to Wuta," implying that this death of Zra Wuvè was a result of magical revenge, a suspicion that had already been voiced in the village. Within minutes, the place was empty but for some older smiths, the corpse, and me. The smiths quickly unwrapped the body and two of them took the body to a nearby stand of trees—quite close to the compound, in fact. In haste, they dug a shallow grave, dumped the body in it, and filled it up, just covering the corpse with some earth and stones. To be honest, I was shocked with this abrupt ending of a funeral. In Kapsiki, one's funeral is the best day of one's life, an outpouring of grief that forms the highlight of village life, a celebration of a lasting identity of the deceased and the village. Suddenly, Zra Wuvè was not only found guilty of the ultimate transgression in Kapsiki life, but also he was defined as a nonperson, someone without identity who should not have "been there," who in retrospect had no right to a life. His name (Wuvè means shit[2]) now became an ironic commentary. The name had been given to him at birth for a completely different reason, but *"nomen est omen"* and his end did justice to his name.

It is a chain of evil deeds, magical revenge, and social retribution that we are looking at here, among the Kapsiki and Higi of North Cameroon and Northeastern Nigeria.[3] There are many ways in which people can harm each other, so many routes by which evil[4] can enter one's life. In Africa, witchcraft is usually the most obvious one, but that is not what we speak about here. Kapsiki society is not witch-ridden and sees *mete* (witches) or *hweteru* (evil eye) mainly as a threat against children, since adults can quite easily protect themselves against these. Our focus is on the principal Kapsiki definition of evil, *beshèngu*, black magic, as well as the ways people are entitled to ritual revenge, and to the escalation of evil that the occult arena entails. The classic distinction between sorcery and witchcraft (Evans-Pritchard 1937) holds for the Kapsiki: conscious manipulation of objects and words versus an inborn proclivity to harm. As the Kapsiki divinatory systems do not name specific culprits or perpetrators, revenge never comes in against witchcraft. People just cry out in the night that the witch has to desist or else . . . , a vague threat that should be sufficient.[5]

However, revenge comes with other types of afflictions. There is open revenge and the hidden kind. Open revenge was part of the warfare the Kapsiki have engaged in during the past centuries, up until the colonial pacification. Scourged by slave-raiding from the outside by Moslem emirates bent upon "harvesting" from the pagan Mandara Mountains, the Kapsiki villages also fought each other in a low intensity internal war.[6] Unrelated villages—usually those further away—fought with poisoned arrows and caught slaves. Any casualties in such a war could not be revenged other than instigating a similar war and killing some enemies. In fact, any of these internal wars ended once there were casualties: burying one's dead was more important than getting back at the enemy. That is open revenge, and the basic notion of negative reciprocity reigned: a life for a life. There was nothing particularly bad or evil about this enmity; the "other" was simply an enemy, hated because he was from elsewhere, despised because he was not kin. Victory over him, or defeat by his hand, was a question of dexterity and strength, nothing shameful or hidden.

Some villages were and are related, and between them neither slaves should be caught, nor poison used, as they were "brothers of the same father" (brothers of the same mother are much closer in Kapsiki). Still, casualties were inevitable, as the use of spears and knives was allowed. If so, a system of blood payment, the *keluhu,* set in. The *keluhu,* "blood money," was claimed by the mother's brother of the slain one. Because he had lost a sister's son, a coveted relation in Kapsiki culture, he could walk right into the slayers' village without any risk; nobody could object or protest and since he came unexpectedly, even hiding one's possessions was hard. He would never venture alone, but came with a retinue of his clansmen, all sharing his uterine relation with the slain one, and together they could take from the culprit village whatever they could find: cattle, money, goats, sheep, gowns. The crucial element was that the payment was to be theirs, not for the lineage of the victim. Precisely this rule made exacting the *keluhu* much more interesting than avenging a death for a death, so the simple fact that it was the mother's family who collected the blood prize between these villages prevented feuding. If the brothers of the slain one would try direct revenge by killing a brother of the culprit in the other village, the latter's mother's brothers would have the right to collect another *keluhu* in the first village. So any revenge killing would simply produce a second *keluhu* claim.

Evidently, this arrangement is more than just a mechanism against feuding and is an expression of the importance of the maternal side of the family in Kapsiki social structure. During a war, the only way to halt the fighting was to send in a *wuzemakwa,* the "son of a bride." Between the fighting parties would appear a youngster, the son of a bride originating from the enemy village who had married into their own village. Since a *wuzemakwa* was inviolate for both groups, the fighting would halt immediately. Also negotiations afterward had to be done by him, as he linked his patrilineage with his mother's family. A crucial distinction runs through the Kapsiki marriage, that is, the one between two kinds of married women, those marrying for the first time, *makwa,* "bride," and all secondary marriages, *kwatewume.* As most brides tend to marry inside their own village first and move to a husband in another village later—as *kwatewume*—the "son of the *makwa*" binding two villages was rare and therefore a precious link. War, after all, is an expression of a relationship, and the rules of war, in the Kapsiki case those of a segmented society, illustrate that. One does not fight strangers, one fights enemies and those one knows!

Thus, Kapsiki was never a feuding society, and revenge was and is limited to those ills that stem from humans who are relatively close, but not precisely known; it is against their—mainly occult—attacks that defense is difficult and revenge forms an important option. So it is an occult arena we are entering now. The main threat here is, as said, not witchcraft, but sorcery, and then especially that branch of sorcery the Kapsiki call *beshèngu*, black magic. The use of *beshèngu* is the epitome of evil in Kapsiki society, a type of magic practiced by someone who aims at harming others, by killing them through magic. The term *beshèngu* denotes not a specific object or combination of things, but a number of different ways of harming the other. Some of those are well known (e.g., the whiskers of the leopard), others are very secret and known to a specialist only. Making *beshèngu* is a specialist's job, done professionally by smiths mainly, the ritual intermediaries par excellence in Kapsiki culture. But the smiths just sell the stuff to customers, and are deemed not to use it, so its use is for anybody's own responsibility.

A number of ways to make the stuff are given by the Kapsiki, all in the most general terms, because everybody emphatically disclaims having inside knowledge. The main fascination centers on the distribution of the harmful substance. One major image is flies: sorcerers are reputed to train flies to bring the beshèngu over to their victims or to change themselves into flying creatures in order to administer their wares. Or, more mundane and believable, sorcerers might personally bury it in the footpaths. The Kapsiki feel sure that all "important" men do have such magic, which they bought from a specialist in another village. Though it is not the possession of *beshèngu* that is evil, but its use, this powerful stuff is not to be trifled with, as we shall see.

One may defend oneself against possible attack, as there are recipes for protection, as well as the know-how of specialists. In many ritual texts and public discussions, curses are formulated against the perpetrators: "Anyone who walks with *beshèngu* [i.e., who carries it with him in order to use it], let him drop dead in his tracks." Still, according to some informants, those curses are often mouthed by the very people who own the stuff.

Other than the threat of witchcraft, that emanates from within the compound, the enemy within the gates so to speak (van Beek 1994), the threat of black magic comes from outside the immediate compound. Yet, it does not stem from real strangers, not from far away. In the ideas of the Kapsiki, *beshèngu* is sought after by people who are kinsmen, probably agnates, jealous of their clan- and lineage-brothers with a vested or occasional interest in their misfortune. A large inheritance may trigger the use or accusations of *beshèngu*, usually between the agnates competing for the inheritance.

Treating an affliction resulting from *beshèngu* is difficult and must be done by the same type of specialist who can produce the harmful magic himself.

These rites are very secret. The information I have on this treatment indicates that these curative rites are highly idiosyncratic, varying from specialist to specialist. Protection against *beshèngu* is more important than treatment and constitutes a continuous focus of daily Kapsiki religion. Whoever has gained some social prominence must live carefully in order to minimize the dangers. Protection against this threat focuses on the ways of transmission: how to keep the trained flies away, how to protect the compound against flying creatures, etc. A constant vigilance is needed, and any protection one may have against beshèngu must be kept in good shape. When *beshèngu* succeeds, it kills, so we will locate our revenge story in the aftermath of a funeral, the one we saw in our opening pastiche.

REVENGE: THE RITUAL

There is a good death, and there is a bad death. When a man dies after a long, eventful, and productive life, with his wives, children, in-laws, brothers, and friends mourning him, dancing frantically around him as he is seated astride the shoulders of the smith, with the drums going all out and the clans charging each other with clubs and spears, and with the boys and girls amusing themselves on the sides—that is a good death. All people die, but they do have some right to a life. When a man is robbed of such a life, when death is premature, and especially when someone has not only wished his death but actually produced it, when he cannot see his children grow up and his grandchildren enter this world—that is a bad death. And that death raises questions, important questions.[7]

In order to provoke these questions, a death should be sudden, without obvious cause, and untimely, that is of someone who should have more years ahead of him or her. More than anything else, the suspicion of *beshèngu* calls for revenge. But knowing the culprit is hard in this culture. None of the many Kapsiki divinatory practices—the crab, pebbles, cowries, the tweaking bird—are geared to deliver the names of culprits. They can indicate the influence of the ill will of a third party, but cannot go any further. So here enters the "art of revenge," the ways to get even with an unknown opponent, a hidden evil. Since the culprit is unknown this has to be an occult arena, as any revenge can only be done by ritual means, and in Kapsiki, this ritual is called *wuta*. The name is the word for a large jar, used for brewing beer, but seemingly also indicates a village in Nigeria—that is, the village where the ritual is performed. Actually, no Nigerian village bears this exact name, but the expression is *kadza wuta*, to go down to Wuta, and the village in question is far away, on the border with

Kilba country. This is one ritual I never witnessed—never could witness, in fact—but which I am sure was actually performed, and I will use one specific case for its description.

We saw Masi enter the throng of people waiting to dance with the corpse of Zra Wuvè and utter the fateful words: "Such is the taste of death." She was a widow who lived close to our compound, whom I knew well. Disaster had struck, as her son suddenly died, still quite young. A diviner indicated *beshèngu*, a probable diagnosis as the family had already suffered a loss: Masi's husband Tizhè had died almost a year before, which made the family vulnerable. So after her son's funeral she "went to Wuta." Two weeks after the funeral, a smith from Rumsiki, Ndewuva, came along with Masi to show her the way. They left at night because nobody should know about the date of her journey lest the culprit sorcerer would try to be there first. Masi brought along a lot of money, a large gown, iron bars, and a pair of leather sandals made from a real Kapsiki bull,[8] plus one thing belonging to her son, a medicine holder, mblaza. At sundown on the third day, they arrived at the village, in the ward Bassala. On the road they had encountered people, who had asked—a usual question— where she was going, and she had duly answered, "I am going to mourn someone." Any smiths and blind people she had met on the road, she had handed some money with the words "*A shala ke'yanga*" (May god guard you). The ritual expert, Tange, welcomed them in their own language and immediately poured water in a large *wuta*, the beer jar that stood out in the courtyard. She explained why she had come and gave him the money, the iron bars, the gown, the pair of sandals, and her son's mblaza. Medicine holders, usually small oblong iron containers, are worn on the body and are immensely private, an obvious choice for a magical referent.

Masi told me that the whole atmosphere of the place was quite business-like, everything focused on the ritual itself, which took place in the early morning. Tange came out with a calabash, a knife and his rhwɛ hidden in a bundle of straw and crouched by the jar with Masi next to him. He rattled his *rhwɛ* and shouted, "Come now!" Some tweeting sounds were heard from the water, which only he could understand,[9] not Masi, for, as she explained, in the *wuta* the spirits (*shinangkwe,* shadows) of her son plus all living people around him were assembling. Tange went on to interrogate them; Masi just heard some tweeting, but for him it was understandable language. He asked her son who had killed him, and when he learned the name, he summoned the culprit's spirit, interrogated him, and extracted his confession. As everyone has to tell the truth in the *wuta,* the truth came to light quickly. Tange said to him, "Come and drink beer," and when the culprit's spirit rose to the surface,

Tange wiped the dust from the water's surface with his straw, and stabbed his knife into the water. "It is finished," he told Masi, "do you want one dead or more?" It was now for Masi to decide how many people would die, and then he would stab as many times into the water. But she decided that only her son was dead, so only the real culprit had to die.[10] And anyway, if too many people were to be killed by this revenge, death would not stop but would proceed as an epidemic. Tange told her the spirits of kinsmen of the culprit might try to protect him in the jar, but then they would also risk being stabbed. To finalize the ritual, Tange wiped the water surface to see whether the culprit had indeed died, and he burned the straw under the *wuta*. Of the pair of shoes, he returned the left sandal to Masi, who then left him without saying anything and without looking back.[11]

About the return trip, Masi did not remember much and back in Mogode she shut herself in her own hut and stayed there for three days; for a deceased woman, it would have been four days. On the third day, she cooked *zhazha*—a meal of beans and maize that is central in the closing rites of the funeral— called in the children of the neighborhood, and had them eat it. Then she went to the blacksmith and had her head shaven, a sign of mourning again. By now everybody in the village knew that she had been to Wuta, and the great waiting for death started. Tension reigned in the village, but when weeks passed without anything untoward happening, life gradually took its normal course.

The sign people wait for is simply the first death of anyone who might be construed as the culprit killer. That can take weeks or even months, but each death is in principle suspect. In the case of Masi, it took three months, and she was in another village when she heard the news: Zra Wuvè had died, and quite a few members of his lineage were ill as well. Zra Wuvè was in fact a lineage brother of her late husband Tizhè, so for Masi, the suspicion of his involvement with both deaths, her husband's and her son's, came easily. Singing the dirges of mourning, she hurried back to Mogode, and there waited until the smith had taken the body on his shoulders in order to start the dance. The words she shouted, "Such is the taste of death," form the standard expression of revenge. So, immediately, the smiths understood what she meant and stopped the whole funeral. That was the moment of our opening case. But the situation was tricky, as Zra was very close with Masi and her late husband. Tizhè had been Masi's levirate husband, he had "inherited" her, so the immediate suspicion was jealousy between two "brothers of the same father," a ready locus for suspicion in Kapsiki; after all, these kinsmen tend to be more rivals than allies, and accusations between half-brothers are not uncommon, so in this case, the verdict was plausible: Zra Wuvè had "done it."

Yet, in these cases some doubt lingers on, as the possibility that the revenge death was "accidental" can never be excluded: if people accidentally touch or come near a strong *beshèngu*, it can hurt others than those intended, as there is a perennial risk of contagion. Magic is ungovernable and has its own agency. Ndewuva, who had accompanied Masi, tells of another case, from the village of Sir. That man's son had also died because of *beshèngu*, and he had taken it upon himself to revenge the death. After coming back from Wuta, he fell ill himself: he was the culprit, unknowingly and unwittingly. His own *beshèngu*, even if well hidden, had attacked and killed his son. The man had tried to accuse Ndewuva in a court case, but the village chief immediately dismissed the case because the man had possessed beshèngu and so had called death upon his own house.

So far, the wuta revenge follows the Kapsiki logic of inherent justice: the purported culprit is punished in kind. But the general tenor of occult revenge is one of excess, adding evil upon injury, for death through *wuta* is contagious: one does not punish by a death, but in principle through a string of deaths. At least Masi had restricted the revenge to the culprit, but some people are thought to be more vengeful and take out a whole family, and in any case, *wuta* is tricky, as this kind of death does not stop easily. It is, in principle, a small epidemic projected into a home. There is a way to counter this threat of an epidemic—to contain the "sorcerer's apprentice"—as it were, and that is where the left sandal comes in. As soon as people construe the death as provoked by wuta, all close kinsmen of the deceased rush to the one who has taken the revenge—in this case, to Masi. And that was exactly what happened, in her hut after the abrupt ending of the burial. All family members hurried, gave her some gifts and begged her to help; she took out the sandal and with it softly struck each of the family members on all their joints, from the left foot over the left side to the head and then down to the right foot. As one of them explained, as a family they were intrinsically involved: "If my brother kills someone and is summoned to *wuta*, his shadow will struggle in the jar. Just like his brother, my shadow will also be called to help him. Maybe I am also wounded somewhere. If the claimant comes back, and my brother dies, I will gather money to ask him to stop Death. We really have to beg, and have to give a lot. If she agrees, she taps us with the real Kapsiki shoe."

A sense of justice is culture bound, at least the measure of retribution is, and for the Kapsiki, revenge-by-epidemic seems fully commensurate. Death on the battle field is a normal risk, but being killed by *beshèngu* is not. Such a killing is covert, sly, and cowardly, an evil act; it is a hideous deed also, as it punctures one's privacy, breeching the many defenses a person has set up. Elsewhere (van Beek 1994), I have argued that Kapsiki protective magic aims at erecting a double defensive shield around the individual. The first one is the wall around his home, which is in fact very physical and eminently visible, but which has to be protected ritually in regular intervals, usually during home sacrifices (van Beek 2012, 60) in order to serve as a shielding second skin around the family. The second line of defense is the skin itself, which can be reinforced to withstand the attack of the trained flies, of the projected evil. Many concoctions of plants aim at just that, making the skin impenetrable. These ritual defenses all have to defend the cherished privacy and autonomy of the individual, inside and outside his home. So part of the very evilness of the dastardly deed of *beshèngu* is that it fundamentally ruptures identity: even inside one's own skin one cannot be oneself any longer.

To punish someone who purportedly used *beshèngu,* only a type of vengeance seems to suffice that smashes the identity of the culprit. Here the rules of the *keluhu* do not apply: there is no mother's brother to collect a rightful claim and no *wuzemakwa* to jump into the fray between these parties. Evil, in Kapsiki, is done purely individually, but it is so bad that it is contagious, an epidemic. All who would defend an evildoer would be in his league, so retribution would come their way as well, in fact the constant referent is that of an epidemic, so the whole family of the culprit is open for retribution from the start. They have to distance themselves from him, denouncing not only his act, but ritually severing their kinship relation with him. When the avenger strikes them on the joints with his Kapsiki sandal, she symbolically disengages the kinship bond between the family and their evil member, who just got what he deserved. The rapid, improvised grave is an even stronger indication of the end of kinship. The studious neglect of the proper rules of burial not only denounces his acts, it pushes the dead out of the realm of his descendants. They cannot inherit his qualities any longer, they do not unite at the graveside to build up the tomb as a symbol of his continuous fatherhood, and there will be no upright stones on his grave to indicate his progeny (van Beek 2012, 267). Also, when in January all tombs are finished and for all other deceased the new sacrificial jar filled with their beer of the grave is brought back to their son's compound, the son of the evildoer will have no jar representing his father and, therefore, no proper start of his own sacrifices. When performing his sacrifices later, he will not address his father. He has lost his father, completely, and the latter's unmarked shallow grave will be forgotten as soon as possible, as if he never existed. So the vengeance is terrible, an identity smashed post mortem through a complete denial of existence. Regular funerals allow for a long period of "deconceiving the deceased" as Barley calls it (1995, 132), but this reaction is "deconceiving his very existence," and that in one moment.

Though few people have actually witnessed the *wuta* ritual, it is not a secret, simply a ritual that few specialists master and one seldom uses. Recently, more smiths have taken up this ritual, and it seems to be done in Mogode as well, but then for clients from other villages.[12] A *wuta* specialist is never consulted by his own village. This is one ritual that is always performed in a distant village, for several reasons. The first reason is the general notion that magic from abroad is stronger than the homegrown variety, and, second, because one has to exert oneself for this kind of ritual; this kind of ritual force should not come easily. A third reason is that such ritual represents a violent intrusion into other people's lives and as such has to be done from afar. Kapsiki life is colored by the notion of privacy, and *wuta* is a serious invasion in privacy. One's own village is simply too close. Also, the guide comes from another village. Ndewuva, whom we saw feature in Masi's case, has specialized in guiding people to Wuta, based on a local knowledge he jealously keeps to himself. It is a lucrative business, and as such had to be earned.

> Ndewuva is from Rumsiki, a village at the Cameroonian side with close links to Nigeria. He had learned the whereabouts from his father and is the only one in Rumsiki who knows. Some years ago he spent five days in Uba, the main town of the Kilba people, in order to get to know the actual wuta specialist. It had cost him three large gowns to get that information, in a trial-and-error procedure where he had to try out who was the effective wuta performer. Now he knows, and he gets one gown for each time he guides. He explains that a person can claim the services of wuta only once in his or her life. And also for him, going back with the same person would become dangerous.

The occult arena is always multidimensional in African religions, with backdoors and sideways. First, the claimant seeking revenge can be evil: if he (or she) wants to inflict major damage on the culprit, he puts seeds on the grave of the deceased, and takes these to wuta. When the specialist puts these in the jar, an epidemic such as smallpox (still the most feared of all epidemics) will ravage the village. Ndewuva claims that he refuses to guide someone who aims at doing this. But, this is indeed an occult arena, and people hide their secret agendas. Each ritual specialist, especially a smith, knows magical means that will keep him from being summoned to *wuta*, means about which tall tales circulate in the village, involving stealing honey at the market or staying over in a tree for a night, etc. One specialist has a unique recipe for avoiding *wuta*: "One takes a melon, cuts it, and leaves the pieces in a pot with water for some months. When the melon has rotted, one drinks the liquid and buries the rest in a pot under the refuse heap. After a year one digs it up and makes a sauce out of the remains, and after eating that sauce one's spirit will not go to *wuta* anymore. Curiously enough, it is also a recipe for a long life."[13]

THE POWER OF REVENGE

After another death in the family much later, Masi went back for a second *wuta* session, but Ndewuva refused her and sent her home. He told me that he thought she had turned quite vindictive, seeking not so much revenge as simply to kill, to accrue destructive power. In Kapsiki cosmology, the sense of justice is crucial. The power of revenge stems from being in the right and the vulnerability for revenge from one's *fete*, guilt, being wrong. The notion of *fete* is crucial and shows two other ways people can inflict harm onto each other, ways which are not considered evil, but fully legitimate. One is the curse, *bedla*, and the other is the magical means to collect a debt, *sekwa*.

A curse can come from any kin: father, brother, father's brother/sister, initiation-father, or even mother, but from the mother's side it is most powerful. After all, the Kapsiki reason, those are the people who should love you; so if they curse you, they will have a very good reason. For instance, as the closest relative is one's mother, an ill wish from the mother outweighs anything else. Her brother comes as a close second, for if a nephew does not show proper respect for him, he may resort to a formal curse. This does not imply a great deal of ritual but is simply spoken: "If so-and-so has misbehaved against me in that manner, then. . . ." A wide variety of afflictions can be projected in this way, and the closer the relationship between the parties, the more dangerous the curse. The mother and her brother need, in fact, only to think the curse. The image of a mother chewing softly on her nipple and whispering some threats is an image that frightens any Kapsiki, for if nothing is done, all children that drank from that breast will die. I never witnessed a woman actually do this, but when enraged, they sometimes gesture toward a breast.

For any curse to be effective, the notion of one's own guilt, *fete*, is crucial. As the formula used in the *bedla* indicates, it is only effective in cases of factual and serious misbehavior, of real *fete*. If the accused one has done nothing wrong, he has nothing to worry about, the threat is fully conditional. Also, a stranger who does not have that relationship with the curser, is completely safe. But if the curser is "right," and especially if the cursed one is wrong, has fete, then the *bedla* hits in full force. So the power is in the relationship, the guarantee is in proper behavior, and the means to inflict harm is through thoughts and words.[14]

To reclaim unpaid debts, magical means are used, called *sekwa*, in which the same principle is operative, even stronger. In principle, *sekwa* is a means of ensuring the repayment of outstanding debts: when someone refuses to repay a debt, a creditor may put his *sekwa* in the debtor's compound and death will strike that compound like an epidemic, wiping out the debtor's household as well as anyone else who has ever eaten there. This *sekwa* may be used as a threat, but one that is seldom carried out. It is considered a perfectly legitimate means of enforcing repayment, and neither its manufacture nor its possession bears any social stigma. There is in principle no remedy against it except paying the debts immediately. When actually applied, it is put in the middle of the court-yard, visible to everyone, but things rarely go that far. It consists of a bundle of objects, and its composition is generally known. The crux is that it only works in cases of a real debt, for without it, the *sekwa* is just stuff that anybody can touch or remove.

Both *bedla* and *sekwa* are socially legitimate, even if the official courts in the Kapsiki area forbid the latter's use, claiming that it just aims to kill; yet, they are definitely not considered evil. One has to be pretty desperate to use them, for such measures are only justified after all moderation has failed. But both aim at the guilty ones, those who have *fete*. Both also share the notion of an epidemic in the family: the culprit may die, but he may take along his kinsmen as well, the same mechanism we saw in the *wuta* ritual. Both also are post hoc interpretations of mishaps or afflictions that may strike: one administers the curse, the *sekwa* or the *wuta* ritual, and then simply waits.

Sekwa and *bedla* are in themselves already expressions of revenge, of getting back at a debtor or a misbehaving kinsman. Both share the occult arena with the *wuta* ritual, and all three of them are based upon guilt, *fete*. Revenge is part of a sense of justice, or, to be more precise, it is an integral part of a sense of injustice. It is the wrongness that renders the culprit vulnerable, open to occult attack, and without defense. Rules for proper behavior are many, but never precisely formulated, but *fete*, wrongs, are easily recognized and widely debated. Guilt is clear, precise, and contagious.

Curses work, as we saw, only conditionally: "If he is my child, and if he has done that to me, then. . . ." These conditions are already fully met when one starts the formula, but the conditional wording is crucial. The cursing one has to be right, and the cursed one wrong. In *sekwa* debt collecting, the debt has to be there, acknowledged, and not yet repaid. *Wuta* only works when the summoned one is thought to have performed the ultimate evil act of *beshèngu*. And as the identities of kinsmen intermingle and merge, close family members can only be protected by taking their distance from their guilty kinsman.

Against an occult revenge, no defense is possible, as one's guilt weakens one's identity. The power of revenge stems from a clear and unambiguous recognition of wrongs, in fact from a recognition of suffering: the one who has suffered, who has been robbed of the proper rewards of his exertions and sufferings, accrues supreme power and is even inviolate. The mother's brother who lost his cherished *wuzemakwa* is inviolate in an enemy village, the groom who has worked hard and long for his bride may enter with complete immunity the enemy village where his bride has disappeared—if only once (van Beek 1987)—and the one who suffered a great loss through the evil of beshèngu cannot be slighted nor denied: accusation is enough for a full conviction, albeit post hoc. It is the combination of suffering and loss in the avenger and being wrong on the culprit's side that renders revenge so inordinately powerful. Rightful vengeance is so powerful that handling it calls for moderation, as justice and not killing should be the issue. Justified revenge is a terrible and irresistible force and demands great care; in fact, it should be performed only once in a lifetime. The catch, evidently, is in the moderation, as the occult arena tends to multiply afflictions, instead of solving them.

Where, in all this, is the "other world"; where are the gods and the ancestors? Ancestors in the classical African sense are absent in Kapsiki religion, and at the center of the Kapsiki cosmology is *shala*, a complex concept. *Shala* is one's personal god and, at the same time, the supreme deity. The difference is indicated usually by adding "my *shala*" or "*shala* in heaven." There is also the *shala* of a house, a group of people, a lineage, a ward, a village, so any relevant social echelon, in fact even any ad hoc group, has its proper *shala* (see van Beek 2012, chapter 6).[15] Two characteristics of this intricate cosmology are germane here: there is little distance between *shala* and the people, and the other world is fundamentally ambivalent and fuzzy. As each person has a personal god who easily blends into gods of other people, the relation with the other world is in principle close and does not need mediation, hence the absence of ancestors. As for the ambivalence, in principle *shala* does not do evil, that is for humans, but some *shala* may be tricky, such as those of enemies, of a strange village, or of the deep bush. One simply never knows with *shala*.

Though the other world is tricky, it is not evil, guided as it is by the same measures of justice that rule the human world. *Shala* will punish fete, though one never knows how and when. When people are afflicted, divination has to sort out the background reasons; in doing so, the diviner sets out the problem or affliction against the history of the client. Many afflictions stem from dissatisfaction of the other world, but in principle they are reparable; there is redress, because one can restore the relation with one's own *shala*. And ultimately, the interests between a person and his *shala,* the Kapsiki surmise, run parallel. Life is not expected to be without problems, but the hitches in one's life course should be within bounds.[16]

Evil deeds are quintessentially human. Having an unpaid debt is not evil, and being inconsiderate to one's mother's family is not necessary evil either, rather it is bad manners. But actually killing someone can be an evil act; even in killing an enemy one had to be careful, for revenge may just be as forceful or other worldly. It is the occult killing in one's own group that is fully evil, first because it is inside one's own group, but mainly because it is hidden, done by cowardly looking for breeches in the personal defenses of the intended victim. For this evil there is no excuse, and whoever has perpetrated it is wide open for full-scale magical revenge. Evil is the denial of relationships, of normalcy, and such is not ambiguous or ambivalent, but absolute. Both daily life and the other world in Kapsiki are characterized by ambivalence and fuzziness, and that is just what can be expected. But evil is the beyond the pale of normal ambivalence, evil acts are those that deny the fuzziness of human life and relations, the deep black between the paler shades of gray in human existence.

All three occult vengeances imply that retribution is in principle an escalation of the problem, not a solution. The reaction on perceived evil or injustice significantly adds to occult evil and does not redress wrongs, because occult arenas tend to multiply interpersonal problems; the threat with occult vengeance may refrain people, but its implementation multiplies wrongs, morphing a debt or guilt into an epidemic. In this essay, we have followed the emic Kapsiki definitions of evil, injustice, and retribution, as anthropologists are wont to do, but that leaves open one major analytical as well as existential problem. I started out the *wuta* story with my shock in seeing Zra Wuvè reduced to nothingness within half an hour. Someone I knew and had respected was denied a funeral, robbed of his kinship network, and his children were orphaned. I understand the sense of Kapsiki justice in this and can fathom their definitions of evil and retribution, but I do not share them. Anthropologists routinely follow a program of emic understanding and use a vantage point of methodological agnosticism in order to refrain from any truth questions. So much is standard practice, and for very good reasons. We learn to shift between worldviews and juggle as it were systems of understanding, feeling with our informants, bodily experiencing their events, and we are proud to do so. But the professional accolade inherent in this "methodological ludism" (Knibbe and Droogers 2011), this ability to play with hidden worlds, runs into trouble when dealing with notions of evil, and especially with retributions on purported occult evil. People do suffer because of these imagined wrongs and their all-too-concrete retributions. In that respect our Kapsiki case is still a rather benign one, as Zra Wuvè was hurt after his death more than before, and though the notion of *beshèngu* does generate some existential anxiety, that is still limited. Whatever one's methodological stance, there is no discussion with suffering. Elsewhere in Africa, witchcraft accusations, for instance, ruin lives and even lead to murder, for ontological reasons which I deeply believe to be absent, and the many victims of social retributions against imagined occult aggression deserve the support of such a statement.[17] Occult arenas are a case of "culture against man," inherently dangerous, easy to think of, and hard to get rid of, and we saw how an imagined affront in such an arena quickly leads to escalation, sliding rapidly from superficial justice to profound injustice.

NOTES

1. All personal names have been altered for reasons of privacy.
2. That part of the name is real.
3. The people are called Kapsiki in Cameroon and Higi in Nigeria, but they have to be considered one ethnic group (see van Beek 2012). Research among the Kapsiki/Higi started in 1972/1973 and has been going on since, with follow-up studies every four to five years; the last one was in January 2012. The financial assistance came from WOTRO (the Dutch Foundation for Tropical Research), Utrecht University, Tilburg University, and the African Studies Centre at Leiden, plus several other sources. The author gratefully acknowledges his debt to Michigan State University Press in being allowed to rework a part of the material presented here, as far as it relates to smiths.
4. The notion of evil as an analytical category has been introduced by the volume of David Parkin (1985).
5. For the specific properties of the Kapsiki witchcraft discourse, see van Beek (2007) and Danfulani (2007).
6. For a general description of the precolonial insecurity in the area, see Vaughan and Kirk-Greene (1995) and Reyna (1990). For an elaboration on the intricacies of the smith role in Kapsiki revenge magic, see van Beek (2015).
7. See for a general treatment of death rituals, Barley (1995), Metcalfe and Huntington (1991), and Bell (1997).
8. The Mandara Mountains house their own species of short-horned West Africa Bos taurus cattle, the "Boeufs Kapsiki," that have a special ritual position as well (van Beek 1998).
9. The Kapsiki know a divination technique using tweeting sounds, the *kwahɛ*, in which tweeting sounds are translated as the tonal layer of a sentence. See van Beek (2015, chapter 7).
10. Her husband had died in an accident.
11. Not looking backward is standard in Kapsiki rituals that emphasize separation; the same happens at various points of the funeral rites.
12. Gamache Kodji (2009, 49) reports having assisted at one such ritual in Mogode in 2008.

13. Melons are an important symbolic item. When a girl has delivered her baby under her father's roof—which is a large taboo—the groom (and presumed father) takes a similar melon, operates on it by cutting it open and removing the seeds, in order to sow these later. After all, one cannot operate on the mother, but one can on a melon. This ritual, in this case, also constitutes the wedding ritual, replacing the wedding feast as well as the bride's initiation rituals, just leaving a small bride price to be paid. See van Beek (1987).

14. For an extensive treatment of *bedla* and *sekwa*, see van Beek (2015).

15. For a comparison with the neighboring Mofu, see Vincent (1987, 2008).

16. For a thorough analysis of a similar cosmology, see Whyte (1997).

17. Ngong's argument that anthropologists tend to unwittingly and unwillingly legitimize witchcraft discourses is apt here (Ngong 2012). The distinction between the real and the imaginary is neither easy nor straightforward, and the general stance in this book is that making an a priori ontological distinction is not productive. However, at the end of the academic road, the discourse on evil makes a completely neutral stance dubious. As anthropologists, we do not want to take sides, but any discourse on evil in ontological terms—which is what emic systems engage in—more or less forces our hands. As an example of a more active stand, see Kgatla et al. (2003).

REFERENCES

Barley, Nigel. 1995. Dancing on the Grave: Encounters with Death. London: Abacus.

Bell, Catharine. 1997. Ritual, Perspectives and Dimensions. New York: Oxford University Press.

Danfulani, Umar H. D. 2007. "Anger as a Metaphor of Witchcraft: The Relation between Magic, Witchcraft and Divination among the Mupun of Nigeria." In Imagining Evil: Witchcraft Beliefs and Accusations in Contemporary Africa, edited by Gerrie ter Haar, 143–184. Trenton, NJ: Africa World Press.

Evans-Pritchard, Edward E. 1937. Witchcraft, Oracles and Magic among the Azande. Oxford: Clarendon Press.

Kgatla, T. Simon, Gerrie Ter Haar, Walter van Beek, and Jan de Wolf. 2003. Bridging Witchcraft Barriers in South Africa: Exploring Witchcraft Accusations: Causes and Solutions. Utrecht, the Netherlands: Faculty of Social Sciences Press.

Knibbe, Kim, and André Droogers. 2011. "Methodological Ludism and the Academic Study of Religion." Method and Theory in the Study of Religion 23:283–303.

Kodji, Gamache T. 2009. "Traditional Beliefs in Modern Society: The Case of the Kapsiki Blacksmiths of Mogode, North Cameroon." Master's thesis, Visual Culture Studies, University of Tromsø.

Metcalfe, Peter, and Richard Huntington. 1991. Celebrations of Death: The Anthropology of Mortuary Ritual. 2nd ed. Cambridge: Cambridge University Press.

Ngong, David T. 2012. "Stifling the Imagination: A Critique of Anthropological and Religious Normalization of Witchcraft in Africa." African and Asian Studies 11, no. 1/2:144–181.

Parkin, David, ed. 1985. The Anthropology of Evil. Oxford: Blackwell.

Peek, Philip, and Walter E. A. van Beek. 2012. "Reality Reviewed: Dynamics of African Divination." In Reviewing Reality: Dynamics of African Divination, edited by Walter E. A. van Beek and Philip Peek, 1–16. Berlin: LIT Verlag.

Reyna, Stephen R. 1990. Wars without End: The Political Economy of a Pre-colonial African State. Hanover, NH: University Press of New England.

Van Beek, Walter E. A. 1987. The Kapsiki of the Mandara Hills. Prospect Heights, IL: Waveland Press.

———. 1992. "The Dirty Smith: Smell as a Social Frontier among the Kapsiki/Higi of North Cameroon and Northeastern Nigeria." Africa; Journal of the International African Institute 42, no. 1:38–58.

———. 1994. "The Innocent Sorcerer: Coping with Evil in Two African Societies, Kapsiki and Dogon." In Religion in Africa: Experience and Expression, edited by Tom Blakely, Walter E. A. van Beek, and Dennis L. Thomson, 196–228. Oxford: James Currey.

———. 1998, "Les Kapsiki et leurs bovins." In Des taurins et des hommes: Cameroun, Nigéria, edited by Christian Seignobos and Eric Thys, 15–39. Paris: Office de Recherche Scientifique et Technique Outre-Mer.

———. 2007. "The Escalation of Witchcraft Accusations." In Imagining Evil: Witchcraft Beliefs and Accusations in Contemporary Africa, edited by Gerrie ter Haar, 293–316. Trenton, NJ: Africa World Press.

———. 2012. The Dancing Dead: Ritual and Religion among the Kapsiki and Higi of North Cameroon and Northeastern Nigeria. New York: Oxford University Press.

———. 2013. "Crab Divination among the Kapsiki/Higi of North Cameroon and Northeastern Nigeria." In Reviewing Reality: Dynamics of African Divination, edited by Walter E. A. van Beek and Philip M. Peek, 185–210. Berlin: LIT Verlag.

———. 2015. The Forge and the Funeral: The Smith in Kapsiki/Higi Culture. East Lansing: Michigan State University Press.

Vaughan, James H. Jr., and Anthony H. M. Kirk-Greene, eds. 1995. The Diary of Hamman Yaji: Chronicle of an African Ruler. Bloomington: Indiana University Press.

Vincent, Jeanne-Françoise. 1987. "Le prince et le sacrifice: Pouvoir, religion et magie dans les montagnes du Nord-Cameroun." Journal de la Société des Africanistes 2:89–121.

———. 2008. "Statut et puissance du 'Dieu-du-ciel' en Afrique de sahel." In "Dieu seul!" Le Dieu du ciel chez les montagnards du nord des Monts Mandara, edited by Joseph Fedry, Gabriel Djibi, Antonio Michielan, and Jeanne-Françoise Vincent, 147–178. Yaoundé: Presses Catholiques.

Whyte, Susan Reynolds. 1997. Questioning Misfortune: The Pragmatics of Uncertainty in Eastern Uganda. Cambridge: Cambridge University Press.

9 DISTINCTIONS IN THE IMAGINATION OF HARM IN CONTEMPORARY MIJIKENDA THOUGHT

The Existential Challenge of Majini

DIANE CIEKAWY

In discussions about spirit aggression and human agents of harm, Mijikenda,[1] whose lifeworld is centered in the coastal hinterland of Kenya, assert particular views about the importance of moral action. Their claims are imbedded in a complex of thought and practice that has been described by various works on Mijikenda religion, most notably by David Parkin in *Sacred Void: Spatial Images of Work and Ritual among the Giriama of Kenya* (1991). His comprehensive volume details central dimensions of Mijikenda thought and practice and offers conceptual schemes that provide a foundation for contemporary scholarship.

This essay examines what Parkin broadly refers to as eastern and western orientations in Giriama thought in an effort to understand Mijikenda conceptualizations of harmful magic. Eastern and western orientations will be used to explore ideas and practices in Aravahi and Arihe Mijikenda communities as they respond to two recent tragedies. In their discussions about the tragedies, Aravahi and Arihe focused on a particular class of spirit agents, *majini*, and the importance of the gerontocratic society of *kaya* elders who were called upon to provide a ritual response. As I discuss a range of views about harmful magic, therapeutic practices, and spirit and human agents, I rely on my work through successive courses of research in Mijikenda communities that began in 1982. My understanding of Mijikenda religion has greatly benefited from the work of David Parkin, Linda Giles, Monica Udvardy, and Jeanne Bergman.

THE UNPRECEDENTED VIOLENCE
OF TWO ROAD ACCIDENTS

In April 2011, a road accident of unprecedented proportions shocked residents of the Kenya Coast. A few minutes before nightfall, a group of passengers were hit by an oncoming transport truck as they disembarked from a crowded public vehicle known as a *matatu*. The *matatu* had been traveling on the Kaloleni-Mazeras road and had stopped at a regular vehicle station. Six people were killed and many others severely injured.

The accident was particularly unsettling for members of the Mijikenda subgroups whose homes and farmlands are located on either side of the Kaloleni-Mazeras road: Aravahi, Arihe, Akambe, and Agiriama. The road cuts through land that historically has been associated with each subgroup's community. All but one of the accident victims were Mijikenda. Thus the accident that killed many Mijikenda had occurred on what was conceptualized as Mijikenda soil.

Any accident involving extreme and sudden violence is disturbing in itself, and especially for older Mijikenda who tend to categorize such violent deaths as "bad death" (Parkin 1991, 130) that carry polluting potential. More significantly, this accident was unusual in both size and scope. Mijikenda in this hinterland region were not been able to recall an accident on the Kaloleni-Mazeras road where so many people were killed and injured and where so many Mijikenda lost kin and neighbors. Another reason why Mijikenda were so alarmed by this event was that earlier that year another bad road accident had taken place. The first one occurred in Ribe, only three months before the second accident in Rabai, and only a short distance north on the same road. It claimed the lives of two young women.

Witness accounts of the second accident left much to speculate about. It was odd the way the truck, careening down a hill, came to approach the disembarking passengers. It is common for *matatu* vehicles on the Kaloleni-Mazeras road to stop at known travel stations, and there are always some late *matatus* at twilight and after dark. But this truck, lights switched on, seemed not to slow down nor be able to veer away from a collision course. One witness recounted his wonder as he watched the lights of the truck illuminate the entire road, including the *matatu* and its passengers. Surely, the witness reasoned, any driver with full mental faculties would have seen the passengers and could have avoided them for there also seemed to be plenty of room on the side of the road where the truck traveled. According to another witness, as the truck approached the accident site it swerved from side to side while continuing to return to the same focused course, as if the driver were wrestling with another person who also held the wheel.

As hinterland Mijikenda residents reflected on these two events, stories of the deceased youth held their attention most: the doubly tragic situation of the girl who was on her way to her father's funeral, and the brother and sister who were returning to their respective schools in Kaloleni and Ribe. Youth snatched from the world before their prime, before reaching an expected stage of development, was a central theme that not only heightened their families' loss, but also recognized the disruption of reproductive power that would provide lineage continuity. Central in discussions about the accident were remarks about its extreme violence, with the spilling of so much blood that desecrated the soil in Rabai and Ribe.

INTERPRETATIONS: A CASE OF *MAJINI*?

The search for satisfactory explanations for why two terrible accidents occurred, in the space of three months and within a short distance from each other, dominated discussions for months after the events. Almost two years later, Mijikenda in Rabai and Ribe continue to speculate about the accidents and remark about their extraordinary qualities. Not only are community members still grieving and taking care of the injured, but they also continue to debate about how their communities might respond to similar tragedies in the future. People still wonder what these accidents indicate about the existence of spirit aggression and human malevolence that might have directed this violence. They continue to discuss their options for acting collectively to prevent such accidents and reflect on the solution that was chosen in 2011.

A series of discussions and interviews conducted by Harold Kodo provide insight into the perspectives of Aravahi and Arihe community members regarding the two road accidents.[2] These discussions and interviews reveal three patterns in thought and argument. The first is that that nearly all of respondents thought that *majini* (sing. *jini*) were the spirit agents that caused both accidents. Only two of the respondents viewed the accidents as the exclusive fault or negligence of the driver, without the intervention of harmful magic involving *majini*. The second is that nearly two thirds of all the respondents thought the most appropriate way for their communities to counter the threat of *majini* and to deter practitioners of harmful magic was to rely on the cleansing and protection rituals of *kaya* elders, a group of men who belong to a gerontocratic male secret society. A smaller number of respondents, nearly one sixth, considered or advocated another action in response to the accidents: hiring a witch-finder. The third is that almost half of the respondents stated or suggested that the human agent(s) that instigated the harmful magic resided in the hinterland and were probably Mijikenda.

What does it mean for Mijikenda to suspect the involvement of *majini* in the creation of harm? As long as I have been engaged in discussion of magic that results in harm to human beings, which in Kimijikenda is glossed as *utsai*, I have heard both Mijikenda religious specialists and lay people describe *majini* as powerful spirits that can create great harm (Ciekawy 1992). Over the past twenty years, some of the ideas that Mijikenda have expressed about *majini* have remained relatively stable, while others seem to have emerged more recently.

My own work focuses on Mijikenda whose primary lifeworld is in the coastal hinterland, and whose conceptual frameworks draw from Mijikenda religious thought. They share with other people of the Kenya Coast a wealth of ideas about the etiology of illnesses, healing practices, and various classes of spirits (see also Giles 1989b). It is generally assumed that a person who engages in magic for the purpose of obtaining wealth or power might cultivate relationships with *majini*, which are one among many classes of spirit agents. *Majini* are extremely powerful and can exert extraordinary violence in human life. *Majini* desire the blood of animals, including human beings, and over time they increasingly ask their human partners for more and bigger sacrifices. In 1987, an Aravahi *muganga* (healer) shared with me some of the dynamics: "*Majini* want blood, the blood of animals. They can begin drinking from animals that are sacrificed for them, such as goats and sheep, but with time they will want larger animals, and more blood. They will progress to want to take the life of humans. The person who started with them, who has been benefitting from what they bring him/her, will face problems later, for the demands of *majini* increase and increase. The person who starts with them (*majini*) is not thinking of what the demands will be later."

Eventually *majini* require the lives of human beings in order to satisfy their appetites and to continue working for their human partner. Thus, the general understanding is that *majini* are used by practitioners of magic to acquire wealth or power, but that this wealth and power comes at a huge human price. Among Aravahi and Arhihe Mijikenda living in the hinterlands, this use of harmful magic (*utsai*) is viewed in opposition to magic used for healing (*uganga*).[3] Among Aravahi and Arihe Mijikenda living in the hinterlands, it is commonly thought that both kin and neighbors are the most frequent victims in a practitioner's use of this kind of magic (Ciekawy 1992).

In the mid-1980s I engaged a range of Mijikenda religious specialists consisting of *kaya* elders, diviners, and healers in discussions about changes in the incidence and spread of *majini* in coastal Kenya.[4] These religious specialists perceived a shift in the relative influence of spirits who acted in their hinterland world. They not only recognized the increased influence of spirits associated with Islam, but the increasing influence of *majini* within the entire Kenya Coast (Ciekawy 1992). All of the interlocutors conceptualized the influence of *majini* with a spatial dimension and assumed that *majini* were used by Swahili and Arab practitioners.

They argued that there were two reasons why in the hinterland the lower incidence of human misfortune was a result of *majini*. One was that there were few magic practitioners of *majini* in the hinterland, but there were many on the coast. This view assumed that the knowledge and skills in the use of *majini* were held by Swahili and Arab practitioners and had not been adopted by Mijikenda living in the hinterlands. They reasoned that there were fewer Mijikenda than Swahili or Arab practitioners of *majini* because Swahili and Arab people who wished to learn about *majini* lived in closer proximity to teachers of those skills and were familiar with other Swahili magic forms that would assist them to learn about *majini*. Swahili and Arab magic practitioners therefore had easier and greater access to the magic traditions that concerned *majini*. The second reason given for the lower incidence of human misfortune in the hinterland as a result of *majini* was that it was difficult for *majini* to reach Mijikenda in the hinterlands. The religious specialists assumed that *majini* sent by magic practitioners from the coast could not travel far. In these and other discussions about *majini*, Mijikenda conceptualized clear associations between *majini* and magic practitioners who were Swahili and Arab.

Another set of reasons offered by a small number of religious specialists was based on differences between Mijikenda, on the one hand, and Swahili and Arab peoples, on the other. A few Mijikenda healers I spoke with presented *majini* as an extreme form of *utsai* that Mijikenda did not engage. One healer claimed, "Aravahi are Mijikenda, and Mijikenda do not keep *majini*," seeming to make an ontological claim about the kinds of spirits that were partnered with Mijikenda. Another Aravahi healer expressed his doubt about Mijikenda healers' interest in learning how to use *majini*, even ones trained in what he called Swahili healing traditions. He made the following statement: "Yes, there are some healers among us who rely on skills and knowledge of all those spirits on the side of Swahili, and those that we can access by becoming Muslim. But we are not Waswahili or Warabu . . . we cannot mix with *majini*. *Utsai*, it is here, but those *majini,* they are not for we Mijikenda. We refuse those *majini. Majini* can come to interfere with our lives, but we do not keep *majini.*" In this statement, the healer appears to be making an argument for a distinctive Mijikenda moral sensibility. He implies that Mijikenda draw a line when it comes to using the power of *majini* for harmful purposes, but Swahili and Arab peoples do not.

In both statements, the healers not only contrasted the practices and inclinations of Mijikenda with those of Swahili and Arab peoples, but they seemed to suggest that the choice to not engage *majini* was guided by ontological principles. The distinction made between the two groups that was offered by the second healer can be interpreted as an idealized Mijikenda-centric view of moral behavior. Assessing the relative potential for Mijikenda, Swahili, and Arab peoples to engage in acts of harmful magic, he distinguishes the superior moral qualities of Mijikenda peoples. And although he did not assert the ontological superiority of Mijikenda outright, he implied that Mijikenda were destined to follow some moral principles that Swahili and Arab peoples did not.

Some twenty years later in 2006 and 2008, conversations I had with Mijikenda religious specialists indicated that there were new trends in thought about *majini.* Like the perspective expressed in previous decades, many Mijikenda said they thought *majini* acted mostly on the coast and especially in Swahili communities. But many of the people I spoke with in 2006 and 2008 also said that *majini* could travel long distances in order to attack human victims. Some imagined that *majini* could travel throughout the Kenya and Tanzania coasts. As in the past, interlocutors claimed that the influence of *majini* was greater than in previous decades. In these conversations about *majini,* I also heard more about Arab medicines and the role of Islam than in previous decades.

MORE INTERPRETATIONS OF THE ROAD ACCIDENTS

Returning to the discussions and interviews conducted by Harold Kodo concerning the road accidents in Rabai and Ribe, interlocutors revealed other opinions and lines of reasoning that permit a greater understanding of some of the communities' conclusions and actions. Many interlocutors explained why the larger and more devastating accident occurred in Rabai. Among all of the hinterland Mijikenda communities, they argued, Rabai has the largest number and density of magic practitioners. It was therefore more likely to have a practitioner of *majini* among the residents. Many commented that the accidents demonstrate a decided trend in the hinterland for magic practitioners who desire wealth and power to become more adventurous in learning magic techniques that include *majini* and who were more inclined to use magic that results in greater harm to human beings. Others observed that Mijikenda in the hinterlands seemed to be increasingly motivated to acquire wealth than they were in the past. The majority of the interlocutors also assessed that there have not been sufficient ritual means to prevent the work of practitioners of harmful magic, and that more regular solutions should be employed by Mijikenda communities.[5] In most of the discussions, Aravahi and Arihe demonstrated concern about the best ways to deter *utsai* practitioners. All thought that it was important to cleanse the land, but as noted earlier, not everyone thought that the actions of *kaya* elders were sufficient for the prevention of future problems. Those who advocated using a witch-finder were following the logic of another common practice, but one that has the potential to be socially divisive and volatile.

These discussions and interviews indicate that a significant group of Aravahi and Arihe think that Mijikenda magic practitioners who reside in the hinterland have mastered skills to manipulate relationships with *majini*. This perception parallels their observations about general trends in the Mijikenda desire for wealth and implies that Mijikenda behavior toward harmful magic is in transformation. This implies that if Mijikenda of the hinterlands are now expected to rely on *majini*, then they probably expect the extreme forms of harmful magic to increase. Aravahi and Arihe seem less likely now than in the past to assume that there is an ethical limit on the part of Mijikenda practitioners, a limit that once resulted in their refusal to engage in magic relying on *majini* and that used to be associated with Swahili and Arab practitioners.

CONCEPTUAL DISTINCTIONS BETWEEN
THE EAST AND WEST

It is important to remember that the perspectives and thoughts expressed by Aravahi and Arihe discussed here are shaped by what I can refer to as a hinterland positionality. These Mijikenda occupy a particular place, in terms of both the political economy of their hinterland existence and their exposure to particular kinds of therapeutic practices. They solely or primarily reside in hinterland communities and have continual exposure to a discourse about harmful magic in relation to Mijikenda personhood and sociality as influenced by a religious complex rooted in the centrality of the *kaya* and cyclical rituals of cleansing and protection.

Key aspects of this complex are examined by Parkin (1991) in *Sacred Void: Spatial Images of Work and Ritual among the Giriama of Kenya*. Parkin presents a series of contrasts that shape Giriama perceptions of themselves, compared to other peoples and lifestyles in their region. While Parkin's arguments are specifically based on his research in Giriama Mijikenda communities of Mijikenda, I find that his general observations are also applicable to Rabai and Ribe hinterland communities. Parkin's presentation of conceptualizations of Giriama notions of space is especially useful in this discussion. He examines Giriama notions of space as relational and organized through an opposition between the east and the west (Parkin 1991, 18–25). In this binary, the west comprises the sacred *kaya* forest and a lifestyle dominated by pastoralism and some forms of agriculture ("the traditional"), standing in contrast to the east, which is characterized by mixed boundaries, a lifestyle shaped by a blend of different peoples and wage labor, which also presents to the west the danger of cultural contaminants from Islam, tourism, upcountry migrants, Christianity, and expanding consumerism (Parkin 1991, 7, 14). He characterizes the representations of the east and the west as the eastern gaze and the western gaze.

As Parkin states, "the western gaze is, then, an expression of cultural identity. Paradoxically, the more the Giriama become involved in the ethnic and economic diversification and dependency of the coast, the more the western hinterland takes on the character of an autochthonous region considered essential for the preservation of Giriama identity" (Parkin 1991, 21). Giriama in the 1990s imagine the kind of lifestyle and moral universe that ideally characterize them, in contrast to their relevant others, the Swahili.

Claims about the differences between Mijikenda and Swahili as presented in discourses about spirits and power have been well documented by Giles (1989a, 1989b). She shows how the dominant economic position of Swahili in the past and present clearly informs imagination about Swahili skills in spirit aggression. This theme can be observed in Mijikenda discourses concerning witch-finders and politicians over the past thirty years (Ciekawy 2006, 2014a). Contrasts between Giriama and Swahili also have been addressed in the work of McIntosh with respect to the Malindi area of the Kenya coast, where she finds that *jini* spirits are associated with forms of mobility that come with trade and commodity markets (McIntosh 2009). In all of the preceding works, distinctions concerning the lifeways of the two ethnic groups dialectically shape distinctions between their perceived magical powers. I will return to these beliefs and their relationship to spatial contrasts in order to further interpret the ways in which healers in Rabai and Ribe present their views about the uses of harmful magic and *majini* in the hinterlands.

SPIRIT AGENTS, HUMAN AGENTS, AND
THE POWER OF THE KAYA

For Aravahi and Arihe, as for other peoples of the coast, *majini* are generally associated with Islam and the power of the Swahili Coast and wider Arab
world. Along with many other spirit pantheons found throughout East Africa,
they can be understood to represent various forms of hegemonic power that
historically have exerted influence over the lives of Mijikenda. Mijikenda understandings of the nature and behavior of *majini* are grafted onto historical
memories of the slave trade and the political and economic disadvantages they
experienced as Swahili, British, and up-country Kenyan peoples managed to
gain control over various forms of wealth produced at the coast. Like other
discourses concerning spirits and human agents, they can stand for Mijikenda
marginalization within the postcolonial state as they fail to achieve sufficient
power to reclaim and protect what they consider to be their rightful resources
and to successfully participate in the political and economic life of the coast
(Ciekawy 1992, 2009, 2014a, 2014b).

Discourse about *majini* can be examined for its assertions about sociopolitical relationality, pointing to the ways in which Mijikenda positioned in the
hinterland perceive the qualities of their own communities in relation to other
groups in Coastal Kenya. If we return to the case of the two accidents, and the
general public's diagnosis of *majini*, we can consider how Aravahi and Aravi
who identify with the (more) "western" orientation might respond to the challenge of unprecedented violence and spirit aggression, discursively identified
with *majini*.

Aravai and Arihe communities suffered greatly in 2011, both in terms of
accident victims and in terms of the polluting effects from the accident. Their
soil was in a state of desecration as a result of the violence of these deaths.
Many people worried because they assumed *majini* and human agents were
responsible for the tragedies, and they wondered whether more harmful activities would occur in the future.

In the precolonial past, most matters that broadly affected Mijikenda life
were directly and indirectly controlled by *kaya* elders. At times of collective
threat, the guidance and intercessory power of the *kaya* framed events. *Kaya*
wisdom and *kaya* action were considered to be the primary means to protect,
renew, and cure many large-scale problems and contagious diseases, including
the threat of contamination from bad death and other challenges to the purity
of the land.

MIJIKENDA *KAYA* INSTITUTIONS AND *KAYA* SOLUTIONS

Until the mid-nineteenth century, each Mijikenda subgroup was identified with a ritual center located in a forest called a *kaya* (pl. *makaya*). In each forest there was also a fortress constructed for defense against the raids of pastoralists and slave traders (Spear 1978). Progressive advancement in the age-set system and induction into secret societies provided both men and women with status and sociopolitical power (Spear 1978; Brantley 1978, 1981). The senior men of the male age-set system participated in a discussion and decision-making institution called the *kambi,* constituting the central governance institution in each subgroup. In the late nineteenth century, as Mijikenda increasingly constructed dispersed settlements outside the *kaya,* clan and lineage senior men largely replaced the authority of the *kambi* (ibid.). Many of the religious, legal, and political practices of the men's secret societies continued in modified forms and are considered to be central functional and symbolic features of Mijikenda life today.[6] Most of the women's social and political organizations declined, although some of their forms of knowledge and practice are reproduced informally through enculturation and in healing societies.

By the late nineteenth century, it became increasingly more common for Mijikenda to seek the assistance of independent healers *(aganga;* sing. *muganga)* in addition to the Mijikenda elders whose knowledge and skills were based in closed societies. Both groups diagnosed and treated problems concerning physical health, social relationships, and misfortune. *Aganga* have drawn their knowledge and skills from many different traditions, some of which had been established in Mijikenda closed societies, and others that were learned from neighboring groups, particularly Swahili. By the mid-twentieth century there were distinctive fusions of Mijikenda and Swahili healing traditions available in both coastal communities and in the hinterland, which Parkin identified as a particular form of ritual syncretism (1970).

In Kimijikenda, men who have been inducted into any of the secret societies of the *kaya* can be referred to as *azhere a kaya* (elders of the *kaya*). In English, these men are called *kaya* elders. Reflecting on the use of the term in the 1980s and 1990s among Giriama, Parkin (1991, 38) finds that the term *kaya* elder has "come to refer to many influential elders who are not exceptionally senior, but who participate in the judicial and ritual activities from and in the name of the *kaya.*" The range of activities understood by Mijikenda to fall under the province of the *kaya* and popular representations of *kaya* work vary considerably, having been subjected to great popular political controversy over the past twenty years (Ciekawy 2009, 2014a; Mitsanze and Giles 2013).

As part of their induction into a *kaya* organization within a Mijikenda community, *kaya* elders receive formal training in the knowledge and practices of the organization and informal training through their participation in meetings that require oratorical skills and philosophical debate (Ciekawy 1997, 2000). Like many other Mijikenda elders, they are experienced judges and arbiters in legal councils, but they have more specific knowledge of Mijikenda philosophy and *desturi* (tradition) (Ciekawy, Parkin 1968). They also provide Mijikenda with blessings to ensure success as they undertake a change in status, engage in a legal trial, or are involved in a competition (Parkin 1991).

Kaya elders singularly maintain the knowledge and skills to use certain forms of esoteric power and the ability to collectively mediate relationships between living Mijikenda and the spirits of important deceased lineage elders (*koma*).[7] Within *makaya*, there are locations reserved for the rituals devoted to this purpose. These locations are considered to be especially sacred within the entire *kaya*, which is itself already sacred with respect to the rest of the land considered to be historically connected to early Mijikenda settlement (Spear 1978; Parkin 1991). Those who do not adhere to rules concerning access to the *kaya* might pollute the *kaya*, which would require *kaya* elders to conduct cleansing rituals in order to restore the *kaya* to a state of wholeness and purity.[8]

The work and responsibilities of *kaya* elders, compared to those of the *aganga*, maintain a greater focus on collective rituals and on the collective welfare of Mijikenda (Ciekawy 1992). Where strong *kaya*-based secret society organizations still exist, such as among Aravahi and Agiriama, *kaya* elders conduct rituals to protect and ensure human and crop fertility and to prevent epidemics (Ciekawy 1992, 1997; Parkin 1991). Other subgroups of the Mijikenda have discontinued the institutions or have smaller and less regular practices (Ciekawy 2014b). Over the last decade there has been a revival of many *kaya* organizations and a new wave of innovations in *kaya* organizations, particularly among Agiriama (Mitsanze and Giles 2014; Tengeza and Nyamweru 2014).

Aravahi *kaya* elders view their responsibilities with great seriousness and devote a large amount of time each week to particular social, political, and material activities concerning the *kaya*. In addition to weekly meetings with other *kaya* elders, conducting prayers and engaging in collective rituals, Aravahi *kaya* elders participate in efforts to educate Mijikenda people about both customary Mijikenda medical perspectives and biomedical ones.[9]

For most Mijikenda, *kaya* elders, the *kaya* forest, and the knowledge and rituals associated with the *kaya* form dominant reference points. Both *kaya* elders and *kaya* forests are central to Mijikenda identity, but are understood or imagined differently in ways that reflect the changing lifestyles of Mijikenda people (Parkin 1991). Regardless of the variety of meanings the term *kaya* carries, Mijikenda generally agree that the term *kaya* stands for Mijikenda tradition and continuity in a larger society characterized by legal and religious pluralism.

After each accident in 2011, the strong organization of Rabai *kaya* elders discussed the problem in their weekly meetings and then presented their ideas to influential community leaders. In March 2011 and September 2011, cleansing and protection ceremonies were held in both communities. They were made in both the locations of the accidents and at the homesteads of most of the deceased. Thus they addressed both individual family and larger collective concerns, responding to problems of social rupture and the restoration of the purity of the land. Because Arihe do not have a stable organization of *kaya* elders, their need for the rituals was met by the *kaya* elders of Rabai. According to several *kaya* elders in Rabai, their work in Ribe was also noteworthy because in the recent past it has not been common for *kaya* elders of one subgroup to conduct rituals for another subgroup.

As in other discussions about harmful magic, Mijikenda in these communities were able to critique uses of power (Ciekawy 1998, 2001). They examined their moral standards and decided on courses of action regarding unacceptable acts of violence. Aravahi and Arihe people's overwhelming support for *kaya* elders to conduct rituals asserted the value of Mijikenda ways of approaching moral problems. The ritual of cleansing is accompanied by a ritual of protection, which is considered to stifle the actions of *atsai*. These decisions and actions affirm the wisdom of Mijikenda-centered approaches to large-scale threats. Contained within this solution is the assumption that human beings have both the choice to undertake harmful magic and the choice to combat it.

WHAT KIND OF HARM, AND IS IT EVIL?

Citing the distinction made by Middleton (1960) between the witch and the sorcerer among Lugbara, as the "understandable witch" and the "truly evil one," Parkin (1991, 205) makes a parallel to Giriama conceptualizations. He argues that Giriama distinguish between a person who becomes a witch as a result of circumstances and whose resentment is partly excusable, which he describes as an "indigenous Giriama witchcraft which can be controlled by traditional means" (ibid.). This can be compared to "the image of autonomous coastal witches who are said to have increased in recent years as a result of the new climate of material desire at the coast under modern influences" (ibid.). Thus, Parkin implies that Giriama imagine that the coast harbors a kind of harmful magic that has different moral implications than the kinds practiced among Giriama associated with the western orientation (see also Parkin 1985). It is possible to wonder whether Giriama might view the kinds of harmful magic of the eastern orientation as evil, in contrast to the lesser forms that are common in the western orientation.

In my own work in Rabai and Ribe from 1984 to the present, I have found that most people make distinctions in their interpretation of the actions of a *mutsai* (pl. *atsai*), but I cannot characterize this distinction as binary.[10] I have found that many Aravahi and Arihe distinguish among *atsai* by qualifying the kind of harmful magic used and categorizing it as "small," "lesser," and "greater" (Ciekawy 2001). In assessments about human involvement in an act of *utsai,* discussion is characterized by a great deal of contextual analysis. Opinions most often evolve through gradual qualifications in a conversation rather than being offered with an immediate assessment or proclamation. Discussions also involve the measurement of parameters such as the degree of harm done to human beings and the *mutsai*'s intention, which is usually assessed according to the degree of selfishness involved (ibid.). Thus, greater uses of *utsai* are marked, but they are not necessarily categorized in an unambiguous manner that might be described as evil.

In the views expressed by Aravahi and Arihe about the road accidents in 2011, there is no doubt that the accidents represented a great kind of harm. This perception is consistent with the larger discussion about *jini*-led accidents in Coastal Kenya. For Aravahi and Arihe, the extreme degree of human suffering brought about by the actions of these *utsai* practitioners occupied the far end of a continuum. The accidents were also understood to come from an extreme act of human malevolence, which is perhaps as close to a notion of evil as most Mijikenda might entertain.

Majini have been present for some time in Mijikenda healing practices as members of a broad spirit pantheon inhabiting the Kenya and Tanzania coasts. For Aravahi and Arihe Mijikenda, *majini* have often been associated with Islamic therapeutic practices and practices of harmful magic. More recently, perhaps since the early 1980s, they began to articulate a perception that the actions of the violent and harmful *majini* were increasing in power and in geographic scope. Discussions about the recent accidents in Rabai and Ribe indicate that some Mijikenda in the hinterland think Mijikenda magic practitioners in the hinterland use *majini* and that this partnership was responsible for the two road accidents. Compared to the views about *majini* in the 1980s, this seems to suggest Mijikenda magic practitioners in the hinterland are perceived to cross moral lines that previously distinguished them from Swahili practitioners.

Discourses about both *majini* and *kaya* continue to offer ways for hinterland Mijikenda to conceptualize a variety of peoples and processes that stand in hegemonic relationship to hinterland life and their more idealized notions of Mijikenda collective identity. These hegemonic peoples and forces are conceptualized through acts of historical memory. Applying Parkin's understanding of the contrasts Giriama make between an "eastern orientation" and a "western orientation," where the hinterland is opposed to the coast and the rural is opposed to the urban, Mijikenda can be generally positioned in opposition to various alter egos in addition to the historically dominant Swahili alter ego. The range of peoples and processes that have undertaken action opposing Mijikenda interests is wide. For hinterland Mijikenda, discourses about *majini* can perform a certain kind of work that examines the relatively marginal social, political, and economic position Mijikenda have held in the wider affairs of the Kenya Coast and to subject to moral scrutiny the problems generated from immense inequalities.

It is possible that the fear that *majini* represent to hinterland Mijikenda peoples, while engaging a history characterized by the force of dominating groups and the loss of Mijikenda opportunities, also can be understood to reflect a more recent existential crisis. It is perhaps influenced by the perception of a world more out of control than the recent past indicates and one that is even less responsive to cultural and social values of the past (see Ciekawy 2001, 2014a). In the case of the road accidents described in this essay, it is also possible to view discourse about *majini* in opposition to *kaya* as a measure of the degree to which people situated in a Mijikenda ethnoreligious space choose to assert their distinctive worldview and the usefulness of their own practices. Overall, they affirm the value of their own ethnoreligious response.

Mijikenda who view *majini* as a form of *utsai* consider both *majini* and the human practitioners of magic who cultivate and harbor *majini* also to be a threat to moral existence. *Majini* destroy healthy bodies and sever bonds that promote fruitful collective existence. For the hinterland Aravahi and Arihe Mijikenda discussed in this work, *majini* represent a threat that their *kaya* institutions were prepared to counter. Under the leadership of *kaya* elders, a clear response was formulated and executed through cleansing and protection ceremonies. By mid-2012, many Aravahi and Arihe reported to Harold Kodo that they were satisfied with their communities' response and considered it to be the best solution. It is also noteworthy that the Aravahi *kaya* elders offered their expertise to the Arihe Mijikenda community that did not have *kaya* leadership. Here, ethnoreligious solidarity was extended and celebrated.

In 2011, a boundary concerning moral existence was challenged and tested in both communities. *Kaya* elders and community members, drawing on the collective imagination of the purity and autochthony of what Parkin terms a western gaze, advanced their ideas about what qualities and powers define their world. The decision to support *kaya* cleansing and protection rituals in response to the spirit aggression of *majini* and the interests of amoral *atsai* continued to inscribe one of the grand oppositions that have characterized Mijikenda thought and action. *Kaya,* as a symbolic assertion of not only Mijikenda but human possibilities, can be further understood as an affirmation of the power of human moral choice. *Kaya* offered a particular path of collective wisdom and action. In this hinterland lifeworld there is a strong will to maintain the moral commitment to collective wellness and to use the power of a time-worn religious tradition to respond to the threat of superlative harm.

NOTES

I thank William Olsen for his dedication to the creation of the panel for which this essay was originally written. I am grateful to the following people whose comments have improved this work: Rebecca Gearhart, Linda Giles, William Olsen, and V-Y. Mudimbe.

1. Mijikenda are a people composed of nine closely related subgroups that share a common language and history (Parkin 1972; Spear 1978). The groups that compose the Mijikenda include the Adigo, Aduruma, Akambe, Achonyi, Aravai, Arihe, Agiriama, Ajibana, and Akauma. Most rural Mijikenda speak both Kiswahili and their subgroup dialect of Kimijikenda. Mijikenda reside in all parts of Kenya, but the majority settle on the coast, and the majority on the coast live in rural areas often referred to as the hinterland.

2. Harold Kodo and I have cooperated on research projects over the past twenty-five years. Harold Kodo conducted the interviews and discussions on which this section of the essay is based. From July 2011 to September 2011 and from February 2012 to June of 2012, he held thirty-seven discussions and conducted formal interviews with twenty-three adult men and women who live in the Aravahi and Arihe communities. He and I established the questions and discussed responses through email correspondence.

3. *Uganga* is a Kimijikenda and Kiswahili word that refers to diagnostic, protective, and curative skills that usually involve medicines, although it can refer to any act of healing. These skills are acquired through training, and with the assistance of spirits, healers treat problems of misfortune and illness.

4. Mijikenda religious specialists provided more elaborate knowledge of *majini* compared to laypeople and made many distinctions among kinds of *majini*. While laypeople usually referred to these spirits in the plural, placing the *ma* prefix on the singular term *jini*, healers and others with specialized knowledge of the spirit world placed emphasis on individual *jini* and referred to them by name, such as Jine Bahari. Aravahi

and Aduruma healers often used a slightly different pronunciation for *jini,* placing an "e" at the end of the word (*jine*). As Giles (1989b) explained in her work on Swahili and Mijikenda understandings of particular spirits from the 1980s, both *mashetani* (sing. shetani) and *jini* have the potential to assist human beings in the orchestration of processes and events that both (heal) or harm the human beings to whom magic is directed. We can note that the dominant view expressed by Mijikenda laypeople in my work conducted in the 1980s, later echoed in 2006, is that *majini* facilitate magic that results in harm to human beings.

5. The perception of growing threats from *utsai* and insufficient ritual means to prevent *utsai* has been a continual feature of all of my work over the past twenty-five years. The political implications of this perception are discussed extensively in Ciekawy (1992, 1998, 2006).

6. Both Parkin (1991) and Willis (1993) understand contemporary academic and local Mijikenda notions of the *kaya* in terms of historical contingencies. Parkin's (1991) argument about *kaya* as "sacred void" enables us to understand the range of referents, past and present, that connect notions of *kaya,* including the meanings that have been grafted onto *kaya* since the advent of more commoditized notions of medicine, collective identity formed in dialogue with processes of globalization, and the growing perception among Mijikenda that they are culturally, politically, and economically marginalized within the country of Kenya.

7. Both through personal interest and the encouragement of lineage members, Aravahi *kaya* elders have studied from two to fifteen years to become members of *kaya* societies (Ciekawy 1997, 2000).

8. Refer to Parkin (1991) for extensive discussions on notions of purity in relation to the *kaya.*

9. Since 2001, Aravahi *kaya* elders have asked Harold Kodo, a community health specialist, and I to organize workshops to discuss selected biomedical ideas in accessible terms. We have organized nine of these workshops on issues such as HIV/AIDS transmission, mother-to-child HIV transmission, and prenatal care.

10. In my own framing of the problem of *utsai,* I have been critical of the use of the terms *witchcraft* and *sorcery* because of the wide range of semantic imports, from Euro-American societies and other anthropological discourses, that often overshadow discussions about harmful magic in African societies (Ciekawy 1998).

REFERENCES

Brantley, Cynthia. 1978. "Gerontocratic Government: Age Sets in Pre-colonial Giriama," *Africa; Journal of the International African Institute* 48, no. 3:248–264.
———. 1981. *The Giriama and Colonial Resistance in Kenya, 1800–1920.* Berkeley: University of California Press.
Ciekawy, Diane. 1989. "Spirit Possession on the Swahili Coast: Peripheral Cults or Primary Texts?" PhD diss., University of Texas at Austin.
———. 1992. "Witchcraft Eradication as Political Process in Kilifi District, Kenya, 1955–1988." PhD diss., Columbia University.
———. 1997. "Human Rights and State Power on the Kenya Coast: A Mijikenda Perspective on Universalism and Relativism." *Humanity and Society* 21, no. 2:130–147.

———. 1998. "Witchcraft and Statecraft: Five Technologies of Power in Colonial and Postcolonial Coastal Kenya." *African Studies Review* 41, no. 3: 119–141.

———. 2000. "Mijikenda Perspectives on Freedom, Culture and Human 'Rights.'" In *African Visions: Literary Images, Political Change and Social Struggle in Contemporary Africa*, edited by Cheryl B. Mwaria, Sylvia Federici, and Joseph McLaren, 15–27. Westport, CN: Praeger.

———. 2001. "Utsai as Ethical Discourse: A Critique of Power from Mijikenda in Coastal Kenya." In *Dialogues of "Witchcraft": Anthropological and Philosophical Exchanges*, edited by George C. Bond and Diane Ciekawy, 158–189. Athens: Ohio University Press.

———. 2006. "Party Politics and the Control of Harmful Magic: Moral Entrepreneurship during the Independence Era in Coastal Kenya." In *The Power of the Occult in Modern Africa: Continuity and Innovation in the Renewal of African Cosmologies*, edited by James Kiernan,126–152. Berlin: Lit Verlag.

———. 2009. "'Demonic' Traditions: Representations of Oathing in Newspaper Coverage of the 1997 Crisis in Coastal Kenya." In *Media and Identity in Postcolonial Africa*, edited by Kimani Njogu and John Middleton, 287–307. London: International African Institute.

———. 2014a. "Fake Kaya Elders and Fake Oaths: Reflections on the Immorality of Invented Tradition in the 1997 Crisis in Coastal Kenya." In *Recontextualizing Self and Other Issues in Africa*, edited by V-Y. Mudimbe, 195–131. Trenton, NJ: Africa World Press.

———. 2014b. "Kajiwe's Witchfinding Movement as a Challenge to Swahili Cultural Hegemony." In *Contesting Identities: The Mijikenda and Their Neighbors in Kenyan Coastal Society*, edited by Rebecca Gearhart and Linda Giles, 169–188. Trenton, NJ: Africa World Press. Giles, Linda L. 1989a. "The Dialectic of Spirit Production: A Cross-Cultural Dialogue," *Mankind Quarterly* 19 (Spring): 243–265.

McIntosh, Janet. 2009. *The Edge of Islam: Power, Personhood, and Ethno-Religious Boundaries on the Kenya Coast*. Durham, NC: Duke University Press.

Middleton, John. 1960. *Lugbara Religion*. London: Oxford University Press.

Mitsanze, John B., and Linda Giles. 2014. "The Kaya Legacy: The Role of the Mijikenda Makaya and Kaya Elders in Postcolonial Kenya." In *Contesting Identities: The Mijikenda and Their Neighbors in Kenyan Coastal Society*, edited by Rebecca Gearhart and Linda Giles, 201–244. Trenton, NJ: Africa World Press.

Nyamweru, Celia. 2014. "Identity Politics and Culture in Coastal Kenya: The Role of the Malindi District Cultural Association." In *Contesting Identities: The Mijikenda and Their Neighbors in Kenyan Coastal Society*, edited by Rebecca Gearhart and Linda Giles, 245–267. Trenton, NJ: Africa World Press.

Parkin, David. 1968. "Medicines and Men of Influence." *Man* 3: 424–439.

———. 1970. "Politics of Ritual Syncretism: Islam among the Non-Muslim Giriama of Kenya." *Africa: Journal of the International African Institute* 40, no. 3: 210–233.

———. 1972. *Palms, Wine and Witnesses: Public Spirit and Private Gain in an African Farming Community*. London: Intertext Books.

———. 1985. "Entitling Evil: Muslims and Non-Muslims in Coastal Kenya." In *The Anthropology of Evil*, edited by David Parkin, 224–243. Oxford: Basil Blackwell.

———.1991. *The Sacred Void: Spatial Images of Work and Ritual among the Giriama of Kenya*. Cambridge: Cambridge University Press.

Spear, Thomas. 1978. *The Kaya Complex*. Nairobi: Kenya Literature Bureau.

Tengeza, Amini H., and Celia Nyamweru. 2014. "Symbols of Indigenous Identity: The Ndata Leadership Staffs of Kaya Elders in Kilifi District, Kenya." In *Contesting Identities: The Mijikenda and Their Neighbors in Kenyan Coastal Society*, edited by Rebecca Gearhart and Linda Giles, 225–244. Trenton, NJ: Africa World Press.

Willis, Justin. 1993. *Mombasa, the Swahili, and the Making of the Mijikenda*. Oxford: Clarendon Press.

10 HAUNTED BY ABSENT OTHERS

Movements of Evil in a Nigerian City

ULRIKA TROVALLA

In comparison with other cities in Nigeria, Jos has often been depicted as relatively peaceful, a place where all of the country's different religious and ethnic groups live together in harmony. In this vein, the violence that broke out in the city of Jos on Friday, September 7, 2001, and which came to be known as "the crisis," threw a once-familiar city into disarray and confusion. It came to be viewed as a turning point—a start of a cycle of escalating violence that to date has brought with it repeatedly renewed violent hostilities. On that Friday, a cleansing from within began as Muslims in mainly Christian areas and Christians in mainly Muslim areas were targeted. By the next Thursday, when the fighting ceased, thousands of homes, businesses, churches, mosques, and other buildings had been destroyed. It was estimated that sixty thousand people had been displaced (IRIN WA 2001), between one thousand and three thousand people had been killed, and many others were missing (see Bawa and Nwogwu 2002, 110; Danfulani and Fwatshak 2002, 249; HRW 2001, 10; IRIN 2004).

With the crisis, people's patterns of movement changed drastically and so, too, did Jos. In places where one had felt at home before, one was now a stranger or even an intruder. Former friends became enemies, and as Christians and Muslims moved apart an increasingly religious and compartmentalized landscape emerged (see Egwu 2004, 32; Je'adayibe 2008, 171). Part of the intangible qualities inherent in any city is different conceptions of fear and danger, galleries of friends and enemies, and mental maps outlining safe versus threatening places and times. Mirroring the transformation of Jos, its cosmologies of evil also changed. As people moved away from each other, gates were closed, and no-go areas emerged, the "other" was increasingly conjured up in terms of fear and hate. As borders between different areas became more pronounced people stopped crossing them, but this did not instill people with a sense that "evil" was contained. Other malevolent entities seemed to increase in reach and mobility. Seemingly mundane matters such as medicine, phone calls, and rumors that could traverse boundaries that people did not dare to cross came to be imbued with the essence of evil. In their capacity to move beyond their makers, they became manifestations of an enemy residing in an elusive "elsewhere." In a very real sense, places became haunted by absent others.

As the presence of these entities became more palpable, the landscape increasingly became instilled with notions of hidden aggression that could be lurking around any corner and that were prepared to surface at any time. Suspicion, fear, and hate became everyday companions and the city was no longer experienced as the home it once was felt to have been. The surrounding urban landscape was increasingly seen in terms of threats—invading forces beyond people's control. Rather than feeling part of the city, people often felt insecure, exposed, and out of place (see Jackson 2005, 26, 130). This text analyzes a landscape ever more characterized by divisions and a fear of evil matters—poison, evil phone numbers, and infectious rumors—that moved across the borders that separated people.

PRESENCE AND ABSENCE: A CITY OF DIVISIONS

In Nigeria, an intensified power struggle between adherents of Islam and Christianity has instigated a fervent religious battle over public space as well as an on-going struggle for souls, attention, dominance, and access to state resources. Over the years, the other has increasingly become demonized, and attitudes of intolerance and suspicion have come to dominate the relationship (see Hackett 2003, 51, 62; Obadare 2006a, 667–671, 674–675; Ojo 2007, 175, 186); both sides have come to "conjure the devil in the name of the other" (Marshall 2009, 230). Located in between the mainly Muslim north and Christian south, Jos is part of a region where the tensions between Christianity and Islam have acquired their most combustible force (see Alemika 2002, 9–10; Best 2002, 273–274; Okpeh 2008, 31; Tyoden 1993, 19, 103). But more than this, the crisis, as well as succeeding acts of violence, has gained force from a specific fusion of ethnicity and religion in the concept of "indigeneity" (see Andersson Trovalla 2011, 16–20, 35–40; Suberu 2001, 17). On the one side are Christians belonging to ethnic groups seen as indigene to the area, and, on the other, are people viewed as Muslim settlers, mainly belonging to the ethnic group Hausa. Even if matters of belonging as well as the continuation of conflicts also are connected to more complex relationships, these two stereotypes carry a great force in shaping the conflicts, the emergent city, as well as its inhabitants' views of their life within it.

With the crisis, the image of Jos in many ways became a religious map indicating how many Muslims and Christians lived in different areas and to whom the areas belonged. The city came to be redefined into Muslim- and Christian-"controlled zones" (Danfulani and Fwatshak 2002, 253). A landscape of fear and ownership claims emerged in which Christian-dominated areas received informal names such as "New Jerusalem," "Jesus Zone," and "Promised Land," while the Muslim-dominated areas were named "Sharia Line," "Angwan Musulmi," "Afghanistan," "Jihad Zone," "Saudi Arabia," and "Seat of [bin] Laden" (see Danfulani and Fwatshak 2002, 253; Harnischfeger 2004, 446; Murray 2007).

If the spatial order is an ensemble of possibilities and interdictions—different ways in which different people can or cannot move (de Certeau 1988, 98)—Jos's inhabitants became increasingly aware of them. In people's talk about Jos as a place, there was a new attentiveness to how they were able or not able to move—how the environment moved them (see Vigh 2008, 18). Emanuel—a Christian man, who had been born and brought up in Jos—described how, with the crisis, Jos had become divided into what he called a "Hausa zone"[1] and a "main zone." With the crisis, he had become an enemy in the first zone and could no longer enter it. He said he was afraid that they would lynch him but that it was likewise for the others; they would not dare to go into his zone, either. Jonathan—another of Jos's middle-aged inhabitants—explained similarly that while there had been a line before, that line had become thicker after the crisis and places had become no-go areas. Christians and Muslims no longer crossed the lines; Muslims would not enter Christian areas and Christians would not enter Muslim areas. Even though the idea of a place is always constituted in relation to other places—"an idea of difference" (Hetherington 1997, 197)—Jos was a city in which places were increasingly made sense of in direct opposition to each other.

Just as specific places—in the case of no-go areas—were feared because of the presence of certain people, specific times were also feared. Places that could be visited during a certain time would be avoided at other times because of this felt presence. People warned each other to be extra careful on Fridays, Sundays, and days of religious celebrations, when moving through Jos. For Christians, the mosque was a threatening place, especially on Fridays, where people were thought to go to secretly make plans, and for Muslims, the church and Sundays were similarly intimidating places and times. Time, place, and people's movement were fused together to form a landscape not only of no-go areas, but also of no-go times.

A reporter who portrayed Jos as a city divided between Muslim and Christian areas, observed that when one enters a Muslim area one would see "women walk[ing] the streets with their heads covered in Islamic headscarves while the men wear long flowing gowns and the colourful, fez-shaped 'Hula' hats typical of Muslims in northern Nigeria. But turn a corner and the atmosphere and clothes change straight away. Suddenly there are endless signs advertising different churches, while the men are wearing western-style suits and the women are keen to show off their elaborate hair-styles" (Winter 2003). In Jos as an urban landscape, places were shaped by the absence as much as the presence of certain activities, people, and buildings. It was increasingly formed by who was—and who was not—living in a particular area or walking down a certain street (Andersson Trovalla 2011, 43–77). In the tension that stemmed from what was no longer there, new forces were gaining strength.

MATTERS OF POISON

During a conversation in 2004, one of the women who worked for the polio immunization program in Jos described how they targeted different areas in Jos, one week at a time. They would knock on people's doors and offer the oral vaccine for free to children under five years old. While most people agreed to give their children the vaccine, she acknowledged that Hausas often did not. This, she said, was connected to family planning and AIDS. Many Hausas believed that the vaccine gave people AIDS and that it was intended to make their children infertile. It was all part of a plan to reduce their numbers. Around the same time, four women and a man who were wearing green aprons and said that they were working for the polio program stopped by Maryam's mud house, which was located in a village on the northern outskirts of Jos. Maryam was a Hausa woman in her sixties who had been practicing traditional medicine ever since her father taught her at a young age. When they left, Maryam explained that they usually came by every other month to give the vaccine to children between six months and two years of age, but that not everyone wanted to give it to their children. I asked if her grandchildren had taken it and she answered that some of them had. I told her that I myself had had polio vaccinations twice, once as a child and one more time before I came to Nigeria. She answered that we ought to know best how to use our own drugs, but if you told a Nigerian that he or she would need to take it more than once, they would think you were trying to cheat them out of their money.

Among Muslims in Nigeria, Western medicine and its services have long been seen as activities of Christians, and. as such, they evoke a certain degree of suspicion (Last 2007, 613). At the time, voices questioning the oral polio vaccine were being raised all over the mainly Muslim northern Nigeria, and people made a sharp distinction between vaccines administered at postnatal clinics during routine immunizations and those handed out by "roaming vaccinators" who went to people's homes (Yahya 2007, 195). A man from Kano explained: "If I go to the hospital, even simple Panadol (paracetamol) for a headache, I cannot buy and these people are following us into our houses, forcing us to bring our children for free medicine for polio" (ibid., 202). A man from the northern city of Zaria explained: "We are looking for medicine in the hospital to give to our children and we can't get it but this one, they are following us to our houses to give it. I don't trust this polio vaccine" (Renne 2006, 1862).

The controversy about the safety of the oral polio vaccine had started back in 2003, when five of the northern states in Nigeria banned its use on children. It all happened during the World Health Organization program "Kick Polio out of Africa," and in the middle of 2003, the controversy surrounding the program set the Muslims of northern Nigeria against the World Health Organization, UNICEF (U.N. Children's Fund), and Nigeria's federal authorities (Obadare 2005, 265ff., 279). The controversy reached a peak when Dr. Dattii Ahmed, who was on the Kano State Sharia Supreme Council, declared that as part of its war against terrorism, the U.S. government had deliberately contaminated the vaccine in order to reduce the Muslim population (see Fleshman 2004, 188; Obadare 2005, 275; Yahya 2007). In contrast to the doubts in the northern part Nigeria regarding the vaccine, people in the south "simply could not fathom why anybody would decline a vaccine declared safe by the WHO" (Obadare 2005, 268–269). The dangerous other whose medicines you had to safeguard yourself against was not the same for the southerners as for the northerners.

With the crisis, the other's medicine more and more turned into poison; it became lethal. When I, in 2004, settled down with three of Jos's Christian practitioners of what in Jos is perceived as "traditional" medicine relative to the more "modern" Western medicine, it was very clear who the feared other had become. Two of them explained that they used to go to Muslim barbers to get shaved but no longer did, because it would be too easy for them to slit their throats. The discussion switched to issues of medicine. It did not take more than a few minutes until they all emphasized that they would not take any medicine from a Muslim. They concluded that at present, no Christian would do so, just as no Muslim would take medicine from a Christian, for fear of being poisoned. While the other's medicine more and more turned into matters of poison and borders were emphasized by which medicine people used and feared, the roaming vaccinators that crossed borders into the different neighborhoods gained additional dimensions in Jos. In the way that their movements came to merge with the increasingly compartmentalized landscape, they came to connect to a pattern of poison—a matter that increasingly was infused into the urban landscape.

With the crisis in Jos, rumors of mass poisoning emerged, much like it did in Biafra during the Nigerian civil war in the 1960s. Then, rumors had it that the Nigerian federal government had poisoned the university students' breakfast, and that food and drugs offered by the British government were turned down by the Biafran government because they were poisoned. Other rumors claimed that the increasing number of stillbirths was caused by a form of poison that the Nigerian Air Force had spread. When kwashiorkor, a disease that is caused by protein deficiency in the diet and which had been known to affect children, also started to affect adults, it was likewise thought to be caused by poison spread by the Air Force (Nkpa 1977, 399, 341).

In Jos during the years after the crisis, the magnitude and the prominence of poison rumors, accusations, and fears escalated to the point that they became an integral part in people's everyday lives. Among others, there were rumors that the Christian local government had poisoned the water going into some Muslim areas. People were warned not to drink it. There have been continuous rumors about the meat being sold in Jos. Both cattle herding and slaughtering have traditionally been in the hands of Muslim ethnic groups, and among Christians, persistent rumors appeared about poisoned meat, and they warned each other not to buy meat from Muslims. While a lot of the slaughtering in Jos during the recent years has been taken over by the Christian community, similar rumors have appeared on the other side. There are also a lot of rumors moving across the city connected to *suya,* the barbeque meat sold along the streets. Traditionally, this is a business run by Hausas. Among Christian communities, warnings have been spread against buying this meat, because of the risk of being poisoned.

As specialists on preparing poison, as well as curing and composing protective medicines against threats generally seen as uncontrollable and impossible to detect before it is too late, there is no group that throws light on these issues as well as the practitioners of traditional medicine. Like the rest of the city's inhabitants, they have had to deal with the emergent landscape and with the new dangers that have been fused into it. The problems they tackle are the same as those of all people in Jos, but their line of work forces them to deal with these problems even more directly than others have to. In other words, their work concretizes processes, and their struggles magnify questions, of importance for the city as a whole.

Pam, one of the practitioners in Jos, explained that traditional medicine, unlike Western medicine, could treat conditions caused by poison, witchcraft, and spirits. He stated, "No orthodox doctor, no surgeon in an orthodox job can cure this poison, never." Pam went on to relate that there were practitioners who could make different forms of poison. Some used hair, some charcoal, and others lizards. He added thoughtfully that they could poison the meat you ate. Isaac, another practitioner, similarly described how traditional medicine was not just the only medicine that could deal successfully with poison, but that Western medicine would even worsen the condition. He picked up a nail from the floor and showed it to me, commenting that this was an ordinary nail, but that for no more than 20 Naira[2] a traditional "doctor" could send it across any distance and harm a person with it. They could harm your children by sending needles, seven to be exact—one to the forehead, three to the chest, and three to the stomach. The child would not notice anything and you as a parent would not see anything, but after some time, the child would begin to have headache followed by pains in the stomach and chest. If you took the child to a Western doctor and gave it an injection, the child would become sicker and eventually die. However, if you took the child to a traditional doctor, he would just hit the child on the different places where the needles had been inserted and the needles would fall out directly into his hand. He would then just let the needles fall to the ground and the child would be healthy again.

Among the traditional practitioners there was a great fear of others' medicine—a fear that with the crisis in 2001 surpassed all previous levels. Many of them were members of the Nigerian Union of Medical Herbal Practitioners— an association that was established in the beginning of the 1980s. To be able to survive union politics one needed to have strong medicines that protected against the strength of other practitioners' medicine. Not having medicine that was strong enough could have fatal consequences (see Last 1992, 404–405). Isaac described that when he had moved to Jos, in 1997, he was a newcomer, but he was prepared. He arrived at his first union meeting in Jos with very strong medicines that would protect him against all the tests that were going to be thrown at him, and the protective medicine in his pocket had just crumbled in response to all the pressure put on it during the meeting. As a result of his strong medicines, he left the meeting not only unharmed but also as the newly elected public relations officer of the union in Jos. Isaac concluded that one has to come prepared to meetings; without protection, they were very dangerous events.

While issues of both politics and religion were given increasing prominence within the union in Jos with the crisis, new divisions and borders emerged among its members, just as in the landscape of Jos. The union split into two factions—indicative of life in the Nigerian city of Jos, where divisions, tensions, conflicts, and fears were growing in importance. On one level, the union was broken up into a "Hausa faction" and an "indigene faction"; on another, Jos was divided into Christian and Muslim areas. As a result, the union's weekly Tuesday meetings rarely took place anymore. What had been a meeting point for people became marked by distrust. Emanuel, who had stopped attending, explained that if he went to a meeting and spoke his mind, he knew that people who got annoyed or angry would never tell him to his face but would secretly send medicines that would make him ill. Being that people before the crisis had participated in large numbers, while after the crisis most meetings had only a few participants, if any, Emanuel and Isaac concluded that the reason the union was currently in such a poor state was that everyone was too afraid of each other's medicines.

In fact, with the crisis there was a steadily growing pattern among the practitioners of dealing with and interpreting conflict through poison or suspicions and accusations of poisoning. During a conversation between Mohammed and Samuel, two of Jos's practitioners, regarding how various people in Jos were trying to poison each other, Mohammed stated, "Exactly, that is the real problem even within our own movement." Poison was a topic that engaged, and Samuel filled in and agreed with Mohammed's interpretation of the situation. "Everybody who is within the medicine trade knows that you cannot be a chairman of the union without being tried. . . . Even our secretary has been tried," Samuel said. I asked Mohammed, who was the secretary, who had tried to poison him. He answered, "Our people," and Samuel added, "Enemies." Mohammed referred to problems with the Hausa faction and said that he had been warned, because he was standing in their way. If he was not careful, they were going to kill him. Samuel added that they would not kill him themselves, "physically," but through "poison." They would "either send poisonous missiles or injections."

The practitioners highlight a fear, which embraced the whole society, of poisonous forces moving across the urban landscape. While Jos's inhabitants moved to areas where they felt safer, closed gates, avoided no-go areas and no-go times, and stopped attending meetings, both the magnitude and prominence of these kinds of accusations and fears escalated. In general there were no distinctions made between poison as a harmful substance that could be mixed with food or smeared on an arrow and poison as a spell, needle, or talisman that worked through spiritual means. In understanding poison, it was not the exact manner in which it functioned that was important. What gave poison its characteristic was rather its obscurity—how its maker, path, and presence were veiled. You would not know that somebody had poisoned your meat or sent a poisonous needle until you fell sick. Unlike other forms of violence, like the brute presence of the other during a cut of a knife, poison was marked by a striking absence of the other. For that reason, moving away did not decrease the felt presence of poison but, rather, increased it. Through its ability to move beyond the physical limitations of the other, poison brought an absent other to a presence. Michel de Certeau wrote, places people live in are like the presences of diverse absences" (de Certeau 1988, 108). They are full of things that are no longer there, that can no longer be seen, but can still be sensed. Just as the burnt down house in Jos brought forth the presence of the neighbor who used to live there, poison made places seem "haunted, by an absent other" (de Certeau 1988, 154).

EVIL PHONE CALLS

Other matters were also increasingly bringing absent others to a presence. In 2001, when the Global System of Mobile Communication (GSM) was introduced in Nigeria, the telephone industry was extremely stagnant. With a population of over one hundred million there were around five hundred thousand landlines in use and over ten million Nigerians queuing for an installation—with an average queue time between eight to ten years (Obadare 2004, 8; Onwumechili 2001, 223–224, 2005, 24ff). With the introduction of GSM, Nigeria's telecommunication system took an enormous leap (Elegbeleye 2005, 197). By the end of 2003, the newly introduced GSM market had around four million subscribers, and, by 2007, over forty-three million GSM lines were estimated to be in use (Badaru 2007) and Nigeria was depicted as one of the fastest growing GSM markets in the world (Jonah 2007). It was concluded: "Every major city and many small towns are now connected, and countless rural and urban communities that have no running water and little or no electricity service are integrated into the country's vast and expanding mobile telephone network" (Smith 2006, 498). Today, there are around a hundred million active lines in use (NCC 2012).

The mobile phone in Nigeria has come to be seen in the light of fantasies about improved futures. Ebenezer Obadare wrote, "At the very least, mobile telecommunication was expected to accomplish some of the 'miracles' associated with its introduction in other parts of the world, for instance, 'abolishing' distance by facilitating the conduct of business and interpersonal relations" (2006b, 101). As poison in Jos could bring forth the presence of an absent other, so, too, could the mobile phone. Through the mobile phones, the sound of people could move beyond their physical limitations as never before. Rumors, gossip, and news of violence could spread immediately across the city and the nation as well as to other countries at speeds and with a reach unheard of before. Mobile phones have enabled people to move beyond the "friction of distance" in ways that contradicted all previous experiences. They have become tools that were part of forming a "time-space compression" to the degree that they allowed people, in a sense, "to be in two or more places at once" (Larsen, Axhausen, and Urry 2006, 261, 263, 273). James Katz argued that there was a seemingly magical quality to how the new technology worked and to the power that it transferred to its users, who could just "wander around and yet invisibly connect to just about anyone" (2006, 6). The mobile phone quite literally became a "portable power" that could immensely amplify a person's reach and power to affect circumstances that would otherwise be out of reach (ibid., 10).

However, through the same channels that you could reach and be reached by others, there were also other entities that could reach you. With the introduction of GSM, there followed an increasing tension between an "acoustic revelatory presence" and a "visual hidden presence" (Feld 2005, 186). A form of "spatio-acoustic confusion" emerged in which "delocalized sounds" could move without restraints (Yablon 2007, 641). In a fashion similar to poison, the phone call could travel any distance, locate you anywhere, and enter your home.

In July 2004, I was sitting on a bench on the grounds of the University of Jos, talking to a woman who worked at the university. Our conversation eventually turned to the increasing use of mobile phones. She told me that there existed a phone number that you could die from; if you answered when this number called, you would die immediately. This rumor came to circulate all over the country in a speed previously unheard of. As a result, some Nigerians stopped answering calls coming from numbers they did not recognize, and a steadily increasing list of "killer numbers" was shown on television. People stopped using commercial mobile phone centers; some stopped using their own phones; some memorized the killer numbers; some stored them on their phones under the name "evil"; some argued for the ban of GSM (Adam 2004); and many, after receiving calls, went to hospitals for checkups (Agbu 2004, 16). "A company was reported to have alerted its employees by posting the following on a notice board: 'Please beware of these strange GSM numbers: 08011113999, 08033123999, 08032111999 and 08025111999. In short, any number that ends with 333, 666, 999. They are killing! This is nothing but reality, you are warned!'" (Agbu 2004, 17).

These evil phone calls were referred to as "satanic calls," "killer calls," and "doomsday calls," and many Nigerians saw them as a sign of the "end times" (Agbu 2004, 18–19). Two weeks after the conversation on the bench, the rumor about the phone numbers that killed people had grown to such an extent that I received a text message from MTN, my GSM provider, that declared: "Y'ello Customer, we assure you that the rumour about an evil GSM number is unfounded and scientifically impossible. Please disregard this rumour. Thank you."

The evil phone numbers came to tap into the increasing feeling of being haunted by malevolent forces that were circulating across the urban landscape. As something that, like a poisonous needle, in obscure ways defied any distance and found you anywhere, the mobile phone was both fearsome and had great potential. Through it a person could gain the ability to move in ways that defied physical constraints. In your hands, it embodied enormous possibilities, as the mobile network provider GLO indicated. In 2007 GLO covered Jos, like the rest of Nigeria, with advertising posters with the tagline "Rule your world." The new GSM system had brought with it not only a changed landscape in the form of commercial posters and small commercial phone places with highly visible signboards and umbrellas, but also highly moveable and invisible forces that carried the ambiguous potential of either ruling one's world or helping one rule it.

The ambivalence of the mobile phone resembles that of medicine as a simultaneous source of enormous curative powers and poisonous forces; on the one hand, a healing or protective tool and, on the other, something hostile that invaded people's bodies. In Jos, they were part of an increasing feeling of being acted upon by forces beyond people's control. Through the "killer calls," the phone became the portal for a life-threatening evil force. It was a move between being a tool that enhanced people's abilities—seen as a part of them, being under their control or subject to their will—and something that invaded them—experienced as alien, controlling, or overpowering (Jackson 2005, 130–131).

VIOLENT RUMORS

Ambiguous forces that were based on a tension between presence and absence were recurrent companions in Jos. As in the case of the poisonous needles and evil phone numbers, it was extremely hard to know what was going on behind the scenes. Suspicions of hidden agendas and hidden aggressions that could surface at any time were constant. Just as there was a fear connected to what the other was planning in the church or in the mosque, there was a fear of what the other was doing behind your back at the meeting or in his or her area. Ordinary day-to-day events such as eating or taking medicine became marked by a fear of being killed by poison. It was no simple task to detect what was going on, and people tried in different ways to tune into the state of the city. Before leaving their homes in the morning, people checked the news on the radio. When he was on the move, Mohammed, like many others, carried a small radio with him. All over the city, you could see small groups of people gathered around radios. When tension increased, the use of the radio also increased. It became an essential piece of equipment; it was not just a matter of satisfying curiosity, but also a matter of life and death.

On the other hand, the radio had its clear limitations as a tool for understanding what was going on—not listening could actually save your life. This predicament became apparent when Esther told me about her experiences during the crisis of 2001. Living on the outskirts of Jos, she had wanted to go into the center to buy some food and visit her Bible study group on the fourth or fifth day of the crisis, and she had heard on the radio that everything was calm and that everyone should go about their business as usual. From one of the larger roads heading into Jos, she and a friend succeeded in finding a taxi to take them to the center. Absence of sound and passing cars was an indication that something was wrong in the city, but since there were taxis passing, Esther and her friend assumed that everything was okay. They asked the driver to take them to their Bible study group inside Jos. When they got there, it turned out to be closed and they decided to walk to the bank. As they were leaving the bank, they heard gunshots. Now very afraid, they tried to find a taxi or any other vehicle to get a ride out of Jos, but without any success. Instead, they found temporary shelter in the house of a friend in the area. Because they knew, after some hours in hiding, that people at home would be very worried about them, they then left the house and started to walk toward home even though they were still hearing gunshots. After some walking, they met a soldier, who asked them what they were doing outside. They told him that the radio had said that everything was calm in Jos. The soldier answered that this was clearly not the case and they should go home. The soldier helped them stop a car, and they were eventually able to get home.

When violence again struck Jos in 2008, similar stories emerged. People complaining about the lack of information from the local media—at the same time that people could see smoke rising all over Jos, there were no comments about the violence (Audu and Ajakaye 2008; BBC 2008). One man cried out, "We have three radio stations in Jos and they are only playing music and telling us about what happened yesterday. Nobody is telling us what happened now" (BBC 2008). As one of the most important news media in Africa, the radio has had clear limitations when it comes to satisfying its listeners' questions.

In comparing the radio to what he translated from the French expression "radio trottoir" as "pavement radio," Stephen Ellis illustrated several instances when the latter—conversations in bars, markets, living rooms, and taxi-parks as well as on pavements—had been much more accurate than the former (1989, 321, 325–326). While most people did try to tune in to Jos through the radio, the most important medium by far was the rumors that were in the air. They were a vital part of knowing what was going on in Jos, just as Veena Das observed in relation to her work in India during the 1980s: "Being able to interpret the rumours correctly became a matter of life and death for many" (1998, 120). Listening to rumors about the situation in Jos might save your life, since what the news broadcast did not necessarily correspond to any experienced reality. On the other hand, there was no guarantee that the rumors did not portray a reality dreaded or wished for rather than one experienced. People found themselves in a "twilight zone in which it was difficult to know whether it was wiser to believe in rumours or in the official versions of events" (ibid., 119).

In Jos, tensions constantly appeared between the news on the radio and the news on the pavement radio. In the beginning of April 2004, a phone call came to the family I was staying with. The caller wanted to warn us that there was trouble in Jos again and said that it had started during the night. At ten o'clock in the morning, we were listening to the local news when we heard the chief of police of the neighborhood in question talking. He explained that armed robbers had attacked some houses during the night. The public had phoned it in and the police had been on the scene immediately. I later found out that five Muslim houses had been robbed and that people living in the area had thought it had been Christians attacking. The chief of police went on to encourage people to stop spreading rumors. There were no problems in Jos. Similarly, in 2004, the local government authorities tried to counteract the rumors that were being spread when Plateau state, which Jos is the capital of, after escalating violence, was declared to be in a state of emergency. It was just a week after the day of the declaration that I heard for the first time a message—or rather a jingle—on the local radio channels that would be repeated continually through the six-month long state of emergency. It declared that people should stop spreading rumors; they should stop spreading hearsay that they had not seen proof of; and if they had important information they should report it to the proper authorities.

Rumors were something to be greatly feared. During the crisis in 2001— just as in previous conflicts in Jos (Plotnicov 1971, 301–302)—rumors had played a large part in the escalation and spread of violence (Danfulani and Fwatshak 2002, 254; HRW 2001, 7). As with medicines and mobile phones, rumors carried an ambiguous potential. They could inform you and quite literally save your life, but they could also spread and increase violence. In the midst of violence in 2010, one resident of Jos explained: "Rumours are being spread and that is making people afraid. People are panicking and telling their loved ones to come home" (BBC 2010b). Just like Michelle Osborn in her work in Kenya illustrated how rumors intensified feelings of fear and panic and accelerated and increased violence (2008, 316, 318, 321, 324), Das described how during her work in India rumors brought a new "form of death into existence" (1998, 125).

What makes rumors powerful and fearful is not whether they are true or not, but the power they possess to shape the world—people's perception and actions. By building on arguments by Austin et al. in their classic work *How to Do Things with Words* (1976), Das analyzed the "perlocutionary" force of rumors "to do something by saying something." The power of rumors, just like poisonous needles or killer numbers, is connected to their ability to detach themselves from their makers or senders. The perlocutionary force in the case of a rumor "would be lost if it was tethered to the words of the speaking agent" (Das 1998, 127). The very power of rumors emanates from the fact that they lack signatures, from the absence of their being tied to an individual agent (ibid., 125). Through not being attached to a specific person, rumors, like poisonous needles and evil numbers, could move very far, cross almost any border, and affect people like a "contagion and infection" (ibid., 116).

In this manner, localized conflicts often went national. The violence during the Jos crisis in 2001, like many other conflicts in Nigeria, spread to the most northern and southern cities in Nigeria as reprisal attacks took place (Danfulani and Fwatshak 2002, 253; HRW 2001, 20). During continually renewed outbreaks of violence in Jos, police all over Nigeria in apparently peaceful cities took to the streets to prevent possible spillover. During the January 2010 violence in Jos, the police public relation officer of Kaduna state to the northwest of Plateau state made assurances that the "Operation Yaki squad"—a specialized police unit equipped with "state of the art patrol vans, motorcycles, bulletproof jackets, GPS and latest communication gadgets"—was "battle-ready to deal with any possible spill-over." While the squad furnished with the newest tools for communication patrolled crisis-prone areas in "full battle-ready uniforms" (Alkali 2010), there were other forces that had also embraced the new technology.

With the growing ownership of mobile phones, both violence (Last 2007, 606) and rumors gained a new potency that enabled them to spread faster and further. In Jos, as in Kenya, rumors acquired "an instantaneous spread"—they could go national in minutes (Osborn 2008, 315–316). What were referred to as "short text hate messages," which had initially circulated around Jos, now spread across Kaduna as well (Alkali 2010; BBC 2010a). In Jos, the inflammatory text messages had fueled and escalated the violence that had spread across the city. According to some figures, over 145 different messages had been circulating. One of the reported messages declared: "War, war, war. Stand up . . . and defend yourselves. Kill before they kill you. Slaughter before they slaughter you. Dump them in a pit before they dump you" (BBC 2010a). Another one warned Christians not to buy food from Muslims because it was poisoned. Another, addressed to Muslims, claimed that Jonah Jang, the governor of Plateau state, in an attempt to kill them, had ordered the water supply to Muslim-dominated areas in Jos to be cut off (Alkali 2010; BBC 2010a). Other messages warned Christians that Muslims were going to attack churches over the weekend (BBC 2010a).

As local authorities in Jos previously had encouraged people to stop spreading rumors, authority figures in Kaduna now urged people to ignore the text messages that were being sent with intentions of creating hatred and mistrust between Christians and Muslims. A Christian leader said: "We are living together peacefully in Kaduna, so there is no iota of truth in the text messages being circulated. Let both Christians and Muslims ignore the SMS messages because God is the only one who can protect us all; so let us all believe in Him and go about our daily activities without fear or favour" (Alkali 2010). A Muslim leader appealed in a similar manner to people to ignore these messages and delete any they received. In his words, "they are only meant to cause panic and crisis in the state. So, when you get such SMS do not forward them to anyone" (Alkali 2010).

By not being attached to a specific agent, the rumors, the text messages, the killer calls, and the poisoned needles were all felt to uncontrollably move and spread over the city. By not being anchored anywhere they were possibly everywhere and yet nowhere to be found. In a way, they were no longer just extensions of absent others, but uncontrollable forces in their own right—evil entities in and of themselves.

THE INVISIBLE SIDE OF JOS

Ideas of evil are a contextual and situational matter. With the crisis in 2001, divisions and emotions of suspicion and fear became an intrinsic part of the Nigerian city of Jos. At the same time that people moved apart to feel safer there emerged a new fear—a fear that brought a novel anxiety and presence into the urban landscape. While the others more and more became contained in their area, there were evil manifestations that were not felt to be confined by the borders that separated people. Moving, avoiding areas, or blocking other people's movements could not obstruct or fool these forces because, emerging from an absent other, they could travel any distance, cross any border, and find you anywhere. It was an urban landscape that increasingly was shaped by the tension between presence and absence.

In a landscape of divisions, these entities were highly relational and ambiguous matters. What was one person's medicine was another's poison. With the crisis, not only did these forces increasingly appear to be out of control, but their frequency was also amplified. The other's medicine turned more and more poisonous and ever more present in the form of suspicions and accusations of poisoning as well as poisoned food, medicines, needles, or missiles that were felt to move across the city. The growing ownership of mobile phones enabled people to communicate beyond distances but also to be found by others in ways never imagined before. In its wake, a new presence emerged—the killer calls. In a city where tensions and the fear of the other kept rising, so did the discrepancy between the radio waves and the rumors that were in the air. As an essential tool for grasping a world that emerged in unpredictable ways, rumors increased, and with the help of the mobile phone they spread with unprecedented speed. In the wake of this sped-up rumor mill, violence spread in a way previously unseen.

The landscape became imbued with feelings of hidden aggression that could be lurking around any corner, ready to surface at any time. A fear of absent others was evoked. In *Kinshasa: Tales of the Invisible City*, Filip de Boeck described how there existed both a visible and an invisible city. Behind the visible city, he wrote, "lurks yet another city, an invisible but very audible city of whispers, . . . consisting of fleeting words, questions, harmful suspicions and treacherous accusations" (2004, 50). Although they emanated from absent others, suspicions of poison, killer numbers, violent rumors, and hate text messages were ever present. They were the invisible side of Jos—what could not be seen, but felt.

NOTES

1. As the name given to the zone indicates, it was common to refer to the two stereotypes in terms of religion, ethnicity, or indigeneity alone–like "those Hausas," "those Muslims," "those settlers," "those indigenes," or "those Christians"–rather than all three or any two characteristics (see also HRW 2005, 21–22). These terms were used

interchangeably to depict a world that was becoming increasingly divided according to the clustering of indigeneity, religion, and ethnicity.

2. In 2004, the official exchange rate between the US dollar and the Naira was 1 to 127–130.

REFERENCES

Adam, Sagai John. 2004. "Do You Want To Die? (All the GSM Killer Numbers)." *GSM Today,* March 31. http://www.mail-archive.com/gsmtoday@freelists.org/msg00140.html.
Agbu, Jane-Frances. 2004. "From 'Koro' to GSM 'Killer Calls' Scare in Nigeria: A Psychological View." *CODESRIA Bulletin* 3 and 4:16–19.
Alemika, Etannibi E. O. 2002. "Sociological Analysis of Ethnic and Religious Conflicts in the Middle Belt of Nigeria." In *Ethno-Religious Conflicts and Democracy in Nigeria: Challenges,* edited by Etannibi E. O. Alemika and Festus Okoye, 1–24. Kaduna, Nigeria: Human Rights Monitor.
Alkali, Ali. 2010. "Nigeria: 13 Men Arrested With Guns in Kaduna." *Leadership,* January 24. http://allafrica.com/stories/201001250015.html.
Andersson Trovalla, Ulrika. 2011. "Medicine for Uncertain Futures: A Nigerian City in the Wake of a Crisis." PhD diss., Uppsala University, Sweden.
Audu, Onoja, and Rafiu Ajakaye. 2008. "Nigeria: 50 Killed, Two Generals Wounded in Plateau LG Poll Crisis." *Daily Independent,* November 28. http://allafrica.com/stories/200812010690.html.
Austin, John L., James O. Urmson, and Marina Sbisà. 1976. *How to Do Things with Words.* Oxford: Oxford University Press.
Badaru, Shina. 2007. "Nigeria: Telecoms Subscriber Base Hits 45.5 Million." *Thisday,* October 29. http://allafrica.com/stories/200710291366.html.
Bawa, Idris, and Victoria Ijeoma Nwogwu. 2002. "The Jos Crisis." In *Hope Betrayed? A Report on Impunity and State-Sponsored Violence in Nigeria,* edited by World Organisation Against Torture and Centre for Law Enforcement Education, 105–128. Geneva: World Organisation Against Torture and Centre for Law Enforcement Education. http://www.omct.org/files/2002/09/1231/nigeriareport0802.pdf.
Best, Shedrack Gaya. 2002. "The Challenges of Peacemaking and Peace Building in the Middle Belt of Nigeria." In *Ethno-Religious Conflicts and Democracy in Nigeria: Challenges,* edited by Etannibi E. O. Alemika and Festus Okoye, 267–286. Kaduna, Nigeria: Human Rights Monitor.
British Broadcasting Corporation (BBC). 2008. "Poll Riots Erupt in Nigerian City." *BBC News,* November 28. http://news.bbc.co.uk/go/pr/fr/-/2/hi/africa/7754883.stm.
———. 2010a. "Nigeria Text Messages 'Fuelled Jos Riots.'" *BBC News,* January 27. http://news.bbc.co.uk/2/hi/africa/8482666.stm.
———. 2010b. "Nigeria Violence: Eyewitness Stories." *BBC News,* March 8. http://news.bbc.co.uk/2/hi/africa/8556566.stm.Danfulani, Umar Habila Dadem, and Sati U. Fwatshak. 2002. "Briefing: The September 2001 Events in Jos, Nigeria." *African Affairs* 101, no. 403:243–255.

Das, Veena. 1998. "Specificities: Official Narratives, Rumour, and the Social Production of Hate." *Social Identities* 4, no. 1:109–130.

De Boeck, Filip, and Marie-Françoise Plissart. 2004. *Kinshasa: Tales of the Invisible City*. Ghent, Belgium: Ludion Press.

De Certeau, Michel. 1988. *The Practice of Everyday Life*. Berkeley: University of California Press.

Egwu, Samuel Gabriel. 2004. "Ethnicity and Citizenship in Urban Nigeria: The Jos Case, 1960–2000." PhD diss., Department of Political Science, University of Jos.

Elegbeleye, O. S. 2005. "Prevalent Use of Global System of Mobile Phone (GSM) for Communication in Nigeria: A Breakthrough in Interactional Enhancement or a Drawback?" *Nordic Journal of African Studies* 14, no. 2:193–207.

Ellis, Stephen. 1989. "Tuning in to Pavement Radio." *African Affairs* 88, no. 352:321–330.

Feld, Steven. 2005. "Places Sensed, Senses Placed: Toward a Sensuous Epistemology of Environments." In *Empire of the Senses: The Sensual Culture Reader*, edited by D. Howes, 179–191. Oxford: Berg Publishers.

Fleshman, Michael. 2004. "Nigeria Dispute Endangers Global Polio Drive." *Africa Recovery*. February. http://www.un.org/ecosocdev/geninfo/afrec/newrels/polio.htm.

Hackett, Rosalind I. J. 2003. "Managing or Manipulating Religious Conflict in the Nigerian Media." In *Mediating Religion: Conversations in Media, Religion and Culture*, edited by Jolyon Mitchell and Sophia Marriage, 47–63. London: T. & T. Clark Publishers, Ltd.

Harnischfeger, Johannes. 2004. "Sharia and Control over Territory: Conflicts between 'Settlers' and 'Indigenes' in Nigeria." *African Affairs* 103, no. 412:431–452.

Hetherington, Kevin. 1997. "Place of Geometry: The Materiality of Place." In *Ideas of Difference: Social Spaces and the Labour of Division*, edited by Kevin Hetherington and Rolland Munro, 183–199. Oxford: Blackwell Publishers.

Human Rights Watch (HRW). 2001. *Nigeria: Jos: A City Torn Apart*. HRW 13(9A). http://www.hrw.org/node/76878.

———. 2005. *Revenge in the Name of Religion: The Cycle of Violence in Plateau and Kano States*. HRW 17(8A). http://www.hrw.org/en/node/11755/section/2.

Jackson, Michael. 2005. *Existential Anthropology: Events, Exigencies, and Effects*. New York: Berghahn Books.

Je'adayibe, Gwamna Dogara. 2008. "Religious Conflicts and Internally Displaced Persons in Nigeria." In *Population Movements, Conflicts and Displacements in Nigeria*, edited by Toyin Falola and Okpeh O. Okpeh, Jr., 155–177. Trenton, NJ: Africa World Press.

Jonah, Nathaniel. 2007. "Nigeria: GSM—We Are Tired of Constant Poor Network Service—Nigerians." *Leadership*, October 4. http://allafrica.com/stories/200710040590.html.

Katz, James E. 2006. *Magic in the Air: Mobile Communication and the Transformation of Social Life*. New Brunswick, NJ: Transaction Publishers.

Larsen, Jonas, Kay W. Axhausen, and John Urry. 2006. "Geographies of Social Networks: Meetings, Travel and Communications." *Mobilities* 1, no. 2:261–283.

Last, Murray. 1992. "The Importance of Knowing about Not Knowing: Observations from Hausaland." In *The Social Basis of Health and Healing in Africa*, edited by Steven Feierman and John M. Janzen, 393–406. Berkeley: University of California Press.

———. 2007. "Muslims and Christians in Nigeria: An Economy of Political Panic." *The Round Table: The Commonwealth Journal of International Affairs* 96, no. 392: 605–616.

Marshall, Ruth. 2009. *Political Spiritualities: The Pentecostal Revolution in Nigeria.* Chicago: University of Chicago Press.

Murray, Senan. 2007. "Profile: Joshua Dariye." *BBC News,* July 24. http://news.bbc.co.uk/1/hi/world/africa/6908960.stm.

Nigerian Communications Commission (NCC). 2012. "Subscriber Data." http://www.ncc.gov.ng/index.php?option=com_content&view=article&id=125:art-statistics-subscriber-data&catid=65:cat-web-statistics&Itemid=73.

Nkpa, Nwokocha K. U. 1977. "Rumors of Mass Poisoning in Biafra." *Public Opinion Quarterly* 41, no. 3:332–346.

Obadare, Ebenezer. 2004. *The Great GSM (Cell Phone) Boycott: Civil Society, Big Business and the State in Nigeria.* Dark Roast Occasional Paper Series 18, Cape Town: Isandla Institute.

———. 2005. "A Crisis of Trust: History, Politics, Religion and the Polio Controversy in Northern Nigeria." *Patterns of Prejudice* 39, no. 3:265–284.

———. 2006a. "Pentecostal Presidency? The Lagos-Ibadan 'Theocratic Class' & the Muslim 'Other.'" *Review of African Political Economy* 33, no. 110:665–678.

———. 2006b. "Playing Politics with the Mobile Phone in Nigeria: Civil Society, Big Business & the State." *Review of African Political Economy* 33, no. 107:93–111.

Ojo, Matthews A. 2007. "Pentecostal Movements, Islam and the Contest for Public Space in Northern Nigeria." *Islam and Christian-Muslim Relations* 18, no. 2: 175–188.

Okpeh, Okpeh Ochayi, Jr. 2008. "Inter-Group Migrations, Conflicts, and Displacements in Central Nigeria." In *Population Movements, Conflicts and Displacements in Nigeria,* edited by Toyin Falola and Okpeh O. Okpeh, Jr., 19–84. Trenton, NJ: Africa World Press.

Onwumechili, Chuka. 2001. "Dream or Reality: Providing Universal Access to Basic Telecommunications in Nigeria?" *Telecommunications Policy* 25, no. 4:219–231.

———. 2005. "Reaching Critical Mass in Nigeria's Telephone Industry." *Africa Media Review* 13, no. 1:23–40.

Osborn, Michelle. 2008. "Fuelling the Flames: Rumour and Politics in Kibera." *Journal of Eastern African Studies* 2, no. 2:315–327.

Plotnicov, Leonard. 1971. "An Early Nigerian Civil Disturbance: The 1945 Hausa-Ibo Riot in Jos." *Journal of Modern African Studies* 9, no. 2:297–305.

Renne, Elisha P. 2006. "Perspectives on Polio and Immunization in Northern Nigeria." *Social Science and Medicine* 63, no. 7:1857–1869.

Smith, Daniel Jordan. 2006. "Cell Phones, Social Inequality, and Contemporary Culture in Nigeria." *Canadian Journal of African Studies* 40, no. 3:496–523.

Suberu, Rotimi T. 2001. *Federalism and Ethnic Conflict in Nigeria.* Washington, DC: United States Institute of Peace Press.

Tyoden, Sonni Gwanle. 1993. *The Middle Belt in Nigerian Politics.* Jos, Nigeria: AHA Publishing House Ltd.

United Nations Integrated Regional Information Networks (IRIN). 2004. "Nigeria: Plateau State Violence Claimed 53,000 Lives." *IRIN News,* October 8. http://www.irinnews.org/Report.aspx?ReportId=51641.

United Nations Integrated Regional Information Networks for West Africa (IRIN-WA). 2001. "IRIN Update 1060 of events in West Africa." *ReliefWeb/Latest Updates,* September 12. http://www.reliefweb.int/rw/rwb.nsf/db900sid/OCHA-64C9N6 ?OpenDocument&rc=1&emid=FL-2001–0521-TCD.

Vigh, Henrik. 2008. "Crisis and Chronicity: Anthropological Perspectives on Continuous Conflict and Decline." *Ethnos* 73, no. 1:5–24.

Winter, Joseph. 2003. "Nigeria's Elections in Plateau State." *BBC News,* April 18. http:// news.bbc.co.uk/2/hi/africa/2958541.stm.

Yablon, Nick. 2007. "Echoes of the City: Spacing Sound, Sounding Space, 1888–1916." *American Literary History* 19, no. 3:629–660.

Yahya, Maryam. 2007. "Polio Vaccines: 'No Thank You!' Barriers to Polio Eradication in Northern Nigeria." *African Affairs* 106, no. 423:185–204.

11 ATTRIBUTIONS OF EVIL AMONG HAALPULAAREN, SENEGAL

ROY DILLEY

The linguistic root *bon* in Pulaar, the main language spoken in northern Senegal, is usually translated in English by words related to the concept of evil. Thus the noun *bone* means "evil," and as an adjectival root it denotes the "evil eye," as in *yiitere bonde*, or "malicious or evil speech," *konngol bonngol*, or "evil gait," *yaadu bondu*. However, the semantic field marked out by terms that share the same linguistic root is broad, and it encompasses terms that English speakers would denote by the two separate words *evil* and *bad*. So *bonde* is the verb "to be bad or evil," and the adjective *bondo* can be used to denote a bad or evil person (*neddo bondo*), or one who is also hostile, nasty, mean, and wicked. The Pulaar root *bon* has yet further extensions and associations: the noun *bonande* refers to "damage, mess, waste, tragedy and destruction," and *bonnude* is a verb meaning "to spoil, tarnish, impair, pervert, spoliate." This single root *bon* refers therefore not merely to the idea of evil/bad but also embraces notions of physical incompleteness, unwholesomeness, and physical imperfection.

Parkin (1985b) has noted the elasticity of the term evil in anthropological and popular usages, and any attempt here to achieve linguistic clarity clearly misses the central point. While we may seek analytical or conceptual exactitude, the fuzziness attached to our own and others' linguistic terms opens up windows for different sorts of investigation. While theologians, of both Christian and Muslim persuasion, have worked to refine our sense of the meanings of evil,[1] the differentiations at the level of linguistic labels in abstract discourse become even more opaque when considered with respect to how native speakers deploy these terms and concepts in relation to concrete social situations. While linguistic items may have been given more or less precision in theoretical discourses, their attribution to everyday practice, world events, and human predicaments remains contested and for the most part ambiguous.

Another Pulaar term related to the root for bad/evil is *bonki* or "sin." Sin is often regarded as the root of much evil, whose ultimate source for Muslim Haalpulaaren ("the speakers of Pulaar") is Satan, known locally as *seytani* and in the form of evil spirits and jinn as *seytaneeje*. There are a number of different types of experts in esoteric arts, some of which are reputed to use the powers of these spirit beings, and they include witch-hunters and curers (*wileebe*), magicians (*nyengotoobe*), diviners (*tiimoobe*) and even some Muslim marabouts These sorts of practice are the focus of much debate among ordinary people about what kind of spiritual force lies behind a specific body of expertise. Are they good spirits or are they evil ones? What are the intentions of the practitioner? Does he or she wish to bring about good or ill in the world and in the lives of those people who surround them?

One day I was talking to a Haalpulaar man in Senegal whose family belonged to the rank of Islamic clerics and whose sister was married to a teacher of Arabic. The teacher was also the imam of the local mosque and he had leanings toward Islamic radicalism rather than toward mysticism that is a large part of Muslim practice associated with local Sufi brotherhoods. My informant's brother-in-law was steeped in the writings of Islam, and around his room were stacked handsomely bound copies of the Quran, the Haddith and various commentaries and law books in Arabic. Sitting in the brother-in-law's room, my informant's first reaction to the topic of our conversation—the varieties of Islamic practice in Senegal—was to condemn outright all practices of "magic" (*sihr*) as animistic and bad. All these practitioners, including those marabouts who prescribed the wearing of Qur'anic verses as a form of protective magic, were committing the sin of *shirk*, an offense within Islam of attributing partners to Allah, thus undermining His position as the one and only God. These were some of the worst sins (*bonki* or *"akbarru kabba iri"* was the phrase he used) that could be committed by man.[2] He argued that Islam states that man should not profit himself from the use of such "animistic" powers (he used the French term *animiste*), and that it was for Allah to judge and bring retribution to sinners. It was not for man to intervene in the course of events for his own ends and purposes, which was the result of wickedness in the world. These sentiments were obviously felt strongly and his case was put over to me very passionately.

The conversation then moved on to the subject of sports, in particular the summer football season and an upcoming wrestling match that was on everyone's lips, for these were examples of events that involve "illicit" maraboutic practice. The wrestling match was to be held between the top two wrestlers in the country. It had been trailed in the newspapers, was discussed on the radio, and was to be televised. And those lucky enough to have a television would be particularly popular neighbors on the evening of the fight. Both wrestlers employed marabouts who administered a whole range of medicines, amulets, and potions to their prized fighters. Sometime later, on the night of the fight, the wrestlers entered the ring adorned with strings of talismans, and one of the men was covered in a slimy, milky substance that had been poured over him as part of a libation to the spirits or jinn. One fighter was a Lebu, a coastal dweller and sea fisherman from the Cap Vert region; the other was a Serer, a much darker giant of a man, from the central southern region. Everyone I spoke to said the Serer was bound to win since he would have more magic (*xamxam* in Wolof) than the Lebu would, and this magic was blacker (as was the wrestler) and more potent than anything the Lebu could conjure. In fact, the match was becoming billed as a spiritual contest of battle-magic between the two respective marabouts who would use any means, any powers, or potencies to ensure that their man would win. At one stage in the fight, the smaller Lebu lost one of his amulets from around his forehead, and the assembled audience groaned in disbelief since he was bound to lose now that his most potent weapon had gone. In fact, the match, which dragged on for forty-five uneventful minutes, ended in an unsatisfying draw.

The point of this digression is to highlight the switch that can occur in people's attitudes toward local practices once they are no longer talked of in the abstract but are experienced as part of people's lives. The use of marabouts to lend magical support to sportsmen and sporting activities in general is a common practice that is integral to the conduct of games. It is a practice that is condemned by Islamists as a sin, and for them, the practices harness evil forces. Indeed, my interlocutor, having first condemned the use of maraboutic medicines in general, then related how he, as the trainer of the local youth football team, relied upon an extremely effective marabout who helped the team prior to every game. Medicines could be produced to affect the opposition's star players such that they might get injured or have an off day, and magic could be used to secure the right result and protect one's own team. I was struck by the obvious change of attitude toward marabouts once discussed in the context of football, and my friend's condoning of, if not his sense of pride in, the exploits of his team's marabout. Here condemnation had turned to jocular boasts about his team's performance aided by magical means; no longer were these practices outlawed simply as *shirk,* but they were a coherent part of a social practice in which he was engaged. The theological arguments no longer seemed important about who and what the agents of these interventions in everyday happenings were. His concern was with (literally) results, or, more generally, the conduct of worldly affairs in terms beneficial to him and his group.

I frequently encountered during fieldwork such seemingly contradictory stances regarding the nature of religious practice. Indeed, many Senegalese often joked about whether a statement referring to Islam reflected local practice or the religion of the book. Local Muslims are involved, therefore, in their own debates about what is and what is not good Islamic practice; they are aware of the distinction between theoretical statements on an issue, no doubt echoed in an imam's sermon, on the one hand, and reflections on actual social practice on the other. There is an inherent ambiguity about the status of certain activities, and the concerns of everyday life seem to demand that forms of action be taken to secure particular kinds of outcome.

The accommodations and condemnations of particular kinds of practice are responses or stances that inform part of a local debate about where the lines of demarcation should be drawn around forms of religious conduct. They are attempts to define what should or should not be accepted by Muslims, what should and should not be included as good Islamic practice. Perhaps it is not for analysts to say where this line should be drawn by comparing local forms of Islam to some pure or parent type of the religion, but it is for them to highlight the contours of local debate and discourse, as well as the kinds of issue that come under scrutiny. The contours of that debate are now changing, and much more extreme positions are being adopted by Muslim radicals who condemn outright specific practices. These practices are, they point out, the workings of Satan, in the guise of the *seytaneeje* or evil spirits or jinn whose aim is to sow misfortune and darkness in the world. Moreover, their condemnations are catching on, and others influenced by these reformist religious ideas have taken on such an outlook.

This shift can be seen specifically in attitudes to specialist songs performed by members of particular social categories. The traditional songs of praise-singer and musician groups—for instance, the *dille* of the weavers, fishermen's *pekaan*, and so forth—have often been condemned and interpreted by Islamic clerics as anti-Islamic. Popular among the young and sung by members of low "caste" groups, these songs were often banned by local religious authorities. Such proscriptions were and are a feature of stricter Islamic communities and have been reported in a number of cases.[3] These dubious activities, thought by marabouts and imams to be linked to magic (*sihr*) and spirit possession, were seen as a menace to morality and sharia law. Ba reports (1985–1986), for instance, that a form of song popular (*leele*) at the turn of the twentieth century sung by Haalpulaar *wambaabe* singers mocked the town of Cilon, an important center of Islamic learning and Muslim authority in Fuuta Toro. He adds that other forms of song (e.g., *cooloo*) were even more offensive to Muslim morals, for they employed vile language and obscene gestures. These different types of song are interpreted by Ba as a form of expression of popular resistance to Islamic authorities in Fuuta Toro (1985–1986, 39–44). Marabouts have, therefore, two means by which they can condemn members of these marginal castes or social categories: they find repulsive yet also hard to resist the demands of praise-singers and entertainers who are given rewards by them, their patrons, in return for praising members of these high-status families. In addition, members of the same social categories of praise-singers, etc., are at odds with local Muslim leaders who disapprove not only of their "begging," but also of the moral content of their activities and songs.

The weavers and their songs are a case in point, and their changing social and historical situation is worth examination. A *dillere* or weaver's song, for instance, is sung in a particularly stylized manner similar to a chant or plain-song and is delivered in a louder and slightly higher pitched voice than is normal. There is no strict metrical structure or constant rhythm that dictates the tempo of the recitation, because different parts of a song develop their own pace. This can be seen in different sections such as the languid and more melodic sections often repeating a refrain, or as in the staccato, highly punctuated and rhythmical recital of *askos* or pedigrees.[4] A third type of highly rhythmical recital, also often inserted into these songs, comprises incantations (*cefi*) performed in "the language of the spirit" (that is, not in Pulaar or at least standard versions of the language). These *cefi* are powerful oral media that are devised, controlled, and performed only by members of specialist marginal social categories, and they are not an area of Muslim expertise. By contrast, one form of poem adopted by clerics to teach subjects associated with Islam is a *qasida*, often written in Pulaar but using Arabic script (known as *ajami* text) and following imported rules of composition. These poems too have a strict metrical structure.[5] The sonority of recital; the stylistic embellishment of performance; and the use of allusion, image, and metaphor in such songs and poetry mark them out as distinct genres of expression that have particular means to move listeners emotionally. The praise-songs of a *gawlo* praise-singer are said in particular to affect people, especially a patron who listens with pride to the deeds of his illustrious ancestors. He is said to feel a heightened sense of pride and of elation in response to the praises being bestowed upon him via his forebears. Some people say, after hearing their praises sung by a skilled praise-singer, that they could take on almost any challenge. The language in poems or verse form has a power that is effective through its aesthetic quality, through its poetic intensity and the use of allusion, and through its effect on the imagination and sense of social pride of the listener. Language in the form of praise-songs has a power that inheres in the speaker's ability to use words to convey messages about the social standing and prestige of a patron; a praise-singer, however, has the ability not only to praise but to defame and slander as well as. Moreover, the incantations or *cefi* inserted into songs are regarded as powerful magical words by singer and audience alike, and the mere pronunciation of these words can bring about powerful effects in the world.

In this example, praise-singing and Islam can be seen in a dynamic and evolving relationship that brings together members of low caste social categories, on the one hand, and mainstream Islamic groups, on the other. The relationship is complex, ambivalent, and multilayered: traditional songs of the praise-singer have for a long time been the focus of a variety of interpretations and the topic of much social commentary. They have been construed as anti-Islamic propaganda; they are thought to encourage immorality and licentiousness among the young; and they are condemned for containing sections in which forms of words are uttered that are non-Islamic and potentially threatening to the status of the religion in the eyes of the ordinary believer. But there is now something more profound about the charges being laid at the door of traditional songs. A weaver informant reported to me in 1995 that weavers' songs or *dille* were no longer sung for they were "evil" (*bonde*). Many people would die the following morning as a result of singing such songs the previous night, he told me. This is a significant shift, for the very specialists whose expertise this once was in the past, are turning their backs on the performance of a form of poetry and song now condemned by their own words in the harshest terms and associated with the most grave of consequences.

These critiques form part of a wider movement of opposition to aspects of West African Sufism, and they stem from either Western-educated elites versed in secular rationalism and or from *arabisants* and Islamists versed in ideas of Middle Eastern origin. Both parties have attacked the metaphysical core of Sufi brotherhood practice, and this assault touches the popular view of legitimate religious authority. A bifurcation of the Muslim community has occurred around opposition to Sufi mysticism. Western-educated Senegalese intellectuals and Arabic-educated Islamists make odd bedfellows in their stance against Sufi brotherhoods. These attacks on Sufi mysticism with its particular esoteric construction of knowledge and power are also by implication attacks on the similar construction of knowledge and power among praise-singer groups. But more particularly, the condemnations of their song and poetry as evil, and that they have wicked consequences, are developments that have emerged over the last twenty years or so. What were once complementary modes of knowledge and power are now regarded as being in competition with each other; indeed, they are seen as a moral antithesis. A parallel development has been, however, that these very same praise-singers who no longer perform their traditional songs have taken up singing the praises of religious figures such as marabouts and Muslim holy men. Their expertise has been turned away from activities that are dubious in the eyes of the Islamic faithful to ones that attract the acclaim of the Muslim community and the prestige of their fellow members of society.

The case of the traditional songs of Senegalese praise-singers highlights the historical shifts in the way that songs and their singers have been regarded by the Muslim community, or at least aspects of that community. I now turn my attention to another area of social life that is associated with the idea of evil. In particular, I examine the status of specific acts and practices conceived unambiguously by the vast majority of folk as sinful and bad or evil. This topic is witchcraft. There exist, however, ambiguity and tension around witchcraft accusations, for although people are convinced of the inherently evil nature of witchcraft, there is uncertainty about whether a particular misfortune has been caused by a witch and, if there is agreement that it has, then the question arises of who can be identified as the witch causing the affliction. The discourse of witchcraft in the abstract is relatively clear (see Dilley 2004a); it is the application of these ideas and concepts to the specifics of any particular case that is more tangled and contested.

The case of a young man who was suffering from pains in his stomach is illustrative of the kinds of ambiguities that inhere in any attributions of evil within a community. The afflicted man was in so much pain that he cried out pitifully. His mother, a woman who unusually had a number of domesticated snakes living in the house with her, used some of the magical charms she possessed to try to alleviate the affliction, which she thought was caused by witches (*sukunyaabe*) (see Gaden 1931, 220–221). Witches are universally condemned as evil, for they eat human flesh and drink blood, and they are thought to be in league with spirits or jinn of the bush, whom they summon from tamarind trees to help them. These spirits assist in securing the shadow-self (*mbeelu*) of the witch's victim, which is held in safe-keeping until the witch demands its return, when it will be consumed. To capture a victim, a witch operates at night and transforms itself into an animal, such as a vulture, so that it can fly in search of its prey. Alternatively, a witch might transform itself into a snake that bites its victim, who is sent into a coma.[6]

The young man's mother tried in vain to cure her son, but the illness grew worse. The man ate little and when he ate it seemed to him that he was swallowing snakes or worms. When he had to get out of bed one day to relieve himself, he fell over and cried out that a snake was threatening him and was about to throw itself at him. He was only calmed down once he returned to his room. A healer, a *bileejo,* was consulted and he proceeded to extract from the young man the name of a woman thought to have bewitched him and caused the malady.[7] The woman in question earned her living by tending the sheep and goats of the village and had been suspected for a long time of being a witch although no proof was to be had. The man's illness provided this evidence. He remembered how one day earlier in the year, he had bought milk from the old woman and had had an argument with her about the price she was asking, and she had threatened him with the words: "You are nasty, you will see what will happen to you." It seems as though everything was clear: the woman had seized the man's shadow-self by changing herself into a snake, which is why he felt as though a snake were about to pounce on him. The old woman was eventually persuaded to let the young man's shadow-self go, for she had not yet eaten it as she might have done, and the man was cured. She, however, protested her innocence. The evil of witchcraft, it appeared, had been neutralized and disaster averted.

Sometime later, the young man went to see another specialist healer of great renown who lived some way from his own village. The healer prepared an amulet for his client, which had to be worn at all times, and gave him incantations to recite each night prior to going to bed for protection from the evil intentions of predatory witches. The young man died some time later in circumstances that remain unclear. But what killed him? Whatever it was, it was without doubt evil in the eyes of his family; this was a young man cut off in his prime. However, was it the witchcraft of the old shepherdess with whom he had argued over the price of milk? Or was it, others speculated, his mother who indulged in the strange habit of keeping poisonous snakes in the house? What kind of power did she need to achieve this sort of thing? Precisely the powers perhaps that witches possessed. And what role did the renowned *bileejo* play in this? Was he righting some wrong that the young man had done to another? Misfortune must have a cause, and that cause for most people who knew the young man was considered to be evil. That people know that misfortune is caused by evil is not doubted. But attribution of evil is a complex and multilevel process.

The possible role of the *bileejo* in the case of the young man just considered highlights another area of ambiguity surrounding attributions of evil: that is, if the healer was righting a wrong that the young man had done to another, then there are two very different sides to the matter. The young man's death could thus be seen by the victim or his or her relatives, on the one hand, as a good done to them; the young man's kin, on the other hand, would be hard pressed to regard the misfortune as anything other than the workings of evil. As Peter Lienhardt once pointed out, the problem of attributing the moral evaluations of good and evil to specific acts of magic is akin to viewing shot silk: its color depends on the angle from which it is seen (1968, 51).

I now turn to another specialism, a magical power practice called *nyengo,* which is not caste-specific but is open to anyone. Members of caste social categories are regarded as having an affinity with the arts of *nyengo,* but it is not exclusive to them alone. *Nyengo* or *nyengi* is performed by a *nyengotoodo,* a specialist magician or sorcerer whose training takes the form of an initiatory process entailing contact with powers otherwise hidden and condemned as dangerous and malevolent by ordinary people. *Nyengo* is universally condemned by ardent Muslims and by those less self-conscious about their religious practice as a reprehensible form of magic. It is considered by them to be evil and self-serving. Although it is open to all to learn, few people would openly and publicly admit to practicing the art.

While a Muslim marabout deals with afflictions of the soul and illnesses of the body often caused by jinn, the *nyengotoodo* seeks out the patronage of jinn and other spirits in order to accomplish his art. While a person may come to *nyengo* through the teaching of a specialist, the art itself is only fully developed by means of a tutelary spirit helper. A person enters into a pact with a jinni, and the two are joined in a mutually beneficial relationship. The spirit will ask the person for a sacrifice, perhaps his little finger or even one of his own children. If the person agrees, the finger will be accidentally cut off or badly damaged and have to be amputated for medical reasons; alternatively, the child will die of a mysterious illness or be killed in an accident. It is said that some *nyengotoodo* opt for a slow, painful, and lingering death in exchange for the absolute powers a tutelary spirit can bring. Once a seal has been set upon this gruesome Faustian pact, the practitioner can ask the spirit to carry out his instructions. It will steal things for its patron, it will set fire to the crops or possessions of his enemies, or it will change the shape of things in order to bring about some effect; for instance, the spirit might transform a sandal into a snake that bites the intended victim, leading to his or her death. (One observer noted that spirits do not actually change the shape of things, so rather than transforming a sandal into a snake, the spirit removes the sandal and replaces it with a snake!) Whatever the mechanism involved, the intended effect on the victim of the practice is the same.

Nyengo involves, therefore, an initiatory process in the creation of a relationship with a tutelary spirit, whose knowledge and powers are subsequently put into the hands of the magician for his own personal benefit. *Nyengo* nonetheless differs from many other forms of power-practice for it rarely involves the manipulation of material objects to bring about its intended effects as other techniques, such as *dabare,* do. In the case of *nyengo,* a specific agent—a spirit—is the power that brings about effects, and the potency of *nyengo* is thus represented as an abstract, discrete, and separate force that does not inhere in material things or technical manipulations. These features can be contrasted with those forms of magical efficacy, such as the respective arts of the *bileejo* and of the marabout, which rely upon the manipulation of things—herbs, potions, paper, ink, and so forth. While *dabare,* the making of charms (*nyawndude*), and the confection of talismans and Qur'anic script-potions may be considered to embody forms of potency, it is a potency that is accomplished through operations applied to material things. Embodied in the very material procedures of the certain arts—both "black" and "white"—are potencies that have an effect on the world. This can be contrasted with *nyengo* practices whose operations lie essentially in the ability to "call up" or "invoke" a tutelary spirit (*noddude jinne*).

There is, however, a way in which the procedures of *nyengo* find an echo in the techniques of master marabouts (*sirruyankoobe* or "masters of secrets"), whose advanced methods of divination and spiritual consultation (*khalwa* or "spiritual retreat" and *listikaar* or "dream interpretation") also entail entering into the revered presence of divine forces.[8] Brenner (2000b) makes an important point regarding the perception of the activities of marabouts and even *walis* or "saints": the view from above is that miracles and marvels are seen as signs of a person's spiritual elevation and are not of their own making; the view of ordinary folk from below is that the person is seen to have spiritual power that they are able to employ as they wish. This distinction appears in another form: namely to what extent do marabouts actively summon the presence of divine forces—the view from below—or do they passively prepare themselves in a state of purity and piousness to receive the divine word—the view from above? There are other points of comparison that could be drawn out with respect to *nyengo* and the arts of the Muslim marabout. For instance, Brenner reports that sand-writing, a form of Muslim geomancy (*khatt ar-raml*), taught through a series of initiatic stages, involves at the second stage a "'mystical marriage'" which places the apprentice in contact with the occult forces which will "'open the eyes' of the diviner" (2000a, 54).

The point here is that those individuals (marabouts or magicians) who actively seek out the help, support, and tutelage of a spirit being (whether catego-

rized as good or evil) are more easily suspected by ordinary folk of unwhole-
some motives and malevolent actions than the individual who is regarded as
preparing him- or herself passively for divine inspiration. Contact with the unknown, the invisible, the hidden, and esoteric is a cause of concern for folk who
are left to question what is really going on. It is in this space of uncertainty that
the concepts of both good and evil enter, since no one is really sure what forces
the religious expert is drawing on. People can only judge by the outcomes of
the expert's secret deliberations, and as we have seen these outcomes can be
differently interpreted.

There are also parallels that can be drawn between the stages of craft apprenticeship that I have analyzed elsewhere (Dilley 1989, 1999) and the practice
of *nyengo*. The *maabube,* the social category of weavers, are for instance often
said by others (and this is indeed admitted by the weavers themselves) that
they are "close to the jinn" (*maabube ina badi jinneeje*), and this is a relationship that few ordinary Haalpulaaren would purposefully seek out. Part of the
weavers' system of craft apprenticeship involves preparing the young weaver
for potential contact with the jinn he might come across during the course of
his occupation.

One of the master weavers with whom I learned the craft used to practice
nyengo magic, but gave it up a long time ago on the advice of a Muslim religious
leader because it was "not good" (*ina mojaani*). The weaver confessed to using
it primarily to steal other people's property and possessions. There is, however,
an obvious affinity between the art of the *nyengotoodo* and the activities of the
craftsmen and singers in general, because craft occupations bring their practitioners into a relationship with the jinn that animate the craft or that are associated with aspects of production. Craftsmen by virtue of practicing a craft
are required to forge relationships with jinn, and it is by virtue of this relationship, I argue, that the lore and knowledge of their trades is classified as black
(*balewal*) in contrast to the white (*danewal*) lore and knowledge of the Islamic
clerics (see Dilley 2004a). The *nyengotoodo* similarly creates a connection with
a jinni, although the nature of that relationship and its intended consequences
might be different from those of craftsmen. There is, therefore, an elective affinity between the two activities (*nyengo* and crafts) regarding their connections
to the spirit world, and although it is by no means true to say that only craftsmen practice the art of magic, they are thought by others to have a proclivity
toward it and a propensity to do well in it.

The idea of a pact between man and spirit in *nyengo* gives us another point
of comparison with the relationship between a weaver and the craft's mythical
ancestor, a half-man, half-spirit named Juntel Jabaali. Compared with the *ny-*

engo pact between practitioner and spirit, often sealed after the man has offered a large personal sacrifice to the spirit, the weaver-ancestor relationship is much more substantial in the sense that Juntel is a forefather of many lines of weaving ancestry, and as kinsmen, the descendants share common substance (blood or *yiiyam,* and bone or *yiyal*). The master weaver, Seydu Gisse (Seydou Guisse), claimed direct ancestry from Juntel Jabaali, some sixteen generations back. Although admittedly a historical person in the sense of being separated by time, the mythical ancestor was nonetheless a contemporary presence for the master weaver, with whom he would commune (see Dilley 2004b). Juntel appeared in the weaver's dreams at night to give him spells, incantations, words for his songs (*dillere*), and other forms of knowledge related to the range of specialisms he pursued. Here we find echoes of the relationship between a practitioner and his tutelary spirit in *nyengo,* the difference being that no price is paid for the knowledge and power (*gandal*) gained through the relationship with a weaving ancestor—it is a matter of social being. The weaver gains access to what is part of his spiritual patrimony by virtue of his membership of a particular social category, because he is who he is. There is a price to be paid, however, in a relationship with a tutelary spirit: the *nyengotoodo* sells his soul.

The practice most frequently defined as evil by the vast majority of Haalpulaaren, it could be concluded, is *nyengo.* Witchcraft is similarly regarded. In both cases, the intentions of the practitioner are held to be harmful and wicked, and real misfortune is thought to result from these types of nefarious activities. As Parkin states for Swahilis on the East Coast of Africa (1985a), and so too I might add for Haalpulaaren of Senegal, Satan is inherently evil and is regarded as the source of wickedness in the world.[9] The evil that ensues allows people, Parkin argues, to engage in dialogue about and reflect on the boundaries of the human (1985b, 23). This dialogue and these reflections often take place with respect to specific incidents and events that require some sort of interpretation by local actors. Parkin states that by naming experiences as evil, people generate the opportunity to distinguish between types of evil, thereby excusing some of them (1985a, 227). In addition, once the types are named, people may no longer continue to view those experiences as absolutely evil and feel morally ambivalent about them. My point in this chapter is to argue that discussion of good and evil in the abstract, which takes place at one remove from incidents and events, is more readily cast in absolute terms in comparison with those discussions of specific concrete occurrences that involve particular human actors in known contexts. People may not necessarily excuse some types of evil, but their views of the sorts of causes of misfortune and the forms of agent involved are perhaps, more to the point, less susceptible to absolutist terms of reference.

An analytical consideration of the processes, evaluations, and discussions surrounding concrete social situations has shown that relativistic elements are included as part of the picture drawn by people, who attempt to grope toward some sort of understanding of the world around them.

NOTES

1. See for example discussions of "evil," "the devil," and other entries in Hastings (2000), Cross (2005), and Newby (2002).

2. This phrase is derived from the Arabic *al-kaba'ir*, "great or mortal sins" and contrasts with *al-sagha'ir*, "small or venal sins" See Abun-Nasr (1965).

3. See Ba (1985–1986, 47); Leblanc (1964) on restrictions of singing and dancing in the village of "Amadou Ounaré"; and Tall (1984, 190) on the strict regime of the Haalpulaar Muslim enclave Medina Gunass in southern Senegal.

4. These pedigrees are given either in the form of *kaari jibini karri*, "so-and-so begat so-and-so," or as an ascending list of names reaching back to an apical ancestor. This latter takes the form of, for example, Mamadou, Samba, Koda, Abdoulaye, Yerro, and so on. In passages where a group of relatives with the same forefather is recalled, the performance often takes on a highly rhythmical style: for example, Yerro Ali, Bubu Ali, Bukar Ali, and so forth.

5. See Gaden's analysis (in Tyam [1935]) of the structure of Mohammadou Tyam's (Caam's) *qasida* in praise of the life and deeds of El Hajj Umar Taal.

6. In parts of the Middle East a "ghoul," a desert-dwelling shape-shifting demon, can assume the guise of an animal, especially a hyena. The creature is thought of as evil for it leads travellers astray to the desert wastes where it kills and eats them; it also preys on children, drinks blood (like witches do), robs graves, and eats the dead. Among Haalpulaaren, the hyena (*fowru*) is an image of evil too: "the hyena is bad, the old hyena is bad above all else" goes a popular saying. The animal goes by a number of sobriquets: *njarki* means the galloper owing to its lumbering gait; *wasooru*, "the poor"; and *baleeru*, "the black," as in the phrase *ndu bawli reedu* or "he of the black stomach" or "with evil intentions." The hyena is, however, a multidimensional character that is not simply evil but also greedy, awkward, and clumsy; a hypocrite; and the butt of ruses played by the hare in popular fables. This figure of evil has comedic value too. (See Overing in Parkin [1985] who claims that the Piaroa find humor in the figure of evil.)

7. Old women are often accused of having evil tongues and doing harm to others through their malicious words (*konngol bonngol*). A frequent target of accusations of malicious intentions is the figure of the "evil stepmother," *yumma bondo,* a bad mother who has the evil eye for the children of the other women of a household, especially the cowives of a polygamous husband. A woman will take the first mouthful of food she has prepared for the children of the household to show to everyone that she has not cast a spell on the meal. The father of the house might say of this: "*ittu yitere yumma,*" or "the removal the mother's [evil] eye."

8. See Dilley (2004a, chapter 6) for further details.

9. There is a debate in both Islamic and Christian thought about the inherent evil of the devil or Satan, and some lines of theological argument suggest that absolute moral evaluations are not wholly appropriate. Iblis, the fallen angel and bringer of evil in Mus-

lim cosmology, was condemned by Allah for not bowing down before Adam, the first man who was made of clay, for, as Iblis pointed out, he himself was made of fire. Some commentators have argued that Iblis's fall was due to his pride, but other interpretations suggest instead that he refused to worship Adam because this act would be tantamount to ascribing partners to Allah, the sin of *shirk*. There are echoes here of Milton's portrayal of Satan as the "Patron of liberty" in *Paradise Lost* (see Hastings 2000, 164–166; Newby 2002, 189–191).

REFERENCES

Abun-Nasr, Jamil M. 1965. *The Tijaniyya: A Sufi Order in the Modern World*. London: Oxford University Press.

Ba, Omar. 1985–1986. Le rôle des écoles islamiques dans le développement de la culture arabo-islamique dans le bassin du Fleuve Sénégal." PhD diss., University of Paris IV—Sorbonne.

Brenner, Louis. 2000a. "Muslim Divination and the History of Religion in Sub-Saharan Africa." In *Insight and Artistry: A Cross-Cultural Study of Divination in Central and West Africa*, edited by John Pemberton, 45–59. Washington, DC: Smithsonian Institute.

———. 2000b. "Sufism in Africa." In *African Spirituality*, edited by Jacob Olupona, 324–349. New York: The Crossroads Publishing Co.

Cross, F. L., ed. 2005. *The Oxford Dictionary of the Christian Church*. Oxford: Oxford University Press.

Dilley, Roy M. 1989. "Secrets and Skills: Apprenticeship among Tukolor Weavers." In *Apprenticeship: From Theory to Method*, edited by M. W. Coy, 181–198. New York: State University of New York Press.

———. 1999. "Ways of Knowing, Forms of Power: Aspects of Apprenticeship among Tukulor Mabube Weavers." In *Cultural Dynamics* 11, no. 1:33–55.

———. 2004a. *Between the Mosque and the Termite Mound: Islamic and Caste Knowledge Practices among Haalpulaaren, Senegal*. African Monographs Series. London: International Africa Institute.

———. 2004b. "Time-Shapes and Cultural Agency among West African Craft Specialists." In *The Qualities of Time: Temporal Dimensions of Social Form and Human Experience*, edited by Wendy James and David Mills, 235–248. London: Tavistock.

Gaden, Henri. 1931. *Proverbes et maximes peuls et toucouleurs traduits, expliqués et annotés*. Travaux et Mémoires de l'Institut d'Ethnologie 16. Paris: Institut d'Ethnologie.

Hastings, Adrian, ed. 2000. *Oxford Companion to Christian Thought*. Oxford: Oxford University Press.

LeBlanc, Colette. 1964. "Un village de la vallée du Sénégal: Amadi Ounaré." *Cahiers d'Outre-Mer* 66:117–148.

Lienhardt, Peter A. (ed. and trans.). 1968. *The Medicine Man: Swifa Ya Nguvumali*. Oxford: Clarendon Press.

Newby, Gordon. 2002. *A Concise Encyclopedia of Islam*. Oxford: Oneworld.

Parkin, David, ed. 1985a. "Entitling Evil: Muslims and Non-Muslims in Coastal Kenya." In *The Anthropology of Evil*, 224–243. Oxford: Basil Blackwell.

————. 1985b. Introduction to *The Anthropology of Evil*, 1–25. Oxford: Basil Blackwell.

Tall, Emanuelle K. 1984. *Guérir à Cubalel: interprétation de la maladie et pratiques thérapeutiques chez les Haalpulaaren dans la vallée du Fleuve Sénégal.* Paris: Ecole des Hautes Études en Sciences Sociales.

Tyam, Mohammadou Aliou. 1935. *La vie d'El Hadj Omar—Qacida en poular. Transcription, traduction, notes et glossaire par Henri Gaden.* Travaux et Mémoires de l'Institut d'Ethnologie 21. Paris: Institut d'Ethnologie.

12 REFLECTIONS REGARDING GOOD AND EVIL

The Complexity of Words in Zanzibar

KJERSTI LARSEN

> For it was safer to have that terrible frightening force held in a shape
> associated with the mythical or the magical, than loose, or as it were at
> large, in a person, and in a person who had the power to move me.
>
> —DORIS LESSING

This essay addresses the moral category of evil from an anthropological perspective. For that reason I shall explore "evil" from a particular ontology rather
than as a universal concept. This is the only approach that could disclose understandings that may challenge the dominant emic Judeo-Christian theological or philosophical framework. Investigating the manner in which evil
is embedded in cosmologies of the everyday, I shall pay attention to practice
including discourse as, within this domain, it would only rarely be elaborated
in any abstract mode. Furthermore, being attentive to how evil is perceived
and identified through its practice renders possible a discussion of its potentially different shapes and divergent qualities. The epigraph from Doris Lessing
(1973, 479) is precisely chosen because it conceptualizes evil not as an exclusive
category external to society, but as a force made part of personhood and activated in human relationships. Inspired by this insight, my aim is to explore
the manner in which evil would be sensed and conceptualized in a Zanzibari,
Swahili lifeworld. By exploring the dynamics of evil and what it opposes to, I
shall focus on questions relating to how evil is perceived, lived, and enacted, the
ways in which evil is identified and how its presence impacts daily life routines
and human relationships. The exploration is based on ethnographic fieldwork
in Zanzibar Town, including both Stone Town or Old Town (*Mji Mkongwe*)

and its suburbs (*ng'ambo*) from 1984 until the present. The women and men I have worked with belong to different communities and economic categories, they are all Sunni Muslims and thus, Islam and Islamic teachings are incorporated into their everyday lives. With the aspiration of being good Muslims, most would understand and negotiate their lifestyle and activities with reference to the Quran and the Hadith as well as to translations provided by local religious scholars (*walimu* and *mashehe*). Not claiming reference to any particular theological position, approaching *evil* as well as encounters associated with potential malice within a Zanzibari cosmology of the everyday, I will thus be focusing on practice and the colloquial discourse, including terms, concepts, and conditions associated with harm.

EVIL AND THE COMPLEXITY OF WORDS

Within a Swahili, Muslim lifeworld, notions of evil included in discourses on morality and malevolence are perceived as potentially manifest in human relationships. The potential of behaving decently as well as causing harm, if not evil, is seen as immanent to human existence. The presence of mythical or magical shapes, including spirits, is not a necessity for experiencing fright or malice, although such potencies also form part of reality.[1] From research among the Swahili on the Kenyan coast, David Parkin argues that "among the Swahili, evil is . . . excessive behaviour, but it is quite unnecessary for humans, having been foisted on mankind by the negative forces of divinity. For the Swahili the problem of what to do with evil is relatively clear: control excess of behaviours and you eliminate it" (1985a, 231). Interesting, regarding this more general understanding among the Swahili, is that with reference to the wider cosmological system and questions of morality, women and men in Zanzibar Town maintained that humans have the potential for doing "both good and bad," as they put it. Only God, they insisted, is beyond mistakes and malevolence—beyond emotion. Time and again, I received the explanation that "Only God possesses *jabari,* this thing that makes God different and above human beings, although, some persons would still think that they too have *jabari;* that they are without any faults and that only they know how to behave and judge others. These people have *kibri;* they are arrogant, proud, and self-important." Persons perceived to embody such above-mentioned features are thus considered responsible for enmity, quarrelling, and malevolence, in both personal and social relationships. Whether such malice should be denoted as "evil," an emic Judeo-Christian theological or philosophical concept, is a question of analogy (van Beek 1994). Potencies that, perhaps, could be seen as somehow analogous to evil are, in terms of a Zanzibari ontology, mainly located within human relationships, something relational, pertaining to emotions such as jealousy, envy, greed, and self-importance.[2] Considering notions of evil and ideas about the propensity for "doing evil," the potency ascribed to words when these are pronounced in particular contexts or also enacted, is notable. Interestingly, while invocations are engaged so as to provide protection, "talk" and nonverbal communication in the form of excessive behavior, are mostly associated with malice. It is, I argue, the emotional or intentional states of human beings expressed though words, talk, and actions (*vitendo*) that are here perceived and considered potentially threatening. Through discord in human interchange, enmity and harm may be evoked, which are considered to be grounded in the emotional condition of human beings. In the following section, I shall further explore in what manner evil as a concept and experience could compare with a broader Zanzibari cosmology. In the process I will refer to vernacular terms applied in situations of enmity as well as in discussions about, and reactions toward, malevolence and, more widely, in what is here perceived as threats against happiness and harmony.

MORALITY, MALEVOLENCE, AND
THE QUEST FOR PROTECTION

There is, in this Muslim society off the coast of East Africa, a constant concern about how to manage public life: what kind of life-situation, behavior, and relationships to disclose in front of others, and what to conceal. People are apprehensive about talk (*maneno*), in this rather small island society.[3] Simultaneously, there is a common awareness that life is multifaceted and not always lived according to the shared ideals and values. Both women and men would often complain that in their society "we all like to talk in derogatory ways about each other (*kejeli*) and, currently, greed has become part of our being or self (*choyo ndani ya nafsi yetu*)." To be talked about or noticed as better off than others—economically, socially, or in matters of attractiveness and with behavior or comportment noticeably different from the dominant trend or fashion— is perceived as potentially dangerous. It is believed to engender jealousy and envy. Such an attitude suggests that the way to deal with emotion and human character, especially of others, becomes a major concern. Jealousy and envy (*wivu*), selfishness and arrogance (*choyo*), as well as self-importance (*kubri*) all are emotional states recognized as destructive—a common understanding rendering most social relationships ambiguous. A main issue for those experiencing malevolence while longing for happiness (*heri*), bliss (*raha*), and harmony (*umoja*) is how to protect themselves from the potential envy and selfishness of others. Through *dua,* supplicatory prayers, favors may be requested as well as protection. Moreover, the words of the Quran being read or invoked are, by themselves, understood to bring protection as well as clarity and wisdom, to heal and remove misfortune.[4] Certain verses of the Quran are learned by heart and recited in situations of anxiety, threats, and when entering the house of someone whose intentions seem unclear. Various forms of ritual readings or invocations (*dua, kisomo, soma, zinguo*) are also performed in order to supplicate protection and healing and as thanksgiving for already performed requests (Larsen 2011). In contrast to *salaa,* that is, the daily prescribed prayers, supplicatory prayers, *dua,* may be rehearsed at any time of the day and anywhere and can be said in any language. Thus, in order to cope with what is perceived as the potential malevolence of human beings, God's protection is called on through various forms of prayers. The various supplicatory prayers include *Halbadiri*, a liturgical invocation used to identify and punish those who intentionally have brought misfortune to others and, especially, to the one on whose behalf the reading is performed. As such, the reading of *Halbadiri* could be seen as an act that is directed toward evil. Yet, the invocation may also engender malice in the sense that it is "read" in order to destroy the person(s) who cause the malevolence.

HALBADIRI

Halbadiri involves the Quran: words of the Quran, God, the angels, the fight against human disobedience, human malevolence, and sacrifice (*sadaka*). The text, *Halbadiri,* amounts to a small book or booklet incorporating passages from the Quran, quoting the names of the participants at the Battle of Badr. The power involved in the reading is said to be that of the angels, whose intervention was decisive in ensuring victory when Prophet Mohammed and his followers went to war at Badr against the nonbelievers, the disobedient. *Halbadiri* is seen as the most potent or severe supplicatory prayer. It is never read carelessly or without good reason. When people experience what they call *zukuzuku,* that is, constant problems in their lives, one problem following in the wake of another, *Halbadiri* is read. "But," said most people, "*Halbadiri* is a perilous prayer (*halbadiri ni dua nzito*), it can destroy people and may even turn back towards oneself." *Halbadiri* is thus read so as to identify and punish the person(s) responsible for malice, those causing discord and misfortune in the lives of others. *Halbadiri* is known to work its way slowly. I was told that it could take up to three months from the time *Halbadiri* is read until God provided the culprit what she or he deserved—*mungu anawastahiki*. It is important to note that while reading *Halbadiri* God is called upon to sentence those responsible for malice. In the end, it is thus God who is understood to interfere, not the person enacting *Halbadiri*. While reading *Halbadiri*, a sacrifice, *sadaka*, has to be provided so as to give thanks for that which has been requested and to ensure that what has been requested may be granted. Let me provide an example emphasizing both the manner in which words may be performed and how malice is seen as incorporated and potentially identifiable within social relationships and yet remains uncertain. It remains uncertain in the sense that no particular person or relationships would ever be clearly identified as being responsible for malevolence. Rather, it is the coming course of events in the lives of those initially suspected of malice that would either confirm or weaken the initial suspicion.

BI SALMA'S *HALBADIRI*

One morning when I was visiting Bi Salma, a woman now in her late forties who I have known since 1985, Bwana Saidi came to read *Halbadiri*. On that occasion, Bi Salma explained her wish to perform *Halbadiri* in the following way: "I want everyone who has good wishes for me to come close and that those who wish me misery would disappear from my surroundings (*Kila mtu anoakheri na mie kaja karibu na kila mtu anaombaya na mie akasfiq*)." Then, Bwana Saidi said he wanted to make sure that I had understood the importance of the sacrifice in *Halbadiri* and in all other situations of prayers or requests made to God. In his elaboration, he clearly placed the ritual reading of *Halbadiri* within the Islamic realm and, moreover, emphasized the relational dimension between God and human beings: "We learned about the sacrifice from the Qur'an. Ibrahim was willing to sacrifice his son Issak when God asked him to. When God realized Ibrahim's submission—his obedience—he sent an angel to stop the sacrificing of Issak and to replace Issak by a lamb. When Ibrahim pronounced the *u* before the *Akubaru*, that is, in *Allah u Akubahru*, Issak was replaced by the lamb. This is why we always express these words while enacting the slaughtering: *Allah u Akubaru*. This is why we have to slaughter, to give *sadaka*, when requesting something."

In advance, Bi Salma had done the necessary preparations: a hen of mixed colors, not white, had been purchased, as well as an octopus, rock salt, raw coffee beans, and lime—all items that are meant to materialize and make sensible that which is sensed as evil. While the hen was to be slaughtered toward the end of the reading, the other items were put on a small tray before the invocation began. Bi Salma sat on a white cloth spread on top of a mat just in front of Bwana Saidi, covering her newly showered body and hair with *khanga*—all preparations meant to materialize purity and cleanness of body and intentions.[5] Bwana Saidi sat on a praying-mat. Eventually, the maid, Hanifa, brought the incense jar; the room was filled with fragrant smoke. Bwana Saidi first recited the Fatiha and, subsequently, a prayer, before Bi Salma presented her justification for this *Halbadiri:* "I have asked you to witness the reading of *Halbadiri* for my protection and the protection of my children, because we have cried due to deception, discord, jealousy and all other things bad. Let God provide them what they deserve, *Allah sa'lahu, bihakimil, hakimia.* Even if it is my mother, the one who has given birth to me, let her from this *Halbadiri* be judged by God."[6]

Then, Bi Salma mentioned the names of other persons close to her, including her own watchman and maid, friends, and the members of the extended family, all those who were close and all those who entered the house. When she finished, Bwana Saidi started to read *Halbadiri.* Regularly and in between the different verses, the maid threw a handful of a mixture of salt, coffee beans, lime, and octopus taken from the tray on a small fire burning outside in the courtyard. All items thrown into the fire are associated with bad smell and thus, in this context, perceived to be as contemptible as malevolence itself. When such items are burned, thrown into the fire, they give off sounds and smells portraying how the words uttered would equally "burn" those who have already committed malevolence; anything and anyone as harmful as what the various ingredients represent would thus have to be eliminated. Finally, when the full text had been read, a prayer was said, and the hen was sacrificed. As expected in all contexts of Islamic ritual slaughtering, Bwana Saidi put on his *kofia* (cap/fez) before sacrificing the hen, which he would afterward take to a particular place where offerings are left (*mizimu*). After this, the *Halbadiri* was concluded and Bi Salma explained that she now had to let the words work their way through the incense and the angels. From then on it was up to God to identify those responsible for her misfortune and suffering. "Only God knows; the one to blame (*laumu*) could even be me," she said. When Bwana Saidi had left, Bi Salma resumed her reflections upon the fragility of social relationships: "One thing is jealousy, but selfishness and greed (*choyo*) is something else. In situations where people feel jealousy they want what others have and feel bad because they do not have it. Selfishness is dangerous because it means that people do not want others to have access to what they themselves have not. To this end they would also do anything to prevent others from achieving what they themselves desire. They would as well do anything in order to take from others what others have; even if it would still be inaccessible to them."

When Bi Salma says that people could do "anything," this refers to gossip, lies, and harmful attitudes, as well as taking recourse to remedies activating sorcery (*uganga*) and witchcraft (*uchawi*). Her contemplation echoes the more general idea of human relationships in this society and, moreover, indicates how all everyday life encounters could be potentially menacing. Such an understanding as the one expressed here, does induce mistrust and worries in social relationships. In such situations, the Quran constitutes a meaningful presence of trust and hope. Women and men in Zanzibar do, indeed, feel the need for its protection (*kinga*).

ISLAM, MUSLIM COSMOLOGY, AND THE INCORPORATION OF EVIL

There is a constant worry about the potential motivation of others to create discord (*fitina*) and quarreling (*ugomwi*) as well as enmity (*hasidi*), harm (*ubaya*), and even deception in the wide sense of the term (*ufisadi*). Against such dangers, the Quran provides a means for maintaining harmony and happiness. The words of the Quran being read or expressed do by themselves bring protection. This could be either as invocations or as "incorporated," that is, written on paper, soaked in water that is then ingested or applied on the body (*kombe*), carried as amulets (*hirizi*), or when encircling the person in the sense of sound when recited (*zinguo*) (see Caplan 1997). Bringing in the Quran, the *msahafu*, I wish, like in the case of *Halbadiri*, to draw attention to the presence of God (*Mungu*, Allah) and Islam, or religion (*dini*) as Zanzibaris would say, in this realm of moral sociality. Referring to Islam and to a Zanzibari, Muslim cosmology I am, as already mentioned, particularly focusing on the everyday life discourse. Hence, unlike many scholars and specialists, I am not claiming reference to any theological discourse. Rather, what I discuss is how common people, all being Muslims, intending to be what they consider "good Muslims," understand religion and the world: what they consider rightful and commendable (*halali*), and what they, in different situations, comprehend as prohibited and forbidden (*haramu*). The reading of *Halbadiri* illustrates how God may be called upon to sentence those who create malevolence. Within this cosmology, God is perceived as the force that eventually could provide protection from everything threatening. Yet, God might also threaten to test the morality of human beings and thus elicit their readiness to submit to or disobey God's will. Such tests (*mitihani*), as people call them, refer to an understanding that humans go through periods of suffering and misfortune during their lifetime. God is testing their observance, inflicting suffering in their lives. In this sense, God is perceived in terms of both protection and threat toward harmony—at least, for an immediate experience of harmony. Such trials are also considered necessary for human beings so as to instantiate their submission to God's will. Thus, from what precedes, I would suggest that within their cosmology it is therefore more disobedience (*ukaidi, uhalifu*) rather than evil that is emphasized. The effects of disobedience seem to be a negation of what would otherwise promote harmony (*kheri, umoja, upatano*). Time and again, women and men have reminded me: "God is the creator of human beings, angels, spirits (*jinn*), and animals. Among the angels, Ibilis disobeyed God when told to submit to human beings. Ibilis was punished for his disobedience (*ukaidi*) and became the enemy of human beings, inducing in them destructive emotions."

Ibilis referred to in this quote is the being or essence that somehow seems to resemble the Judeo-Christian Satan. Yet, attention should here be paid to how Ibilis as a manifestation of disobedience and malevolence in the Islamic cosmology is not represented as being explicitly evil to the same extent as Satan usually is in the case of Christian, protestant cosmology. In this regard, evil, I suggest, appears as internal and, in principle, as a controllable dimension, not an entity in itself that could eventually be eliminated. Rather, Ibilis remains internal to the human realm and should not be destroyed or expelled as an outside external potency. Ibilis is incorporated as a part of the human condition. This further implies that evil is placed inside the moral domain, not outside. Such an understanding engenders a form of existence where, in this case, humans are attributed the propensity to be seduced by their various emotional states and thus to engage in, if not evil acts, at least, disobedience and thus act in ways which will undermine states of harmony.

The different terms and notions discussed to this point denote what are considered harmful characteristics of human beings. These characteristics, all included in discourses on morality are, moreover, equally perceived to be potentially present in all human relationships. Yet, as I shall describe, who or what, exactly, embodies or emanates that which may engender evil seems always to remain disputable and uncertain. The case of *Halbadiri* illustrated how words spoken within such ritual contexts are perceived as potentially mortal. They summon potencies beyond human capacity. Spoken and enacted in daily life, words like excessive behavior are still potent in the sense that they are perceived to reveal or transmit potentially dangerous emotional configurations, but, as I will illustrate, nevertheless, these words and actions always remain within the human realm.

WORDS SPOKEN FOR GOOD AND FOR BAD—
THE ORAL QUALITY OF EVIL

Words are potent within a Zanzibari lifeworld. They can please and bring joy, harm, insult, or flatter. Words are never perceived as being neutral and without effects. Words are not only what they literally mean, they are loaded. Words are thus powerful by themselves—as in the case of the words of the Quran—or can be made such, being as they are the basic means of exchange in human relationships. How words are interpreted does require an identification of the kind and character of the relationships in which they are exchanged. The circumstances in which they enter are crucial to understanding the way words are both produced and received and what exactly they are felt to portray. In a Zanzibari context, words, *maneno,* are steeped in potency.

People turn to the words of the Quran as well as to various prayer books whenever they are up against uncertainties and misfortune; when emotional as well as mundane matters are to be dealt with.[7] The word of the Quran as medicament and protection is, as such, a common shared medium. Yet there are also other kinds of words: talk or gossip, words uttered in daily life as part of daily conversation, exchange of messages; all of these considered potentially harmful. They could be meant to inform, gladden, appease, hurt, or harm or their uttering itself could be harmful. This is what people find threatening. This is what is seen as malevolence and malice. This is where enmity emanates—from the emotions and conditions of human beings. Against such words, protection is needed. The reading of *Halbadiri,* as I have shown, is a last resort. Words, talk, gossip, and rumor can be used to create discord (*kutia fitina*), to produce quarrels (*kufanya ugomwi*), and, when they do so, they are usually seen as motivated by greed (*choyo*), desire (*tamaa*), and jealousy (*wivu*)—all human emotions that potentially lead persons into doing harm. Zanzibaris often express their disillusionment by saying: "*Dunia mbaya, tamaa imesidi; watu wanahisi kama kwanini huyo nacho, mimi sina,*" that is, "This world is bad, greed has increased; people think that why should others have, when I have not."[8] How does the presence of such utterances and alleged intentions impact daily life routines and affect human relationships?

Taking this query into consideration, I shall now turn to words in the sense of talk (*maneno*), in order to show the ways in which they bring malevolence and enmity into social relationships. Here a link between notions of malice and experiences of feeling threatened has to be presupposed. How words are linked to notions of maliciousness (*ushari, ufisadi*) and the manner in which they may form part of practices and activities (*vitendo*) requires some attention. The terms embed references to characteristics or behavior experienced as threatening and potentially destructive to relationships, as well as reflecting attitudes and actions known to create quarreling and discomfort. Whether the meaning of malevolence differs from meanness (*baya*), attention should be placed on local understandings and the way in which malice is perceived within this particular lifeworld; how does it enter everyday life settings through talk and actions?

TALK AND THE PERFORMATIVITY OF WORDS

Maneno, they say, is used to create disharmony, quarreling, and discord in the life of others (*kutia fitina*). Discussing the power of words, it is compelling to include the situation in which they are uttered. It is the context surrounding the spoken words that decides the meaning of what is said (Stewart and Strathern 2004). In this sense, the meaning of words and talk is context-sensitive. The fact that talk or words are perceived as threatening in Zanzibar is, for instance, conveyed by women's and men's constant anxiety regarding the way their manners, engagements, life situation, or private affairs are perceived and revealed by others. To talk and to publicly unveil the secrets of others is taken as a sign of malevolence—of destructive actions (*vitendo vibaya*). The motivation for such behavior is understood to be envy or jealousy, or also as a sign that the person doing so possesses *kiburi* and *jeuri* or *choyo* and *wivu; kiburi* and *jeuri* refer to rudeness and insolence, to arrogance and self-importance, while *choyo* and *wivu* mean greed and selfishness, jealousy and envy. These are all perceived as emotional states that motivate malice. I shall now give an example of the meaning and effect of talk and how it is experienced and managed.[9] This will exemplify how certain rumors and gossip become constitutive of the surroundings they are produced from. In this sense, words become threatening precisely because they are interpreted with reference to events, relationships, and notions already present within the milieu or networks where they are spoken (Stewart and Strathern 2004, 30). Talk feeds from and at the same time feeds into a given set of relationships and ongoing events including the dealings and exchanges involved. The following case, the course of which I was recently able to follow, involved both women and men, although the two main characters were women. The content and dynamic of the event could, however, apply equally to men or to relationships involving both genders.

Maryam and Halima had been close friends for some years. Both were divorced and managing their own households. Yet, their relationship had constantly to be adjusted by Halima, the older among the two, and also the one whose economic position was vulnerable and inferior to that of Maryam. Time and again, Halima felt that her honor (*ari*) was at stake because of Maryam being the one whose economic position could easily put shame on her by making her appear as dependent and thus subordinate. Without entering into details, I have observed over the years how Halima, in spite of her limited means, has made Maryam lose face (*vunja uso*), not by confronting her verbally, but through what she referred to as "actions" (*vitendo*)—for instance, by bringing huge quantities of elaborate food whenever Maryam has invited her and other friends for parties. As reactions, these are, according to Halima, motivated by previous incidents were Maryam had asked Halima to prepare food on order for her parties, parties to which Halima had not been invited, an attitude usually interpreted as performance of social distinction.

Halima explained that actions could be more important than words, and that one should rather convey reactions by actions, not by words (*Vitendo muhimu kuliko maneno, unafanya kwa njia ya vitendo*). This means that the excessive behavior described should be understood in terms of a "performativity of words." Here, it should be kept in mind that words in Zanzibar are conceived as dangerous when spoken. Because words can easily be turned against the one who has initially spoken, Halima explained that she would rather act than verbally expose her criticisms and challenges toward those close to her. Bringing food is, by definition, a gesture of generosity and kindness. Yet interpreting such a gesture as carrying malevolence, as something done in order to bring shame upon somebody, can easily be substantiated through what is observed and sensed, although such an interpretation cannot be claimed or publicly uttered—it would not make sense. It could still be suspected that such an act has been done in order to bring disgrace upon another person. This cannot ever be proved and remains disputable and uncertain. Let me provide another example:

In a certain period when Halima had many guests staying in her house, for days she was too busy to call Maryam—whereas usually they would speak on the phone daily. Once the guests had left, Halima eventually called in order to ask for news. Answering her call, Maryam told her that their friendship was over. In this context, Maryam did not say that she felt offended by Halima's sudden silence, but rather that she was tired of being told by others how Halima talked negatively about her publicly and even revealed her secrets. From then on, she contended, only *Salam Aleikum—Aleikum Salaam* should be uttered between them. On hearing these explicit and thus threatening words, Halima immediately started to mobilize their common circle of friends, making them aware that what Maryam had said was only an illustration of Maryam's own personality. Halima claimed that she had not done anything wrong, nor had any intentions of causing harm, and, moreover, that she had certainly not talked about Maryam's private affairs in public. She then called a larger circle of friends and relatives, explaining to me that it was necessary to tell everybody about what had happened so that they would not come to think (*fikiri*) that she had actually been gossiping. This she did as an act of protection, to make sure that she would be seen as the one wronged and, thus, to prevent being marginalized in their circle of friends. In the following days, Halima would make a point of dropping in on friends and neighbors in order to tell them what had happened. The conversations usually developed into a discussion about the difficult and unpleasant features of Maryam's personality and, moreover, that her personality was the actual reason why she could, in the first place, speak such words to Halima, accusing *her* of gossiping. Words such as *mjeuri, mkorofi,* and *kibri* were constantly mentioned, identifying Maryam as a person who always saw herself as better than others, as being perfect, and others being the ones who made mistakes. "She would criticize everybody, *mkorofi* (pestilent person)," it was said. "She thinks that she is like Almighty God" (*Anahisi yeye ni kama mwenyezi mungu*), meaning that Maryam thought that she could say whatever she liked to other people without them reacting. These ongoing conversations were obviously meant to establish a shared, negative portrait of Maryam within their common milieu. Still, in this situation, the emotional states of greed or *choyo* were not brought up. As it turned out, the main reason for Maryam's reaction was that there had been a gathering at Halima's place where one of the guests—a common friend and a previous lover of Maryam—had said negative things about her without Halima immediately making Maryam aware of this by phoning her. Maryam had later been informed about this slandering by another common friend who had been present; this apparently meant that Halima had failed her by not immediately informing her of this event so that, in turn, Maryam, on her side, could activate other words to protect her own position. As this case also indicates, the mobile phone has obviously increased the circulation of words as well as the expectations of information about words that have been spoken.

When such situations as the one just described occur, the support of other people is crucial (*kutetea*). Gossip and exchange of harmful words, between persons or families, evoke contexts for moral evaluations and judgment. The doings and oral elaborations of each party are open to contention. For a certain period of time, there would, as I have illustrated, be continuous negotiations of how and why, for instance, the quarreling and enmity started and who could be seen as bearing the responsibility for it. In most cases, the result is a reshuffling of relationships, but not a shared or commonly agreed upon understanding of who is to blame. This is perhaps what Stewart and Strathern (2004, 39) call "the interpretative ambiguity of gossip"; thus, in the end, it is the interpretations of situations and events that fashion the outcome. The talking in the preceding case was actually about somebody *said to have been talking*, revealing secrets or private matters about another person who, in the first place, had conveyed these in confidence, that is, in a state of trust (*imani*). Transgression of confidence is perceived as something done intentionally to create discord and enmity in human relationships; it is *maneno ili ya kutia fitina*, words spoken so as to create enmity. It seems, thus, that within this particular lifeworld, malevolence, or malice done with an intention to harm, or even destroy, is what comes closest to what elsewhere could be denoted as evil.[10]

There is a shared understanding that malice, as well as protection against its effects, can be activated through and by words. In this society, words are not ever what they literally appear to be. They are loaded or, rather, although of different kinds, carry a potentiality of enmity and harm and, at the same time, a protection against them. In her book, *Deadly Words,* Jeanne Favret-Saada argues from her research in the French Bocage that "witchcraft is spoken words"—words incorporating power rather than knowledge or information (1980, 9–10). In that particular society, with spoken words, there is no neutral position: exchanging words never only expresses a wish to communicate. In Zanzibar, words are potentially threatening. In both cases, however, it appears that words gain their potency from human intention, whether the intentionality is perceived to emanate from emotional or rational reactions. Yet the wish and willingness to constantly partake in exchanging words, in communicating are also what turn women and men into socially appreciated persons. Consequently, a significant concern in the Zanzibari context relates, exactly, to how best to guard oneself against the destructive potencies forming part of this world. Apart from seeking various forms of protection through the words of the Quran, *Halbadiri* represents, as shown in the beginning of this chapter, one forceful option among several other kinds of remedies. When everything else has been tried, this could eventually provide protection.

Having discussed evil and cosmologies of the everyday by focusing on human engagement in and with words and talk, I have emphasized that evil is perceived as internal to society. Evil then has to be dealt with as part of human existence, as part of sociality. Nevertheless, there also exist within this reality potencies or shapes of a different order than human beings who hold the capacity to cause misfortune and malice. The reason why I find it relevant to bring in these capacities here is that their presence and character further confirm that malice might not be perceived as an entity existing outside human practice and consciousness, but rather is internal to it. Before concluding, I shall thus briefly comment on these, how they are associated with evil and in what manner they not only relate to, but are integral to a human existence.

DOING OR BEING EVIL?

There are particular cultural configurations that are seen as representative of evil. Still, also these are, more or less, incorporated in the human domain. Reflecting on the idea of malevolence, I have, out of curiosity, sometimes discussed the English term *evil* with people in Zanzibar Town who have a certain command over English, asking whether there would be a comparable term in Swahili. Usually they would say, precisely, quarreling (*ugomwi*) and discord (*fitina*), that is, that which negates the possibility of being and living peacefully together (*umoja, upatano*). They would also mention greed (*choyo*), arrogance, and self-importance (*jeuri*), all characteristics considered as relating to human, emotional states that, when uncontrolled, will only lead to suffering and misfortune. Interestingly, nobody mentioned *ushari*, a term that literally translates as evil. Sometimes, after further reflection on translation they would mention *uchawi, mumiani,* and *uwanga* as different phenomena that could be denoted as evil. These are all perceived as different kinds of nonhuman potencies, and yet, at the same time, they are clearly interrelated with what are otherwise seen as human capacities.

Uchawi, a term usually translated into English as witchcraft, refers to a sort of esoteric knowledge that can be activated by humans so as to harm, even kill. A person with such knowledge is called *mchawi* (pl. *wachawi*). A *mchawi* is known to activate and apply various forms of destructive or mortal medicaments. It should be noted that *mchawi* will perform *uchawi* on behalf of other persons who actually seek her or his assistance with the intention of harming somebody (Larsen 2013).[11] As such, *uchawi* refers to knowledge and skills that certain persons hold and use in order to create misery. It is activated in situations where someone, driven by jealousy or greed, intends to harm somebody. Thus in ontological terms, it seems once again that it is humans who are the source of evil and that in order to succeed they may also activate extraordinary potencies.

Furthermore, there exist amoral humans called *wanga*. The term *Mwanga* (pl. *wanga*) refers to a particular kind of human being, a person, different from others and known to take sacrifices from among family members: siblings, offspring, nieces, and nephews. Supposedly *wanga* belong to a particular coterie where, in order to be included as a member, a person has to offer human vic-tims from their own family as sacrifices (*wahanga*). They are said to meet in secret places during the nighttime where they, among other activities, per-form a particular form of dance, *kwanga*, while speaking in a special way all by themselves—to express their happiness for succeeding in their task (*kazi*). Pat Caplan discusses the *wanga* from Mafia Island, who are perceived as sor-cerers associated with the night and corpses (Caplan 1997). In the Zanzibari context, *wanga* will hide their "true" character. Nevertheless, with time, per-sons who actually are *wanga* may eventually be recognized, usually from the way they behave in situations of illness and death among family members and thus by their excessive or peculiar behavior. Interestingly, the destructive deeds ascribed to *mwanga* are not explained by reference to emotional states such as jealousy and envy or, for that matter, related to aspects of personality such as arrogance and self-importance. The reason behind their deeds is not explained by reference to anything other than them being *wanga*.

Mumiani designates another kind of potency, considered to be something of the past, not anymore forming part of the present. It was told that those as-sociated with *mumiani* were persons, almost similar to *wachawi*, who equally had skills that could be activated in order to cause harm. They would conduct their malice due to their own envy and enmity (*hasidi*). Through the use of a mirror, or only by caressing or patting the back of a person's hand, they would be able to dry up this person's blood (*kauka*) and bring about death. Unlike *mumiani*, which belongs to the past, *uchawi* and *wanga* are, certainly, part of the present.[12]

While *uchawi* refers to remedies used by people who intend to destroy some-body through an intermediary who offers such remedies (*mchawi*), *mwanga* is known as an amoral person operating without the use of remedies or an inter-mediary. He or she takes the life of people. In terms of moral sociality, what these two phenomena have in common is that they operate within rather small milieus and among acquaintances. This also confirms that such threats like the threats of talk and disclosure of private matters are usually found within the household itself, in the extended family, that is, always within close rela-tionships. People thus feel threatened by the very same relationships that they need to nurture so as to be acknowledged as full persons in society. Apart from keeping at a distance those suspected or recognized as having the propensity to apply witchcraft or being *wanga*, nothing is usually done to explicitly name, frighten, or punish them. It seems that, while the doings of a *mwanga* as well as *mchawi* are perceived as amoral, the persons suspected to be *mwanga* and *mchawi* are seen as "only" immoral. Although such a distinction is socially marked, their existence is nevertheless unavoidably interrelational with their doings and, thus, equally destructive for a wished-for state of harmony.

In describing these extraordinary phenomena, my wish has simply been to further clarify that, in this society, malevolence is considered to form part of human existence. Among the three phenomena mentioned, *mwanga* and *mumiani* could be seen as "beings of malice." In contrast, *mchawi* is a person who, through her or his knowledge and skills, is able to do malice. Still, *mchawi* would perform malice whenever requested. Thus it is common women and men, due to their jealousy or greed, their emotional state and intention to harm, who actually approach and compensate a *mchawi* to cause malevolence. Simultaneously, there is a shared understanding that in order to know and, in turn, be willing to practice *uchawi,* a person must be bad (*mbaya*). This is why people would usually claim that while others apply *uchawi,* they themselves would only use *uganga,* that is, knowledge and skills used for protection and healing.[13] No one would ever disclose that they visit or seek assistance from *mchawi*—only others do so. In situations of worry, people would seek the help of *mganga* (healer, specialist in Quranic and local medicine) who is able to discover by divination (*tazamia*), for instance, whether *uchawi* is being used against them and, if so, to identify their enemy. In certain cases, it is known that a healer would have to apply destructive medication in order to protect the one who has initially been harmed. The fact that the one to be punished is usually referred to as the enemy (*adui*) implies that the person on whose behalf destructive medication is applied, will, somehow, still claim that she or he is seeking protection, only.

What is here conceptualized as threatening is usually to be cautioned against, particularly, to protect situations of harmony and relative well-being. In this sense evil, as argued by David Parkin (1985b, 18), "denotes a discourse concerning human suffering." The idea of evil seems to serve as a fluid reference for an unidentifiable or unknown potency, which despite its uncertain character, certainly is perceived to cause misery in peoples' lives as well as in society. Yet, I would argue that the same discourse is equally about morality along with its questioning on immorality and whether there exists anything that is properly amoral. Nevertheless, forces or properties that threaten a wished for state of harmony, are obviously experienced and sensed. Most of all, these threats are captured by words such as *choyo* (greed), *jeuri* (arrogance), and *kubri* (self-importance), as well as *fitina* (discord), *ugomwi* (quarreling), and *hasidi* (enmity). When investigating why I hardly ever heard the word *ush-*

ari (evil) mentioned when people discussed malevolence, Bi Salma, mentioned in the beginning of this chapter, replied, "But, *fitina, hasidi, choyo*—all comes from *ushari*—it is this."

In the Zanzibari setting, people would usually hold that human beings embody the capacity to create both harmony and harm. How they live and behave would depend upon their personality or self (*nafsi*), their trust (*imani*), and the kind of relationships they are engaging in. Human capacity thus varies according to personal character and social relationships, which may alter according to context. Even so, emotions such as greed and jealousy as well as characteristics such as arrogance and self-importance are all said to be sources of discord, negating harmony. If the term *evil* were to be applied, it might be as a sort of floating signifier—a notion denoting something pervasive, encompassing all kinds of relationships and encounters.

In approaching *evil* from an anthropological perspective, I have kept in mind the idea that if such a condition could actually be produced in most cultures, it remains each time a notion specific to a particular cosmology. Thus, when referring here to "evil," the discussion is placed in relation to a given ontology as well as phenomenology. By looking at the various component properties of what is experienced or denoted as harmful, we may nevertheless make sense of something sensed as evil. Seen from a Zanzibari lifeworld I would say that malice is, first and foremost, the effect of verbal and nonverbal communication, of excessive behavior following from certain kinds of emotional experiences. Within a Zanzibari Swahili context there is, as I have tried to show, an understanding that humans are full of shortcomings, and that their emotions could be destructive if not socially and psychologically controlled. So, to return to Doris Lessing's observation, I would say that for Zanzibaris "that terrible frightening force is loose, and as it were at large, in persons, and in persons who have the power to move each other" (1973, 249). In certain conversations where the misbehavior of others is discussed, both women and men may apply the term *sheitani* or "spirit," when referring to destructive potency, that a person may be tempted to create enmity in social relationships. As they would say, "*Sheitani ya mtu, ni mtu*"—causing malevolence and suffering, such is the human being.

NOTES

I wish to thank Jean-Claude Galey, Ingjerd Hoem, and, in particular, Gro Ween, for valuable comments on earlier drafts of this text.

1. As I have discussed at length elsewhere, spirits interchangeably referred to as *masheitani* or *majinni* are not evil beings. They are beings created by God, beings different from angels (Larsen 2008). Like humans, they are said to have the ability to do both good and bad.

2. I am aware that in Zanzibar, in other Muslim societies, in Islam, as such, that womanhood/femininity is associated with emotion, while manhood/masculinity is associated with reason. This gender distinction obviously impacts the juridical, social, and economic status that women as women and men as men are granted in society and within the state. Such a gender complex is more widespread than just in Muslim societies and Islam. Nevertheless, here, I have not included this distinction when discussing a link between emotion and evil as both women and men, although in different ways, are perceived to embody emotion as well as reason.

3. Zanzibar is a semiautonomous polity in the United Republic of Tanzania. It consists of two main islands: Unguja, with a population close to 700,000, Pemba, with a population of 350,000, and some smaller islands, the biggest among them being Tumbatu. Zanzibar Town, with a population of about 400,000, is situated on Unguja.

4. Of the five prescribed prayers, *salaa* imply a recitative use of language in harmony with the precisely ordered bodily actions of *rakaa* and must be performed in Arabic. *Dua* could be performed as requests and are not accompanied by specific bodily actions; *dua* could be spontaneous, creative recitations as well as formulaic recitations in which Quranic verses are also included.

5. *Khanga* is a rectangle of pure cotton cloth with a border all around it and printed in bold designs and bright colors. It could be worn as a long skirt or loincloth.

6. *Nimekushuhudia kusoma halbadiri hii kwa niaba ya kinga yangu na mwanangu/ wanangu kila alye nikalia wa ufisadi, uhasidi, fitina na kwa njia yoyote mbaya mstahakie mwenyezi mungu, allahi sa'lahu, bihakimil, hakimina. Hata iwe mama yangu amenizaa kwa hii halbadiri namstakia mwenyezi mungu.*

7. The prayer books would be in both Swahili and Arabic.

8. In relation to this often-heard statement, I wish to say that in Islam the Omniscience of God is not the opposite of free will. In general, it is understood that human beings have been given free will in this life, and that retribution in the Hereafter is based on how one manages one's freedom of choice in this worldly life.

9. Zanzibar is a sex-segregated society. Therefore, being a woman, I have been positioned among women, engaging with men mainly in contexts where the presence of both genders is considered acceptable—which, especially with age, are plenty.

10. Writing about the Swahili and how their Muslim cosmology incorporates evil, David Parkin (1985a, 236) says, "They may be responsible for their own practice of evil, but since it is defined by God, they can hardly be said to have created it."

11. In some cases, *mganga* may have to enact forms of medication that implies that somebody identified as an enemy of the person involved, will be targeted, with the aim of destroying either the effect of medicament applied by this person against the one seeking treatment or even destroying the person. Neither the *mganga* nor the persons seeking help would say that they are practicing *uchawi* or witchcraft; they would argue that they have to use this destructive medication in order to protect the person in question, who is seen as the victim.

12. Some would associate *Mumiani* with the dead bodies of the Parsees. It was said that passing the site of the Parsees' Tower of Silence in the outskirts of Zanzibar Town, one could still be affected by *Mumiani* who would drink all your blood and thus eventually kill you. Others would not link *Mumiani* with deceased Parsees at all. What was shared, however, was the idea that *Mumiani* was a force or potency belonging to the past.

13. A distinction is thus made between *uchawi* and what is known as *uganga*. *Uganga* translates into English as sorcery or magic and is mainly associated with healing practices including the Quranic-related medications called *kombe* and *kafara*, astrology, divination (*ramli*), and various forms of herbal medications. *Uganga* is practiced both in order to heal and to protect; the one practicing it is referred to as *mganga* (pl. *waganga*).

REFERENCES

Caplan, Pat. 1997. *African Voices, African Lives: Personal Narratives from a Swahili Village*. London: Routledge.

Favret-Saada, Jeanne. 1980. *Deadly Words: Witchcraft in the Bocage*. Cambridge: Cambridge University Press.

Larsen, Kjersti. 2008. *Where Humans and Spirits Meet: The Politics of Rituals and Identified Spirits in Zanzibar*. Oxford: Berghahn.

———. 2011. "By Way of the Qur'an: Soothing Emotional and Mundane Matters in Zanzibar." Paper presented at Approaches to the Qur'an in Sub-Saharan Africa, York University and Institute of Ismaili Studies, Toronto, May 19–21.

———. 2013. "Spirits, Magic and Everyday Life Politics in Zanzibar." In *Spirits in Politics: Uncertainties of Power and Healing in African Societies*, edited by Barbara Meier and Arne Steinforth, 73–91, Frankfurt: Campus Verlag. Lessing, Doris. 1973. *The Golden Notebook*. New York: Bantam Books.

Parkin, David, ed. 1985a. "Entitling Evil: Muslims and Non-Muslims in Coastal Kenya." In *The Anthropology of Evil*, 224–243. Oxford: Basil Blackwell.

———. 1985b. Introduction to *The Anthropology of Evil*, 1–25. Oxford: Basil Blackwell.

Stewart, Pamela J., and Andrew Strathern. 2004. *Witchcraft, Sorcery, Rumors, and Gossip*. Cambridge: Cambridge University Press.

Van Beek, Walter E. A. 1994. "The Innocent Sorcerer: Coping with Evil in Two African Societies (Kapsiki and Dogon)." In *Religion in Africa: Experience & Expression*, edited by Thomas D. Blakely, Walter E. A. van Beek, and Dennis L. Thomson, 196–228. London: James Currey.

13 CONSTRUCTING MORAL PERSONHOOD

The Moral Test in Tuareg Sociability as a Commentary on Honor and Dishonor

SUSAN J. RASMUSSEN

Evil often induces human suffering; it may, for example, result in illness. In many African societies, it is often synonymous with witchcraft, possession, and other malevolent practices elaborated in ritual (Comaroff and Comaroff 1993; Ferme 2001; Rasmussen 1998, 2001; West 2005, 2007), and it is often combated through formal religious and political means. I contend that, in addition to these manifestations, evil may also be addressed more informally, in moral testing during deceptively trivial ordinary everyday sociability, not solely in public formal ritual or large-scale political contexts. Preoccupations in such tests include combating literal physical harm, tangible material theft, and/or psychosocial suffering.

I focus here on local cosmologies and concepts of evil as expressed in incidents and cases of testing of persons to construct or deconstruct, reflect upon, and critique moral personhood. The goal is to reveal subjective cultural experiences of evil and danger through exploration of their representations in small incidents and cases involving tests of character and judgments and commentaries on honor and dishonor, with examples from other social interactions and verbal art. I show how, for many Tamajaq-speaking, Muslim, socially stratified, and seminomadic Tuareg in Saharan regions of Mali and Niger, moral testing offers opportunities to weigh "lesser" and "greater" evils and to judge moral character in shifting terrains of uncertainty.[1] Here I draw on data I collected in rural and urban communities of Mali and Niger, with special emphasis on Tamajaq-speakers in a multiethnic town in northern Mali, where many self-identify as Tuareg in cultural and linguistic affiliation and maintain ties with rural nomadic communities. Key in defining and resisting evil are widely held values of respect, honor, and dignity, expressed in not solely offering, but also accepting, generosity and hospitality. Ideally, all parties to interaction—offenders and perpetrators, as well as "victimized" or vulnerable persons in cases of mischief—should approach each other on moral common ground. Honor (*achak*) is important here, but not in the sense of "not giving in." Evil, also "bad" and "dangerous" (glossed as *wa labasen,* a verbal construction used as an adjective) subsumes superhuman, as well as human and social, powers and manipulations that subvert, even invert these key values. Sin (*abakat*) is a more religious-derived concept, used more narrowly to describe the breaking of specific ritual taboos and often Quranic injunctions, for example, sexual restrictions (Rasmussen 2000, 2006). Sometimes, seemingly ordinary everyday incidents—both in life and in verbal art performance illustrate local assessments of moral personhood. Why are these incidents and practices so important to many Tuareg, what wider processes do they reveal in moral cosmologies of evil, and how are they so analytically valuable to anthropologists?

In northern regions of Mali and Niger, major themes in everyday sociability, mythico-histories, poems, songs, and plays concern theft, avarice, or rejecting another's generosity and/or hospitality. In a play based on a religious legend, a merchant is a victim of theft but gives generously to the suspected thieves. In a real-life incident, relatives of a thief did not report the theft to authorities, but they offered a kid goat as compensation to the victim of his theft, and later, the alleged thief approached the victim requesting a gift! Why, alongside compensation to the offended or hurt person, are there also demands to be generous to the offender in forgiveness? Dyadic, "two-way street" relations are mutually constitutive in the construction of moral personhood, and small tests are frequently conducted to judge and comment on this issue. Key persons expected to "pass" these tests include guests, hosts, merchants, customers, and matrilineally related kin, including fictive and classificatory, and even the ethnographer on occasion. A widespread tale motif concerns a maternal uncle who tests the character and intelligence of his sister's son. Another common motif in tales is a lost or endangered sister, whose brothers stop at nothing to find and rescue her. These motifs express longstanding ideals of special, mutually protective relationships between siblings, mothers and daughters, maternal uncles and aunts, and maternal nephews and nieces, from ancient matrilineal influence persisting to varying degrees, in many Tuareg groups' currently bilateral legal systems.[2] Adults frequently play games with small children by pretending to insist they share food to see if they are generous. In addition to these pervasive patterns, there are also dilemmas, double-binds, contradictions, and ambiguities—for example, competing notions that the Islamic God (Allah) is the source of everything, and only Allah can reward or punish, and yet the need, at the same time, for specifying individual human agency in increasingly uncertain circumstances. The source of evil is dispersion of community and breakdown of mutual obligations.

Many Tuareg often ponder and attempt to resolve these predicaments through small moral tests. I ask which social contexts prompt informal moral testing to cope with danger, uncertainty, and evil, rather than prompting more formalized rituals combating *togerchet* (evil eye), *ark echaghel* (sorcery or bad work), evil spirits of the wild (Kel Essuf), or a smith/artisan's dangerous anger (*tegare* or *tezma*) (Casajus 2000; Nicolaisen 1961; Rasmussen 1998, 2001, 2004, 2013)?

My goal is to move beyond the anthropologist's own concepts of evil toward local concepts of evil, as emergent in interpersonal encounters. I attempt to do this by exploring how perpetrators and victims of local concepts of evil acts are socially and culturally constructed through moral tests in sociability and commentary, in coping with ambiguities of good and evil—for example, in dilemmas between Sufi emphasis upon establishing common moral ground and dialogues versus the need for discerning friend from foe in regional political violence. Illuminating here is the central focus, the moral test. I argue that the informal moral test is powerfully used as a system of communication in this society, where there is an ideal of indirect, subtle speech and reserved, dignified, and respectful conduct, but where there also arise dilemmas from competing and ambiguous moral forces in social turmoil and waves of invasion, and consequently, local residents also need reassurance of trustworthiness.

In anthropology, with the exception of more ritualized "witch ordeals," moral tests tend to be underrepresented. Informal, less ritualized incidents of such testing reveal resilience and vulnerability of widely held, but disputed values. The situations where these prevail in Tuareg society are those that feature negotiations and realignments of guilt and innocence, in contests between generosity and avarice, and loyalty and betrayal. I argue that, for many, evil derives not so much from excess (the "root" of evil in many witchcraft cases in much of Africa), but rather derives from deprivation, fear, and very real danger, which entail a loss of honor or dignity, as well as threats to personal safety. This runs counter to some other observations about evil in many African societies that tend to emphasize excess as the root of evil (Comaroff and Comaroff 1993; Ferme 2001). For Tuareg, friend and foe must be discerned in the social turmoil that blurs the boundaries between social patrons, clients, customers, hosts, guests, kin, and nonkin. Moral tests constitute efforts to distinguish between them. Thus these moral tests constitute, in effect, efforts to initiate and/or repair relations that are ideally (hoped to be) reciprocal, but are in jeopardy in their reliability.

I begin with a longitudinal case study and life history featuring trauma, loss, accusation of theft (or at least, appropriation) of property against a close kinsperson, mental breakdown, and rebuffed hospitality. A small incident—a response to rebuffed hospitality—was initially puzzling to this researcher, but later yielded rich insights into the local cosmology of evil when contextualized more broadly.

A Tuareg woman in an urban community in northern Mali accused her brother and aunt of stealing some of her livestock for the aunt's own use to manufacture and sell hide tents. I had earlier lodged with the accuser and her brother in a previous trip to the field, and they had kindly invited me back again to stay during my later research trip, but, sensing the tension in their household upon my return, I indefinitely delayed my move there, and, hoping not to hurt their feelings, gave as a reason their home's distance from the site of my research transcription assistance. Subsequently, the woman generously gave me presents, visited me in my rental lodgings, and made an unusual request of me.

This woman, aged approximately between fifty-five and sixty years old, whom I will call Takhia, resided with her brother in late life, following her geographic and social dislocation during political violence and economic crises in northern Mali. The intimacy and small-scale predicaments in her story are, I show later, connected to larger-scale events and illuminate the construction and deconstruction of moral personhood. I was prompted to examine her life in connection to these issues by a deceptively trivial incident in my relationship with her.

THE CASE STUDY

An Incident and a Life

Takhia, (pseudonym), a friend with whom I had previously lodged in Kidal, a large town in northern Mali, during my earlier research project there in 2002, invited me to again stay with her, her brother, and his two small sons on my return trip in 2006. Although grateful for their kind hospitality, I hesitated to do so, for several reasons. First, I planned to work frequently with the staff at the local radio station in my project on Tamajaq theatrical plays: this station was located in the center of town, while the compound of Takhia and her brother was located in an outlying neighborhood. A second, more personal reason involved my mixed sentiments of sadness, fear, and guilt. On a brief visit to her home shortly after I arrived in town, before moving in as a long-term guest, I found that this was not the same place. The family was experiencing tension and conflict, and Takhia appeared to be suffering from a nonorganic illness, possibly dementia (an illness category locally recognized, called *takhal* in Tamajaq). Although no mutual acquaintances used that term, they hinted they considered her to be insane (using *tanebzeg* and other idiomatic Tamajaq and French expressions, such as *une buole est tombee de sa tete,* or "one ball has fallen from her head"). Takhia did not recognize me at first, the compound was neglected and insect-infested—and neighbors described that place as "the wild (*essuf*)."[3]

After much soul-searching, with much regret, I decided to avoid residing there again. In order to avoid hurting the family's feelings, I gave them my first reason only (geographic distance from the central site of one phase of my study) and stalled on my move indefinitely. In the meantime, I visited often, spent holidays there, and brought numerous presents to the family, which they reciprocated.

For a time, things went smoothly, at least on the surface. Then, one day Takhia came to visit me in my rented room. Suddenly, she asked me if she could bathe in my shower and also use my towel, a request I had never heard from anyone else in Tuareg communities during a brief social visit. Normally, only a long-term guest, or someone who arrives after very lengthy travel, bathes on a visit; this is not a conventional practice during a brief social visit, and borrowing a towel is not normally done. In fact, some Tuareg even shun using the same bar of soap from concern with pollution. Nonetheless, I obliged her, and she emerged after about a half an hour.

In effect, Takhia was attempting to protect our host-guest relationship: perhaps she wished to remind me of our past social intimacy—I, in effect, a fictive sister, niece, or daughter, matrilineal relatives one should be able to count on for emotional support—and she wished to test my willingness to reinforce our reciprocity, for reassurance. But why was this so important to her, and why did her effort take this particular form?

Given the prominent position of many Tuareg women, who enjoy independent property ownership and high social prestige, how did these protective connections unravel? How did Takhia become socially disaffiliated, how did she cope with this predicament, and what connection was there between her conduct with me and her more general strategies to combat dangers in her life?

Significantly, neither Takhia herself nor others who knew her mentioned any malevolent superhuman forces here, or even *tamazai,* a depression often leading to possession by spirits of the wild or solitude (Rasmussen 1995). Although a few mutual acquaintances mentioned the wild in describing her home, and the wild as a spatial category and mental state can include the presence of Kel Essuf spirits of the wild that can lead to possession and then either exorcism or mediumship, no spirit possession rite was held for her.

Takhia had been married several times but was now widowed and divorced. Her sole adult son was killed in a car accident, and she did not have a daughter—the latter a key supportive relative for an older woman among the Ifoghas Tuareg in the Adragh-n-Ifoghas Mountains and surrounding Kidal region, where matrilineal influences remain strong. Relations between brothers and sisters should also be strong and supportive, especially in late life (Nicolaisen and Nicolaisen 1997). Yet these relationships became threatened by the strains among Takhia, her brother, and her aunt, as well as between Takhia and her nephews.

Kidal, a town of approximately twenty thousand in a region by the same name, in the Adragh-n-Ifoghas Mountains, remains largely seminomadic, a settled center many residents leave part of the year for seasonal migration with their herds.[4] Many also intermittently flee sporadic armed conflicts between Tuareg dissident/rebels, the Malian army, and most recently, Islamist reformist militants and the forces of the Al-Qaeda in the Islamic Maghreb. During this researcher's absence of four years, much had occurred there. That May, there had been an attack on the town by dissident Tuareg rebel forces impatient and disillusioned with the progress of the peace pact ending the previous (1990–1996) armed conflict between some Tuareg in the north and the central government of Mali, the latest in a series of conflicts dating back to mid-century Malian independence.[5] There had also been regional droughts and more general national unemployment.

Soon after returning to Kidal, I set out to see this family. Their surrounding neighborhood was much more sparsely populated than usual. Some residents were still temporarily nomadizing with their herds, for the rains had been late that year. Others had fled the town during the resurgence of the Tuareg rebellion. All had experienced looting and damage to their homes. Takhia and Salikhou's compound, tents, and house now appeared dilapidated and deserted. One side of the courtyard (which I later learned was occupied only by Takhia) was now divided off by a low wall, but had not been previously, and was littered with debris. The adolescent who had accompanied me to the residence, echoing a neighbor's view, commented, "It is really *essuf* (the wild—a lonely abode of spirits far from tent and civilization) around here now!" *Essuf*, as already noted, denotes both the literal wild, a space outside the civilization of the maternal tent, village, and camp, and the psychosocial state of loneliness and solitude.[6]

After approximately an hour, a nearly unrecognizable Takhia appeared and entered the compound courtyard haltingly, looking more haggard, stressed, disheveled, and less washed—also much older and vacant-eyed—than she had four years earlier. She initially ignored us, then noticed us, and slowly approached. Upon greetings, somewhat stilted, I noticed that Takhia did not recognize me! Perhaps I, too, had changed? I presented her with a gift, and we chatted stiffly for a while. After about twenty minutes, she finally recognized me, and suddenly warmly embraced me. Her brother Salikhou, she explained, was currently in Tamanrasset, Algeria, but would return soon. She urged me to come stay with them again, to move my bags and supplies over from my present location as soon as Salikhou returned. After we left, the adolescent surmised, "I think she has spent too much time out here alone, in *essuf*." He also speculated that there were "probably plenty of scorpions around here." Scorpions sting, sometimes lethally, and they are much feared. Yet more is at play here: moral and social, as well as physical space had become overgrown with weeds and insects, scorpions (whether literal or figurative) and other antisocial, harmful forces, encroached. In referring to scorpions inside the compound, the adolescent connected Takhia's state of mind to the now "wild," rather than civilized space. Implicitly, he sensed some evil afoot.

On another visit, I found Takhia wandering outside the compound. On a later occasion, around noon, I again found the compound apparently vacant, and left. Later, I learned that Salikhou and his two sons had not heard me calling greetings because they been sleeping inside the house—its door was locked (not normal practice during residents' occupation in daytime), as was his tent door on his side of the courtyard.

Descent into Madness

Larger-scale and more long-term forces, as well as additional local cultural concepts, shed light on this case. Evil was afoot somewhere in Takia's more general predicament of suffering, in her treatment by others with whom ideally, she should have enjoyed close, supportive, and reciprocal kinship relationships. In Tuareg society, persons suffering from nonorganic illnesses considered incurable, that is, those defined as permanently insane are often isolated in a space apart from other family and community members, usually at home. If they wander far out in the desert, either they become lost and tragically die of exposure and thirst, or their relatives subsequently tie them up, an acceptable practice for restraining them, intended to protect them, but also arising partly

from shame—since some afflictions are believed to be the outward manifestations of past sins (*ibakaten*) or the breaking of a sexual taboo—either by the afflicted, or by a close relative, usually the mother during conception, pregnancy,
or breast-feeding (Rasmussen 1997, 2001, 2006).

During my earlier research, extended family relatives had resided in an
adjoining compound next door to Takhia and Salikhou, and all these relatives
had engaged in lively and warm sociability and shared some food and livestock
resources. Later, I learned, there had been a rift: a dispute over what to do with
some herds jointly owned by Takhia and her aunt. Each tent requires eighty
goat-hides, a substantial number, which the aunt sold for a profit, with approval
from Takhia's brother. But herds had dwindled from sporadic droughts, wars,
and thefts in the region, so Takhia had opposed slaughtering more goats for
their hides to construct tents, despite the promise of monetary profits from
their sale, viewing this as risky depletion of their wealth for uncertain returns.
They had quarreled, and the aunt had moved away.

By 2006, although Takhia and her brother Salikhou both remained in
their large compound, they had changed living spaces within it: they now
lived on two different, far sides of it, each space separated by a low stone wall.
Before, they had both had their tents standing in the same open courtyard
alongside each other, and they had cooked, shared food, and often ate together,
both using the kitchen in Salikhou's adobe house and a well in front of it. Now
the adobe mud house was always locked up, and Salikhou and his small sons'
tent also had chicken wire and a lock on it during his absence—which was
never the case before. Salikhou and his two sons, now in primary school, lived
on one side of the compound in a nomadic tent, and Takhia lived on the other
side, in a smaller, low-slung tent, not the female-owned, dignified elliptical
nomadic hide tent, which Takhia was highly skilled at building, but one made
from bits of fabric patched haphazardly together that are prevalent in refugee
camps.

The recurring political turmoil had been devastating. During the 1990–
1996 Tuareg rebellion, Salikhou was in Burkina Faso, though later he returned
and worked first as a journalist at the local radio, and later at a youth-oriented
nongovernmental organization agency. Many residents had to flee Kidal during
the May 2006 attack. Some refugees died, tragically, lost in the desert, far from
water. Others suffered physical and psychological trauma and property theft
and/or destruction in the violence. Children became separated from parents.
Aid and nongovernmental organization programs were interrupted, some suspended. Takhia traveled temporarily to the Adragh-n-Ifoghas countryside, but
while there, she lamented to me, many of her personal belongings were stolen.

A truce arranged by Algeria was eventually reached, but Kidal remained vulnerable to attacks.

Intermittently over the years we were acquainted, Takhia related episodes from her life to me: "My first husband was a cousin; our fathers were brothers, but he left another woman for me, but later reconciled with her, so we divorced." (Many first marriages among Tuareg are arranged by parents, often to a close cousin, in order to keep bride wealth in the family; couples often divorce from such marriages, called "family marriages," and later contract love-based marriages [Nicolaisen and Nicolaisen 1997; Rasmussen 1997]). "My second husband was a Bambara soldier. I lived with him in Bamako for about four years, had two children, one a girl, who died. My son is now about twenty years old, but I have not seen him for eight years [this son was later killed in a car accident in Bamako.] I liked Bamako, but I prefer Kidal because my relatives are here. So we divorced, and I returned here until the earlier (1990s) rebellion broke out, when I had to flee to Mauritania and Morocco (where there were refugee camps).

"My third husband, the Mauritanian Arab, took good care of me: he bought me things and got Bella (former slaves) to do housework. I liked Nouatchott, it was on the ocean and there were plenty of fish, but my husband contracted a polygynous marriage, and I opposed this. So we divorced, I left (Mauritania), but at the borders, some customs agents and soldiers stole my jewelry."

Takhia's marriages to the Bambara and Mauritanian Arab men were not unusual; some sedentarized and urban Tuareg women have intermarried with men in other ethnic and regional groups in adaptation to the loss of their property base, livestock herds. Nor was her motive for divorcing the Arab unusual; most Tuareg women oppose polygyny, even as their husbands technically have a right to the Islamic limit of four wives, and many leave their husbands who attempt this. Takhia now lived in a "reversible world" where former bases of prestige, wealth, affection, and power were inverted.

Takhia and Siliman had been orphaned as very young children, and were raised by their aunt. The siblings, both divorced, had been residing in the same compound for several years, in accordance with custom in late life for many Tuareg siblings or half-siblings, particularly if widowed and/or divorced and/or childless, who should ideally be close and supportive.

Even during my previous stay there in 2002, Takhia had already expressed some disappointment over her losses. In contrast to some other widespread local explanations of evil and misfortune, however, her explanations did not include superhuman causation such as spirit affliction, evil eye, "sorcery," "witchcraft-like" powers of artisans, or malevolent gossip and coveting of property, or even the will of Allah. Instead, she emphasized social, economic, and political upheavals. Her own outlook and logic, despite her Islamic devotion, were firmly in the human domain. It would nonetheless be misleading to attribute this to a more "secular" worldview or cosmology. For some aspects of her moral testing, as well as that of others I describe later, can be found in Sufi influences, specifically, in the need for rapprochement between persons inflicting harm and those they harm on a common ground, as all creations of Allah.

The family's economic situation deteriorated, and social tensions increased. Takhia lamented that her nephews did not listen to or obey her. Eventually, she started spanking them. She explained these discipline problems as a consequence of the inherited, but also the distanced, neglected, and subverted matrilineal descent ties to his errant mother's side: "He (my older nephew) inherited the character (*tasney*) of his mother's side (*tedis*, literally stomach). That explains his sometimes naughty behavior, because his mother is evil (here, *wur tela takarakit, wur tela imojagh,* or approximately shameless, dishonorable, bad, dangerous)."

The nephews' mother, Salikhou's ex-wife, had allegedly become involved with a lover during her husband's absence on travel for medical care. Takhia disapproved of this extramarital liaison, not solely because it hurt her brother, but because it was so distracting that the ex-wife allegedly stopped breast-feeding her son before he was weaned. There is relatively free social interaction between men and women in Tuareg society; women are not secluded, and may receive unrelated male visitors, but courtship involves in principle mostly conversation. Although extramarital and premarital affairs are sometimes tacitly accepted, a mother should refrain from sexual relations for approximately two years following the birth of a son, to breast-feed her baby until weaning age. There is deep shame attached to sexual relations before a child is weaned, and if the mother bears another child too soon, such a child is called *eljenagougou,* or "child of the spirits," and may have a birth defect. Even if the postpartum taboo is broken within marriage, and a legitimate child is thus conceived, many fear the child will also suffer. Salikhou's ex-wife's affair while her then-husband was absent was therefore criticized primarily because she abandoned her two young children; the younger child was not even yet weaned. The ex-wife kept the bride wealth, but the ex-husband received custody of their children, and initially, he gave them to his sister Takhia to raise. Takhia had fed the younger one with goat's milk, and earlier in 2002, had beamed with pride that "the children call me *anna* (mother) now." She also frequently mock breast-fed the younger nephew at that time.

The kinship relationships between mother and children; among aunts, uncles, and nephews; and among ancestors, elders, and children, in effect became subverted from the ideals of economic solidarity and emotional support. As in India and parts of the Middle East (Lamb 2000, 75), a mother's milk among Tuareg is a special substance, mixed with the mother's love and distilled from her body's blood, which creates a special pull over children. Spirit possession, not always evil or destructive, can also be transmitted through the mother's milk (Rasmussen 1995). Living milk herds (*akh ihuderen*), endowments matrilineally transmitted solely to sisters, daughters, and nieces, also evoke such ties.

Later, a marabout and an uncle came by and gently suggested that Takhia be more patient (*tezedegh*) with the children. When I suggested that perhaps the (older) boy had experienced trauma on his parents' divorce, she disagreed, asserting that "only older children are hurt by this, not younger children." She sorrowfully surmised that "neither of these boys will take care of me if I fall ill." She complained of no assistance in heavy household work and alleged that her relatives did not give her money. Her increasingly fragile health and lowered material standard of living only increased her suffering. Concerning her nephews, she added that "[although they are my nephews], they are not [my] children of the stomach; they are different because they are children of my brother, [not my sister]." Yet she opposed her brother's plans to send his older son to school in Gao because, she insisted, she loved the child.

Here, normal matrilineal descent and intergenerational social and spiritual ties were polluted and distanced by the ex-wife's breaking of the sexual taboo. Additional social and economic tensions were also factors in her dispossession (herds are an important source of Tuareg women's wealth) and her disaffiliation (sibling and mother-child relations are an important source of social support), caused in large part by the rift in her family, but also by her own serial divorces, bereavement, drought, war, and perhaps, also, mental decline.

ANALYSIS

Why did Takhia not express her predicament in the idiom of spirits? Surely, matrilineal spirits were disturbed here. Matrilineal spirits—important in herbal medicine, possession rituals, rites of passage, mythico-histories, and mother-child social ties—are not usually evil. By contrast, most Kel Essuf spirits of the wild are evil, even some who possess women alongside matrilineal possessing spirits. Recall that Takhia had been orphaned from her mother at a young age, had no daughters, and her aunt, brother, and small nephews were, in effect, alienated from her. Their relationship became an aberration of the ideal matrilineal ties and also of the ideal frail elder and small children relationship of mutual support (Rasmussen 1997). Sibling separation, not necessarily alienation, in pastoral nomadism is a prominent theme in verbal art, and indeed, is a reality in times of war and refugee flight (Rasmussen 1995). There are many tales with motifs of close but threatened relations with brothers and sisters; a prominent tale-type motif concerns brothers searching for lost sisters who are missing in nomadism, and/or who are sometimes in danger; for example, in one tale, a sister is abducted by the devil, Iblis, or by a spirit, who attempts to make her his wife. Another motif concerns a maternal uncle testing his sister's son by sending him on dangerous errands in the desert; for example, as in a tale related to me by a niece of Takhia's and Salikhou's aunt: a maternal uncle orders his nephew to do a series of very difficult herding tasks, leaving him on his own in the desert. The nephew obeys and succeeds, and later drinks at a pond his uncle led him to, and does all tasks on his own initiative with his own herds. According to local exegesis, this implies that he inherited his herds and also his character from his uncle, "the nephew came out of the thigh of his uncle," and this is a test of moral character as well as of intelligence.

Dispersion of ideally close persons—whether through geographic distance or alienation—is a prevalent cultural preoccupation. Casajus (1987, 2000) has analyzed hints of sibling incest symbolism in Tuareg folklore, conveying the older matrilineal influences predating Islam and Arab, Quranic, and state-derived patrilineal influences, and as expressing the double-bind between the brother-sister and spousal tie in the currently bilateral system prevalent in many Tuareg groups. Nicolaisen and Nicolaisen (1997) described a wedding game of "tug-of-war" over the stomach of the sacrificed animal, which, according to these authors, also symbolically expresses this conflict and struggle between matrilineal and patrilineal ties and identity. In these episodes, not solely romantic love, but also love between brothers and sisters, is often tested and threatened.

In this light, brother-sister love imagery in some other Tuareg folktales and a related matrilineal preoccupation in Takhia's narrative (in particular, her strong but ambivalent sentiments regarding her sister-in-law and nephews, and her emotional and economic stress over her disputed matrilineally inherited property) expose underlying tensions between loyalty to siblings and other competing relationships and obligations, which are exacerbated by social upheavals, dispersions of populations, and their dispossession. Violence from state, militias, and rebel dissidents have, in concert with internal family disputes over herds in pressures from monetarization and unemployment, and also, in Takhia's case, perceived intergenerational pollution from alleged breaking of sexual taboos, disrupted and endangered matrilineal kin relations and wealth. Takhia brought this idiom to her interpretation of the evils causing her problems and also to her moral testing of me, as a way of coping with dispersion, disaffiliation, loss of wealth, dignity, and honor.

Although in some respects, Takhia's case is unique, other, more general aspects of her predicament are widely experienced among many in her community. Many Tamajaq poems, songs, and plays performed today lament the perceived breakdown of family, household, and community—as well as moral personhood according to prevalent ideals—in monetarization, unemployment, dispossession, and violence.

For example, selected verses in many poems and songs express concerns over good and evil and threats to valued social relationships: dangers of betrayal, material gain over emotional ties, distancing of maternal and matrilineal relations, and other dangers. Consider the following:

"Rap" Song (performed by a famous rapper, singer, and comedian at a concert at a youth center):
"My friend [fem.], remember my young soul / That cries, that my mother is dead / That because of this, [one] no longer knows where there is good and evil . . ."

Temel n Annabi, "Praise of Prophet" (performed by women and girls at a baby's name day, Kidal region) (Soloist: a female cousin of mother of baby):
"There is no God but God [Allah] Bravo for Mohamed, Bravo for Mohammed / Bravo for he who does the praise and he who listens also / He listens to them and that pleases him / He would not be in the solitude [*essuf* or *tenere*] / It is Satan [*Iblis,* the devil] who prevents him from listening [to anyone], except to three individuals: Satan, the non-Muslims [*akafir*], and the bad [dangerous] people [*dagadame labassane*] / He is burdened by sins [*ibakaden*] / Oh, God, how terrible is she who is neither myself nor my friend, her unhappiness [should be] my unhappiness, my wealth benefits her also . . ."

Ichumar (guitar) song called *Tamoust* (Identity):
"If there is an identity that must be loved by each other / it is that which lived in suffering and drought [In order to have unity, one must have shared the experience of suffering] / Now there exists a love [cultural unity, but fragile, false] after all that happened, later one will discover that it is not a true or solid unity / When you have a friend you go together to the shadow [shade] and one morning you find that he left you and hid / Treason is a blow / He who receives that that hurts him, that has no remedy / that does not cure me. If it [treason] is not finished or he who betrays becomes conscious of it [i.e., the only remedy is to stop treason]"

Selections from poem recited at garden marketing cooperative meeting by poet and human rights worker:

"One must help one who helps you. / One must not sweep the exterior if the interior is dirty . . . If Tuareg become angry, one makes perfume [i.e., gifts, especially perfume, are believed to diminish bad feelings] / and beautiful clothing and the soul sees what one has done . . . / Kinship [temet] does not buy anything at the market / Knowledge is not found here in the large towns . . . / Love has left the hearts and has entered the pocket / These last years, kinship has become like garbage [i.e., one has abandoned kinship] / Thus that world is dead, it is mixed up."

Chiluban smith/artisan songs—Azel in Assalam in Anasdouban (A Song for Greeting the Bridegroom)—performed at name days and weddings in the countryside:

"Me this morning I have come, I have come / Uniquely [expressly] in order to perform [celebrate, play] well / Do well, and keep away the evil fate [here, specifically evil eye or togerchet], evil eye / Against the young girls of [name of village] / I thank the young girls of [name of village] / For their respond- ing to the call [i.e., for offering cash gift to smith praise-singers, in order to protect from misfortune] . . ."

What precisely is evil here, and what are its sources? Many of these verses address fragile or ambiguous relationships, betrayals, threats of evil eye from jealousy or coveting, lurking invaders, and the need to reaffirm protective hu- man and spiritual powers, thereby illuminating the meaning of moral tests: to reaffirm mutuality and protection in life dangers. Some also praise God (Al- lah), and thus refer to both human secular and superhuman "sacred" powers in causes of, and protection from, danger, harm, and evil.

Takhia's unusual request to bathe on a brief visit, as a test of loyalty and solidarity, has moral import when one considers additional, similar social situ- ations in Tuareg society involving misfortunes, harm (both intentional and inadvertent), and requests for compensation. Illustrative here is another small moral test. In the following incident, a scorpion sting is reported in order to test someone's compassion and generosity.

A traveler once ordered some items from a smith/artisan family. The cus- tomer, following the tradition of the older noble patronage system toward smith/artisans, is supposed to, ideally, bring presents, visit, and socialize with them, as well as make an advance partial cash payment. The traveler neglected to do that, either due to ignorance or other obligations.

While the item was being made, a member of the smith/artisan family paid a visit to the traveler, his veil high over his nose and mouth, a style in Tuareg men's veiling that signifies, variously, formality, respect, defiance, or a potentially dangerous situation. The visitor made a request: "A small child in our family has been bitten by a scorpion. He needs an injection at the clinic. Could you give us money to cover the cost of the injection?" The traveler, though genuinely concerned and wishing to assist, lacked the amount of cash equal to the amount requested; she had attended a name day that same day and had offered the host family a considerable sum—as is also customary. So the traveler offered money to the artisan, but just short of the amount he requested for the injection. The artisan visitor, nonetheless grateful, indicated this amount would help, the remainder could be found elsewhere. Later, the traveler inquired at the artisan's, other Kidal households, and the clinic about the child's health. No one knew of any child who had been bitten by a scorpion recently.

In this scorpion-themed vignette, there are strong hints of a moral test conducted by the artisan to see if the traveler would make a generous potential "patron" and also to see if she felt compassion for an injured child. Recall the adolescent's earlier comment about scorpions invading Takhia's neglected compound, now transformed from tent into wild. These insects, both literally (physically) and figuratively (symbolically) evil, could indeed have stung the child, but whether true or false, the point of the vignette is that scorpions embody evil in the Sahara, and can be used, almost "divination"-like, to discern friend and foe.

Also instructive here is the widely-held value of *(e)shshek,* usually "decency" or "honor." *Eshshek* ideals are expressed in many proverbs that relate to women's position (Kohl 2009, 76), for example, "the woman is the trousers of the man." Women are the pillars of society: they own the nomadic tent, and thus guarantee the stability of the community (Claudot-Hawad 1993, 50). Takhia was without her tent—left with only its shadow or skeleton. Women, through their observance and execution of normative moral concepts of decency in educating children inside the tent, should ideally protect and maintain the entire community (nomadic camp), and thus broader cultural identity *(temoust)*. Takhia's nephews did not receive an education inside her or their mother's tent; instead, they attended "modern" schools due to their parents' divorce and Saklikhou's progressive attitudes and his own educational background. Thus Takhia's role in the transmission of cultural memory and moral concepts to youths was diminished, as was her property, and she felt dishonored.

During her visit to me, Takhia asked about amenities in my rental rooms. She expressed concern, not for herself, but for me: that I was "in the wild or solitude" (*essuf,* or her term, in the regional Tadart dialect, *tenere*) here. Recall that she herself now lived and ate apart from her brother and nephews, separated by a stone barrier and with their house closed up; perhaps she was seeking to identify with me or me with her. She commented, "You have running water here, but in my home, you can see the stars." She preferred her home village/camp, where she spent a year recently, asserting "it is better for livestock and also, that the food and milk and cheese are better and more abundant there." She expressed fear of the center of town "because of thieves," thus revising the cosmological oppositions of tent and wild: traditionally in the nomadic milieu, it is the tent that is associated with social morality and civilization, and the wild is associated with evil spirits and amorality. By contrast, for Takhia, in the sedentarized center, the "downtown" becomes decentered from morality and social ties. Takhia's central concern here was with theft on several planes: her own threatened material belongings and sources of livelihood (jewelry, herds), her fear of my own vulnerability to thieves in the center of town, and her distress at the figurative "theft" or alienation of affection, in her valued relationships, including me as a fictive sibling.

Also instructive here are local concepts of, and moral responses to, thefts and more general deception. In a theatrical play performed by an urban acting ensemble, thieves rob a shopkeeper named Bahmid. Yet in response, he gives them things and helps them because he knows they will ultimately be punished. Eventually, they confess. This play's plot, based on an old religious legend, has a moral, based on the belief that a thief who swears falsely on the Quran will later suffer consequences of illness and/or insanity; for only Allah punishes. If the victim forgives the thief, on the other hand, he or she will be spared. However, the thief must not lie, but instead confess. The play concludes with the following comment by an actor playing one of the thieves: "You must know [that] if you lie one day, the truth is going to stop you. Someday, that is going to catch up with you. You must know what one did to Bahmid. He did [only] good to us, and we had done harm to him. We arrived in Tamanrasset, and then we fell ill [i.e., we were ultimately punished by Allah, not by Bahmid]. You must know that we did harm [bad actions]."

Thus deception, theft, and betrayal of trust must be addressed and redressed, but reciprocally by both parties on "even ground"—not solely by the wrongdoer, but also by wronged person. On one occasion, when an ensemble intended to perform a play for free, (contrary to the usual practice of being paid by the organizer requesting their performance), one actor led the organizer to believe there was the usual fee, and allegedly embezzled the money given for this performance. When this became known, the other actors in his ensemble did not punish him or report him to authorities, even after the "errant" actor spent all the money, allegedly, on "party clothes," and thus could not pay it back. Instead, they gave a small kid goat as a compensation gift to the organizer who had paid unnecessarily for their performance. Later, the "errant" actor visited the organizer and made a request: he hoped to record some songs commercially, needed several blank CDs, and asked the organizer to provide him with funds to do this. In effect, there was the assumption here that the victim of theft should be compensated, but there was also the assumption that the thief, who did not deny his action but confessed, would merit some gift himself.

This incident, initially puzzling, has a Sufi logic that can be explained by the religious legend about Bahmid, who was kind to those who stole from him since he recognized that justice ultimately only comes from Allah. By extension, despite some differences, this logic also applies on some level to my longitudinal case study: Takhia expected me to give her compensation after I had disappointed her, and she also wished to reassure herself she could trust me as a host, if not a guest, during my second research trip. Perhaps, I also needed her forgiveness after a perceived betrayal as would-be guest who refused her hospitality and generosity.

BROADER IMPLICATIONS FOR COSMOLOGIES OF EVIL

Thus Tuareg concepts of honor, dishonor, and evil, and strategies to discern and combat them, are complex, but incidents of everyday sociability, informal commentaries, and verbal art performance yield valuable insights into these topics. Relevant to the local cosmology of evil and practice of moral testing is the Sufi stream in local cultural interpretations of Islam. Although Tuareg vary considerably in their religious devotion, some groups were converted by Sufi marabouts, and their influence persists, at least as an ideal, despite many upheavals (Norris 1990; Kohl and Fischer 2010). The Kel Essuk maraboutique descent group in northern Mali, for example, traditionally bring opposed factions together in peacemaking; their name denotes "people of the marketplace," referring to the idea of a crossroads. Key in the Sufi framework for coping with good and evil is the way in which Sufis attempt to place their experience of the Unity of Being within the Islamic framework. As Bousfield (in Parkin 1985, 194–208) points out, an important theme in Sufi Islam is that everything, including misfortune and evil as well as luck and good, comes from Allah, and no other source (Bousfield in Parkin 1985, 196). Only Allah rewards and punishes; humans should not do this.

Thus the Sufi ideal is to find a ground upon which the unity of experience can be established. This is one level of meaning of the "small moral tests" conducted in social life by many Tuareg. Therefore, evil experienced is not strictly limited to another's compartmentalized greed or avarice; rather, the focus is on a negotiation of moral responsibility between all parties, a common ground to reinforce good and combat evil, and to thereby maintain dignity and honor in moral personhood.

Yet the dilemma for many persons in Saharan regions today is coping with dangers of successive invasions and uncertainties in discerning friend from foe. Hence the need for reassurance that one can trust human agents, and moral tests express these concerns. There is unity in Allah (God) here, but also some human agency. Danger (*wa labasen*), a frequent gloss used for evil in Tamajaq in these incidents, unlike witchcraft, does not operate as a leveling mechanism, however. Despite loss and compensation, the main quest here is not the leveling of material wealth, even in theft, but social validation, purification, honor, and dignity in negotiations and compromises. Many wish to distinguish friend from foe, but at the same time, also wish to keep the moral ground "level" between humans who are (or should be) dependent on each other.

Thus local concepts of evil include danger, harm, and misfortune caused by both human social and spirit superhuman forces, sometimes intentionally, sometimes inadvertently. Responsibility is shared, however, by perpetrator, victim, and bystanders in redressing the suffering.

A case study and life history, tales, songs, and plays do not represent an entire cultural setting or community, or reflect cultural or religious consensus. Quranic and Sufi pronouncements, as well as Tuareg interpretations of Islam, are not unitary. Takhia's situation was not entirely typical, neither was it completely aberrant; many others in her region have also suffered great trauma in recent years, and local verbal art does portray important relevant values for judging conduct. For Takhia, the evil here primarily involved her intrafamilial tensions, in particular those with her close matrilineal relatives, her much diminished female-owned nomadic tent, her appropriated herds and uncertain health, and ensuing challenges to her position as moral center of her household and (formerly, nomadic camp). In the physical and psychosocial limbo, of *essuf* or *tenere*, great creativity or great evil may take place. Takhia's predicament was one of slow abandonment by her family. She did not accuse anyone of *togerchet* "evil eye," *awal* "gossip," or *tezma* and *ark echaghel* "witchcraft" or "sorcery" powers—still commonly evoked by many Tuareg (Rasmussen 2013). The evil here, contrary to many observations on concepts of evil in some other African societies (Comaroff and Comaroff 1993; Ferme 2001; Parkin 1985) was not one of excess; rather, it derived from deprivation and feelings of dishonor. The stomach, milk, and ties and property they represent, associated with matriliny, "children of the stomach," and "milk herds," were not abundant. Brothers did not always protect sisters; aunts did not always give property to nieces, but sometimes even (allegedly) appropriated it; and nephews were not always respectful or supportive.

As many disperse from rural communities and come into towns or cross borders for aid and security, they find fewer rituals to deal with what many Tuareg refer to as illnesses of the heart and soul (Rasmussen 1995); for example, spirit possession ceremonies were banned in Kidal after a possessed person in trance accused a civil servant of corruption. Rites of passage for youths such as the caravan trade have been on the decline. Most urban weddings tend to be shorter and less elaborate than those in the countryside. Live or recorded guitar music, predominantly composed and performed by men, is more frequent than live drumming and songs by a female chorus offering social critique and advice. Islamic scholars, though numerous, respected, and powerful in that town, tend to treat predominantly men with Quranic verses, although it should be recalled that a marabout and uncle did visit the family upon hearing of Takhia's disciplinary problems.

More generally, the value of small moral tests, in their informal sociability, is their situating of cosmologies in context and practice, where the researcher is often drawn into local interactions, thereby minimizing the tendency of the anthropologist to superimpose his or her own concepts of evil. These tests often emerge, not from rigid normative structures, but from dilemmas and double-binds, thereby necessitating a focus on intent and agency in emergent practice. Meanings are more complex than merely attempts to identify and control anti-social actions. Intent, outcome, and unintended consequences emerge from encounters between local cosmologies of evil at the interface of rural and urban, sacred and secular, household, kin and nonkin, ethnic and national forces, as cultural spaces of negotiation (Comaroff and Comaroff 1993; Hutchinson 1996; West 2007).

Much valuable research has been devoted to activation of ritual powers in unleashing and combating evil—among Tuareg (Casajus 1987; Nicolaisen 1961; Rasmussen 1998, 2001, 2004, 2013) and other peoples (Beidelman 1997; Evans-Pritchard 1937; Hutchinson 1996; Parkin 1985, 1991), including evil eye, witchcraft, and other malevolent forces (Pels 1998; Stewart and Strathern 2004; West 2007). The Tuareg case shows how more informal strategies also powerfully reveal conduct to ascertain motivations and modify outcomes. The boundaries around moral personhood are not a matter of rigid "in" or "out" groups, but can be negotiated and revised.

NOTES

1. The present essay is based primarily on data from my field research in Tuareg communities in rural and urban northern Mali in 2002 and 2006, on changing gender constructs and urban theatrical performances, with added insights from my lengthier field research in Tuareg communities in northern Niger, between 1983 and 2012, on spirit possession, aging and the life course, herbal medicine women and other medico-ritual healing specialists and practices, rural and urban smith/artisans, gender, and youth culture. In these projects, I am grateful for support from Fulbright Hays, the Social Science Research Council, National Geographic Committee for Research and Exploration, the Wenner-Gren Foundation, Indiana University, and the University of Houston.

2. Most Tuareg groups (regional confederations and descent groups) today combine, to varying degrees, elements of ancient matriliny and patriliny, the latter introduced during conversion to Islam between approximately the eighth and eleventh centuries CE. Earlier matrilineal practices are more prominent in herbalism, possession, and mediumship; different phases in rites of passage; and special endowments reserved for women called *akh ihuderan* (living milk), property as an alternative to Quranic (Arabic-influenced) inheritance. Patrilineal influences derive from nation-state (French-derived) secular law, outside ethnic practices in sedentarized and urban centers. There are also variations according to classes emerging from the Tuareg precolonial system of stratified, endogamous groups with inherited occupations and client-patron relations (nobles, tributaries, client and servile persons, and artisans) based on descent.

3. *Ettebek* refers specifically to spirit possession temporary "craziness" in being "in the wild or solitude" during trance; *anebzeg* denotes being "permanently insane," in the sense of loss of control over self; and *taghal* approximately denotes "senility" or other generalized dementia.

4. Most Tuareg today are seminomadic, compelled to settle at least part of the time in sedentarized centers, oases, and towns. Most combine stockbreeding with different subsistence patterns such as oasis gardening, artisan work, market and itinerant trading, including both traditional caravanning and trucking, and labor migration.

5. Until recently many Tuareg, particularly more nomadic and aristocratic groups in the northern regions of Mali and Niger, were underrepresented in higher education, functionary jobs, and nation-state governments. For complex historical reasons dating back to French colonial policies of favoring the southern farming groups, there have been armed conflicts between some Tuareg and several central governments. In Mali, the first occurred in 1963, over food distribution during a drought and taxation, when a regional military commander massacred Tuareg elders and marabouts in Kidal. The second rebellion, in both northern Mali and northern Niger, from approximately 1990 to 1996, demanded greater economic assistance to northern regions, more representation of Tuareg in national armies, universities, and government jobs. Beginning around 2006–2007, tensions arose around Arlit, Niger, over uranium mining contracts, and in both countries, there has been massive return of labor migrants, some with weaponry, from Libya. In 2012, in Mali, following a coup d'état in Bamako led by army factions, Tuareg rebel dissidents/nationalists around Kidal declared an independent state of Azawad, but they subsequently faced invasions from Islamist/reformist militants and also allied French and Bamako-based troops. The political fate of the north, as of this writing, remains uncertain.

6. See Rasmussen (1995, 2008). Spirit possession rituals called *tende-n-goumaten* involve medico-ritual therapeutic efforts including music to being the possessed person in trance back into the moral and social community from their state of "solitude, nostalgia," after following the call of the Kel Essuf spirits of the wild.

REFERENCES

Beidelman, Thomas O. 1997. *The Cool Knife: Imagery of Gender, Sexuality, and Moral Education in Kaguru Initiation Ritual.* Washington, DC: Smithsonian Institution Press.

Casajus, Dominique. 1987. *La tente dans la solitude: la société et les morts chez les Touaregs Kel Farwan.* Cambridge: Cambridge University Press.

———. 2000. *Les gens de la parole; langage, poésie et politique en pays touareg.* Paris: La Découverte.

Claudot-Hawad, Helène. 1993. *Les Touareg: portrait en fragments.* Aix en Provence: Edisud.

Comaroff, Jean, and John Comaroff, eds. 1993. *Modernity and Its Malcontents: Ritual and Power in Postcolonial Africa.* Chicago: University of Chicago Press.

Evans-Pritchard, Edward E. 1937. *Witchcraft, Oracles and Magic among the Azande.* Oxford: Clarendon Press.

Ferme, Mariane C. 2001. *The Underneath of Things: Violence, History, and the Everyday in Sierra Leone.* Berkeley: University of California Press.

Hutchinson, Sharon. 1997. *Nuer Dilemmas: Coping with Money, War, and the State.* Berkeley: University of California Press.

Kohl, Ines. 2009. *Beautiful Modern Nomads: Bordercrossing Tuareg between Niger, Algeria and Libya.* London: L. B. Tauris Publishers.

Kohl, Ines, and Anja Fischer, eds. 2010. *Tuareg Society within a Globalized World: Saharan Life in Transition.* London: L. B. Tauris Publishers.

Lamb, Sarah. 2000. *White Saris and Sweet Mangoes: Aging, Gender and Body in North India.* Berkeley: University of California.

Murphy, Robert. 1967. "Tuareg Kinship." *American Anthropologist* 69, no. 2:163–170.

Nicolaisen, Ida, and Johannes Nicolaisen. 1997. *The Pastoral Tuareg: Ecology, Culture and Society.* Copenhagen: Rhodos.

Nicolaisen, Johannes. 1961. "La Religion et la magie touaregues." *Folk* 3: 113–160.

Norris. Harry T. 1990. *Sufi Mystics of the Niger Desert: Sīdī Mahmūd and the Hermits of Aïr.* Oxford: Clarendon

Parkin, David, ed. 1985. *The Anthropology of Evil.* Oxford: Basil Blackwell Press.

———. 1991. *The Sacred Void: Spatial Images of Work and Ritual among the Giriama of Kenya.* Cambridge: Cambridge University Press.

Pels, Peter. 1998. "The Magic of Africa: Reflections on a Western Commonplace." *African Studies Review* 41, no. 3:193–209.

Rasmussen, Susan J. 1995. *Spirit Possession and Personhood among the Kel Ewey Tuareg.* Cambridge: Cambridge University Press.

———. 1997. *The Poetics and Politics of Tuareg Aging: Life Course and Personal Destiny in Niger.* DeKalb: Northern Illinois University Press.

———. 1998. "Ritual Powers and Social Tensions as Moral Discourse among the Tuareg." *American Anthropologist* 100, no. 2:458–468.

———. 2000. "Alms, Elders, and Ancestors: The Spirit of the Gift among the Tuareg." *Ethnology* 39, no. 1:15–38.

———. 2001. *Healing in Community: Medicine, Contested Terrains, and Cultural Encounters among the Tuareg.* Westport: Bergin and Garvey Press/Greenwood.

———. 2004. "These Are Dirty Times!" *Journal of Ritual Studies* 18, no. 2:43–60.

———. 2006. *Those Who Touch: Tuareg Medicine Women in Anthropological Perspective.* DeKalb: Northern Illinois University Press.

———. 2008. The People of Solitude." *Journal of the Royal Anthropological Institute* 14: 609–627.

———. 2013. *Witches, Neighbors, Strangers, and Culture Heroes: Ritual Powers of Smith/Artisans in Tuareg Society and Beyond.* Lanham, MD: Rowman and Littlefield.

Stewart, Pamela, and Andrew Strathern. 2004. *Witchcraft, Sorcery, Rumors, and Gossip.* New Departures in Anthropology Series 1. Cambridge: Cambridge University Press.

West, Harry. 2005. *Kupilikula.* Chicago: University of Chicago Press.

———. 2007. *Ethnographic Sorcery.* Chicago: University of Chicago Press.

14 THE GENDER OF EVIL

Maasai Experiences and Expressions

DOROTHY L. HODGSON

Although there is an emerging scholarship in anthropology on evil (e.g., Parkin 1985a)—its symbolism, manifestations, associations, and changes over time—few scholars have explored whether gender shapes experiences and expressions of evil, and if so how. Women and men appear as agents or victims of evil acts or forces, whether as intentionally negligent mothers (Parkin 1985c) or witches (van Beek 1994), but there has been little systematic effort to analyze what evil acts, beings or forces may tell us about gender relations, or, conversely, how a gender analysis may complicate our understandings of evil. But if, as David Parkin (1985c 10–11) argues, "evil . . . denotes an area of discourse concerning human suffering, human existential predicaments and the attempted resolution of these through other humans and through non-human agencies, including a God or gods," then more attention to *which* humans—men and women, young and old—are implicated and how offers a more embedded, embodied account of evil.

In this chapter, I compare three different manifestations of evil in the lives of Maasai pastoralists in Tanzania in order to suggest the importance of a gendered analysis to our theorizations of "evil": the evil acts (*esetan*) of individuals such as cursing and the "evil eye"; the immoral acts of men that provoke collective retribution by women (*olkishoroto*); and the waves of spirit possession (*orpeko*) that inflicted Maasai women starting in the 1970s. I argue that these seemingly disparate cases illuminate aspects of Maasai gender relationships and demonstrate how making gender a central analytic can deepen and complicate anthropological understandings of evil and related concepts such as morality, agency, personhood, and social change.

THE SPIRIT OF MAASAI MORALITY

Gender and generation have always been the two central organizing principles of life and livelihoods among Maasai pastoralists. Historical evidence suggests that from the time hundreds, if not thousands of years ago, when Maa-speaking peoples migrated southward into present-day Tanzania and Kenya, they recognized different gender-age groups through language, respect protocols, dress, greetings, principles and prohibitions about behavior, and other social and cultural practices (Hodgson 2001, 2005).[1] Gender relations were seen as complementary—men and women of different ages had distinct responsibilities for the household, homestead, and herd, but there was mutual respect (*enkanyit*) and recognition that everyone had to meet their obligations in order for their families to prosper. As both men and women aged, they gained respect, prestige, and power over their juniors. Other hierarchies (of a first wife over junior wives or eldest son over his younger brothers) existed, and some (such as elder age sets over the warrior age sets) were formally institutionalized through rituals (Hodgson 2001, 2005).

Gender has also been a significant axis of difference in Maasai spiritual beliefs and practices. Historically, Maasai women saw themselves, and were seen by Maasai men, as being "closer" to Eng'ai, their divinity, who was understood and referred to in primarily (although not exclusively) feminine terms as the divine principle that created, supported, and nurtured life on earth (cf. Burton 1991). In addition to the female prefix "En," Eng'ai was addressed as, for example, "she of the black garment," "my mother with wet clothes," and "she of the growing grasses" (Voshaar 1998, 137). The alternate meanings of Eng'ai as "rain" and "sky" and the metaphorical references in these sayings and others to wetness, darkness, motherhood, and growth reinforced the association of Eng'ai with fertility, and thus femininity. Women's closeness to Eng'ai was expressed and experienced in many ways, including their shared power to produce and nurture human life.

The closeness was not just metaphorical, however, but material—Maasai men and women who I interviewed in 2000 believed that Eng'ai was present in them through their *oltau*, their heart and spirit. *Oltau* was at once a unique, inner, essence bequeathed to each person by Eng'ai, an agentive force, and the locus of moral value. According to Maasai, "everyone is born with their own *oltau*," which was their closest connection to Eng'ai. Like Western and Christian notions of "spirit," *oltau* resides in individual bodies, but is not contained by them. As Naishepo, an older Maasai woman told me, "Eng'ai created me, and you know that Eng'ai gave you the *oltau* that you have, so if she wants to slaughter a chicken, you slaughter a chicken, because She gave it to you. She gave you the *oltau* that you have, because Eng'ai is the reason you are even walking around." A person's *oltau* could therefore influence their actions, forcing them to do things or go places they might not otherwise choose. Moreover, people could improve or worsen their *iltauja* through their practices, in part by "opening" or "closing" their *iltauja* to Eng'ai: "Eng'ai helps people especially if you open your *oltau* to Her."

In addition to being an agentive force, *oltau* was also the locus of moral value. A good *oltau* was described as being black in color (*oltau orok*), "because black is the color of Eng'ai." In contrast, a bad *oltau* was red, a color associated with power, especially the destructive power of anger and retribution. Certain people were referred to as having "black spirits" because they were perceived as kind, generous, respectful, and moral, with no evil or malice in their hearts, actions, or intentions. Other men and women were said to have "red spirits" because they were selfish, greedy, malevolent, and mean.

Perhaps most importantly for this chapter, the *iltauja* of men and women were understood as having different characteristics. In general, women's spirits were described as closer and more open to Eng'ai, while men's *iltauja* were more distant and closed. As a result, women's *iltauja* were more flexible and receptive to new experiences than men's were. As Letani, a senior male elder commented, "Women are very quick to change their *iltauja*, while men are very hard-headed (*megol ilukuny*)." Similarly, as Esta, the female founder of a Catholic church noted about conversion to Christianity, "It is women who were able to see that there was light, and we tried to persuade the men, but they got stuck, so therefore there are only a few these days [in church]." Thus, although both men and women embodied Eng'ai through their *oltau*, women's *oltau* was characterized as closer and more attuned to Eng'ai's directives and moral sensibilities. As such, women prayed throughout the day to Her, thanking and entreating Eng'ai for the continued protection, preservation, expansion, and prosperity of their family and herds, and incorporating the rich symbolism of grass and milk as signs of fertility, blessing, and bounty (Hodgson 2005).

This gender difference in men's and women's embodied spiritual relationship with Eng'ai has intensified over the past few decades, as many men have increasingly embraced new forms of economic and political control to the detriment of women's property rights, economic security, and political authority. During the colonial period—after first the Germans then the British took control of Tanganyika—colonial initiatives such as creating "Native Authorities," directing all economic and development assistance to men, and ignoring the rights and responsibilities of women, solidified what were gender differences into gender hierarchies. Men were now perceived as the household "heads," livestock "owners," and political authorities. The centrality of women to the pastoralist economy (as milk managers, caretakers for young and sick animals, hide processors, traders, and more) was overlooked, as were their forms of domestic and community authority (Hodgson 2001, 2005).

In response, women emphasized and enhanced their moral and spiritual authority through widespread involvement in the Catholic and other Christian churches (Hodgson 2005). Significantly, many Maasai women said that they joined the church because they were directed to do so by their *oltau*. Conversion (*airuk*, to believe, to agree) was understood as a process occurring by the desire of a person's *oltau*, rather than their will or mind. As Martha, an elderly woman, explained, "No one is forced to convert; each person comes when his/her spirit agrees (*oltau lenye loiruko*), then s/he says 'I will go to church and get baptized.'" Many Maasai confirmed this idea of *oltau*, saying that their *oltau*, their spirit decided, that their spirit led them to church. "My *oltau* wanted to go to church," explained Esta, "so I went and was baptized." Women (and some men) claimed that women's *iltauja* were more open to Eng'ai, closer to Eng'ai, while "the spirits of men just don't want to go to church." Several women described a yearning, a desire, an uncontrollable urge to join the church, all driven by their *oltau*: "my *oltau* demanded that I go to church!" In contrast, some men also invoked their *oltau* as a reason they had not participated in Christianity: "my *oltau* was not interested." One elderly woman even implied that men, like wild animals, had no spirits: "Our [women's] spirits just love [the church]. I mean, if I only knew how to seize/obey my spirit even more, I would do so. But a man is just a wild animal (*olowuaru*) at all times." The invocation of men as wild animals suggests a sharp moral critique of the changes in Maasai gender relations, simultaneously casting men's increased political and economic control as evil and an affront to Eng'ai and affirming the moral superiority of women in the face of such betrayals.

COMPARATIVE MANIFESTATIONS OF EVIL IN MAASAI LIFE

The terms for evil in Maa, the Maasai language, draw on the root *torro*—for evil or bad. Thus the noun for evil things is *entorroni* (pl. *intorrok*), and the adjective is *torrono* (pl. *torro*) (cf. Mol 1977, 63, 1996, 393). The conflation between "evil" and "bad" makes an analysis of evil more challenging, because being bad (such as a bad child) is not the same thing as being an evil person. Evil and bad occupy different points on a spectrum of malfeasance—bad as a moral judgment of an action or person as perhaps a temporary condition, rather than an enduring, permanent condition. In contrast, characterizing a person, action, or force as evil suggests something truly abhorrent to moral codes, whether a onetime horrendous act or a series of actions or events that reveal a pattern, propensity, or character of malevolence.

MODE I: EVIL ACTS AND INDIVIDUALS

Although Maasai seem to have had no concept of evil spirits, they did believe that people, both Maasai and non-Maasai, were capable of intentionally evil actions, including using charms and curses to bring misfortune, sickness, or even death on other people (Hollis 1905; Merker 1910 [1904], 210–211; cf. Krapf 1854, 18). Merker (1910 [1904], 210) claimed that the practitioner of *esetan* (which he translated as "witchcraft")[2] "obtain[ed] his results by the power of his charm only, which power is the outcome of the composition of the concoction, and of repeating of a definite formula, and of the making of particular gestures." Another form of *esetan* was to smear magic medicine under the fingernail of the index finger, point at the person concerned, and murmur a spell (Merker 1910 [1904], 156). As a result, Maasai never pointed (and still do not point) their fingers at other people, and the index finger is called "the magician" (*sakutushoi* or *olasakutoni*).

People accused of such malevolent actions were forced to take an oath or submit to an ordeal to prove their innocence. Most of the ordeals described in the historical sources involved taking an oath of innocence or inviting the retribution of their divinity, Eng'ai, if guilty, and then imbibing certain substances (such as a mixture of meat and roots [Krapf 1854, 27] or blood and milk [Merker 1910 (1904), 219–220]), holding certain things (such as a dry twig and a green twig [Merker 1910 (1904), 219–220]), or other actions. According to Merker (1910 [1904], 220), "The majority of those assembled [to hear an accusation] decide when an ordeal is to be used and which one. The accused, and he alone, must submit to the ordeal, he cannot appoint a substitute. . . . If the accused has come to no harm within ten to fourteen days after the ordeal, he is regarded as entirely free from suspicion." Maasai also believed in "the evil eye," which could sicken both humans and cattle. According to Merker (1910 [1904], 211), "One who is afflicted with the evil eye (*erta gonjek*) may not show himself in the vicinity of a village. Everyone shuns him fearfully, so he builds himself a separate village in which he lives alone with his family. If he ventures to enter a strange village, he must be prepared to be beaten to death."

To protect themselves from curses and the evil eye, men, women, and children wore protective amulets and charms that they made or obtained from *iloibonok* (sing. *oloiboni*, refers to male ritual leaders with powers of prophecy and divination). In addition, Merker (1910 [1904], 210) noted that "women, who go amongst strange tribes from neighboring districts to buy vegetables, protect themselves more particularly against their spells. They smear their foreheads and cheeks with cowdung, or wear a cord round their necks on which is a row of small split wands."

Although Merker and other historical accounts seem to suggest that only men could practice *esetan* or have the evil eye, a conclusion generally supported by my research since 1985 with Maasai communities, there was one set of circumstances when women were susceptible to such accusations—after the birth of a baby. Other premenopausal women, especially women who were barren (or perceived as barren), were careful not to stare at an infant or to praise its beauty or health in case they were accused of being "jealous," or, even worse, because of their jealousy, casting an evil eye on the child so that it might sicken or die. New mothers were cautious about which women they allowed inside their house to see their infant (men—even their husbands—were not welcome) and stayed inside or just outside the house for about three months to not only recuperate from the pregnancy, but protect their newborn child from the possible evil eyes of jealous women and strangers.

MODE II: IMMORAL MEN AND ANGRY WOMEN

A second kind of evil were certain immoral acts by men that were perceived as serious affronts to the fertility and procreative powers of women (and thus, their divinity, Eng'ai), and thus resulted in forms of collective attack and ritual protest by women. One form, *olkishoroto,* was deployed when, for example, a man slept with a pregnant woman or his real or classificatory daughter. According to Hollis (1910, 480), "In the event of a man having intercourse with a pregnant woman, and thereby causing her to abort, he must submit to a punishment which is called ol-kishuroto. All the women of the neighborhood collect together and, having stripped, seize the guilty person and flog him, after which they slaughter as many of his cattle as they can, strangling and suffocating the animals with their garments." Similarly, groups of women would attack men who prevented their wives from participating in the regular collective fertility gatherings of women (*oloirishi*). Interviews with Maasai men and women have confirmed that the practice was much the same as recounted by Paul Spencer in 1988:

Those husbands who beat their wives at this particular time or prevent any of them from joining the gathering, are harried. If the women hear of such an elder, they will storm his village dealing tit for tat. If he has beaten his wife, they will want to beat him and seize some of his best cattle. If he has tried to detain any wife, they will snatch away all of his wives, and leave him to feed the children, milk the cows, and fetch wood and water. No other woman—and certainly no man—would help him. This is a severe degradation, and it is held to be dangerously unpropitious for elders to undertake such tasks. (Spencer 1988, 201)[3]

These forms of collective protest were (and still are) recognized as legitimate and feared.[4]

MODE III: THE EVIL FORCE OF SPIRIT POSSESSION

Finally, a more recent, novel manifestation of evil for Maasai was the spread of *orpeko*, a form of spirit possession, throughout their communities beginning in the mid-1950s. *Orpeko* mainly afflicted women of childbearing age, whose symptoms included shaking, nightmares, sleep walking, refusal to do household chores, burning sensations in their womb and/or stomach, listlessness, and lack of appetite (Hodgson 1997, 114; cf. Hurskainen 1989, 143). The accounts of possessed and nonpossessed women and men from throughout this period (Peterson 1971; Hurskainen 1985; Hodgson 1997) all characterized *orpeko* as an evil, malevolent sickness (*emuoyian*) that came from "outside" and was associated with devastation and disease. Possession fits were often triggered by "foreign" sounds, such as radios and drumming, and some possessed women spoke "strange" languages in which they were not conversant. Most terrifying for some women were the nightmares they had, filled with signs of the invasion of "the other." Many described a sense that "darkness" or "a black cloud" was descending on them, suffocating them, and even strangling them. Consider these two accounts collected by David Peterson in 1971:[5]

> She would wake up at night with a start as "darkness" would come and try to strangle her. Being very frightened, she would cover herself quickly before the "darkness" could cover her and then she would scream. After this she was unable to sleep for the rest of the night. She also began to feel something very heavy on her chest. (Peterson 1971, case 1)
>
> The first occurrence of trouble was in 1969 when this girl became quite sick with a fever. A few days later she saw "darkness," felt that she was being strangled and ran out of the boma. She was caught by her family and they decided she was crazy. From then on she would shake everyday—first on one side, then the other and then her whole body would shake. She always had a burning sen-

sation in her stomach and felt something very hot moving upwards to strangle her. She felt like a dying woman at this time, and she almost did die. (Peterson 1971, case 5)

More recent accounts of *orpeko* by women describe similar symptoms, especially pain, burning, or lumps in the womb (Hodgson 1997, 2005).

Orpeko, as I have argued elsewhere (Hodgson 1997, 2005) was understood by women as a malevolent contagion from "outside" over which they had no control, but which they attributed, indirectly, to the increased materialism and immoral assertions of power and privilege by Maasai men. Their symptoms marked the dimension in their lives where they felt most threatened by these changes—in their roles as mothers. Women feared the effects of these changes in their lives on their capacity and power for both biological and social reproduction. Not surprisingly, therefore, possession was prevalent among barren women, but pregnancy could also trigger possession and possession was in turn said to cause miscarriages (Hodgson 1997, 118).

But the spread of *orpeko* also empowered women by strengthening relationships among them and facilitating the creation of "churches of women." Women came together to support possessed women, holding them, caring for them, and taking over their work while they were incapacitated. But they also found a "cure"—baptism and participation in the Christian (primarily Lutheran and Catholic) churches. As an elder man explained to me in 2000:

> There is a sickness (*emuoyian*) that has spread into this area recently that was not here before, this thing called *esetan,* this *orpeko.* It hasn't entered men, but women. But when you take a woman to the *oloiboni* he says "She is cursed." And if you take her to another, "She is cursed." Basi, . . . this wisdom of Christians showed that a thing called the church (*ekanisa*) could heal (*eishiu*) this sickness. When we put women in there they were healed, really it helped them. *Shie,* why else would so many have joined? Also, it is said that a healthy person who is baptized cannot be possessed.

Orpeko enabled women to overcome the objections of many men to their involvement in the Christian churches as it soon became clear that the only way to permanently prevent its recurrence was baptism. For some of them, as for some priests and pastors, *orpeko* was not just a manifestation of evil, but of the Christian devil, a new form of evil in their lives (Benson 1980; Hurskainen 1985; cf. Meyer 1999). The churches, which were dominated by women, became a space for women to come together to strengthen their ties to Eng'ai and each other as a collective force without directly threatening the increased power of men (Hodgson 1997, 2005).

ANALYZING EVIL THROUGH A GENDERED LENS

So how do we make sense of these three different forms of evil? What do they tell us about gendered expressions and experiences of evil among Maasai, as well as notions of personhood, agency, and morality?

First, Maasai ideas of *oltau*, that is the connection to and influence of Eng'ai in shaping peoples' actions, complicate normative understandings of agency and intentionality in relation to evil acts or deeds. Considering *oltau* as an agentive force—and one that can produce good or evil actions—challenges dominant notions of agency as "free will" that have been derived from Western philosophy. Instead of contained, rational, fully conscious, individuated, autonomous subjects that choose to act in certain ways, Maasai ideas of *oltau* suggest an alternative concept of personhood, subjectivity, and agency in which the role of free will, consciousness, and intentionality in shaping human ideas and practices are ambivalent, if not muted. Since the link between Eng'ai and humans is not unidirectional, however, humans are not simply passive subjects of Eng'ai's will. Instead, they can shape their relationship to Eng'ai by "opening" or "closing" their *oltau*.

Moreover, these ideas of agency and intentionality are further complicated by gender. The first forms of evil, characterized as *esetan* or the evil eye, describe expressions of internalized, intentional evil, primarily on the part of men. If women, through their *oltau*, are perceived as closer to Eng'ai and as guardians of the moral order, then it is perhaps understandable that they are therefore less susceptible to being agents of evil. In contrast, the more closed and distant *oltau* of men makes them more prone to evil actions and deeds, whether *esetan*, the evil eye, or, as described in the second mode, having sex with pregnant women or real or classificatory daughters. The one set of exceptions where certain women are susceptible to evil actions—in response to the birth of a child—speak to the centrality of fertility, childbirth, and motherhood to their sense of being and, by implication, their closeness to Eng'ai, the Divine Mother. In other words, their desire to become mothers is so powerful that it can overtake their innate goodness (their black *oltau*) and the heightened influence of Eng'ai to produce evil acts or intentions in the form of jealousy and the evil eye.

Rather than being the primary agents of evil, Maasai women as individuals instead seem especially vulnerable to evil, despite their closeness to Eng'ai, or perhaps because of it—whether in the form of *esetan*, the evil eye, or, as described in the third case, spirit possession (*orpeko*). Historically, as has already been described, women wore additional protective balms and amulets when they traveled into other communities to trade goods or visit relatives. New mothers were extremely cautious and protective of their newborn infants who, like the women, were believed to be highly susceptible to the evil eye.

Men, both young and old, were also the victims of evil acts, but they had less need of charms, amulets, and other protections when they traveled to other communities. This difference with women suggests that adult men (as opposed to boys) had some kind of innate defense against the potential evil lurking in everyday encounters with other peoples. But men did require additional ritual protection during times when they were seen as especially vulnerable to evil and harm: the ceremonies that marked their ritual transition from one age grade to the other, and occasions when, as young men (*ilmurran*, often glossed as "warriors"), they were being prepared for battle by the *oloiboni* (Hodgson 2005; Merker 1910 [1904]).

The proliferation of *orpeko* during the late 1900s, however, marked a very different kind of encounter with evil. Now the evil was an "other" that infiltrated Maasai communities and homes, manifesting itself primarily among women of childbearing age. Both men and women characterized *orpeko* as a sickness and evil spirit that came from outside. But women associated *orpeko* more clearly with the rapid changes produced by colonial and postcolonial "development" initiatives that were undermining their power, prestige, and respect within their families. *Orpeko* is an indirect critique of the increasing materialism of men, their heightened assertions of power and privilege as household "heads," political authorities, the "owners" of livestock, and other emerging commodities and property forms.

Finally, while individual women may be more defenseless than men against evil acts and forces, they had tremendous power to directly confront and challenge evil as a group. In the case of *olkishoroto* and related collective protests, evil was associated with the actions and aspirations of men, especially when they threatened the fertility and power of women as mothers and guardians of the moral order. More recently, women have waged collective protests similar to *olkishoroto* against what they perceive as contemporary manifestations of evil—corrupt, greedy state officials (all male) who have burned their homes and taken their land to expand lucrative (and personally profitable) conservation and tourism initiatives (Hodgson unpublished manuscript). In the case of *orpeko*, the space of the Christian churches provided a means to challenge and overcome this new evil as a collective.

In conclusion, the Maasai case demonstrates how taking gender seriously as a category of analysis produces a more nuanced, complicated understanding of the modes and manifestations of evil. Maasai believed that men and women had distinct relationships with their divinity, Eng'ai, which shaped their capacity for moral (and immoral) actions through their differential ability to "open" and "close" their *oltau* (heart and spirit) to the influence of Eng'ai. Women were perceived as closer to Eng'ai, more able to open their *oltau* to Her direction, while the *oltau* of men was more closed, making them more prone to evil actions and deeds. Their encounters with colonialism, capitalism, Christianity, nationalism, and other seemingly "outside" forces have exacerbated these gendered differences, as evidenced, in part, by the spread of spirit possession (*orpeko*) among Maasai women in the 1970s and 1980s. But the collective power of women to confront and challenge evil through the continuing practice of *olkishoroto* reveals their power as a collective force, united and empowered by their close relationship to Eng'ai.

NOTES

This chapter draws, in part, on material published in *The Church of Women* (Hodgson 2005) and "Embodying the Contradictions of Modernity" (Hodgson 1997). I am grateful to Bill Olsen for inviting me to participate in this project and encouraging me to deepen my analysis of gender and evil.

1. For sources on the early history of Maasai, see Bernsten (1979), Sommer and Vossen (1993), Sutton (1990, 1993), Galaty (1993), and Waller (1978, 1985a, 1985b, 1988).

2. Krapf (1854, 24) also used *esetan* for witchcraft, claiming that "when the Wakuafi see a book, they take it for esétan or witchcraft." Last (1883, 531) wrote that "Esatan" referred to "the source of evil," as opposed to "Engai . . . as the source of good." In his brief vocabulary list, however, he translated "esatan" as "witchcraft" (1883, 536).

3. These were similar to the Pokot "shaming parties" (Edgerton and Conant 1964).

4. Although I have never witnessed either form of collective ritual protest, I have been collecting accounts from the archives, interviews with Maasai men and women, and colleagues in Tanzania and Kenya who have seen these groups of women in action.

5. I am very grateful to David Peterson for allowing me to use the valuable case studies described in his unpublished paper (1971), which summarized his interviews with nineteen women and one man who had been possessed.

REFERENCES

Benson, Rev. Stanley. 1980. "The Conquering Sacrament: Baptism and Demon Possession among the Maasai of Tanzania." *Africa Theological Journal* 9: 52–61.

Bernsten, John. 1979. "Pastoralism, Raiding and Prophets: Maasailand in the Nineteenth Century." PhD diss., Department of History, University of Wisconsin—Madison.

Burton, John W. 1991. "Representations of the Feminine in Nilotic Cosmologies." In *Body and Space: Symbolic Models of Unity and Division in African Cosmology and Experience,* edited by Anita Jacobson-Widding, 81–98. Stockholm: Almqvist and Wiksell.

Edgerton, Robert B., and Francis P. Conant. 1964. "*Kilipat:* The 'Shaming Party' among the Pokot of East Africa." *Southwestern Journal of Anthropology* 20, no. 4:404–418.

Galaty, John. 1993. "Maasai Expansion and the New East Africa Pastoralism." In *Being Maasai*, edited by Thomas Spear and Richard Waller, 61–86. London: James Currey.

Hodgson, Dorothy L. 1997. "Embodying the Contradictions of Modernity: Gender and Spirit Possession among Maasai in Tanzania." In *Gendered Encounters: Challenging Cultural Boundaries and Social Hierarchies in Africa*, edited by Maria Grosz-Ngate and Omari Kokole, pages. New York: Routledge.

———. 2001 *Once Intrepid Warriors: Gender, Ethnicity and the Cultural Politics of Maasai Development*. Bloomington: Indiana University Press.

———. 2005. *The Church of Women: Gendered Encounters between Maasai and Missionaries*. Bloomington: Indiana University Press.

———. "The Army of Women: Moral Authority, Collective Action and the Pursuit of Justice by Maasai Women." Unpublished manuscript.

Hollis, Alfred C. 1905. *The Masai: Their Language and Folklore*. Freeport, NY: Book for Libraries Press.

———. 1910. "A Note on the Masai System of Relationship and Other Matters Connected Therewith." *Journal of the Royal Anthropological Institute* 40, no. 21:473–482.

Hurskainen, Arvi. 1985. "Tatizo la Kushikwa na Pepo Umasaini Tanzania" (The Problem of Spirit Possession in Maasailand, Tanzania). Helsinki. Privately circulated paper, commissioned by the Catholic and Lutheran churches, Tanzania.

———. 1989. "The Epidemiological Aspect of Spirit Possession among the Maasai of Tanzania." In *Culture, Experience and Pluralism: Essays on African Ideas of Illness and Healing*, edited by Anita Jacobson-Widding and David Westerlund, 139–150. Uppsala: Almqvist and Wiksell International.

Krapf, J. Lewis. 1854. *Vocabulary of the Engútuk Eloikb or of the Language of the Wakuafi-Nation in the Interior of Equatorial Africa*. Tübingen, Germany: Lud. Fried. Fues.

Last, J. T. 1883. "A Visit to the Masai People Living beyond the Borders of the Nguru Country." *Proceedings of the Royal Geographical Society* 5, no. 9:517–543, 568 (map).

Merker, Moritz. 1910 [1904]. *Die Masai. Ethnographische Monographie eines ostafrikanischen Semitenvolkes*. 2nd ed. Berlin: Dietrich Reimer.

Meyer, Birgit. 1999. *Translating the Devil: Religion and Modernity among the Ewe in Ghana*. Trenton, NJ: Africa World Press.

Mol, Franz. 1977. *Maa: A Dictionary of the Maasai Language and Folklore*. Nairobi: Marketing and Publishing.

———. 1996. *Maasai Language & Culture Dictionary*. Limuru, Kenya: Kolbe Press.

Parkin, David, ed. 1985a. *The Anthropology of Evil*. Cambridge: Blackwell.

———. 1985b. "Entitling Evil: Muslims and Non-Muslims in Coastal Kenya." In *The Anthropology of Evil*, 224–243. Cambridge: Blackwell.

———. 1985c. Introduction to *The Anthropology of Evil*, 1–25. Cambridge: Blackwell.

Peterson, David. 1971. "Demon Possession among the Maasai." Unpublished manuscript.

Sommer, Gabriele, and Rainer Vossen. 1993. "Dialects, Sectiolects, or Simply Lects? The Maa Language in Time Perspective." In *Being Maasai*, edited by Thomas Spear and Richard Waller, 25–37. London: James Currey.

Spencer, Paul. 1988. *The Maasai of Matapato: A Study of Rituals of Rebellion*. Bloomington: Indiana University Press.

Sutton, John. 1990. *A Thousand Years in East Africa*. Nairobi: British Institute in Eastern Africa.

———. 1993. "Becoming Maasailand." In *Being Maasai,* edited by Thomas Spear and Richard Waller, 38–60. London: James Currey.

Waller, Richard D. 1978. "Lords of East Africa: The Maasai in the Mid-Nineteenth Century (c. 1840–c. 1885)." PhD diss., Cambridge University.

———. 1985a. "Ecology, Migration and Expansion in East Africa." *African Affairs* 84, no. 336:347–370.

———. 1985b. "Economic and Social Relations in the Central Rift Valley: The Maa-Speakers and Their Neighbours in the Nineteenth Century." In *Kenya in the Nineteenth Century,* edited by Bethwell Ogot, 83–151. Nairboni: Anyange Press.

———. 1988. "Emutai: Crisis and Response in Maasailand 1883–1902." In *The Ecology of Survival: Case Studies from Northeast African History,* edited by Douglas Johnson and David Anderson, 73–112. Boulder, CO: Westview Press.

Van Beek, Walter E. A. 1994. "The Innocent Sorcerer: Coping with Evil in Two African Societies (Kasiki and Dogon)." In *Religion in Africa: Experience and Expression,* edited by Thomas D. Blakely, Walter E. A. van Beek, and Dennis L. Thomson, 196–228. London: James Currey.

Voshaar, Jan. 1998. *Maasai: Between the Oreteti-Tree and the Tree of the Cross.* Kampen, The Netherlands: Kok Publishers.

PART III

EVIL AND MODERNITY

15 NEOCANNIBALISM, MILITARY BIOPOLITICS, AND THE PROBLEM OF HUMAN EVIL

NANCY SCHEPER-HUGHES

In this chapter I address a controversial topic in contemporary biopolitics/ necropolitics (Mbembe 2003): the biomedical abuse and plunder of dead bodies, among these, the bodies of enemies, with the complicity and collaboration of militarized states. Although biopiracy of human biomaterials is not new, the technological capacity to harvest and to distribute these anonymously worldwide through "cannibal markets" in blood, skin, bones, organs, bodies and body parts, DNA, and reproductive material to feed the desires of these new commodities for transplant medicine, for science and research, for commercial pharmacology, and for recreation and display is a late-twentieth-century innovation.

The emergence of death camps, torture camps, and refugee camps alleged to be organ harvesting camps in the late twentieth and early twenty-first centuries points to the demise of classical humanism, holism, and history—the end(s) of the body and the ends of history as we once knew it (or believed we did). Partible/divisible bodies, part-histories, part-truths, and new and robust critiques of moral anthropologies have replaced Enlightenment certitudes and universal codes of human rights and ethics.

In each of the cases to be described here, some in the passing, others more thickly described—a psychiatric "camp" (in Argentina during and after the Dirty War); the National Forensic Lab in Tel Aviv, Israel, during and after the two intifadas; the alleged but still unconfirmed murder of Serbs for their organs in transit-detention camps in Kosovo at the end of war in 1999; questionable allegations of child kidnapping for organ theft in Mozambique; private exchanges of tissues and organs harvested without consent by the university-linked pathologists in Cape Town and Pretoria, South Africa, during the antiapartheid struggle when police morgues were overcrowded with the bodies of township "terrorists"; a US scheme involving corrupt funeral parlors that tossed dead bodies in alleys outside funeral parlors for disarticulation artists to dismember and sell internationally—the research is based on my work as an anthropologist-ethnographer, medical human rights activist (director of Organs Watch), and as a witness or consultant in criminal prosecutions.

Human trafficking for the removal of kidneys from the living is today a widely recognized (Delmonico 2009; Francis and Francis 2010; Ambagtsheer and Weimar 2012), but rarely prosecuted medical human rights abuse (Scheper-Hughes 2013). Surgeons involved in providing their operating rooms and transplant services to an Israeli organs broker, Isaac Rosenbaum, who provided illicit transplants for Israeli transplant tourists with fresh kidneys taken from internationally trafficked kidney providers (Scheper-Hughes 2011a) were not held culpable and the broker received a lenient sentence of two and a half years in a low security prison in New Jersey (Scheper-Hughes 2011b). Similarly, in the South African Netcare Case, surgeons were given a stay of prosecution and the brokers, one nephrologist, and the Netcare Medical Corporation that owned the private transplant units where 109 illegal transplants took place between 2001 and 2011 paid financial penalties in plea bargains (Hassan and Sole 2011). Not one of the convicted saw the inside of a prison cell.

In contrast, the plunder of dead bodies, especially of prisoners, enemies of war, the mentally incompetent, and children are perceived differently, as heinous crimes, crimes against the state, and (in the case of the allegations in Kosovo) as crimes against humanity. Allegations of the plunder of Palestinian enemy bodies in the Israeli National Forensic Institute at Abu Kabir (Scheper-Hughes 2011a) were treated in the Israeli media as a blood libel against Israel; the president and prime minister demanded retractions of the original news story published in *Aftonbladet* by a Swedish journalist (Boström 2009). After the allegations were proven to be true, although partial, there was no international media blitz to clear the names of the whistle-blowers (Scheper-Hughes and Boström 2013). The topic was simply toxic and that toxicity poisoned the whistle-blowers.

In the case of Michael Mastromarino (see Commonwealth v. Mastromarino 2010) the New York dentist turned body snatcher in 2001–2005 was sentenced from eighteen to fifty-four years in prison for his organized crime, deception, corruption, and theft of body parts (including leg bones, hearts, heads, and torsos) from more than 1,600 bodies through arrangements with private funeral parlors in New York, New Jersey, and Pennsylvania. One prosecutor referred to Mastromarino as evil incarnate. Relatives of his victims referred to him as a "ghoul." Mastromarino's death in prison of bone cancer in 2013 was widely applauded and described as "poetic justice," and as "God's punishment for his mortal sins." One of Mastromarino's victims who developed hepatitis after surgery with contaminated tissues that had been procured through the former dentist called him "sick and disgusting" when she confronted him in court. Even Mastromarino's wife, Barbara, commented wryly on her husband's death, that he was just "skin and bones" at the end. Some even suggested that it was wrong for a priest to give Mastromarino the sacrament of last rites before he died in prison. There were some forms of evil that even God could not (or should not) forgive.

TOWARD AN ANTHROPOLOGY OF EVIL

> It seems to me that when we act in critical situations of the sort that Scheper-Hughes describes, we leave anthropology behind. We leave it behind because we abandon what I believe to be a fundamental axiom of the creed we share, namely that all humans are equal in the sight of anthropology. Though Scheper-Hughes does not put it this way, the struggle she is urging anthropologists to join is a struggle against evil. Once we identify an evil, I think we give up trying to understand the situation as a human reality. Instead we see it as in some sense inhuman, and all we then try to understand is how best to combat it. At this point we [leave anthropology behind] and we enter the political process.
>
> —PAUL RIESMAN
> (Riesman cited by Scheper-Hughes 1988, 456n4)

A key question we are posing in this volume is whether anthropology of evil is a feasible or anthropological project. I first addressed the topic in a heated discussion with the late Paul Riesman at a panel of the annual American Anthropological Association soon before his untimely death several months later. My AAA paper was later published in *Culture, Medicine and Psychiatry* (1988). I then addressed this conundrum in the D'Andrade–Scheper-Hughes controversy in *Current Anthropology* (1995). Like D'Andrade (1995), Didier Fassin (2008) argues in "Beyond Good and Evil" that "evil" was a normative concept, a political and a moral and even a philosophical topic, but it was not an anthropological topic. Moreover, he argued that anthropology must be defended on its scientific and empirical grounds from those who (like Pierre Bourdieu [2000]) advocated an engaged anthropology that did not shy away from making moral-political judgments. D'Andrade did not want to see anthropology transformed from a discipline based on an *objective* model of the world to one based on a *moral* model of the world, which he saw as dangerously driven "to identify what is *good* and what is *bad* and to allocate *reward* and *punishment*" (D'Andrade 1995, 399, emphasis in original). In "Beyond Good and Evil," Fassin (2008) reflects on Foucault's ethical sensibility that would bracket the categories of good and evil in his search for a posthumanist radical sense of human freedom. Like totemism for Claude Levi-Strauss, evil might be "good to think with," but absent a moralizing rhetoric. Fassin's argument, like that of D'Andrade, while derived from a different philosophical tradition, is based on basic intellectual grounds. Evil can be studied like any other "object" in the world—totemism or sorcery—neutrally and dispassionately, for the information it can give about the concept itself rather than for our political or moral response to it. Both D'Andrade and Fassin argue that an objectivist approach to "evil," maintaining evil as a culturally constructed and neutral category will ultimately provide a better understanding of how the world works. A more Foucauldian/Nietzschean sensibility begins with a critique of the dangerous dualism between good/evil and the necessity to get "beyond good and evil" to recognize evil in the "undeserved suffering imposed by practices protecting the reassurance (the goodness, purity, autonomy, normality) of hegemonic identities. [Thus] to reach beyond the politics of good and evil is not to liquidate ethics but to become ashamed of the transcendentalization of conventional morality. It is to subject morality to strip searches" (Connolly 1993, 366).

If morality should be subject to periodic strip searches (to see what is hidden behind moralities) then rogue states also need to be subject to anthropological strip searches. Here Agamben's (1998) philosophical-historical-medical-legal reflections on the *homo sacer,* the accursed ex-human, the socially dead, dehumanized, stripped down to a beastly form of corporality, *zoe*—a zoological specimen, the one to whom anything can and must be done, who can be killed with impunity—is a common referent point, often deployed wildly out of context. Agamben identified the reemergence of the obscure Roman figure, *homo sacer,* to the late modern concentration camp, the transit camp, the detention camp, the refugee camp, the pathology lab, the police morgue, and the transplant ward. Agamben was perhaps illustrating his opposing ethical sensibility toward the disgraced, the indecent, the indigestible, and the illegible ex-humans. I am not afraid to call the category of *homo sacer* an evil institution. It assumes no duality. It does not imply what a good opposing figure might be. Franco Basaglia, the radical Italian psychiatrist would have more simply defined *homo sacer* as a violent image produced by violent institutions (Scheper-Hughes and Lovell 1986). Primo Levi would have used the Musselmann rather than the Homo Sacer to describe the stripping away of all human status from the body of the enemy, including the dead body. Finally, in response to D'Andrade, Foucault, and Fassin, I perceive epistemological certainty and extreme cultural relativism as potentially evil, including any exclusion of evil as a lived, phenomenological subject-object relation in the real world (Ricoeur 1967; Staub 1989).

PARADOXICAL AND MIXED METHODS

In its odd juxtapositions of ethnography, fact-finding, documentation/surveillance, human rights advocacy, and collaborations with police and prosecutors, the Organs Watch project blends genres and transgresses sacred distinctions between anthropology, political journalism, social science, moral philosophy, and human rights. In the following ethnographic engagements with the bare life and necropolitics in prisons, camps, forensic institutes, and police morgues, nothing can be taken for granted, and a hermeneutics of suspicion replaces methodological anthropological trust and suspension of disbelief. If these transgressive uses of anthropology make some of my colleagues uncomfortable, know that neither am I comfortable with the subject I have taken on. The view from the "death camp" as Agamben (1997) uses the term and the view from the mortuary slab involve following the bodies and counting them wherever that is possible. Problems remain with respect to incomplete data, to evidence based on rumors and innuendo as well as on fieldwork, hundreds of transcribed interviews, forensic reports, legal proceedings, and collaborative bioarcheological research.

My ethnographic examples include a psychiatric camp in Argentina during and after the Dirty War); a militarized National Forensic Lab in Tel Aviv, Israel, during and after the two intifadas; a transit-detention camp (in Kosovo); and the human rights abuses concern missing or disappeared bodies, illegal dissections and harvesting and stockpiling organs, tissues and other body parts from the bodies of enemies, terrorists, and combatants. In each case, fact and fiction, the social imaginary, and the hallucinatory collide in media and in forensic, medical, and scientific reportage. Motives attributed to each case illuminate matters of social hygiene, including the profoundly mentally disabled and abandoned within a public asylum in Torres, Argentina; political-ethnic conflict and revenge cannibalistic violence against Serbs in Kosovo; the desecration of dead bodies of Palestinian enemies in the Israeli case; the harvesting of tissues and solid organs from black and colored bodies in the state police mortuary in Cape Town during the antiapartheid struggles. These motives were often as contradictory as they were complex.

The ordinary, banal violence practiced against dead bodies, illicit and covert harvesting, become war crimes when they are deployed as effective weapons to terrorize, humiliate, demoralize, and psychologically defeat the enemy. The allegations against the Abu Jabir Forensic Institute in Tel Aviv involved routine biopiracy and organ-tissue prospecting without consent as well as strategic abuses against targeted ethnic groups, including Palestinian "terrorists."

The case of allegations of murder-for-organs of Serbs by former Kosovo Liberation Army (KLA) militants in detention centers in Kosovo and Albania at the end of the Kosovo War in 1999 have never been proven, but hundreds of Serbs are still missing.

Theft of Life—The Real, the Unreal and the Uncanny

The Organs Watch project began in 1997, when I began to investigate rumors and strange allegations bearing on what appeared to be a collective human nightmare—the fear of being kidnapped, executed, and dismantled, with ones' organs or those of one's children stolen and distributed to strangers. These rumors surfaced in the early 1980s in Brazil, Argentina, Central America, Russia, South Africa, and other countries that were under military dictatorships or in transition from them (Interlandi 2009). I interpreted these body thefts as symbolic expressions of the cumulative experiences of poverty, chronic want, labor exploitation, political oppression, and deadly debts. A resident of the Alto do Cruzeiro in Brazil put it quite bluntly in 1987: "They, the big shots, the bosses, the rich, os grandes, are eating us alive, siphoning away our strength, our sex, our babies, and our organs." In South Africa, in the years during and immediately following the end of apartheid, I heard similar stories of body and organ theft in the townships and new squatter camps surrounding Cape Town. A stone's throw from the famous Groote-Schuur teaching hospital of the University of Cape Town where the late Christiaan Barnard (Barnard and Pepper 2006) pioneered the first human heart transplant, Black South Africans in nearby townships expressed fearful, suspicious, and negative attitudes toward organ transplantation. Among older residents and recent migrants from the homelands, the idea of medicalized tampering with the dead body and organ harvesting bore an uncanny resemblance to witchcraft and to alleged ritual murders for human body parts for sale to deviant practitioners of traditional medicine, sangomas and inyangas, some of whom used body parts in covert rituals of magical increase, to promote the wealth, strength, business interests, political power, property, health, and sexual potency of their clients.

An elderly Xhosa-speaking woman and recent rural migrant from Transkei living in a squatter camp along a stretch of the N-1 highway leading from the old Malan airport to Main Road and to the University of Cape Town's prestigious medical school, replied in disbelief when first confronted by me with the bare facts of transplant surgery: "If what you are saying is true that the white surgeons can take the beating heart from one person who is dead, but not truly dead, and put it inside another person to give him strength and life, then these doctors are witches like our own." Nomfundo was referring to evil uses of *muthi* or magical medicine and to local practitioners accused of killing people for human body parts.

Younger and sophisticated residents of urban townships in Cape Town and Johannesburg who were more knowledgeable about transplant medicine than older or rural people are critical for another reason. "Why is it," I was asked, "that in our township we have never met or heard of a person who received a new heart, or new eyes, or a liver while we know of families whose dead have been tampered with in the police mortuaries?" Township residents are quick to note the inequality of exchanges in which organs and tissues, taken from young, productive, black bodies—the victims of violence caused in large part by substandard housing, poor street lighting, bad sanitation, and hazardous public transportation, and the political violence of the antiapartheid struggle that continues to this day in a new form—are transplanted into the bodies of older, affluent, mostly white bodies. In their view, organ transplantation, even in the new South Africa, reproduced the body of (medical) apartheid.

During my field research in 1998, a state pathologist at the University of Cape Town told me that that he had been approached on more than one occasion by a local *sangoma* looking for spare body parts from the police mortuary and medical legal institute at Salt River. Of course, he said, he had refused the request, but I could not refrain from noting that the same pathologist, a complicated and emotionally intense professor of forensic medicine, was then currently accused of violations of bodies of township residents brought for autopsy to the police morgue during the antiapartheid struggle years. These were old accusations, but they ended up in court and at the South African Truth and Reconciliation Commission hearings in Cape Town.

The senior pathologist and his associates affiliated with a prestigious medical legal institute in South Africa participated in quasi-legal but mostly covert arrangements to transfer surplus tissues (corneas, tendons, heart valves, and other usable and transportable human parts) to medical centers in Europe and the United States. The allowable processing fees rather easily evolved into illicit sales to international biotechnical firms, organs and tissue banks, and academic research institutes. In the course of my investigations in 1993–1994, 1996, and again in 1998 and 1999, I learned that corneas, heart valves, and other human tissues were harvested by state pathologists and other mortuary staff and distributed to surgical and medical units usually without asking the consent of family members. The "donor" bodies, mostly poor, blacks and coloreds, victims of violence and trauma, were sent to police mortuaries for autopsies that sometimes ended up in dissections and organ and tissue removal.

I identified another site of corruption in organ and tissue harvesting at an academic organs and tissues bank in Pretoria, South Africa. The medical director was providing hundreds of Achilles tendons to a business man in Tampa, Florida. The tissue bank director received a paltry fee, a few hundred dollars per tendon, which were processed and resold in the United States for $1,200 each, a tidy sum for the Florida-based entrepreneur. The case was never prosecuted although the customs official served as a whistle-blower. In their defense, the pathologists referred to a loophole in the 1983 Organ and Tissue Act that allowed appropriate officials to harvest needed organs and tissues without consent when "reasonable attempts" to locate the potential donor's next of kin had failed. Since eyes and heart valves needed to be removed within hours of death and given the difficulty of locating families living in townships and squatter settlements without adequate transportation and communication systems, some pathologists use their authority to harvest valuable tissues and organs without giving much if any thought to the feelings of the next of kin.

The pathologists justified their actions as motivated by medicine and science. The organs and tissues could be used to enhance the lives of patients in need of bone and tissue transfers, while other body parts were invaluable for the development of scientific research. In return, the organ providers gained the gratitude, professional friendship, and the respect of the prestigious transplant teams who then were in their debt. Corneas and heart valves were sold to the hospitals and clinics—domestically and in the case of heart valves internationally—that request them. Unreported gratuities and honoraria were paid on the side to cooperating mortuary staff. Small gratuities were paid, for example, by a local independent eye bank to transplant coordinators for the favor of carrying donor eyes designated for air transport to the local airport. However, in one case, the mother of a young man, Andrew Sistshetshe, from Guguletu Township, whose eyes were removed at the Salt River Mortuary in 1992, brought the case to the attention of the courts and later to the South African Truth and Reconciliation Commission. The Sistshetshe case resulted in an active debate among pathologists, forensic specialists, lawyers, bioethicists, and theologians about tissue harvesting from the dead (Scheper-Hughes 2006). The Truth and Reconciliation Commission treated the case as a kind of class-action suit about medical human rights abuses in organs and tissues harvesting from the black victims of political struggle and violence.

Organs Theft Stories Combine Aspects of the Real, the Unreal, and the Uncanny

There are many social and political realities that render ordinary people vulnerable, gullible, and terrified. In times of political chaos or natural disasters, people do disappear and fears and allegations of kidnapping and murder for organs proliferate. They surface from the *political social imaginary*—where state power biopower and necropolitics occupy a zone between the real and the imagined. They express the "worst fears" of vulnerable populations in the face of real acts of bioterrorism, as in Argentina during the Dirty War and in Kosovo at the end of the war there. Bodies have gone missing. Where are they? Why have their graves not been found? Could the missing and unaccounted for dead have fallen into the hands of medical executioners looking for their organs? I have argued that the organs theft rumors were at the very least metaphorically true, operating by means of symbolic substitutions. They witnessed the ontological insecurity of classes of people to whom almost anything could be done, reflecting everyday threats to bodily security, urban violence, police terror, summary executions, and body mutilation, all of which were daily occurrences.

Mozambique 2003

Obviously not all allegations of body and organ theft are true, and they are quite dangerous. In 2003 in Nampula, Mozambique, the politically fragile nation was rocked by allegations by Catholic and Anglican missionary nuns of child kidnapping, murder, and organs trafficking. The allegations were picked up by the international media, including the Vatican press. International human rights and humanitarian organizations applied pressure on the president of Mozambique and a Catholic archbishop that resulted in an investigation by a state prosecutor who exhumed several graves without the capacity to conduct forensic examinations. Two white "settlers," a Danish woman and her husband from Zimbabwe, who had purchased an estate next door to the convent were accused by the nuns of bringing street children into their home, physically and sexually abusing them, killing them for their organs, and burying their remains in clandestine graves (Campion-Vincent and Scheper-Hughes 2001). The primary source of these allegations was Sister Elilda, a Brazilian nun, who had worked with street children in Rio de Janeiro and Sao Paulo who had been killed by extermination groups there in the 1990s amid allegations and urban legends of murder for organs. Sister Elilda brought her prior knowledge and experience of death squads targeting street kids, which is well documented, and her palpable trauma resulting from these experiences to Nampula.

Sister Elilda was not alone in her suspicions. The other nuns in her convent were alarmed by the numbers of missing children and the strange goings on at the big estate house, the *casa grande* next door. There were "wild" parties involving local youth, some of whom later disappeared. The nuns and the parents of missing children lobbied the Catholic Church and the president to open an official investigation but without success. When during this same period an American Protestant missionary nun, fifty-three-year-old Doraci Edinger, was found murdered outside her home in Nampula, Attorney General Joaquim Madeira opened a federal investigation that included ill-designed exhumations. Local tribal leaders brought the nuns with them to help identify the remains found in the disturbed graves. The bodies were decomposed, but in a few cases, the state prosecutor was able to state that bodies were missing organs, including hearts, livers, and genital organs.

The foreign couple were arrested, their home ransacked, and the oversized freezers were found to be empty except for some frozen chickens. The organs thought to be in the freezers and that were allegedly being sent by private plane to South Africa for black market transplants, were not found. The primary witness, Sister Elilda, accepted my invitation to the University of California at the expense of Organs Watch. I spent a week going over her data, which included two suitcases of filed complaints and photos of missing children, affidavits by local leaders, and transcriptions of street children who testified to physical abuse suffered at the home of the of the white people. Elilda presented her slides at a conference on violence I had co-organized. I was distressed to learn at that public presentation that Sister Elilda's primary references to organs trafficking were my published articles (Scheper-Hughes 2000, 2003a, 2003b, 2004). She noted that international organs brokers had infiltrated large South African hospitals in Cape Town, Johannesburg, and Durban in the early 2000s. Since children were, in fact, disappearing, since some exhumed bodies were missing organs, since the white strangers befriended young children and invited them into their home, because the couple had installed industrial-sized freezers, and since they traveled frequently back and forth to South Africa in a private plane, Sister Elilda concluded that they were trafficking the missing children's organs that were kept in the freezer and taken to transplant units in South Africa. She concluded her presentation to an audience that included several seasoned human rights activists including a forensic specialist in exhumations, that the missing street children of Nampula were a clandestine source of the international transplant tourism that I had identified in South Africa. The well-meaning nun was devastated when I told her that her intuitions were understandable but were not supported by the evidence. I explained that the South African Netcare scheme relied on the trafficking of living kidney sellers from Romania, Israel, and Northeast Brazil. She was correct that under age minors were among the kidney sellers, but these were teenagers who had signed up through local brokers and in one instance, had arrived in Durban with her family—mother, father, and daughter sold their kidneys to transplant tourists from Israel.

Bad things were going on in Mozambique, but the presence of *mutilated* bodies—like Bakhtin's *grotesque* bodies—carry many different histories and many different truths. In this case, the evidence pointed to corrupt *curandeiros* and *feticeiros* rather than corrupt surgeons. The investigation was closed, much to the dismay of my key informant, Sister Maria Elilda, who considered my conclusion to be a personal betrayal to her and a betrayal of my own human rights watch project. How could I suggest that among the people she knew as devout Catholics were Catholic-animists who sometimes relied on the magical power of human body part *fetishes* rather than on rosary beads or holy relics? Yes, I agreed that crimes had been committed to be sure, but not in the interests of transplant medicine.

Other allegations of organs trafficking from the living and from the dead, from strangers and from enemies, were proven to be factual. As my investigations shifted toward a kind of forensic or detective ethnography, I followed rumors of illicit organs trafficking networks from Africa to the Middle East to Southeast Asia to South America, Europe, and the United States. In Israel, I learned from transplant patients and brokers about transplant tours to Turkey with kidney sellers trafficked from rural Moldova, Romania, and the Ukraine, some were gypsies, others were displaced persons. I followed the clues to several small villages in Moldova in 2001 and in 2009. There, I met with dozens of kidney sellers who had been recruited by brokers—kidney hunters—who offered the men work abroad and an escape from their hungry hardscrabble villages. Some knew that the work was selling a kidney; others were deceived and defrauded of their money, their health, and an organ. Many of the men ended up in the private transplant clinic owned and operated by Dr. Yusef Sönmez (Jimenez and Scheper-Hughes 2002), now a fugitive from the current European Union prosecution of illicit transplants in the Medicus clinic in Kosovo, and a suspect in the allegations of war crime organs harvesting in Kosovo in 1999 (Fatmir 2012). The stories told by the trafficked Moldovan kidney sellers were chilling. After waking up from the anesthesia and in great pain following their kidney removal, they were put on busses to return to Moldova without painkillers and in some cases with as little as $1,000 tucked in their pocket or even under their surgical bandages. They referred to Sönmez's clinic as a slaughter-house and to the surgeon as a butcher who would as soon cut off their balls, if there were a market for them, as one of their kidneys.

Most of these human trafficking for organs crimes fit into the paradigm of what Franco Basaglia called peacetime crimes, *crimini di pace,* the violence by state bureaucrats, social workers, teachers, public health officials, hospital ad-ministrators, doctors, surgeons, and psychiatrists against the sick-poor, the im-migrant, the refugee, the displaced, the dispossessed, and the mentally or cog-nitively challenged. But peacetime crimes can also be deployed as war crimes and, in the worst instance, into crimes against humanity. Dr. Yusef Sönmez may have been guilty of both.

The chaos of war—civil wars, dirty wars, and genocides—provides an ideal cover for the inhumane treatment of the bodies of the enemy, the terrorist, and those seen as mentally or morally deficient, as "better off dead" (Harrison 2013). In each of these cases—and there are many others in the Organs Watch archives—the war crimes and the crimes against humanity continued under the radar, unacknowledged by Human Rights Watch and other humanitarian organizations. They were protected by the belief that such crimes are techni-cally impossible, that organs harvesting and transplant could not be conducted under unstable and technologically primitive conditions.

CASE 1—THE GHOSTS OF MONTES DE OCA—ARGENTINA

For decades allegations of blood, cornea, organ, and baby theft, as well as medi-cal experimentation at Argentina's National Colony for the Mentally Deficient during the 1980s–1990s were dismissed as leftist propaganda by Argentine and U.S. officials, by transplant professionals, and by scholars and folklorists. In his 1994 government report to the United Nations, "The Child Organ Trafficking Rumor: a Modern Urban Legend," Todd Leventhal, a U.S. State Department disinformation specialist, described the organs trafficking allegations at Mon-tes de Oca as an intentional disinformation campaign led by Latin American Marxists to stir up anticapitalist sentiments (Leventhal 1994). The allegations of tissue and organ theft were a propagandist attack on the Argentine govern-ment, the Ministry of Health, and its U.S. allies.

Leventhal's conclusions were based on his reading of media reports, he told me. He admitted that he conducted no fact-seeking investigations for the U.S. State Department. His report, insofar as it bore on the case of Colonia Montes de Oca, reflected U.S. policies toward Argentina when during the Dirty War

(1976–1983) the Ford and Reagan administrations sought military aid for junta, supported the regime diplomatically, and covered up its atrocities. Secretary of State Kissinger denied human rights abuses in Argentina.[1]

In January 2000, Dr. Hernan Reyes, medical specialist on Detention-Related Activities for the International Committee of the Red Cross, and I paid an unannounced visit to the Colonia. We were accompanied by a private Argentine detective who provided an alibi for our entry into what was a locked facility. What we discovered was far worse than the allegations of illegal cornea, blood, and organ harvesting. We had stumbled on what could only be described as a psychiatric death camp of emaciated inmates, naked and shivering following cold showers used to calm the inmates. The untrained asylum-dependent staff knew no better, as they were born into four generations of local families who were raised in the Colonia. They struck as equally the captives of a violent institution.

Two subsequent field investigations (2008, 2011) confirmed that medical human rights abuses at Montes de Oca—malignant neglect; premature and inexplicable deaths; missing inmates; blood, organs, and tissue thefts—against the mentally deficient intensified during the Argentine Dirty War, an insane period when the state turned itself against its citizens. Many of them were ordinary people suspect of lacking sufficient loyalty to the fascist regime. Although it has never been acknowledged, there is evidence that during the Argentine Dirty War (1976–1983), the administration of Colonia Montes de Oca was applying a regime of malevolent and malignant neglect of the mentally deficient population concentrated at the national mental colony, leading to more than 1,200 premature and unexplained deaths (Scheper-Hughes 2015).

General Jorge Videla, the political engineer of the Proceso, the *Guerra Sucia*, appointed Dr. Florencio Sanchez, an Opus Dei Catholic, a man of many stripes—a therapist who also claimed to be a surgeon, a forensic pathologist, and a physical anthropologist—as director of the Colonia. Under his regime, deaths and disappearances of inmates rose to extraordinary proportions. In the name of progressive psychiatry, inmates were allowed to refuse food, clothing, and medications. General Videla had interned his own "profoundly deficient" but healthy, first-born son, Alejandro, at the mental colony. The boy, otherwise robust, died suddenly at the age of nineteen, one of many unexplained deaths. In 1992, nearly a decade after the end of the Dirty War, Dr. Sanchez was arrested at the Colonia and charged with embezzlement of state funds, cocaine trafficking at the Colonia, and the inhumane treatment of the inmates he called his darling *chiquitos*. Sanchez died suddenly in his jail cell in Mercedes before he could give testimony in court.

I argue that a petite war, a war within the war—against the "germ" of mental deficiency was being waged by Sanchez at the Colonia Montes de Oca. The method was simple, "letting [patients] die" in the name of psychiatric reform. The open door policy led not to freedom but to a swamp, to the cistern, to the woods outside the perimeters of the Colonia. During this period, Montes de Oca served Argentina as the country's primary reservoir of fresh corneas, heart valves, and other biomaterials retrieved from the dead and of blood supplies from the living delivered to the military (according to staff at the Colonia) and illegally to private blood banks. A driver for the Colonia reported taking inmates to local hospitals for operations, from lobotomies to nephrectomies (kidney removal). Omar, an inmate photographed by Argentine human rights lawyer Liliana Magrini, bore the scar of a nephrectomy, but when questioned about it the staff said that the patient had injured himself. Interviews with the judge in Mercedes and with an order of Catholic nuns who ministered to the needs of women at the Colonia, revealed that there were many unreported pregnancies and births, some delivered at the Colonia. Many births were not reported and were adopted through informal networks. There were suspicions of traffic in babies born to inmates following a pattern of sexual abuses by staff and visitors.

While the tragic history of state terror, kidnappings/disappearances, torture, murder, and strange scatterings of human remains has been painstakingly documented (Robben 2005), the specifically medical and psychiatric abuses let loose during that period have never been acknowledged. Because the allegations were so readily dismissed by the experts as implausible, the abuses continued long after the return to democracy, until 2006 according to an informal, but thorough, unannounced investigation by the former judge of Mercedes who wrote a report documenting the corruption, medical abuse, and drug trafficking at the Colonia. Media coverage following the report exposed a detention camp for a category of subhumans abandoned by their families and unwanted by the modern state.

After sending an eighty-page report on the Ghosts of Montes de Oca to several officials in the Ministry of Health and to the new interim Director of the Colonia Dr. Jorge Roseto, I was invited to return in 2008 to witness the current reform. Today the nursing staff have begun to recognize that the muteness of the "deaf and dumb" inmates, the inability of the so-called crawlers to walk, the incontinence of the inmates, their so-called refusal of clothing and of so-called food—an indecipherable mush—that had been served out of plastic buckets were artifacts of what Franco Basaglia labeled the "violent institution." Freed from their cells, given proper food and clothing, the mute speak, the crawlers walk, and the "nudists" argue endlessly about their shoes, their sweaters, their shawls, and their cravats. Contraceptives are given to the women, and staff are told that sleeping with inmates is abusive not recreational.

But the whereabouts of several hundred unaccounted for inmates and the premature deaths of hundreds of others during and after the military state are still unknown, as are the homes of confiscated infants. Medical staff are still prickly about my investigations. One older medical attendant at the Colonia complained: "When we kept them in cages we were criticized, when we gave them the freedom to roam, and they chose to flee, we were criticized; when we allowed them to be without clothes and to have sex, we were criticized; when we placed their infants in good families we were criticized. Tell me something, Nancy, would you let your own son or daughter work in an impossible place like this?"

In 2011, I interviewed the practical nurse, Dr. Zanutti, who admitted that he worked closely with Dr. Sanchez in a basement laboratory where bloods were routinely drawn for genetic and other medical and scientific research studies, for delivery to private blood banks, and sometimes recycled within the Colonia, which, by that time, had a great many anemic inmates. His main job, however, was the extraction of eyeballs that were carefully preserved and delivered to the Laglezie Eye Bank in Argentina as well as to private organ banks. Like many of the older staff, Zanutti was somewhat abashed, neither apologetic, nor boastful. While refusing to answer my questions about kidney trafficking at the Colonia, he was willing to state that there was an active promotion of the right to sex for the mentally deficient, and that the pretty ones were often pregnant. Following the several weeks that painters were brought to the Colonia prior to my official visit in 2008, several women were found to be pregnant by the contract workers.

CASE 2—THE BODY OF THE TERRORIST—BIOPIRACY AT THE ISRAELI FORENSIC INSTITUTE AT ABU KABIR, TEL AVIV

There was trophy collecting of skinned tattoos taken from the bodies of Russian new immigrants and from prisoners, at Abu Kabir. Tattoos were an oddity in Israel where they are still associated with the Shoah. But there was also a taint of suspicion about the new immigrants from the former Soviet bloc states, who were privately suspect of being economic rather than cultural refugees, claiming a tenuous at best Jewish identity. Eye globes and sheets of skin were taken from the backs of Palestinian combatants, whose bodies would be returned to their family members in tightly bound sheets and with eyes glued shut to avoid detection (Dr. Hiss, director of the institute, explained). But some family members (as in the case of South Africa) carefully uncovered and inspected their "war" dead and were horrified at seeing the second death to which their loved ones had been subjected.

The moral collapse at Israel's National Forensic Institute at Abu Kabir led by the director and state-appointed senior pathologist, Jehuda Hiss, and his staff was complete, lacking any vestige of human decency in their official stewardship and protection of the bodies of the dead. The abuses were facilitated by the military conflict during and between the two intifadas, which produced abundant supplies of dead bodies from Palestinian militants, soldiers of the Israel Defense Forces, and victims of suicide bombings and military-civil emergencies.

There was a hierarchy of bodies and a confusion of motives that ranged from the banal to crimes against humanity. The abuses could be arranged along a continuum from the stockpiling of hearts, glands, long bones, and brains (even heads) for profit; for "science"; for recreation; and for power, patronage, and reputation. The stockpiling of tattoos skinned from the dead bodies of new immigrants was an act of hostility toward new immigrant refugees from former Soviet states, although linking it to a nascent form of race hatred might be going too far. A knowledgeable source from within the forensic institute pointed out that the man responsible for the tattoo collecting was himself a Russian and a Jew. The desecration of the dead bodies of Palestinian combatants is toward the far end of the medical human rights abuse continuum—a crime against humanity.

For more than two decades, the Israeli government and Ministry of Health denied "blood libels" accusing the government's state pathologists of harvesting organs and tissues from the bodies of "enemy" combatants, terrorists, and teenage stone-throwers from the occupied territories. In August 2009, another organ-trafficking story broke, one that linked Rosenbaum's U.S.-Israel organ-brokering and money-laundering schemes with much older allegations of organ and tissue stealing from the bodies of Palestinian "terrorists" and stone-throwers following autopsy at Israel's National Forensic Institute in Abu Kabir, a neighborhood of Tel Aviv.

These allegations, dating back to the early 1990s, were reopened by a Swedish journalist Donald Boström in a banner headline story—"Our Sons Plundered for Their Organs"—in a left-leaning Swedish tabloid, *Aftonbladet*, on August 17, 2009. The story was a mix of organ theft accusations, seemingly far-fetched connections to the arrest in Brooklyn of an orthodox rabbi and transplant broker, and a dash of political rhetoric. The story, based on Boström's earlier research in the Occupied Territories during the first intifada, and published in his 2001 book, *Inshallah,* repeats the story of family members whose killed sons and husbands were harvested at the Abu Kabir Forensic Institute where they were brought for autopsy only. Boström argues that Palestinian bodies were being harvested as the "spoils of war." The *Aftonbladet* story, instantly translated into Hebrew and English, created a firestorm of international protest that included a libel suit by antidefamation lawyers in New York City and a boycott of Swedish industries. Boström was labeled an anti-Semite and the story he dredged up from the sewer was labeled a despicable "blood libel" against Israel and the world's Jews.

I read these news reports with mounting horror.[2] The only question that was not being raised in the avalanche of articles, editorials, and news columns published in Israel, Europe, and the United States was: "Is the story true?" I knew the answer. I was in possession of the proverbial smoking gun—an audio-recorded interview with the director of Abu Kabir, the National Forensic Institute, Dr. Jehuda Hiss. The interview was conducted at the institute in July 2000, when I was in Israel investigating the growth of organized transplant tours and organs trafficking by underworld brokers in Israel. A human rights lawyer in Bethlehem asked me to investigate complaints by Palestinian families about illegal harvesting of eyes, solid organs, and skin at the National Forensic Institute. I was given the photo and files of a young man whose autopsy appeared to end in dissection.

In his interview with me Dr. Hiss was open, energized, and brazen in defending his method of "informal" procurement of organs and tissues from the bodies of the dead brought to the institute for autopsy. He did so, he said, as a patriot and to serve the needs of his country. When he first arrived at the institute in 1987 as chief pathologist, there was no organ or tissue harvesting. An absurdity, he called it. He instituted his own version of "presumed consent" for organs and tissue harvesting. That is, he presumed to know what was best for his country without the knowledge, backing, or consent of the victims, the Israeli population, or the law. It was justified behavior, he said, for a war-torn and traumatized country such as Israel. From his medical perspective as a state pathologist, little harm was done to dead bodies by the careful removal of skin, tissue, bone, and organs that would never be missed by the deceased and which could be hidden from the families of the dead. "We were very careful in peeling the skin," he said, "it wasn't like skinning a rabbit—We took only from the back and the back of the legs."

Special care was taken with the harvesting of Palestinians and Arab-Israelis, Christian and Muslim. Hiss explained to me without any embarrassment that his team was very careful to sew the empty eye sockets shut so the families could not see that the eye globes has been removed. When hospital pathologists were brought into Abu Kabir to assist with the organ harvesting and refused to comply, plastic surgeons were recruited by Hiss, and at least one was hired.

Hiss was not so much "above the law," as representing a higher law, *his law,* which he felt was supremely cool, rational, and scientifically technically correct. The country was at war, blood was being spilled every day, soldiers were being burned, and yet Israelis refused to provide tissues and organs needed. So, he took matters into his own hands. While I did discuss the interview with a lawyer for the Ministry of Health, I never published it. Fearing the unintended political consequences of making it public, the tape sat, more or less untouched, in my archives for ten years. But after the Boström firestorm in 2009 and at the request of some Israeli colleagues who knew about the interview, I released the tape to Israeli TV journalists who used it as part of their own investigative report that aired in December 2009.

After segments of my interview with Professor Hiss were aired on the Israeli national nightly news on Channel 2 TV, government officials for the army and the Ministry of Health admitted that organs and tissues had been harvested (without permission) from dead bodies throughout the 1990s, but that the practice ended in 2000 (the date of my interview). Dr. Hiss, however, publicly denied everything on tape—including his words to me. Today, he says that he denies it all—the stockpiling of body parts, the perjury in autopsy reports concerning enemy combatants and Palestinian civilians, and organ harvesting. He denies everything. He says that everything was all done according to the law, and that all the families consented to harvest for transplantation. No organs were taken for research, and none were ever sold, none at all. However, the Segalison committee determined that Hiss had lied to the police investigators and that he knew that the harvesting of organs and tissues without consent was illegal.[3]

Hiss's denials were passionately rebutted at an Organs Watch Conference in Combating the Traffic in Organs in May 2011 by a former associate of Dr. Hiss at Abu Kabir Forensic Institute, Dr. Chen Kugel, a retired military officer and a distinguished pathologist. Kugel reported that the situation was far worse than what Hiss had told me. Kugel worked as one of Professor Hiss's younger assistants who as soon as he arrived at the institute in 1999, pointed out to his superior that his behavior was deviant. Kugel dared to tell his boss said that it was wrong to harvest organs and tissues without permission, and that "giving false evidence in court about autopsies conducted there" was also "not okay."

Kugel and three other doctors from the institute wrote a letter of complaint to the Ministry of Health, outlining the illegalities. The Ministry of Health reacted with alacrity: they fired the three residents and punished Kugel, who, as a military officer working for the Israel Defense Forces, could not be fired. Then the four told the entire story to the media. In other words, the story of criminal behavior at the Abu Kabir institute was an old story, long known to the population, and the false alarm about the Boström report was disingenuous. Organ theft at the institute was a dirty, public secret, and one to be kept inside the borders of Israel.

According to Kugel, "The organs procured there were sold to anyone; anyone that wanted organs just had to pay for them." While skin, heart valves, bones, and corneas were removed and sent to hospitals to be used for transplants and other medical procedures, solid organs—hearts, brains, livers—"were sold for research, for medical presentations, for drills (training) for medical students and surgeons." There was a price for these organs, low—just $300 for a femur, for example—and should a client want all the organs from a body, or a full range of solid organs taken from several different bodies, that, too, could be arranged, Kugel said, for about $2,500.

From whom were the organs taken? They were taken from everyone, from Jews and Muslims, from soldiers and from stone-throwers, from terrorists and from the victims of terrorists, from tourists and from new immigrants. There were only two considerations—the physical condition of the body and its organs, and the ability to conceal what they were doing. Some victims were not even subject to autopsy, they were simply harvested. Organs removed with the sole purpose of distributing them for use in medical research, hearts, for example, that were in great demand, had to be complete. Dissection of the heart for the purpose of autopsy would render it useless for medical research. According to Kugel, any hearts that were retained (and stockpiled for sale and distribution) were removed illegally in each case. The forensic team hid the damage by using pipes and glass eyes, broom sticks, toilet paper, and plastic skull caps to cover the place where the solid organs or the brain was removed. The institute, Kugel said, was counting on one thing: that most Israelis do not view the body after death except once, to verify that the body is the correct one. The body is wrapped in a winding sheet, or might be wrapped in plastic sheets for the burial company to come for it. In that case, the staff would warn the burial employees, who were not well educated, not to open the sheet because the body was contaminated with an infectious disease. It was more difficult to take organs from soldiers because their bodies were supervised by the military, which was more difficult to fool. "But even so organs were taken from soldiers,"

Kugel said. It was easier to take tissues and organs from the new immigrants, and, needless to say, easiest of all to take from the Palestinians. They would be going back across the border, and, "if there were any complaints coming from their families, they were the enemy and so, of course, they were lying and who would believe them?"

The motives had nothing at all to do with science. According to Kugel, the illicit harvesting was about power and immunity. In the end, the hoarding and trading in body specimens, the stockpiling of organs, long bones, sheets of skin, and solid organs turned the National Forensic Institute into a factory of bodies. It was motivated, Kugel argues, by a traditional authoritarian paternalism of the kind that says, "We know what's good for you, we can and we will decide what happens to you, the dead person doesn't know anything. We alone will decide." Chen Kugel asserted that the organ theft did not end in 1999, the time of my interview with the director of the institute. Rather, the practice was routinized and continued through 2011 when the police finally raided the institute.

Among the dozen civil law suits that have been filed against Dr. Hiss, some concern the desecrated bodies of Israeli soldiers. These suits are given the greatest attention because in Israel the body of the soldier is at the top of a hierarchy of bodies in the nation as in the forensic institute. There are, as yet, no suits from the Occupied Territories against the institute. Perhaps the families have other concerns about the dead and their offspring that are more pressing. Among the victims are both Israeli and Palestinian soldiers, Israeli citizens who were killed in suicide bombings, and the body of an American activist from Oregon, Rachel Corrie, who was crushed to death on March 16, 2003, by an army Caterpillar bulldozer. She was killed while demonstrating in Gaza against the demolition of Palestinian homes when the tank plowed into her. Her body was taken to Abu Kabir and subjected to autopsy during which "body samples" and organs were taken and "misplaced" according to Dr. Hiss's testimony in court.

In 2012, government investigators and police descended on the Institute of Forensic Medicine at Abu Kabir and discovered 8,200 body parts stockpiled. And, finally, the government recognized that the illicit and free-for-all harvesting had become a norm and that it was criminal, unethical, and had to be acknowledged; that families had to be compensated; and the bones, tissues, organs, and other body parts had to identified and returned to the victims' families. Jehuda Hiss, who was once praised and rewarded as a national hero and paid the highest federal salary in the nation, was suddenly recognized as a criminal. Finally, Hiss was forced to retire, though he kept his full pension if not his reputation. He was forced to leave his position as director of Abu Kabir. Today Hiss's lawyers are actively defending him in dozens of individual and collective lawsuits by Israeli families of his victims. Most are the parents of soldiers killed on duty, who were subject to what Boström thought was only the plunder of the enemy. He has not, however, been prosecuted by the state for fraud, deceit, organs trafficking, violation of Israeli organ and tissue laws, or any other federal crimes. Hiss was allowed to go silently into the night with his pension, but who knows how well he is able to sleep at night.

As for the courageous Israeli pathologist, retired Lieutenant Colonel Chen Kugel, former assistant to Jehuda Hiss who was forced out of his position as a disloyal, internal whistle-blower and treated as a pariah for having the moral courage to confront the abuses head on, no matter the consequences for his own career, mental health, and well-being, he has to his own amazement been appointed the new director of the Abu Kabir Institute and he is in the process of repatriating thousands of body parts to the relatives of the victims of his former superior's handiwork (Scheper-Hughes and Boström 2013).

CASE 3—DID KOSOVO ETHNIC ALBANIAN MILITANTS REALLY MURDER SERBIAN CIVILIANS FOR THEIR ORGANS AT THE END OF THE KOSOVO WAR (1999–2000)?

In recent years, the newly independent nation of Kosovo has been at the center of two controversial investigations. The first began with a report by prosecutor Dick Marty delivered to the Council of Europe in December 2010 asserting that KLA militants kidnapped and murdered some four hundred Serbian civilians or former militants in secret detention centers, some in Albania, at the end of the Kosovo War in 1999. The bodies of these disappeared Serbian minorities and some gypsies have never been found. Marty's investigation followed allegations by Carla Del Ponte, former prosecutor of the U.N. International Tribunals, that some of the missing Serbs were preselected and killed by the former KLA militants for the purpose of harvesting their organs (mostly kidneys), which were allegedly flown to Turkey.

U.N. investigators, stationed in Kosovo, engaged in a frustrating attempt to track the disappearances of the missing Serbians who disappeared after the arrival of NATO (North Atlantic Treaty Organization) troops and UNMIK (U.N. Mission in Kosovo). Unlike the thousands of Albanians killed during the Bosnian War whose graves were located, the missing Serbs vanished without a trace. While there were casualties on all sides, the 2008 joint study by the Humanitarian Law Center (a nongovernmental organization from Serbia and Kosovo), the

International Commission on Missing Person, and the Missing Person Commission of Serbia made a name-by-name list of 13,472 war and postwar victims in Kosovo killed in the period from January 1998 to December 2000. The final toll of the war was 9,260 Albanians, 2,488 Serbs, and 1,254 victims that could not be identified by ethnic origin. The disappeared numbered in the thousands for Albanian ethnics and most of their bodies have been found. Of the roughly four hundred Serbian civilians who disappeared in the chaos, few of their bodies have been found, leading to allegations of Serbs having been kidnapped and trafficked by KLA militants across the border and into Albania where they were allegedly killed in detention camps.

There were many rumors that the missing Serbs had been captured and taken over the border to Albania where they were held in secret detention facilities run by operatives of the KLA, the ethnic Albanian rebel group whose leaders occupy key positions of authority in the newly independent country today. According to a few protected witnesses, mostly former KLA operatives, a small subset of the captive Serbs were subject to "special treatment," told while in transit that their fate would organs harvesting. The witnesses testified that doctors would be brought to these special detention centers to conduct medical tests on the captives, selecting the younger and healthier specimens whose deaths would begin or end with the removal of solid organs. The witnesses, including KLA drivers, heard that the organs would be shipped by air to Europe or to Turkey where they would be received by agents for the black market.

It was not clear whether the detention centers were used only to hold and transfer those selected for harvesting to a clinic closer to Albania's Tirana airport. Nor was it clear from the testimonies whether the organs were removed before or after the patients were killed. Sources (unnamed) told the Guardian newspaper that Yusuf Sönmez may have been involved in the receipt of some of the Serbian organs. The Marty report named a possible transit-detention center, a dilapidated farm house in Albania, dubbed the "Yellow House" that had been identified by Michael Montgomery, a Berkeley investigative journalist who was in Albania reporting on the aftermath of the Kosovo War. Montgomery later accompanied U.N. officials to investigate the two-story dilapidated farmhouse at the end of a rutted track in a remote area of central Albania. The U.N. team was accompanied by local police, forensic experts from Peru, Norway, and France and retired police detectives from Finland and the United States.

The inhabitants of the farm—a large, extended family—and other villagers some of them old women wrapped in colorful shawls and wearing thick rubber boots, milled around, gawking as the investigators donned mysterious protective gear. The team began searching the property, first the perimeter, including a barn and garbage dump, and then the small rooms at the ground level. They found blood stains on the floor of one of the rooms and discarded surgical equipment—needles, syringes, and containers of muscle relaxant drugs. The family members were separated and gave wildly divergent stories. One identified the blood stains as the traces of a hemorrhage during a birth when the house was used as a small clinic by a local nurse-midwife. Another spoke of operations on sick farm animals by a veterinarian.

A U.N. report was filed along with the material evidence and results of the investigation. An extremely redacted version of the report can be found, with some difficulty, on the Internet. When the UNMIK left the country, the transfer of power to the Kosovar authorities was messy, and the U.N. files in several cardboard boxes were accidentally destroyed in a warehouse. Meanwhile, the story of the Yellow House entered the folklore, while another investigation organized by the Council of Europe proceeds at a snail's pace.

However, complicating matters considerably, on December 4, 2008, Kosovo police and a EULEX (the European Union's Rule of Law Mission) prosecutor raided a private transplant clinic, "Medicus" in a suburb of Pristina, a few kilometers from Kosovo's international airport. According to the indictment, the Medicus clinic lured poor people from Istanbul, Moscow, Moldova, and Kazakhstan, falsely promising to pay them up to upward of $15,000 for their organs. Most received far less than what was promised, and some received no payment at all.

At least thirty operations involving illegal kidney transplants took place at the clinic in 2008. Seven Kosovan doctors and their surgical assistants, believed to be linked to an international network of transplant traffickers, were arrested and accused of conducting illegal transplants for foreign medical tourists— mostly Israelis, Europeans, and Canadians—with kidneys taken from trafficked Russians, Moldovans, Kazakhs, and Turks brought to Kosovo by known organ traffickers.

Following the raid, and an investigation, E.U. Prosecutor Jonathan Ratel filed the Medicus indictment in Pristina, in October 2010. Among the five Kosovo-Albanians charged with participating in the organs trafficking crime syndicate was Ilir Rrecaj, a former senior health ministry official. Yusef Sönmez, and his partner, Dr. Zaki Shapira and Moshe Harel, were indicted and listed as fugitives. Zaki Shapira was listed as a person of interest. The specific charges included trafficking in persons, illegal organs harvesting, unlawful exercise of medical activity, and abuse of power. The accused included the clinic's director,

Professor Lutfi Dervishi who was allegedly aided by Sönmez, who escaped and is wanted on organ trafficking charges in several countries, and Moshe Harel, an Israeli of Turkish origin, who operated as a key broker/fixer, finding both donors and recipients and handling and laundering the funds. Harel escaped the sting in Kosovo, went to Turkey and from there to Israel, where he was arrested but released without facing prosecution.

I was not surprised, having tracked the Turkish surgeon, Yusef Sönmez and his Israeli partner Zaki Shapira since 1997, that mapping their dealings spanned continents: from Turkey, to Russia, Moldova, the United States, the Ukraine, Azerbaijan, Kosovo, Cypress, South Africa, the Philippines, Colombia, Panama, and Honduras. Despite multiple arrests, neither man ever spent more than a night in jail. In 2008, Sönmez dared to attend a transplant conference in Kiev, the Ukraine, where he boasted of performing more than 2,400 transplants with trafficked kidney suppliers from the under classes and ethnic minorities of Eastern Europe, the Balkans, and the Middle East. The transplants were, he said, without the benefit of human leukocyte antigen tissue-matching.

The question I am raising here is whether the two incidents—the Medicus clinic (still in prosecution) and the earlier allegations of the KLA murder of Serbs for their organs in the immediate aftermath of the Kosovo War—were linked. If so, a key suspect would be Dr. Yusuf Erçin Sönmez who had lost credibility in the Turkish transplant profession since Turkish TV journalists caught him performing an illegal transplant with a trafficked donor.

When Sönmez and Shapira started talking business, they came up with a perfect solution. They would organize, with the help of savvy Israeli brokers, black-market transplant tours that would bring well-insured transplant customers from Israel to Istanbul, where they would be transplanted at various rented private clinics in hospitals in Istanbul and Adana. To expand their supply of fresh organs, both surgeons used kidney hunters to locate and convince the desperate and the dispossessed from Iraq, Moldova, Romania, Bulgaria, and the Ukraine to sell their kidneys in Turkey. What Turkish newspapers called an organs mafia, Shapira and Sönmez called an international transplant coordinating company.

I met Zaki Shapira during meetings of the Bellagio Task Force on Organs Trafficking in 1996–1997 at the Rockefeller Foundation's conference center in Bellagio. Shapira confided to me that he was a bit "involved" in commerce in organs and had been chastised by an ethics board, the Cotov Commission, for arranging paid kidney donors from Palestinian guest workers from the Occupied Territories. Shapira decided that outsourcing kidney transplants with reimbursements via Israeli medical insurance was the only solution.

In 2001, I made an unannounced visit to Dr. Sönmez's private hospital Ye-silbehar on the eastern side of Istanbul, where three Israeli patients waited in one section of the two-story, paint-chipped Victorian house and four Moldo-van/Romanian peasants in another room; both patients and sellers were fright-ened. A few days later, Sönmez was arrested for the second time, and released, and then in 2007, both Shapira and Sönmez were arrested in a shoot-out at the Yesilbehar hospital in what was a (according to Israeli press) a police sting and reported in the Turkish news as the rescue by angry relatives of a family mem-ber who was about to be defrauded of a kidney. Freed from jail, Sönmez was banned from practicing transplant surgery in Turkey and the stubborn pair continued, as they had been for years, looking for alternative sites, extending their reach and arranging new transplant tours to the United States, Russia, China, the Ukraine, Azerbaijan, and, in 2007, to Kosovo where Sönmez and Shapira assisted Turkish doctors at the Medicus clinic.

Despite his central role in the global human trafficking for organs trade, Sönmez remained elusive, mobile, and always a few steps ahead of the authori-ties and medical anthropologists on his trail. Sönmez is alternately loathed and loved. Even his ideological foes within Turkish transplant circles will admit that he was one of Turkey's most talented transplant surgeons. A graduate of Istanbul University Medical College, Sönmez observed an interesting phe-nomenon early in his medical career that suggested an extraordinary business proposition: the willingness of Turkish kidney patients to risk traveling as far as Bombay and Madras, India, for transplants with paid kidney sellers. The waiting lists in Turkey (as elsewhere in the Middle East) were long and the chronic shortage of deceased organs made illicit transplants with paid donors a very tempting proposition.

"We were dealing with more and more patients who had traveled abroad in postoperative care," Dr. Hamdi Kocer, a former colleague recalled. "Sönmez first hit on the idea to have Indian donors come to Turkey." But that scheme was bureaucratically complex and expensive even though the Indian kidney sellers were willing to sell cheaply. But by the mid-1990s, the mercurial surgeon was already becoming something of an embittered outsider. He had been fired from his job at the university hospital over a dispute with its director, and then was banned from practicing transplant surgery at a second state hospital called Haydarpasa because of allegations of Sönmez's aggressive harvesting of organs from very sick and traumatized persons who were harvested without the ben-efit of a brain death diagnosis. Dr. Vulture became Dr. Frankenstein in the Turkish and Moldovan media. Finally, shunned and shut out of the country's public health system, Sönmez decided to ignore the ethical standards of his profession and to recruit kidney sellers from among the poor in Istanbul and among immigrant guest workers easily recruited from Moldova, Romania, and the Ukraine.

Shapira provided him with a steady stream of patients, while Dr. Sönmez relied on a local network of so-called kidney hunters to supply him with the organs. In the beginning, there was a ready market of sellers in Turkey who asked for $10,000–$30,000 for a kidney. Israeli "transplant tourists" were charged between US$100,000 and US$180,000 for surgery, postoperative care, and medication. Istanbul turned out to be an excellent city from which to coordinate the trade. With its east-west trade routes and relatively sophisticated health care system, it had all the elements necessary for the market to thrive. Just as the Bosporus Strait, the famous waterway, links Europe and Asia, so too did the city bring together the European patients with the poor sellers from the hinterland. Collaborating with Shapira, Sönmez could perform hundreds of surgeries in rented operating rooms of both public and private Istanbul hospitals, often late at night after other physicians were long gone. With a skeleton staff of hired nurses, and a few trusted junior colleagues and anesthetists, Drs. Shapira and Sönmez were able to operate on two kidney patients per session. A transplant could take as long as four hours: The harvested organ was flushed with cold preservation solution, placed in a bowl, and carried into the adjacent operating room where it was transferred into the abdomen of the waiting recipient. It was fast, easy, and extremely lucrative. After their escape from Kosovo, Shapira returned to Israel where in his semiretirement he acts as a guarantor of cross-border transplant schemes wherever his trusted or not so trustworthy brokers establish relations with surgeons and hospitals willing to go along with the scheme.

HUMAN BIOPIRACY AND THE SPOILS OF WAR

Human trafficking, kidnapping, and disappearances for the purpose of illicit organs harvesting are motivated by greed for the display of power and authority, for currying favor with colleagues and government officials, and for political motives. Human trafficking for organs is not uncommon in war zones, during (and after) political conflict, in transitional states as well as during natural disasters, such as during the earthquakes in Turkey (1999) and Haiti (2010). All of these create the public chaos that provides a cover for illegal harvesting and plundering the bodies of the dead.

Some of these allegations are false, based on moral panics, posttraumatic stress disorders, and the anxiety and "worst fears" of vulnerable population and ethnic groups who have experienced the disappearances of their loved ones, and to whom (they know quite well) almost anything could be done, even the murder of their children for organs. They imagined their lives were not worth 20 centavos in the minds of the organs traffickers. This was the case with respect to the allegations in Mozambique. The fears were based on a sense of political and existential bioinsecurity.

In Kosovo, the allegations of killing Serbs in retaliation for the genocide in the former Yugoslavia was fueled by the disappearances of several hundred Serbs at the end of the Kosovo War. The U.N. and E.U. investigations were detailed by what were politically generated disinformation campaigns, including the release of a tape in Serbia in September 2012 in which a former KLA militant described the illegal harvesting of a heart from a Serbian prisoner at a detention center near the Albanian town of Kukes in the late 1990s and the transport of the heart in preservative solutions to the airport in Tirana, the capital of Albania to be sold on the black market. The witness was unreliable and contributed to the decision by the European Union and the European Parliament to table the investigation altogether. But the fears expressed were not irrational or absurd. An international scheme of illicit transplant and organs harvesting of trafficked person nested inside Kosovo, resulting in the deaths of the transplant patients and the kidney suppliers. In this instance, the European Union was forced to act, and a long prosecution resulted in convictions of local doctors and international brokers. The primary defendant, the Turkish doctor, Sönmez, is still at large, though he was reportedly seen in South Africa and in Azerbaijan, in public, drinking and carousing, showing that he feared nothing, least of all the Interpol detectives.

In the case of the abuses of the bodies of the mentally deficient at Colonia Montes de Oca during and after the Dirty War, the introduction of rumors and urban legends and the mysterious disappearance of a sympathetic doctor (Dr. Cecilia Giubileo) contributed to a hallucinogenic cordon sanitaire that protected the criminal behavior on the part of administration and staff, and allowed the abuses to continue well into the beginning of the twenty-first century. The Colonia administration defended its practices of harvesting blood, tissues, and corneas as being based on a legal contract with the National Organs Harvesting Institute in Buenos Aires, which today is called INCUCAI. Blood taken from the inmates on a regular basis was sold to private banks, sent to the military, and sold to individuals who were required to bring a quantity of blood to the hospitals where they would have surgery. During the period of the Dirty War, the inmates were also used in clinical trials and medical experiments, admitted Director Florencio Sanchez of the Colonia in his prison memoir. As we have seen here, Argentina was not the only modern military state to recognize the value of the human body—whether the body of the enemy or the body of disposable subcitizens and whether living or dead—to supply scarce and valuable medical, surgical, and reproductive material. In its worst form, however, the abuses at the mental colony were egregious, almost in a class by themselves.

During and following World War II, the U.S. government sponsored violent research on prisoners and war resisters at their disposal. Keyes led a study of the biological and psychological effects of "controlled" starvation on a "captive" population of young male conscientious objectors. The experiment was conducted over several months in a laboratory beneath the football stadium at the University of Minnesota. The men's daily caloric intake was reduced to concentration camp levels while the scientific team measured, weighed, and observed the effects on the bodies and minds of the clinical subjects, reproducing an American version of the mad science of Nazi doctors (Keys et al. 1950). Although the subjects gave their consent they did so, Keys acknowledged, because of their conflicted feelings and guilt in resisting a war seen as heroic. But consent to inhumane treatment is a red herring. In 1946–1948, the U.S. Public Health Service sponsored (and the U.S. Surgeon General approved) a "syphilis experiment" in Guatemalan prisons and psychiatric institutions for the mentally impaired, using female sex workers, intentionally infected with syphilis, brought to the involuntary, uninformed, but willing clinical subjects. When the rates of sexual transmission of the disease were not satisfactory, the U.S. government allowed the scientists to directly inoculate the prisoners with the infectious material, killing some research subjects in the process before they resorted to treating them with penicillin.[4]

When military interests and public health projects are enmeshed, as in the examples presented here, moral reasoning is reduced to a kind of megalomaniacal hubris, which Ostrovsky and Hoy (1990, 335) describe as "the feeling you can do anything you want to whomever you want for as long as you want because you simply have the power to do so." Under these circumstances, those in power believe they are themselves in combat with a larger evil force, be it a lethal disease or political enemies of the state.

Primo Levi described the malevolent hierarchy of bodies at Auschwitz in Nazi-occupied Poland. At the lowest rung were the prisoners called the Musselmann, those who were like walking dead men, their eyes having receded into their sockets, their legs unsteady, unable to stand, without the will to survive, unable to flee. Central to Agamben's thesis is the figure of the Musselmann, the man or woman in an advanced state of starvation, stupefaction, and living-in-death, a life reduced to silence, awaiting death, with no other destiny. While I am suggesting that the inmates of Montes de Oca occupy a similar status, both Musselmann and the ghosts of Montes de Oca are the extreme cases, even for the concentration camps, even for the wretched madhouses that have housed the profoundly mentally deficient.

Camp life at Montes de Oca, hardly the pleasant nudist camp of vacationers that Florencio Sanchez alluded to in his prison diary, reproduced the ethnomedical folk categories that ranged from the "high functioning," the violent, the dangerous, the aggressive, the oversexed, the useful, and the ambulatory, to those at the bottom of the heap—the nobodies, the "depositos," and the "gatosos," the cats, the pissers, and the crawlers—those who seemed to have surrendered any claim to human status and were not so much despised by their caretakers for their inability to keep themselves minimally intact, but symbolically "disappeared," rendered invisible. But in "suffering," the "Musselmanner" of Montes de Oca stands as an indictment of the social and medical system that created them, even in their own likeness.

Crimes such as these, ones that are often referred to as heinous crimes, unpardonable crimes, crimes "that cry out to heaven for vengeance," are protected by the emotions of disgust, repugnance, and fear of seeing, let alone handling, dead bodies. Death anxiety and death pollution—the fear and avoidance of confronting the dead body—create a hermetically sealed environment for abuses to take place. Such was the case at the Israeli National Forensic Institute at Abu Kabir. The elegant building housed a genetics/DNA lab on the top floor that was clean, pure, completely segregated from the morgue in the basement. Those of the third floor did not know what crimes were being committed beneath the clean scientific labs of which they were so proud.

What explains the complicity of the forensic pathologists? (Cantraovitch [1990].) Perhaps during the worst times of political conflict there was a moral dispensation, even a belief that the desecration of the dead was necessary. One thinks of many other similar cases, such as the collapse of morality at Abu Ghraib. Perhaps it began with the body of the enemy, the Palestinian "terrorists," and gradually the practice of autopsies turned into ad hoc dissections that spread to other populations.

Finally, a lack of awareness of the minimal technical-medical-surgical requirements of organ and tissue harvesting and transplantation in unruly times and places—such as Argentina during and after the Dirty War, the National Forensic Institute of Israel during and between the first and second intifada, and in Kosovo during the dangerous transition following the end of the Kosovo War and to this day—made these cases difficult to adjudicate. Even seasoned prosecutors are often confused about the difference between organ and tissue harvesting from dead bodies, from brain-dead (decreased) donors, from executed prisoners, and from living, trafficked kidney suppliers.

The allegations against the Israeli Forensic Institute of plundering the bodies of the enemy, of the terrorist, were easily dismissed as blood libels perpetrated by anti-Semitic foreigners as political propaganda against Israel. When we began our independent investigations of Abu Kabir, neither Donald Boström nor I knew that an internal whistle-blower, Dr. Chen Kugel, a Israeli forensic pathologist and a military officer, had been working behind the scenes with three other younger pathologists to stop the plunder of the dead and the stockpiling of body parts at the institute. These "perversions," as he called them, filled Lieutenant Colonel Kugel with righteous anger at the corruption, deceit, and abuse of the dead by public officials whose obligation was to be their final guardians. Kugel paid a heavy price for his interventions. He was forced out of his position at the national institute and was treated as a traitor and, worse, as a "leper," he told me.

The anthropologist and ethnographer's norm of reluctance to judge or to second-guess what we are told by our informants, takes on a different shape when one is working in the field of criminal behavior. Our discipline's moral reticence may be a gentlepersonly vestige of our postcolonial conventions of political reticence, one that has sometimes turned us into willing bystanders when crimes, including crimes against humanity, are taking place in our field sites. Documenting such crimes require collaborations with forensic pathologists, police and detectives, bioarcheologists, and ethnographers with experience working in war zones. Anthropologists can assist government and international investigations of organ trafficking not only from the living but also, and perhaps even more urgently, from the dead, including those scenarios in which the bodies of the enemy become the spoils of war. Thus, for example, the collaboration of three oddly associated professionals—the Swedish journalist, the American anthropologist, and the Israeli pathologist and military officer—brought about an unanticipated outcome. The Ministry of Health and the Israeli government accepted our conclusions and were able to conclude their own internal investigations that led to the "early retirement" of Dr. Jehuda Hiss and the appointment of Dr. Kugel as his successor.

"The dead body has rights and a dignity of its own," Dr. Kugel told me as he took me, Meira Weiss and Zvika Or, on a private tour of the morgue at Abu Kabir in 2013, now under his direction. "Bad things may happen here, as in any forensic institution," he confided as he rolled out a dead body from its refrigerated cubby. "But I can promise you that these bodies under my care will be safe.

It won't matter if these are Jewish bodies, Muslim bodies, Christian bodies, whether they are Israeli bodies or Palestinian bodies or undocumented guest worker bodies, Russian bodies. There is only one body here and they were all to be treated in the same way."

According to this secular and dedicated Israeli doctor to the dead and proud Israeli military officer, the dead body is not an empty nothing. It is not an evacuated object. Dr. Kugel often substituted the word *person* for the "deceased," and he never used the words *corpse* or *cadaver*. The dead body was a person, an individual who had parents, siblings, loved ones. The body had a history and a life. The dead bodies had grieving relatives. There were no hierarchies of dead persons. He said that the choice to practice forensic pathology meant that the pathologist and the dead were joined at the hip, the heart, the lung, and the skin. What happened during those two decades of corruption of the morgue was a violation of the body politic. It was an evil, a term most secular Israelis reserve for the Shoah, for terrorist bombings, for suicide attacks. Translated into secular language, the dismemberment, disarticulation, distribution, and the stockpiling of skin, bones, organs, genitals, tissues of the dead was, indeed, to Lieutenant Colonel Kugel a crime against humanity.

The role of heavily militarized states in organ theft from the bodies of the enemy combatant (the militant, the terrorist) or from the bodies of the enemy within (the undocumented, the new immigrants, the mad, mentally incompetent) is a special case in the larger realm of global organs trafficking. It is the moment when during wartime, peacetime crimes are employed on a larger, political stage and with political intent. Such may have been the case with the missing Serbs trafficked from Kosovo to detention centers in Albania after the war. While the detention, murder, and organ extraction by KLA militants after the war has never been proven, it cannot be dismissed as impossible or even as improbable. Victor Ostrovsy (1994, 24) described a parallel case of the medical abuse of Palestinian prisoners held at a special detention facility, Nes Ziyyona, near Tel Aviv, as described to the author by an ex-Mossad operative. The Palestinian captives brought to the detention center for interrogation also served as human guinea pigs at Mossad's secret ABC—atomic, bacterial, and chemical—warfare laboratory. It became a death camp in the end.

Finally, violations at the Israeli Forensic Institute were a mix of base corruption and human rights abuses against the bodies of Israeli citizens, as well as military war crimes against the bodies of Palestinian militants. That Hiss and his staff also illegally harvested from Israeli soldiers and even the victims of terrorist attacks is beyond explanation, an institutionalized moral collapse, with violations so abhorrent that even among secular Israelis they would fall under the category of evil, another time when, in the words of Jan Gross (2001) "the devil entered history."

PUBLIC DOCUMENTS AND REPORTS ON
GLOBAL ORGAN TRAFFICKING

World Health Organization. 2004. Resolution on "Human Organ and Tissue Transplantation." Publication WHA57.18. May 22. Geneva, Switzerland: World Health Organization. http://www.who.int/transplantation/en/A57_R18-en.pdf.
    Commission of the European Communities. 2007. "Communication from the Commission to the European Parliament and the Council of Organ Donation and Transplantation." Brussels: European Commission Parliamentary Assembly, 2010. "Inhuman Treatment of People and Illicit Trafficking in Organs in Kosovo." Rapporteur: Dick Marty, Switzerland, Alliance of Liberals and Democrats for Europe. Draft report http://www.assembly.coe.int/Committee Docs/2010/ajdoc462010prov.pdf

APPENDIX A

Obstacles to the Recognition, Investigation, and Prosecution
of Crimes of Biopiracy

1. The political manipulations of allegations organs theft. Accusations, counteraccusations, public denials, and the intentional insertion of disinformation and propaganda have been used to confuse and create chaos amid official government and international investigations.
2. The common misunderstanding that "harvesting" from the dead and from the living in clandestine locations and even under fairly primitive conditions is impossible. ("You cannot harvest organs in the bathtub of a cheap hotel.")
3. The aura of respect, fear, and wonder surrounding transplant medicine as a transcendental practice and the accompanying rhetoric of "saving lives" protects outlaw surgeons and makes seasoned prosecutors loathe to question let alone prosecute surgeons suspected of egregious human rights abuses, even when these are crimes against humanity.
4. The lack of resources, of legal precedents, of jurisdictional problems, and the lack of political will to investigate organ and tissue trafficking crimes that are reframed by academic scholars, lawyers, and bioethicists as "ethical" issues to be debated (e.g., "the right to buy and sell spare organs") rather than as medical human rights abuses and crimes to be prosecuted.

5. Prosecutions are inhibited by the difficulties of different international legal jurisdictions, incompatible laws, conventions signed but never ratified, and refusals to extradite defendants.

NOTES

1. Daniel A. Grech (2003), "US Approved the Dirty War: New Evidence Suggests that Henry Kissinger Gave the Argentine Military 'a Green Light' in Its 1970s–80s Campaign against Leftists." *Miami Herald,* December 4.
2. Like Boström, I was greeted on an Organs Watch visit to Israel in 2003 with an ugly headline and centerfold ("New Blood Libel on French TV—Israel Steals Kidneys of Orphan Children in Moldova") in *Makor Rishon,* a right-wing tabloid. The feature story reviewed a TV documentary by French filmmaker Catherine Bentellier, "Kidneys Worth Their Weight in Gold" that followed my research in Moldova, Turkey, and Israel. In Moldova, we interviewed people in villages that had been ravaged by human traffickers recruiting young men to Turkey, the Ukraine, and Georgia to provide kidneys to Israeli transplant patients. The "blood libel" accusation featured medieval woodcuts and a blurry photo of me holding the hand of a Moldovan orphan in his crib, during which I described the scandal of kidney selling in Moldova and its links to child trafficking that were sometimes merged in journalistic stories (as they had been in Brazil).
3. An Israeli government committee looking into this issue; the report was in Hebrew. See Reznick, Shadmi, and Itim (2003); Scheper and Boström (2013), 25, n20, n21.
4. http://www.hhs.gov/1946inoculationstudy/factsheet.html.

REFERENCES

Agamben, Giorgio. 1997. "The Camp as Nomos of the Modern," trans. Daniel Heller-Roazen, in *Violence, Identity and Self-Determination,* edited by Hent de Vries and Samuel Weber, 106–118, Stanford: Stanford University Press.

———. 1998. *Homo Sacer: Sovereign Power and Bare Life.* Stanford: Stanford University Press.

Allain, Jean. 2011. "Trafficking of Persons for the Removal of Organs and the Admission of Guilt of a South African Hospital." *Medical Law Review* 19, Winter:117–122.

Ambagtsheer, F., and W. Weimar. 2012. "A Criminological Perspective: Why Prohibition of Organ Trade Is Not Effective and How the Declaration of Istanbul Can Move Forward." *American Journal of Transplantation* 12, no. 3:571–575.

Barnard, Christiaan, and William Pepper. 2006. *One Life.* New York: Macmillian Company.

Boström, Donald. 2009. "Our Sons Are Plundered of Their Organs," *Aftonbladet Kultur,* August 26, 2009, http://www.aftonbladet.se/kultur/article5691805.ab.

Bourdieu, Pierre. 2000. "For a Scholarship with Commitment." *Profession* 1, no. 1:40–45. http://www.jstor.org/stable/25595701..

Campion-Vincent, Veronique, and Nancy Scheper-Hughes. 2001. "On Organ Theft Narratives." *Current Anthropology* 42, no. 4:555–558.

Cantraovitch, F. 1990. "Values Sacrificed and Values Gained by the Commerce in Organs." *Transplantation Proceedings* 22, no. 3:925–927.

Connolly, William E. 1993. "Beyond Good and Evil: The Ethical Sensibility of Michel Foucault." *Political Theory* 21, no. 3 (Aug. 1993):365–389.

D'Andrade, Roy. 1995. "Moral Models in Anthropology." *Current Anthropology* 36, no. 3: 399–408.

Delmonico, Francis L. 2009. "The Implications of the Istanbul Declaration on Organ Trafficking and Transplant Tourism." *Current Opinion in Organ Transplantation* 14, no. 2:116–119.

Fassin, Didier. 2008. "Beyond Good and Evil? Questioning the Anthropological Discomfort with Morals." *Anthropological Theory* 8, no. 4:333–344.

Fatmir, Aliu. 2010. "Medicus Clinic Was 'Part of Wider Crime Syndicate.'" *Prishtina,* September 4.

Francis, Leslie, and John G. Francis. 2010. "Stateless Crimes, Legitimacy, and International Criminal Law: the Case of Organ Trafficking." *Criminal Law and Philosophy* 4:283–295.

Gross, Jan. 2001. *Neighbors: The Destruction of the Jewish Community in Jedwabne.* Princeton, NJ: Princeton University Press.

Harrison, Simon. 2013. *Dark Trophies: Hunting the Enemy Body in Modern War.* New York: Berghahn Press.

Hassan, Fatima, and Sam Sole. 2011. "Kidney Gate: What the Netcare Bosses Really Knew." *Mail* and *Guardian,* April 29. http://mg.co.za/article/2011–04–29-kidneygate -what-the-netcare-bosses-really-knew/.

Interlandi, Jeneen. 2009. "Organs Trafficking—Not Just an Urban Legend (A Report on the Research of Nancy Scheper-Hughes and Organs Watch in the USA)." *Newsweek,* January 19.

Jimenez, Marina, and Nancy Scheper-Hughes. 2002. "Doctor Vulture—The Unholy Business of Kidney Commerce," *Toronto National Post,* March 30.

Keys, Ancel, Josef Brožek, Austin Henschel, Olaf Mickelsen, and Henry L. Taylor. 1950. *The Biology of Human Starvation.* 2 vols. St. Paul: University of Minnesota Press.

Leventhal. 1994. *The Child Organ Trafficking Rumor: A Modern Urban Legend. A Report Submitted to the United Nations Special Rapporteur on the Sale of Children by the United States Information Agency.* Washington, DC: USIA.

Mbembe, Joseph-Achille. 2003. "Necropolitics." *Public Culture* 15, no 1:11–40.

Ostrovsky, Victor, and Claire Hoy. 1990. *By Way of Deception.* New York: Saint Martin's Press.

Reznick, Ran, Haim Shadmi and Ha' Itim. 2003. "IDF To Bury Tissue of Soldiers Kept at Forensic Institute." January 26. Haaretz.com.

Ricoeur, Paul. 1986. *The Symbolism of Evil.* Boston: Beacon Press.

Robben, Antonius. 2005. *Political Violence and Trauma in Argentina.* Philadelphia: University of Pennsylvania Press.

Rothman, David, et al. 1997. "The Bellagio Task Force Report on Transplantation, Bodily Integrity, and the International Traffic in Organs." *Transplantation Proceedings* 29:2739–2745.

Sanal, Aslihan. 2004. "'Robin Hood' of Techno-Turkey or Organ Trafficking in the State of Ethical Beings." *Culture, Medicine and Psychiatry* 28, no. 3:281–309.

Scheper-Hughes, Nancy. 1988. "The Madness of Hunger: Sickness, Delirium and Human Needs." *Culture, Medicine and Psychiatry* 12, no. 4:1–30.

———. 1995. "The Primacy of the Ethical: Towards a Militant Anthropology." *Current Anthropology* 36, no. 3:409–420.

———. 2000. "The Global Traffic in Organs." *Current Anthropology* 41, no. 2:191–224.

———. 2003a. "Keeping an Eye on the Global Traffic in Human Organs." *Lancet* 361:1645–1648.

———. 2003b. "Rotten Trade: Millenial Capitalism, Human Values, and Global Justice in Organs Trafficking." *Journal of Human Rights* 2, no. 2:197–226.

———. 2004. "Parts Unknown: Undercover Ethnography of the Organs-Trafficking Underworld." *Ethnography* 5, no. 1:29–73.

———. 2006. "Biopiracy and the Global Quest for Human Organs." *Nacla Report on the Americas* 9, no. 5:14–22.

———. 2011a. "The Body of the Terrorist: Blood Libels, Bio-Piracy and the Spoils of War at the Israeli Forensic Institute." *Social Research* 78, no. 3:849–886.

———. 2011b. "The Rosenbaum Kidney Trafficking Gang." *CounterPunch Magazine*, November 30.

———. 2013. "Organ Trafficking—A Protected Crime." *The Conversation*. http://the conversation.com/organ-trafficking-a-protected-crime-16178.

———. 2015. "The Ghosts of Montes de Oca: Buried Subtext of Argentina's Dirty War." *The Americas* 72, no. 2:185–219. (The Academy of Franciscan History).

Scheper-Hughes, Nancy, and Anne M. Lovell. 1986. "Breaking the Circuit of Social Control: Lessons in Public Psychiatry from Italy and Franco Basaglia." *Social Science and Medicine* 23, no. 22:159–178.

Scheper-Hughes, Nancy, and Donald Boström. 2013. "The Body of the Enemy." *Brown Journal of World Affairs* 19, no. 2:243–263.

Staub, Ervin. 1989. *The Roots of Evil: The Origins of Genocide and Other Group Violence.* Cambridge: Cambridge University Press.

16 THEFT AND EVIL IN ASANTE

WILLIAM C. OLSEN

In July 2002, I rode a taxi east from the town of Mampong toward a diviner's village to interview him and his staff. The drive is along a dirt and clay road through two small towns before reaching Apiakrom, where the road then narrows off into the bush. The trip generally lasts about twenty-five minutes. On that day, I saw something unlike anything I have ever seen before. It was both strange and horrible. A young man around the age of twenty was running in the opposite direction of our taxi. He was completely naked and dripping with sweat; on his face was a look of absolute terror. It was not at all clear to me what the man had done and why he was running, but the answer came just minutes later. A crowd of roughly one dozen people then passed. Angered, and with a look of vengeance, they were carrying heavy clubs and farm implements. They were yelling and appeared to be in pursuit of the young man. Uncertain about what was unfolding, I asked the driver what was going on. His banal reply was short and entirely unalarmed: "That man is a thief. They will kill him."

A similar event took place in 2005 in the Kejetia of Kumasi. A European tourist yelled out that his wallet was stolen as the thief ran away. The shouting attracted the attention of dozens, and soon the thief was apprehended, held to the ground, and beaten to death by a crowd that was unacquainted with the victim of the crime. The tourist tried to halt the aggression. But he was told immediately by one of those involved in the beating, while being handed his money and wallet, "This isn't your issue anymore; it is our issue. You need to back off." Years after this public killing, I was assured by some in the gathering that the event of 2005 was not the first nor the last time a crowd of people responded with such precision in apprehending and punishing a thief. Some who saw the 2005 incident related the original details in a conversational manner and were entirely unalarmed by the violence. Their remarks gave a banality to the response to evil.

Lesser forms of theft may result in lesser penalties, but the burden of justice through action remains. In 2004, my students and I watched a large group of young teenagers milling around some shops on the morning of a national holiday. Suddenly the crowd roared in commotion, and they began a collective pursuit for a boy of sixteen who ran away from the town's central square. The boy had taken an amount of money, and he was attempting also to sell "weed." When the crowd of teens caught the thief, they cut off his index finger at the last digit. They explained that this "marked" the boy as a thief, and it served as a reminder of the results of his actions. The rise of various kinds of robbery and their associated violence and vigilante justice prompted the following review in an Accra newspaper:

> Incidences of armed robbery in the country increase every day, and are mostly perpetrated by the youth, who are the future leaders of the country. It has become almost a weekly ritual for either a robbery incident to occur, or for a robber to be gunned down or beaten to death by a mob. Is Ghana gradually turning into a den of armed robbers, where no one can be fully guaranteed his or her safety? The frequent occurrence of robbery in the country is slowly, but gradually polluting the hard-earned peaceful atmosphere that the nation has enjoyed over the years.

This chapter addresses the culture of evil in Asante, especially as evil is associated with acts of theft. I will analyze the culture of theft, and I will highlight the immediacy of responses to theft. Responses are punitive and often public, and these public dramas allow us to understand an Asante ethos of fairness, justice, and retribution.

In Asante, most kinds of theft are considered evil as well as criminal acts. This is because theft disrupts the social flow of people, commodities, and money. Theft displaces persons whose social routines feature the interpersonal exchanges found within bonds of friendship and family. Obligations of mutual assistance, trust, goodwill, and relative brotherhood define the ties between family members and among friends who live within a close proximity to each other. Assistance and lending form the basis of a social security network between individuals, families, and households. Money and goods are shared and lent in an informal basis to specific individuals in support of bonds of social welfare. Persons are identified by their ability and willingness to exchange and contribute to the physical welfare of others at times of need, such as funerals and other occasions. This exchange of money and objects defines not only persons, but also the goods that are transferred. As argued by Appadurai, the demand for and movement of an object, including its "real or imagined exchange," contribute to the value of that object. The source of value of an object is derived from its distribution and exchange among persons within a social network, and by exchanging that object, the persons themselves derive value from the meaning given to the object (Appadurai 1986, 4). Value of objects, including money and commodities, evolves from their exchange within a social network: "their meanings are inscribed in their forms, their uses, their trajectories" (Appadurai 1986, 5). Theft assaults this system by illegitimately removing that object or money from its personal and social contexts. Theft radically disrupts this normal flow of people, goods, and money. This assault is seen in Asante as largely an affront to the individuals themselves. Theft alters the future of social networks: persons, families, and their relations. Theft is a kind of material excess because it potentially disrupts human bonds and because it gives material and financial advantage to the thief in a corrupt way. This is done when robbery removes objects or money used to build future plans. It is also done as a thief changes his own destiny—or that of someone else—by robbing that person through witchcraft. Thieves are identified as criminals, and their actions are evil and must be curtailed by force, if necessary. In extreme cases, theft is so radical that its evil character even produces analogies to the evils of witchcraft.

The setting for understanding this culture of evil and theft is the town of Ashanti-Mampong, located forty-seven miles northeast of the city of Kumasi. Mampong has a diverse population of nearly forty thousand people and another twenty thousand in nearby villages. Livelihoods in Mampong are earned largely by store owners, whose goods and services include beauty and hair styling, carpentry and finishing, household supply, photography and processing, farm implements, banking, printing and photocopying, cell phone cards, small food stores, toiletries, electrical and paint equipment, and television repair, etc. Most households maintain active farming plots for growing crops consumed in the home or sold at Wednesday market. Staples of maize, plantains, cassava, palm fruit, and yams help form the daily diet. Most of the population of Mampong are Christian. They identify themselves as Catholic, Methodist, and Presbyterian. These are mostly Akan-speakers, and they include people from the immediate region and the coast. Other forms of Christianity are found within charismatic churches that appeal to those whose interests in orthodox Christianity has declined. A growing Muslim population represents migrating labors from the North of Ghana (Gonja, Mamprusi, etc.) or Fula and Hausa from Burkina, Niger, or Nigeria. Within a ten-mile radius, I have participated in the rites of six witch-finding shrines, where divination reveals answers to those who seek mystical resolutions to practical problems. Even in a population of largely Akan-speakers, uniform consensus on the meanings of behaviors and of ideology is not possible. Global forces abound in everyday life in Mampong. Nevertheless, a moral culture remains and helps define perspectives of what may be termed "evil," or *bɔne* in Asante Twi.

EVIL

To identify any action as *bɔne*, or a person's hidden character as *bɔne*, requires deeper description of both the specific event and the individuals involved. The word carries three meanings of crime, sin, and evil. All forms of activity that are *bɔne* fall within a realm of actions that are deemed unacceptable and deplorable within one of the three meanings. Few events within the daily stream of experiences are classified as evil. Such evil events would involve witchcraft (*bayeε*), cursing with intent to harm or kill, or sending sickness onto someone or bringing illness upon an infant (*asram*). However, more common forms of evil include jealousy and envy (*ahoɔyaa*), hatred, bad thoughts toward another, and children showing open disrespect for adults. Sinful actions may involve religious precepts within the confines of Christianity, Islam, or offenses toward the local spirits (*abosom*), or the ancestors. Such behaviors include lying (*nkontompo*), cheating, gossiping (*nkɔnkɔnsa*), adultery (*awareseε*), prostitution (*adwaman*), homosexuality—particularly when two men (*berima neberima naa*) or two women (*ɔbaa ne ɔbaa nna*) wish to marry—and sex relations in the bush or forest between a man and a woman. The concept of crime and *bɔne* is nearly always associated with murder, armed robbery, and with theft or *krɔnoo*.

Asante identify three features associated with actions or persons that are *bɔne*. These are *ahinta* (hidden), *mepeεse* (intention/desire), and excess, or *emorosoɔ*. Thoughts and actions that are *bɔne* include at least one of these characteristics. Within the Asante moral ethos, various kinds of behaviors have been designated by numerous people in Mampong as having explicit elements of *bɔne*, and as thereby being reprehensible and undesirable modes of public or private conduct. *Ahinta* means hidden or purposely concealed. I was told: "*Ahinta* is something which is inside the person, something which is hidden somewhere. It is something which is hated, such as *bayeε*." *Ahinta* presumes *bɔne* generally and is commonly associated with business failure, impotence, and illness. "Before one can do *bɔne*, you must have *mepeεse* (literally "I want"). *Mepeεse* can be good or bad. It is like a wish. You would want to do something." Inclinations to work hard and to marry and have children are regarded as good *mepeεse*. Acquiring wealth and a good income stem from good intentions. However, wealth through bribery, theft, corruption, or graft will be identified as *bɔne;* and wealth consumed in greed and avarice represents not only *bɔne,* but also a use of money. Such acts are selfish and are contrary to public morality, as they are in Igbo (Smith 2001). But wealth may also indicate a personal capacity for *emorosɔɔ,* which further identifies the person as *bɔne,* because excess denies traditional social dimensions of sharing and exchange of such things as food, money, and goods. For reasons identified in the following, a person's *emorosɔɔ,* especially regarding money, is considered as *bɔne,* and it should be limited or contained before too much excess becomes harmful. Wealth becomes harmful and *bɔne* when family and close friends are excluded from the bounty. Because open acts of theft demonstrate a thief's character to have both *mepeese* and *emorosɔɔ,* such deeds are viewed as evil. The unmerciful taking of goods also resembles the actions of a witch, and in this regard theft is especially evil.

A prime illustration of theft and all aspects of *bɔne* as previously mentioned concern recent trends in armed robbery being pulled off in larger Ghanaian cities by thieves known as Sakawa Boys. These are small gangs of young men (ages eighteen to twenty-eight), living in urban areas such as Accra, Takoradi, and Kumasi, who acquire military fatigues, vehicles, and weapons and then pose as police. In small bands, these imposters accuse motorists of breaking motorist laws. The driver is threatened with jail time or large fines unless he can pay out large sums of money on the spot. The phony officials enter the car and extort hundreds of *cedis* by threatening arrest. To avoid penalty or incarceration, the driver is taken to a nearby ATM to withdraw the funds. *Kawa* means "ring," and the boys are given a ring when they join as Sakawa. The ring has mystical powers. It can talk to you, protect you, and help you understand new ways of illegal deals, graft, threats of violence, and all manner of theft. I was told repeatedly there are no Sakawa Boys in Mampong; although at least one youth was known to leave the town for Accra to enter into the league of Sakawa Boys. Brazen public arrogance, posing as imposter military or police, and the swindling of large amounts of cash from innocent motorists are all mentioned as forms of *bɔne* in this manner of theft.

Parkin gives a useful premise for understanding evil within a cultural setting. He argues that personifying evil through cultural manifestations provides "a means of placing it cosmically, often with a view to containing it, sometimes to the extent of negotiating with it" (Parkin 1985, 19). In so doing, it may be possible to manage evil, bring it under control, resist it, reduce or limit its effects, cast out the effects of evil from the community, or perhaps pass judgment on its dispositions and thereby transition beyond the evil event. Such maneuvering regarding evil may very often involve empirical results and processes. When *bɔne* includes criminal activity, it is nearly always associated with theft. And theft and violence are often linked together in the criminal enterprise. The crime may be against the state, or it may be a tort action between individuals or groups or persons. Eliminating effects of the offense often cannot be accomplished without seeking some sort of legal, moral, or mystical remedy. Evil may be thus contained by swift and decisive measures.

THEFT AND JUSTICE

In former times, a thief was brought before the paramount chief of the town for matters of judgment and punishment. Or the thief was also arraigned before a shrine priest whose religious remedies of justice included summoning the intervention of mystical forces to reveal and then smite any guilty parties. Two sides of the case were heard, and justice was rendered according to the measure of theft and the harm done to the individual. Imposed by this court, remedies included recompense or repayment of money or goods. The guilty person may be marched around the community in front of townspeople and children, who would ridicule and mock him for being so foolish, disrespectful, and careless. Theft was also a crime which brought offense to the land or place where the theft occurred. Such an offense rendered the land barren or unproductive until recompense was offered through sacrifice. Sacrifice of a hen or egg on that location served to cleanse the land of any burden and sense of wrong. Protective witch-catching shrines appeared in abundance in the early 1920s throughout much of the Akan-speaking regions. As the shrines multiplied, local populations noticed less crime, including theft, and more abundant harvests and greater fertility among young wives (NAG: a.d.M. 11/1243).More serious crimes of theft called for harsher penalties. For example, T. E. Bowdich reports accusations of gold theft that could be remedied only by judgments rendered by a shrine priest (1819, 263–264). Also, King (Asantehene) Mensa Bonsu freely extolled the virtues of state-imposed judgment of capital punishment for thieves in the late nineteenth century (WMMS 1876, box no. 265, #1269): "In Ashanti we do not allow people to abuse the name of God. As to keeping theSabbath, we have always kept it. If a man steals, we kill him, as the English killed a man in Kumasi for stealing."

The nineteenth century brought about legitimate commerce in West Africa. The period represents a moral and fiscal decline in the power of the Asante state and a tremendous shift in state revenue (McCaskie 1995). Political power and state wealth of the past were undermined from mid-century through its end by the fiscal incompetence, political myopia, personal greed, and debauchery of corrupt heads of state. Kumasi was burned in the Anglo-Asante war of 1873–1874, and the state was soon to be sacked. In the place of the power of the king came a more private form of lucrative commerce. Personal wealth was experienced by ordinary citizens for the first time, and since "the guarantors of society were corruptly criminal, then why should the citizens not emulate their superiors and steal what they could?" (McCaskie 1986, 6). In the early twentieth century, people increasingly defined themselves by wealth through private enterprise and separate from the ideology of the state and its icon the Golden Stool. Such wealth was based on retail trade, money lending, cocoa farming and harvesting, and on banking. Entrepreneurs became rich citizens of the colony, and for the first time in state history commoners became as rich as the ruling elites. A business class soon arose, and these were the new elites. Commercial interests in cocoa and other raw goods brought the Gold Coast economy further into global capitalism. As the kingdom was annexed, state restrictions that limited accumulation of resources and any indulgent excesses of consumption were overshadowed by colonial jurisdictions. State penalties for high crimes gave way to colonial overrule for cases of murder, grand theft, and even witch-finding. In less serious cases, the thief was released after the public ridicule and mocking.

Legal procedures became aligned with colonialism and with Western ideas of jurisprudence and human rights. People nowadays discuss with contempt and some disdain current realities of personal legal rights and legal values of "due process" in cases of theft because the legal outcome likely serves the criminal defendant more than it does the plaintiff. The contempt comes from the presumption that Western law is too soft on criminals and punishments are not nearly excessive enough to be considered deterrents. Current formal legal procedure often appears to benefit the guilty party rather than those who have been offended. For example, I was in Mampong on the day in June 2012 that Charles Taylor, former Liberian head of state, was sentenced to fifty years in prison by the International Criminal Court in The Hague. News of the sentencing spread quickly via the local radio station and national television. The response was disbelief and disgust. Incredulity led to outrage. The common retort was voiced by statements such as: "He will live out his life while so many of his terror victims are dead or brutally maimed." "Taylor lives now in a prison cell. He lives a comfortable life; he is well fed; and he will never face the children he injured." And "Taylor should have been beheaded like so many of his victims." Such putative final outcomes would be consistent with the sense of street responses experienced in serious crimes. That would be justice. Bitterness is expressed at the lack of justice in formal cases where guilty persons are not fully held accountable for their deeds. In such cases, real justice does not prevail. Police and courts are viewed widely as ineffective in enforcing true justice, and their remedies are seen as largely ineffective in deterring similar crimes. Ghanaians consider their country to uphold a much higher standard of law and order than what is found in nearby Nigeria, Liberia, or Benin. Nevertheless, corruption is considered to be an integral part of the operations of police and judges: "Going to the police is a waste of time. Either nothing will happen or the thief will bribe the police and then go free." Criminals entering into the legal system are as likely to be set free due to bribing a court official as they are to be sent to prison.

The lack of credibility in government processes and skepticism over Western forms of legal procedure have served to inspire action within the community. An example of justice at the local level was narrated to me by shrine workers in the village of Penteng near Mampong.

> Last year, in 2011, a woman of thirty-five years, who was a market trader in Kumasi Central Market, was brought to the diviner's shrine by her mother, father and brothers. She had committed several crimes, including theft; but she had never been caught. Her family knew of some of the crimes, and suspected others. She was brought before the shrine priest, known as an ɔkɔmfɔ, to confess her crimes to the *abosom*, or prevailing spirits. But instead of confession, she sought the protection and power of the *abosom* to be a greater thief and to be never caught by the police. This desire or request was granted her by the *abosom*—but only for a brief moment. She then "committed herself" to being a thief. But because she did not confess her greatest crime, which was the infertility sent upon her mother's sister, she was killed by the *abosom*. The woman began having symptoms of diarrhea. These symptoms convinced the family to take the woman to the ɔkɔmfɔ. The bodily defenses of the woman declined and her health deteriorated as she continued to assert lies and a desire to be a thief. She went into a coma not long after being taken to the hospital. In the hospital bed, she declared, "somebody slapped me"; and everyone knew this was a manifestation of the *abosom*. She died soon thereafter.

THEFT AND THE SOCIAL LIFE OF THINGS

Market economies are known for their production of credit systems and the exchange and barter of money and commodities. Credit exists to retain the viability of exchange of money and goods over time as prices rise and decline according to demand and wider global forces. Traders in West African markets are as dependent on credit extensions for business deals as are traders anywhere else. Asante market traders, for example, access capital through informal credit systems in order to retain business vitality through good and bad harvests. Money exchanges are thus built upon a system of loans, debt, and repayment among traders, and between women traders and their suppliers (Clark 1994). Who exchanges what, and how much, and with whom, are all understood matters of the formal matrix of trade. Stipulations for all returns and repayment of credit amounts are negotiated and logged. Market credit allows possession of manufactured or farm goods "at a distance" to be sold from hundreds of miles away. And the formal use of credit also reduces the buyer and seller to a mutual status that is close to being "anonymous and impersonal" because of the distance involved (Bloch and Perry 1989, 6).

Informal exchange networks also maintain viability by adapting similar dimensions of hierarchy and structure and a sense of obligation. Informal networks differ from formal systems because exchange distances are close at hand and the nature and timing of the return remains uncertain. Returns may even be political or symbolic rather than material. Emphasis focuses on the social network in question rather than the objective quantified obligations of credit and finance. During a series of conversations with seven men and two women who have lived their entire lives in Mampong, I listened to descriptions of the nature of lending and the exchange of objects and money. They described with whom they give and take money as lenders. They also described the household commodities, farm produce, and money that changed hands. And they explained what expectations for return are generated as a result of such exchanges. Their narratives focused on labor and close ties of family. This flow of goods and money involves trust in lending and friendship. Family and neighbors may come and go within a household, thus allowing in the past for an absence of door locks. Goods are borrowed, while others were exchanged with the understanding that commodities circulated within given social networks. Insofar as individuals produce wealth from hard work, Asante identify themselves in a personal way with their money and possessions. Wealth is then idealized as the model of transaction in which one person may be of assistance to others who are in need. The exchange of wealth is symbolized by sharing of a food bowl, commonly found in much of Ghana (Robertson 1984). A family or some adults may share a common bowl of *fufu* by dipping into the dough and taking their meal. Thus, evening food is consumed by sharing from a commonly prepared source.

Commensality follows a recognized and limited network of friends and relatives, one that involves more than food exchanges. The cooperation in sharing a meal flows from the wider exchange of commodities among friends and family. Asante men and women are recognized as legitimate social beings by their qualities of cooperation one with another. Asante see the person much the same way as other populations of West Africa where the person "consists in having regard for others and showing them respect—recognizing their status, paying them their due, contributing to their well-being" (Jackson 2012, 148). Each transaction of exchange assumes two broader premises. First, the object must not be obtained illegally, and it must not be acquired through mystical means of witchcraft. Second, if the income or object is gained by one's own hand, then he "can give life to his wealth through his toil and hard work." Such perceptions of wealth are common to West African societies that regard wealth as a natural part of life, and the obtaining of wealth is similar to other forms of life that are understood to exist in nature (Ellis and Ter Haar 2004, 119). In this regard, the transformative capacity of a commodity or of money, its exchangeability, demonstrates its "socially relevant feature" (Appadurai 1986, 13). As cultural meaning is given to objects in one's possession, the movement of those objects within a defined network of persons supplies additional value of both goods and people. The path of distribution of objects is "both reflective and constitutive of social partnerships and struggles for preeminence" (Appadurai 1986, 19). The social life of objects in such exchanges is illustrated by the nature of the objects exchanged; the rate of exchange and route of distance traveled to make the exchange; and the operation of informal exchanges despite the presence of a more formal economy. While market values define objects of transaction within the global or formal economic system, the informal system identifies "reputation, name, or fame" (ibid.) as the real nexus of commodity transaction. Elsewhere in West Africa, this interchange between people and objects is conceptualized as a path, wherein "greetings, goodwill and goods and services move to and fro within a community, keeping the paths open, as Kuranko say, keeping relationships alive" (Jackson 2005, 36).

Attention to personal borrowing networks has recently been given to African contexts by Shipton, who identifies such transactions as forms of entrustment. Entrustment involves material or financial transactions over some elapsed period of time. Repayment of one form or another is understood, and bookkeeping is informally relegated to trust and confidence of a future settlement (Shipton 2007). Emphasis is on informal exchanges among friends or family. "People borrow and lend, entrust and repay, for many sorts of reasons: to share, to spread out risks, to hide their wealth or shelter it from third-party claimants, to speculate on seasonal or longer-term price fluctuations, to take advantage of local imbalances in resource endowments, to establish or clarify status hierarchies, to gain voters or supporters, and to create or maintain social relationships useful or satisfying in themselves" (ibid., 101). The point here is that these exchange transactions involve both interpersonal and commercial agendas between individuals as they interact in financial matters along familiar social networks, and as they accomplish desirable results of material satisfaction and economic liquidity. As explained to me by one life-long resident: "A person can yield the results of labor and investing by using that wealth to help others within his social security network, and also by employing others so that can also get money by working for him. A poor use of the funds or money or harvest would be to simply use the money upon himself and his own interests." Three business banks and one credit union in Mampong supply loan equity for entrepreneurs who acquire assets in land, shops, capital for business use, trade, education, and other investments. The formal financial sector is also active as more people than ever save for the future by placing one or two *cedis* per month in savings accounts. Yet, entrustment borrowing is known to be part of the livelihood of every friendship, family connection, and personal companionship. Entrustment is the local social security network that carries individuals through in tough times and when small amounts of money and commodities are needed in the near term. In the words of one informant: "How you use wealth and riches can be good or bad. Some people use their riches in a mean way or are not willing to help anyone or share their money. Money must especially be shared with family. Those who do not are *ne pa bɔne ni,* 'a wicked person.'"

Equally useful to keep in mind for Asante is the illegitimate use of money resources and of commodities. In such a setting, "theft shows disregard to the natural flow of things between people—the things which might allow them to live a peaceful life." The use of money to provide for a family and one's future both fulfill this description. Or, one may also "sow his wealth by using money prudently and wisely and by taking anything extra and perhaps investing the money or using that money to purchase a business or piece of equipment of some other way of gaining money in the future." The person may then "yield the results" by using that income to assist others within his social security network, or, as someone else put it, also by "employing others so they can also get money by working for him."

This formal logic of the economy contains a model for financial survival and liquidity, one that is understood by shop owners and small-scale entrepreneurs. However, limited capital restricts any ability to invest strongly in commercial ventures. Such enterprises are entered into only among those who receive larger sums of income from relatives overseas in Europe, Canada, or the United States. The percentage of people receiving such aid is estimated by many to be 30 to 40 percent of the town's population. The use of money to assist familiars is freely applied to a variety of circumstances within the individual's network of personal acquaintances. It is used on occasions when money is expected to flow to others, such as funerals (de Witte 2001). In such times, donations of money are used to bury the dead, settle debts, make medical or hospital payments, pay creditors, and relieve any tax burdens. Young men preparing for marriage may pass bride wealth to future in-laws. This wealth is acquired by work, by the return of debts, and by service labor. Money, food, or clothing are also used in situations of informal economies when household income is so limited that assistance may be needed from a close friend or family member. In any case of circulation among family, it is acknowledged that any return will likely come at a time of economic windfall, or it may be prompted by need in crisis. Such is the logic of a moral economy found in situations of limited wealth throughout Africa and elsewhere (Austen 1993).

When I asked people to describe the effects of theft upon the entrustment livelihood of the victim and upon this network of exchangeability, I was given emphatic responses condemning theft and its damaging results on the future of the victim. "The mind of every thief is to come and steal and in the process destroy your livelihood." Not all theft has this impact, but all theft intends some degree of disruption of life. One senior man who grew up in Mampong was deliberate in his description. Theft, he said, can be understood by Asantes in only one way. "It is offensive; and it is *bɔne*. The thief takes that thing from someone who planned to use the thing in a way which would be beneficial to owner and perhaps to others. Once the thief steals that object from me, I can no longer make my plans with others because I no longer possess the thing or amount of money to carry out my plans." Thieves can undo one's plans and future use of that resource because they "take things wantonly and with greed. And they do not regard the suffering of their victim. They are very much concerned for their own interests of greed and of *emorosoɔ*." In this manner, Asante encounter the excess of theft in a way similar to how Mitchell identifies excess as a kind of evil: "fear of excess is represented via the complex and often horrific imagery of evil" (Mitchell 2001, 3). The negative morality of any material accumulation seen as *emorosoɔ* condemns both the object and the means by which it was obtained. Moreover, thieves "show disregard to the natural flow of things between people—the things which might allow them to live a peaceful life." One long-term resident expressed this point, "Why should you allow some person—a thief—to take away your livelihood? Without that thing, you cannot do what you intended to do. It may be just five *cedis*. But when the thief takes the money, I cannot do all those things which I planned to do: help my family, grow my business, reduce my debt, and so forth. In doing so, that thief is taking away my livelihood. If we, or I, do not stop the thief now—even by killing him—then he will steal again." This statement of the crime and *bɔne* of theft reveals the social movement and flow of money and commodities. It reveals the source of value of that thing, which is a network of relations who will have contact with it, use it, borrow it, or consume it. The statement makes clear that the thief not only removes that object. Theft also denies a livelihood, an agenda, or the possible use of the resource(s) to enhance the lives of family. While hard work may have created the reality of some material resource(s), theft illegitimately removes the reality by crime. Theft thus cancels out the hard work in the first place. Theft also eliminates what was to become of that resource: the potential for a social network based upon its use.

In this sense, theft in Asante resembles the "occult economies" spoken of in South Africa by Jean and John Comaroff (1999). Occult economies are sustained by evil measures and often through magical means. They are thereby enriched through "illegitimate appropriation . . . not just of the bodies and things of others, but also of the forces of production and reproduction themselves" (ibid. 284).

It is perceived in Asante that theft alters or destroys the future. Material or financial futures thus become a victim of the *bɔne* of theft. The future may no longer take place as planned with the same resources and likely the same individuals. Asante notions of the person dissect the individual into component parts, and one of these components is the person's *nkrabea*, or destiny. *Nkrabea* is a divine endowment from *Onyame* (God), "bindingly approved of by him after being recited in his presence by an individual who was about to be born into corporeal existence" (McCaskie 1995, 107). In life, *nkrabea* determines the life stream and general direction of one's existence, including illness, wealth, and good or bad fortune. Purposeful disruptions in this process are regarded as offensive against both the individual and God. Theft is often viewed as a kind of disruption of someone's *nkrabea*, because it may steal resources that may otherwise be used to build one's future and thereby fulfill someone's destiny. Thus, theft does much more than steal an object. It also steals the future or future plans with which that commodity or sum of money was to become a reality.

Two examples illustrate how theft assaults the entrustment of a social network.

1. A senior woman was once the town's bonesetter; but her strength declined with age. This woman also had sizeable property holdings several miles from town on which she farmed food crops four or five days each week after her morning sessions as a bonesetter. The land is

family-owned. Boundaries indicate where other property ends and her family's land begins. Many decades ago, the woman planted a dozen mahogany trees on the property, which then grew to maturity of fifty to sixty feet. Wood from trees was to be used to build furniture, or the wood would be sold for a sizeable profit. Recently, a thief sawed down several of the trees. He removed some of the wood for sale. The thief also posed as if he were the owner of the land and made sale of some acres to people from Kumasi who were unaware of the real owners.

Word of the fraud and theft circulated among other land holders; and eventually the real identity of the thief and perpetrator was disclosed. The thief lives in town. Before justice was sought, the thief began bringing money to the old woman. Her son told me that the money offering was an attempt to persuade the woman against mystical retribution for the theft, an action which would be entirely justified for such an unprovoked action. Because of the monetary value of the trees, retribution could have been levied in the form of a curse.

2. Someone recently stole several chickens during the night from a family courtyard. An older sister heard the chickens squawking and looked outside in time to identify the thief. The thief was a man in his early twenties. The thief later walked by the courtyard in the daytime, and he was identified by the owner as the chicken thief. The thief did not deny the accusation. The owner then warned him that if any more chickens were stolen he would "knock the man's left eye into his right eye socket" as punishment.

Each example illustrates the *bɔne* of theft and how the stolen objects represented household livelihood potential income, value, real wealth, family resources, and fiscal planning for families. Objects taken were to be used as family resources in either the long- or the short-term. Remedies for the theft were pursued. The thief admitted the crime. However, without an admission in case 1, a curse could have resulted in physical punishment, including stiff joints, headaches, possible HIV, or being "made to walk like a robot."

Theft and thieves may be seen by Asante as the antithesis of entrustment. As in Gisu society, accusations of theft amount to the repudiation of personal responsibility (Heald 1986). For Asante, theft is an action that destroys hard work; it is an assault on individual accountability and on the system of entrustment of money and commodities. Some even spoke of theft within the same actuality of taking human life or of threatening to take the life of someone. "The law says you have inherent right to your life. This means you cannot steal or do something against someone. If you do that, then you are not taking care of that person's rights. You don't have the right to destroy someone's joy, and in Ghana if you do that, they will take instance justice." Actual proof of theft stirs up conditions of immediate actions that both limit the damage of theft and identify the thief as an antisocial character. Theft of objects of value is also an assault to the social network of people who would exchange these objects. Theft disrupts social relations. Theft destroys the fruits of hard work, and theft sets aside planning for the future of families and close relations. In fact, theft is *bɔne*. As such, theft demands retribution for any victims, and it calls for justice to be rendered on the spot. It was said that the man in Apiakrom, the thief who was mentioned earlier, was probably someone who had done this kind of thing before. Perhaps his stealing was repetitive. Maybe he was known as a thief. Such circumstances call for retribution and justice. As described at the outset, this justice is often swift.

It may be easy to argue that limited resources lead to this ideology of austerity that says that theft of even a few *cedis* is considered as repugnant and as *bɔne*. Yet, people in Mampong have for years benefited from increasing wealth. This wealth is the result of family donations coming from abroad. Prosperity is also being realized by careful investing in one of the three banks or lending houses in town. Weekly installments to long-term investment funds are gathered by representatives who call on families in their homes. The money is then taken to the bank and the person is updated on any interest amortization. Savings deposits, investment income, and capital gains are increasingly becoming part of the economic foundation of the lives of families and households. Bank theft is considered as even more brazen and *bɔne* than small-scale stealing. Bank theft brings an immediacy of justice.

INSTANT JUSTICE

Instant justice is known as *ye to no so were*. For reasons of corruption within the court system and injustice in policing previously mentioned, theft calls on the common man to exact instant justice upon the thief. The thief may be a repeat offender. The thief may bribe his way out of prison time. Other legal options for the thief include the protection of a lawyer who is presumed to be able to have persuasion with a judge to pardon the thief or to reduce the prison sentence to almost nothing. A thief is a cunning person who uses their mind and skills in favor of deceit. Instant justice is a legitimized form of retaliation for crime by "any person." This is because the thief poses a "threat to us all" and "it may be me next time" who is to be the victim of the theft. Modern amenities of the law may allow a criminal or a thief more privileges than are accorded to the victim.

The outrage of the 2012 sentencing of Charles Taylor in The Hague recognized that the state will pay tens of thousands of dollars each year to house this criminal in prison for a sentence that amounts to life in prison. One comment was: "If you consider the atrocities he did: killing, war, rape, cutting off the hands of children, he should be given the death penalty. But instead, he is in prison. It is comfortable; he is kept warm and healthy; the state caters to his needs." Rage also reflected on the system under which he was sentenced. As another informant put it: "That is not justice. He deserves to die. And that is why many Africans do not respect or regard Western forms of justice and the court system set up in Africa which models this system. There is never any real true justice. No justice which settles things for those who have been wronged."

Thieves have been known to use violence of the intimidation of violence. This is all *bɔne* because these are qualities of a life that is dishonest, filled with excess, and lacking in hard work. One example of brazen theft and violence includes armed robbery of a local bank.

> Attempted bank robbery took place in Mampong in November, 2002. The botched theft involved four robbers. Two robbers were shot by security while leaving the bank. One died instantly; and the other died later at the hospital. One bank security guard was also shot and killed. The two other robbers were eventually apprehended and brought to the town's central square. Hundreds gathered to witness the following acts of justice. As partial penalty, the robbers' right legs were amputated below the knee. They were then corralled within a circle of tires; the tires were doused with gasoline and then ignited. Two thieves burned to death in the fire.

In such a situation of violence, instant justice becomes a legitimate response because of the general ineptitude of law enforcement and the absence of police on the street. Violence and fatalities of a bank heist were seen as threatening to the general welfare of others in town. The brazen attitudes of thieves display an overall contempt for civil law and for life of those who are honest and hard-working. Such little regard for safety and life is itself *bɔne,* and calculated, threatening actions call for responses that are equally as just and punitive. Harming others through violent means is a greed-driven tactic of thieves and armed robbers. Only instant justice can curtail violence and theft regarded as *bɔne.* Only the immediacy of killing the robbers by instant justice can be legitimized as both punitive and just in such cases. Not one individual with knowledge of this public execution—which includes most of the town—expressed the slightest uncertainty about the fate of these armed robbers. No one questioned the violent justice that prevailed as these men were burned to death in the town square. Rather, statements of outrage echoed the above-quoted refrain as a statement rather than a question: "why should we allow some person to take away our livelihood."

Instant justice is legitimized in Mampong for two other reasons. First, a fundamental feature of *bɔne* is *ahinta*—or hidden, and because *ahinta* is normally part of the personal disposition within one's soul, it cannot be observed. *Ahinta* normally remains unknown and unrecognized in a common manner. By definition, theft discloses one's bad *ahinta*. It makes quite public this undesirable human quality. There is then no equivocating as to the disposition of that person's intentions and desires, one's *mepeese,* in life. Once *ahinta* and *mepeese* are made public, they then become accessible to public scrutiny and possible negative sanctions. Both common sense and criminal law demand punishment of theft. Common sense and law both require justice. The harsh response of violence and death for thieves lead to the final point. Hinton and others have elaborated on the culture of annihilation. One precept of the annihilation thesis states that a particular identifiable sector of the population may be so dissimilar to the rest that they must be fundamentally regarded as "other." As such, the restricted group lives an existence that is essentially different, even contrary, to that of the larger population. Then, within certain economic, historical, and political realities, these differences come to be regarded as extreme, even unacceptable. They may call for the annihilation of that population sector. And this is regarded as a virtuous response for the cleansing and benevolence of society (Hinton 2002). My argument is that these operational features of annihilation appear to be at work at those instances when the killing of a thief becomes both reasonable and legitimized. Theft is perceived as so contrary to normal life that allowing the thief to live may no longer be an option to those around him who have the power to carry out instant justice. In this manner, instant justice annihilates the *bɔne* of theft. In southeastern Nigeria, older males who die unexpectedly are sometimes presumed to have been thieves in a previous incarnation (Offiong 1991, 15). It is a kind of selective justice by mystical means that follows them into their current lives. For the Asante, rather, instant justice for a thief is more brutally immediate and decisive, and it is carried out by those in the town.

THEFT AND WITCHCRAFT

Thieves are persons of either gender and of any age. However, someone decides (*mepeese*) to become a repeat offender usually in their late-teenage years. "Being a thief can start at 15. Most thieves are in their late teens and in their 20s. It is now becoming like a trade." On occasion, a person's *nkrabea* may lead them partially toward bad and evil behavior, but usually, one's *nkrabea* fashions their desires to work, to be a wife or husband, to have children, and to live a good life. When this happens, a person's *mepeɛse* overrules one's own *nkrabea*. Changing the *nkrabea* of anyone is *bɔne,* even if it is one's own self. In such cases, one's own future becomes altered by the decision to be a thief. A future is thus abducted by theft, even one's own future. Anger against this course of action is explained, in part, because of this path in life where a thief may willfully alter his destiny in order to steal, become violent, and to live a life contrary to his destiny. "This may be especially true of the family. There may thus be a sense of judgment toward the person. Rage and anger may be manifest because of the deceit. In some cases, the parents of a child who is a thief will take the child and cut off part of a finger to punish and to indicate to the child that this finger stole that thing. This is a form of retribution within the household. And it also acknowledges the embarrassment brought upon the parents by the child."

A thief may also obtain the assistance of bad spiritual powers, or bad *abosom.* Spiritual powers are used commonly for medicinal healing and protection. However, "there are false *abosom;* but they are not very powerful. They are used to help people such as thieves. They are used by people who seek out mystical powers to do *bɔne.*" For example, it is widely testified that the 2002 bank robbers all wore protective talismans or amulets known as *asumaŋ* that were intended to shield those who wear them against invasive measures of harm or to protect against death. In this case, the *asumaŋ* were worn to shield the guns of police. Bullets would turn to water or to vapor. They would be ineffective on them because they had the mystical shield of *abosom.*

Avarice and greed among youth are suspect in another way, and that is witchcraft. Incomes of most young people limit their abilities to transform themselves into the European or American counterparts they see on the Internet. Shortages of cash, combined with desires to acquire wealth, may lead someone to acquiring "sacrificial money," or *sika duro. Sika duro* may come to someone mystically as he makes a compact with a fetish priest to offer the life of a friend in exchange for vast amounts of money. In one such case, a day laborer was told by the fetish priest to sacrifice his girlfriend by feeding her poison and by placing a toxic mixture in her vagina prior to sex. The girl became suspicious and did not drink the concoction, even though the man was successful with the instructions regarding the woman's genitalia. Attempts at *sika duro* are seen as a kind of theft because they intend to steal the life of someone in exchange for accumulations of money by mystical means. It is all *bɔne.*

In Asante, a witch is motivated by an inexplicable sense of greed and by a desire to destroy. The greed of taking something belonging to another person focuses generally on material goods and money. Theft is identified as part of a broader notion of illegitimate consumption of someone else's personal identity, including not only their material possessions, but also their physical well-being and emotional and mental health. Theft and witchcraft share some common features, including the expropriation of material resources, greedy consumption of individual and family security, the blatant destruction of another person by removing their physical properties, and even the ruin of a person and his family by destroying or threatening someone's future. The future is destroyed by theft when stolen property displaces plans and opportunities considered integral to the future, and it is destroyed by witchcraft in cases where the witch consumes either the life or one's destiny (*nkrabea*). "Both the thief and the witch expropriate the future: the thief takes money (or a basis for the future); and the witch takes the *nkrabea*, of one's children. This alters or destroys the future for that person."

Greed is often associated with theft in that it represents a wanton selfish accumulation of money and material goods. While greed is not illegal, it is considered *bɔne* because no one besides the thief stands to benefit from such an accumulation. Greed and an unrelenting desire to harm others are the foundational features of Asante *bayee*, especially when there is wanton disregard for the suffering of the victim. Trafficking in illegally acquired goods is seen universally in Asante as *bɔne*, and theft may be supported by powers of *bayee*. This reality has been noted to be the case for women traders in Kumasi Central Market:

> Ideas linking witchcraft to theft reinforce the distinction between legitimate prosperity and profit at others' expense. The witch gains economic and spiritual power by feeding on the life force of the very people who should be nurtured, unborn and young children and close relatives. The witch fattens while those around her (or him) wither through illness and misfortune. By analogy, profits generated by a zero sum game metamorphose into actual theft from others, a crime taken very seriously in Asante. Those whose good fortune is conspicuously not shared with fellow members of their lineage or community fall under suspicion of witchcraft. (Clark 2001, 301)

Ultimately, greed motivates actions and desires toward others by means of destructive processes. Witchcraft is forged in a cauldron of power and acquisition; thus, many authors have rightfully noted that the instances of witchcraft and of protection against witches have dramatically increased within the twentieth century with its advent of greater wealth that is unevenly distributed within a given population or community. By mid-century, Margaret Field noted the prevalence of witchcraft among those who used the power for financial gain. "The secondary activities attributed to witches include the power to spoil crops, to spoil cocoa plantations, and to become rich by sucking away the invisible essence of money so that the victim meets financial losses and the spoiler financial windfalls" (ASSM 1945).

Theft in a mystical sense may also include stealing of the spiritual substance of family members, especially children. When this happens, a common result may include sickness or death. When death happens to children, people speak of the event as the witch having stolen one's future. Moreover, some witches have the capacity to alter or disturb the destiny of someone else. This, too, is seen as a form of theft. Access to and acquiring goods is not seen as harmful or wrong. The power and motivation to devour another's health and well-being are certainly seen as evil.

When Parkin wrote of the culture of evil, he stated that evil is often associated with human suffering and with death. Understanding other peoples' ideas of evil "draws us into their theories of human nature: its internal constitution and external boundaries" (Parkin 1985, 6). While one can speak in Asante of degrees of suffering or levels of offence regarding theft, it is also likely that the crime of theft will ultimately be described as evil. Theft is evil in Asante life because it is illegitimate expropriation of property. It is also excessive accumulation of wealth. Indeed, the subject of theft was rarely left out of narratives regarding evil deeds. Theft was, in fact, very often placed at the top or near the top of the list which people might be disposed to do as an evil deed or in association with other evil acts. In part, this is because theft becomes a central core fact in settings where someone's livelihood is threatened, or when one's farm does not produce, or when the harvest is not great, or someone's investments tank. The violence of instant justice is seen as a means of containing the effects of evil. Violence of instant justice appears to restrict the wider spread of theft and its impact on peoples' material lives. Likewise, witchcraft is seen as a collaborating partner and form of theft. It may be assumed in settings of stillbirth, sudden sickness or pain, or when there are unusual symptoms or sudden death. Theft, and its associative qualities linked with *bɔne* are descriptive markers that reveal the motivations behind larger social dramas. They disclose the inner makeup of human frailties and personal deceit. These social facts identify the lives and individual circumstances of everyone in town from time to time: health, wealth, love, poverty, fiscal windfall, financial ruin, goods that disappear, uncertainty, personal suffering, hard times, and failed dreams. All may become associated with the *bɔne* of theft. All may require some kind of immediate remedy in order to limit the wider spread of evil.

PRIMARY SOURCES

ASSM: Asante Social Survey Archives. Cambridge.
NAG: National Archives of Ghana. Kumasi, Accra.
WMMS: Wesleyan Methodist Mission Society. London: School of Oriental
       and African Studies

REFERENCES

Appadurai, Arjun, ed. 1986. Introduction to *The Social Life of Things,* 3–63. Cambridge: Cambridge University Press.
Austen, Ralph. 1993. "The Moral Economy of Witchcraft." In *Modernity and Its Malcontents,* edited by Jean Comaroff and John Comaroff, 89–110. Chicago: University of Chicago Press.
Bloch, Maurice, and J. Parry, eds. 1989. Introduction to *Money and the Morality of Exchange,* 1–18. Cambridge: Cambridge University Press.
Bowdich, T. E. 1819. *Mission from Cape Coast Castle to Ashantee.* London: J. Murray.
Clark, Gracia. 1994. *Onions Are My Husband: Survival and Accumulation by West African Market Women.* Chicago: University of Chicago Press.
———. 2001. "Gender and Profiteering." In *"Wicked" Women and the Reconfiguration of Gender in Africa,* edited by Dorothy Hodgson and Sheryl McCurday, 293–312. Portsmouth, NH: Heinemann.
Comaroff, Jean, and John L. Comaroff. 1999. "Occult Economies and the Violence of Abstraction: Notes from the South African Postcolony." *American Ethnologist* 26, no.2:279–303.
Ellis, Stephen, and Gerrie Ter Haar. 2004. *Worlds of Power.* New York: Oxford University Press.
Heald, Suzette. 1986. "Witches and Thieves: Deviant Motivations in Gisu Society." *Africa: Journal of the International African Institute* 21, no. 1:65–78.
Hinton, Alex, ed. 2002. "The Dark Side of Modernity." In *Annihilating Difference,* 1–42. Berkeley: University of California Press.
Jackson, Michael. 2005. *Existential Anthropology: Events, Exigencies, and Effects.* New York: Berghahn Books.
———. 2012. *Between One and One Another.* Berkeley: University of California Press.
McCaskie, T. C. 1986. "Accumulation, Wealth and Belief in Asante History; pt. II: The Twentieth Century." *Africa: Journal of the International African Institute* 56, no. 1:3–23.
———. 1995. *State and Society in Pre-Colonial Asante.* Cambridge: Cambridge University Press.
Mitchell, Jon. 2001. Introduction to *Powers of Good and Evil,* edited by Paul Clough and Jon P. Mitchell, 1–16. New York: Berghahn Books,
Offiong, Daniel. 1991. *Witchcraft, Sorcery, Magic and the Social Order among the Ibibio of Nigeria.* Enugu, Nigeria: Fourth Dimension.
Parkin, David, ed. 1985. Introduction to *The Anthropology of Evil,* 1–26. Oxford: Blackwell.
Robertson, Claire. 1984. *Sharing the Same Bowl: A Socioeconomic History of Women and Class in Accra, Ghana.* Bloomington: Indiana University Press.

Shipton, Parker. 2007. *The Nature of Entrustment*. New Haven, CT: Yale University Press.

Smith, Daniel Jordan. 2001. "Ritual Killing, 419, and Fast Wealth: Inequality and the Popular Imagination in Southeastern Nigeria." *American Ethnologist* 28: 803–826.

Witte, Marleen de. 2001. *Long Live the Dead! Changing Funeral Celebrations in Asante, Ghana*. Amsterdam: Aksant Academic Publishers.

17 SORCERY AFTER SOCIALISM

Liberalization and Antiwitchcraft Practices in Southern Tanzania

MAIA GREEN

In his introduction to the *Anthropology of Evil*, published some thirty years ago, David Parkin calls for an approach to the social manifestation of evil that extends beyond a narrow focus on witchcraft. If evil is perceived more broadly, as a range of actions that are associated with causing human harm, the categorization can include diverse instantiations of the phenomenon. Moreover, as a classification that is inherently relational, involving the imputation of responsibility to someone or something, the analysis of evil takes us into concerns with wider issues of cosmology and ontology. What is the universe of human and extra human action in which harm can be caused, and to what extent are persons morally culpable? Is evil a capacity of all people? Is it intentional? Or is evil an effect of agents external to the human world? (Parkin 1985a).

The essays in that volume raise important questions about the category of evil and its relation to social orderings. But, in claiming that cosmological orders establish the conditions for the attribution of evil within social relations such accounts occlude the processes and the strategies of actors through which cosmologies of evil come to have social traction. The limitation of this perspective extends beyond this particular work. Arguably, the tendency to approach the study of evil and related phenomena in cosmological terms is constitutive of "normal" anthropology, that is, an anthropology which has, since the pioneering work of Evans-Pritchard (1937), sought to apprehend witchcraft either in terms of its capacity to explain the workings of the world or to articulate structural conflicts. Anthropologists have been far less concerned to explore how ideas about witchcraft and the practices that sustain them enact the social worlds they are assumed to offer a commentary upon (Strathern 1985; Ashforth 2005; Ciekawy 1998). Anthropological accounts of the phenomenon of witchcraft have tended to focus on witchcraft as a framework for symbolic action and hence as a text to be interpreted (Moore and Saunders 2002), or as a vehicle for the articulation of tensions within social orders and hence as a modality for the restoration of order rather than its creation. Such accounts shed light on the significance of witchcraft discourses in various parts of the world, and they clearly articulate various rationalities of witchcraft. While these may indeed be, in Evans-Pritchard's memorable phrase, "imprisoned in action" (1937, 83), such approaches are less able to convincingly explain how such rationalities come to be enacted (Kapferer 1997; Shaw 1997). Through what relational milieus can witchcraft be established as rational? Under what conditions can the "facts" of witchcraft survive (Latour 1987, 251)? What constellations of institutions, power relations, and persons enable the realization of cosmologies of evil in some places and not in others (van Beek 2007)? Through what strategies, and of which actors, is the agentive capacity of evil established? What kinds of institutional infrastructure creates the possibilities for evil to assume capacities for agency in social practice? To what extent can an "occult economy" be brought into existence (Comaroff and Comaroff 1999) unless promoted through the web of transactions and relations that compose a very real "economy of the occult"?

Looking at the phenomenon of witchcraft in various settings, it is clear that the social impacts of ideas about witchcraft do not derive from the power of cosmological notions. As Mary Douglas (1991) has argued, notions of evil are less significant in practice than how people respond to the suffering it is claimed to cause and under what conditions attributions of responsibility lead to some form of restitutive action. While concepts of evil certainly provide an axis against which one's performance as a social being can be subject to moral evaluation (Parkin 1985c, 2), the possibilities for this evaluation to become actionable are highly variable. Not every situation in which there is a strong cosmology of witchcraft results in either the identification of specific humans with witchcraft powers or in some form of action against them. Such actions are usually punitive, ranging from beating and expulsions to killing, or cleansing, in which the polluted nature of the witch is ritually addressed (Douglas 1963; Green 2005). In order for evil to become actionable, it has to be institutionally supported. Social actors must make informed choices about appropriate recourse to such institutions. This essay explores the relationship between human agency and actionable evil in relation to the changing institutional infrastructure that supports the perpetuation of actions against witches in the Ulanga District, Southern Tanzania. Although a range of institutions, not least a large and dynamic traditional healing sector whose members routinely diagnose witchcraft attacks, contribute to creating situations in which acting against witches comes to be a legitimate option in response to the harm witches are believed to cause, taking action against witches requires a level of public support for an action to be perceived as justifiable. This depends, in turn, on the implicit and explicit evaluation of a person's moral capacities based on their public behavior, that is, on their performance of personhood. It also involves the appropriate performance strategies of witchcraft victims in enacting plausible victimhood, with or without recourse to retaliatory action.

The significance of performance in relation to witchcraft struck me with particular intensity when I had returned to my original field site in Southern Tanzania for an extended stay more than twenty years after my first fieldwork. I found myself self-consciously performing relations of obligation within a web of ongoing disputes in which friends were entangled, and which had the potential to escalate into accusations of witchcraft or to subside, depending on how people behaved. Becoming "caught" up in two such sets of relations over a six-month period prompted my critical reflection on moral behavior and on the importance of agency in the social articulation of witchcraft.[1] It also highlighted significant transformations since the early 1990s in the constitution of the relation between ideas about witchcraft and the public identification of witches. Witchcraft in Southern Tanzania continues to prompt action on the part of those who feel that they or their close associates are victims, usually through visiting a diviner in order to get confirmation of suspicions about the identity of a witch. However, what was previously described as "catching" witches (Green 1994) is no longer a frequent occurrence. Catching witches amounted to a form of public accusation and consisted of touching the head of a suspected witch with coins signifying the fee charged by antiwitchcraft specialists for a cleansing ritual known as "shaving witchcraft" (kunyoa uchawi). Although people suspected of witchcraft are less likely to be accused now than in the past, they, along with their accusers, continue to seek the services of antiwitchcraft specialists and shaving remains the standard means of dealing with suspected witches. Going to be shaved is now presented as the outcome of a consensual arrangement between individuals rather than as a result of being "caught" and thus as a matter of personal choice. As witchcraft is reframed as less an issue of public order than as a private dispute, action against alleged witchcraft is becoming more of a private matter. Public consensus around the credibility of an allegation does not inevitably result in public action against the suspected witch. Individuals take action against witchcraft by going to diviners in order to confirm the identities of purported witches, by seeking protective medicines, and by altering their own behavior toward the suspected witch. They do not necessarily take action against "identified" witches.

ACTION AGAINST WITCHES IN ULANGA

During my initial fieldwork in the early 1990s, witchcraft was an everyday concern and the topic of frequent conversations. It was also highly likely to lead to
accusations that could end in alleged witches being taken, often against their
will, to an antiwitchcraft specialist for shaving (Green 1994, 1997). Allegations
of witchcraft did not result in violent expulsions or beatings as they would have
in other parts of Tanzania.[2] The predominantly agricultural community of
small farmers with limited assets in the form of livestock or land maintained
open-ended and malleable networks of relationships that depended on the
proper performance of kinship rather than ascriptive status. Stakes in witchcraft-related conflicts were significant in that relationships could be affected,
but they did not determine access to assets. The particular relations between
persons and property, along with the essential malleability and recoverability
of kinship, doubtless contributed to the creation of an environment in which
alleged witchcraft could be addressed through purification rituals rather than
violent exclusion.[3]

Established antiwitchcraft practice in Ulanga, and indeed in Southern
Tanzania more generally, centers on a package of purification rites and the administration of special medicine that suppresses the "powers" of witches. These
rituals involve shaving off the head hair and, less frequently, the body hair, of
suspected witches. Consequently, shaving was, and is, a widespread euphemism
for witchcraft suppression practices. The ritual of being "shaved" *kunyolewa* is
not restricted to alleged witches. Part of its mass appeal is that being shaved
not only disempowers persons with witchcraft powers, it protects other people
from future supposed witchcraft attacks. Where antiwitchcraft specialists operate from their homesteads, those accused of witchcraft frequently travel with
their accusers, and all participate in the shaving ritual that culminates in eating
a meal together. From the beginning of the twentieth century to around the
mid-1970s, it was usual practice for witchcraft suppression specialists to visit
villages where the logic of treating witches and accusers together justified the
mass shaving of all villagers.

Witchcraft in the late 1980s and the early 1990s was talked about as a
malevolent force experienced through the actions of persons whose access to
powerful medicines transformed them into witches. Although this transformation could be literal in that witches could, on occasion, assume nonhuman
form, alleged witches themselves were not inhuman. They were merely people
whose excessive greed drove their need to consume the very life force of other
people. Witches, as persons empowered through medicines, were supposed to

be humans transformed through excessively human appetites, a transformation that, though intentional, could be reversed through shaving (Green 1996). That suspicion, which led to accusations that led in turn to taking witches for shaving, was enabled by the institutional conjuncture of the time, in which a single antiwitchcraft specialist, an elderly woman known as Bibi Kalembwana, had come to monopolize the provision of antiwitchcraft services throughout much of South Western Tanzania. Kalembwana's monopoly was an artifact of the system of village governance under socialism in which village authorities, consisting of elected villagers who were also holders of authority within the local branches of the ruling party, CCM (*Chama Cha Mapinduzi*, Party of the Revolution), were responsible for dispute settlement in villages as well as granting villagers permission to travel beyond district borders (Green 1997).

As being shaved acquired widespread legitimacy, from around the mid-1980s, among party officials and village residents alike as a means of dealing with witchcraft, it became the usual institutional response to situations in which conflict between kin and neighbors was articulated in terms of allegations of witchcraft. Shaving assumed its unique status as the default response to witchcraft allegations despite, or perhaps because of, the ambiguous quality of the law that made both the practice of witchcraft and the identification of witches illegal, but that did not prohibit activities oriented toward suppressing the powers of witches, as long as witches were not identified during this process. Diviners managed to evade the law by confirming clients' suspicions of witchcraft without explicitly identifying the witch. Shavers of witchcraft ensured that their practices were not directed solely against witches and that participating in antiwitchcraft practices had wider benefits, including protecting people against future witchcraft attacks.

Laws against witchcraft in the 1980s and 1990s were derived directly from colonial legislation, notably the witchcraft ordinance of 1928 (Mesaki 2009). As elsewhere in Africa, at different times, implementation was limited. This was partly an effect of the limitations of a legal instrument in dealing with the intangible in the domain of the unknowable (Fisiyi 1998; Fisiyi and Geschiere 1990) and partly because successive postcolonial administrations took witchcraft for granted as a national cultural institution (Mesaki 2009). While the acceptability of shaving was certainly accentuated by the close political associations between officials of the ruling party in the district, some of whom were close relatives of Kalembwana, two components of her practice enhanced its widespread acceptability. Accusers and accused were shaved together. At no point was any distinction made between those accused of witchcraft and their accusers. Everyone who had been treated by Kalembwana received a numbered certificate to confirm that they had been shaved and hence had their powers of witchcraft suppressed though the ingestion of her unique antiwitchcraft medicines. The shaving, medicine, and certification were held to be an indication of the effectiveness of treatment in the longer term. Any person who had been subjected to shaving could no longer practice witchcraft. If any such person so much as tried to return to their medicines, death would inevitably follow (Green 1994, 1997).

The situation in 2012 displays continuities and change. Witchcraft remains an everyday topic of conversation and gossip that comes to the fore in the immediate aftermath of deaths and during the funeral process. Antiwitchcraft specialists continue to operate in Ulanga District and in neighboring Kilombero. Two of the best known are the grandson and great grandson of Kalembwana herself. Operating under their deceased relative's name each provides a fast and efficient two-day treatment for witches and their accusers at their respective homesteads in each district some eighty miles apart. Village governments are no longer directly involved in witchcraft disputes. If they involve the police in village witchcraft disputes, this is now to protect rather than capture alleged witches who refuse to go voluntarily for shaving. This important change was already in process during the early years of the twenty-first century, not so much due to any alteration in the law on witchcraft, which, though amended, remains essentially the same as its colonial antecedents, but due to the increased emphasis on the human rights of individual citizens that came to prominence as part of the liberalization agenda (Mesaki 2009). Within this discursive frame, individualism and human rights come to stand in for aspirational modernity, the kind of modernity that is presented as antithetical to traditionalism and the backward culture of villagers.

Whereas under socialism, and to an extent under the modernizing colonial regimes of the British administration after the 1940s, support was given to antiwitchcraft specialists as a means of gaining mass compliance from rural populations for collective development endeavors (Green 1997), self-consciously modernist state officials are strongly committed to the rights of the individual, especially where those who resist going for shaving may well, through their class affiliation, share those same commitments to modernism. In the 1990s Kalembwana's claim that by shaving witchcraft, she was providing a service to the development and hence the modernization of the country was supported by local government officials (Green 1994, 1997). Today, officials supportive of antiwitchcraft practices are minded to view shaving as a useful service that helps individuals solve disputes about witchcraft rather than as an instrument in the national development endeavor (Green and Mesaki 2005; Green 2005).

These changes have implications for the numbers of people currently going for shaving. From what I observed on brief visits to the homesteads of these two antiwitchcraft practitioners, the number of clients on an average day is now in the tens rather than hundreds who would have crammed into the thatched shelters built to receive them in the 1990s.[4]

Taking action against alleged witches in the form of catching them for shaving seems to be far less important now than in the 1990s, and the same is true of formal accusations. Seeking the services of diviners to confirm suspicions of witchcraft is commonplace. Whether these suspicions can be acted upon is now more complicated than it was previously as police and state officials protect the rights of alleged witches not to be taken for shaving. Strategies for dealing with suspicion may not necessitate immediate action but may become part of a longer term renegotiation of relationships involving the suspected witch. Individual behaviors are closely monitored for the performance of appropriate morality, especially during funerals or when relatives fall sick. Although ideas about witchcraft play an important role in the management of kinship as a set of public obligations, and the threats posed by witches are ever present, dealing with witches is becoming a more private affair, the focus of conversations within families and visits to diviners rather than public actions. Individuals must continue to deal with witchcraft through protecting themselves from witches' powers, knowing who witches are and acting accordingly, and ensuring that their own behavior does not render them liable to being caught (Favret Saada 1980) in the discourse of witchcraft.

MAMA K'S STORY

That these transformations are in process was suggested by two ongoing workings out of witchcraft within kinship relations that I came to be aware of during my recent visit. Because the person suspected of witchcraft each case was a person with whom I am closely associated, and because these situations are ongoing, my own behavior was potentially implicated in how these cases would develop. This is not because I, as a British foreigner, would be thought capable of practicing witchcraft, which is strongly considered to be a characteristic of people from Africa and Asia, but because my relationship with individuals who were viewed suspiciously could be taken to be benefitting them in some way and hence contribute to their potential accusers' sense of grievance. The first case is straightforward and highlights some key themes in the way that suspicions of witchcraft are frequently not acted upon. A healer lives with his two wives to whom he has been married for over thirty years. I have known all of them for over twenty. All are frail and elderly. The wife who is slightly younger, whom I shall call "Mama K," suffers from a persistent problem with her foot that refuses to heal. Her husband, meanwhile, became afflicted in the space of three months by one serious medical problem after another. Malaria, brucellosis, and a mild stroke cause progressive impairment. The older wife suffers from chronic problems caused by thyroid imbalance and blood pressure. Because all the adult children live elsewhere, the family struggles to clear land and plant for the next season. As the healer gets sicker, he is less able to meet the needs of clients, who begin to fall away. As both women depend on his work for cash income, life becomes progressively more difficult. Trips to hospital in the town are a two-hour walk one way.

Mama K reflects on the situation in relation to her own health, that of her husband, and their diminishing quality of life. After returning from the hospital, she confided in a mutual friend who lives in the town that her cowife has always been jealous of her and is definitely practicing witchcraft. This friend is a man from another part of the district and another ethnic group that has no kinship relation with the healer's family. The younger wife suspects witchcraft but, in telling this outsider, accepts that it cannot be acted upon. Not only is the outsider not in a position to take action of this sort, to assume responsibility for the victim and accompany her to a diviner, for example, but she also knows that her suspicions would not be considered plausible if made public. The other wife is held to be an extremely good and caring person, a person who, though she has not had a child herself, has cared for the children of others. She attends funerals, is a good neighbor, and demonstrates warmth toward her husband and toward his other wife. People say of her that "she has no badness." Nor are there instances in popular gossip that could be invoked to cast doubt on her behavior. She is, people say, "just a good person."

Shortly after Mama K reveals her suspicions about the senior wife, a close neighbor of the healer, another healer, falls ill. An elderly man with a history of chronic drinking, his swollen joints could be attributable to any number of conditions. He is confined to bed, unable to walk more than a few paces. As his illness intensified, so did my own sense of unease that something or someone would be held responsible for this situation. These healers have a long history of competition and conflict. If I am seen to support one family above the other, I could be seen to be abetting someone's malicious intentions. I ensure that I make equal contributions toward their treatment and that these are known publicly. After I leave the district, my friends will ensure that when they visit the first healer to check on him they will also pay a visit to the homestead of the other.

THOMAS AND HIS UNCLES

The second story is contemporary to that of Mama K. It involves a younger relative of the first healer, whom I shall call "Thomas." Thomas is now in his forties. I have known him for twenty years, and we often visit the old healers together. Thomas lives in a house built by his late mother who died in 2001. Like many women in this part of Tanzania (Green 1999), Thomas's mother had several children by different men to whom she was not married. She built her house in a village center on land allocated to her by her mother's father. This village is near to the expanding margins of the district capital and land is under pressure for building as well as farming. Thomas's mother had several brothers and sisters, real and classificatory, including those related through her mother's sisters, most of whom had spent their lives in other parts of the country. When I was doing fieldwork in the 1990s, I rented a house belonging to Thomas's grandmother's sister who was, at that time, living in Dar es Salaam. The owner of the house eventually came back to the village and after her death one of her sons who had recently retired came to occupy the house. This house is directly opposite Thomas's house, on a plot of land increasingly encroached by adjacent plots in what has become a fast growing peri-urban settlement.

The retired son had a wife and seven adult children, two of whom lived at home. He had an older brother living in a town to the north and a younger brother living in Dar es Salaam. All three brothers were close and saw each other regularly. Last year, the brothers organized a family occasion to remember their dead mother and to rebuild the collapsed masonry of their father's grave in the same part of the Catholic cemetery. Such grave mendings and sweepings are an important part of annual *sadaka* to remember the dead (Green 2003). Occasions for eating and drinking locally brewed beer and for reading masses in church for Catholic families, they are also occasions when family conflicts rise to the surface. The brothers assessed what they perceived to be their shrinking plot in a growing village and suggested to Thomas that in fact his mother's house was rightfully theirs because the land the house was on had been the property of their grandfather and siblings should have priority in matters of inheritance. They even went to the land committee of the village government over the dispute. Fortunately, Thomas, anticipating problems, had obtained certification of the boundaries of his holding. The disappointed brothers had to abandon formal pursuit of their claim. They stopped talking to Thomas and his family and no greetings were exchanged between their wives. The *sadaka* over, the brothers returned to their homes.

Shortly after this, soon after I arrived in the village, the middle brother who lived opposite Thomas became unwell. Because the two households were not speaking, we were not aware how ill he had become, but once his condition worsened, we called in to express concern. We did this because we were concerned for his health and believed him to be at risk. We were also aware that not demonstrating concern would have left Thomas vulnerable to being complicit in any negative outcome, a possibility that increased as time went on. The sick man's condition deteriorated rapidly over the space of two or three days. Meanwhile, the oldest brother had come back to the village to finalize the work on rebuilding the headstone. Thomas and I called out for permission to enter (*piga hodi*) the house and were welcomed inside. As we entered the main room, we found the ill man sitting hunched in a chair, pale and breathless, in the company of his wife and older brother. He had been to the mission dispensary but was evidently in need of hospital care. It transpired that his wife had not taken him to hospital as he became sicker because she did not have enough money. The older brother had not suggested this as a course of action, nor had he offered to pay. In the view of the oldest brother, the younger brother was doing fine and probably just needed to have his "blood checked" (*pima damu*), a phrase that covers a range of investigative procedures, in the dispensary. Thomas and I looked at the sick man and at the older brother sitting calmly across from him and the worried wife, waiting for the decisions and financial contributions of other people, and we decided to take action. I asked, "If you had money to go to hospital would you go there? Or would you just go and have your blood tested at the mission?" He rose unsteadily to his feet. "I feel really ill and I am being sick now. I can't eat and I am dizzy when I stand up. I want to go to hospital."

We did a quick calculation of how much cash was needed to get him from the village to admission, including the fare for a *bodaboda* (motorbike taxi) and money for the inpatients' fee, which is known as *kitanda* (bed). I handed the notes to the wife while Thomas used his phone to call a *bodaboda* driver. The last time we saw the sick man alive, he was seated between his wife and the driver on a small red motorcycle heading for the hospital in the district center. He was admitted on a Sunday afternoon, was discharged later that evening, was readmitted on Monday, and was dead by Tuesday. In the immediate aftermath of the death, the family had to organize the funeral, which took place three days later.[5] The dead man's children came from other parts of Tanzania and his younger brother set out from Dar es Salaam, arriving a day later. The death was a serious enough event for animosities between the households to be temporarily suspended. Thomas and his family were fully involved in the organization of the funeral. Thomas's wife helped the other women prepare food, and she sat with other women mourners inside the house with the widow. On the day of the burial, Thomas and his wife acted as full participants in the events, performing the proper roles of related mourners in support of the lead mourners who were the son and wife of the deceased.

Once the body was buried, there was talk from the widow's side of the urgent need to call a family meeting (*kikao*). The issue of land was now deemed unresolved. This mattered to the dead man's brothers because as he had inherited from his mother, there was "no house for the widow." What they were trying to do was to make a claim to property based on the inheritance rights of brothers, using the argument that the deceased brother had not built his own homestead that could then become the legitimate property of the dead man's children and thus that the widow would have had rights to make use of. The widow, whose position was now threatened by the possible loss of the house to her husband's brothers, had very different concerns. She was convinced that her husband had become sick and died, in a matter of days because of witchcraft. Looking to those whom she believed had reason to feel bitterness (*uchungu*) toward her she initially suspected that Thomas had some responsibility for this. At the same time, in the fortnight after the burial, her elder daughter who had returned home for the mourning period began to see visions of her dead father walking with his elder brother in the town. These visions were significant because the young woman was claiming to have seen a person who was actually dead. The elder brother had already returned to his home city. During this period of extreme uncertainty in the first few weeks after the funeral, several members of the dead man's family sought the services of a number of diviners in adjacent villages to explore further the question of culpability. Thomas's wife also went to a diviner.

A couple of months after the funeral, the older brother visited the village once again to check on the progress of a house he had started to build. His presence now made the proposed family meeting seem practicable. A date was set, but it was far from clear what the outcome would be or whether suspicions would be voiced formally. In the few months since the end of the funeral, the framework of culpability had shifted. Thomas had widespread support in the village. He was a respected member of village government and was generally liked. He was perceived to be kind and generous, as was his wife. They were seen to be the kind of people who always take part in funerals, an idiom of cooperation, and help out neighbors and relatives. Thomas's late mother, a nurse, is well remembered as having been an extremely moral person, the kind of person who helped neighbors out with food and medicine; a person who demonstrated through her actions core gendered values of empathy (*huruma*) and love (*upendo*). Despite the attempt by the dead man and his brothers to stake a claim to the house of his late mother, Thomas and his wife had behaved in an exemplary fashion. Rather than escalate the dispute, they had calmly sought involvement of the village land authorities to clarify the ownership of the plot and the boundaries of each person's property. They had helped out and made financial contributions at the funeral. And, in the presence of the older brother who made no contribution, Thomas and I had paid the dead man's hospital expenses.

The dead man and his wife, in contrast, had a history of getting into conflicts with neighbors. They had both been shaved of suspected witchcraft only a year before. The funeral service was taken by a catechist not an ordained priest, because going for shaving results in, as it had during the 1980s, a range of time-bound sanctions against Catholics, including not being able to have a priest officiate at one's funeral. Suspecting Thomas of witchcraft was possible privately, but a public allegation was implausible. Although Thomas's behavior did not seem to support the kind of behavior associated with a witch, someone else's behavior did. The older brother of the dead man was not widely respected in the village where he had not lived since he was very young. He now lived in a city to the north of the country where he was reputed to have several businesses, including a passenger bus. His commitment to the home place was considered to be questionable. He was known to have built a large house where he now lived and had only just started to build a house in his home village. Various stories circulated about the source of his supposed wealth, including allowing one of his children to die in order to augment his own riches through witchcraft. In actuality, this man was a retired public servant who had both business acumen and a lump sum from his pension. Accustomed to emerging urban middle-class norms of comfort and autonomy, it is perhaps understandable that he chose to stay in a guest house in the town rather than the crowded house of his brother. His choice was the newest and most luxurious guest house in the vicinity, aimed at visiting senior officials and wealthy traders, a place of gleaming tiles, full glass windows, self-contained rooms, and electricity. His decision to spend his money at the most expensive lodging in the town at which a single night's accommodation cost three times the daily rate paid to casual laborers added to widespread doubts about his motivation, suggesting a level of decadence that was unacceptable, especially when his relatives considered that their need for support was greater. In addition, paying for a room in the guest house made an explicit moral statement about his preference for the individualized commercial space of the guest house to staying with his family. Staying "at home" does not generate this same issue. Most damaging of all, his decision to stay at the guest house during the funeral before the burial of the body when people, including those who are not related, customarily sleep at the house of the funeral, and men sleep outside, was thought to be shocking, especially so since the dead man was a brother of the closest possible kind, related through the same father and mother.

Talk in the village and that on the periphery of the dead man's family shifted toward a consideration of the potential culpability of the deceased's older brother. His habits and wealth, his disengagement from the obligations of kinship, and his apparent reluctance to contribute to sending his brother to hospital were all cited. Choosing personal wealth over kinship values is a characteristic associated with witches in many countries in Africa, as is not participating properly in funerals. Among Pogoro communities in Ulanga, participating in funerals is a signifier of cooperation and moral personhood. Poor behavior or nonattendance at funerals both indicate witch identity. Even his physical appearance was discussed, especially a hand deformity. The hand further shifted him into a potential category of "witch other" (Ciekawy 1998). Furthermore, evidently using a capacity only associated with witches, he had been seen by the dead man's daughter in the company of the dead person and in one place when he was known to far away in another. The widow was now in an impossible position. Her private suspicion could not be made publicly effective and public opinion, including that within her own family as suggested by the daughter's vision, pointed to a direction that was problematic in that it would intensify her own vulnerability. As a widow, she was solely dependent on her adult children. She thus needed the support of her dead husband's brothers. A public accusation of her brother-in-law might be popularly supported, but if he denied the allegation or refused to go for shaving and the formal reconciliation it implies, the result would be the ending of the relationship, and hence obligation, between them. Fortunately for all involved, the brother returned to his home before the family meeting.

THE CHANGING CONTEXT OF WITCHCRAFT

These two instances, which are at the time of writing ongoing, present a snapshot of how institutions and practices related to witchcraft are changing and how ideas about witchcraft become actionable in these changed times. In the first example, the woman who believes she is a victim of witchcraft is unable to act upon it without the support of her husband and a wider constellation of kin and neighbors who could render the allegation credible. Not only does the senior wife, whom she suspects, publicly display qualities antithetical to those associated with witches, this cowife also has a reputation for acting in ways that demonstrate kindness, lack of selfishness, and generosity. A formal accusation of witchcraft would tear apart the household, which is already strained and at risk of dissolution, when the old man dies. In this instance, suffering is attributable but it cannot be attributed. The woman can take action to protect herself through medicines, and she can seek affirmation from other healers, but she cannot take action against the suspected witch.

In the second example, an older woman suspects her dead husband's relatives of witchcraft. Her suspicions gradually shift from her husband's classificatory nephew to her husband's elder brother. The nephew has widespread support from kin and neighbors and a reputation for helping other villagers. His characteristics are far removed from those associated with witches. Despite this, a plausible allegation could have been made because witches are ultimately unknowable and capable of anything. As things worked out, suspicion settled, at least for a time, on the husband's elder brother. Not only did the older brother not contribute toward the hospital expenses when his brother was very ill, but he also spent all his money on rebuilding their father's grave and on his own construction project. Furthermore, before the brother died and during the funeral, he refused to stay at the family home, an affront to kinship at the best of times but an unacceptable display of antisocial behavior during the funeral process when men and women, even if they are not close kin, sleep at the homestead of the dead person. Finally, although the widow who believes her dead husband was the victim of witchcraft takes individual action against witchcraft by going to a diviner, she initiates no action against the witch. Suspicion of witchcraft and the experience of victimhood do not become the grounds for public action but remain, for the time being, a matter for the immediate family.

These examples are probably not untypical of the ways in which the institution of witchcraft is manifested in Ulanga District in the present. While ideas about witches are very similar to those expressed in the early 1990s and the cosmology of witchcraft is fundamentally unchanged, the assemblage of institutions and relations through which witchcraft comes to operate as "evil" in the sense defined by Parkin (1985c, 6–10), that is as a modality through which suffering is relationally attributable, is changing. Let us start with ideas about witches. Witches are associated, as they have been throughout the twentieth century, with notions of selfishness and greed, with excessive animalistic humanity. Embodying the inversion of normal human attributes, they do their work at night, walk upside down, fly, and are visible only to each other. More mundane witchcraft practices involve the use of powerful substances categorized as medicines (*dawa*), which either enhance the powers of witches or their victims' vulnerability. Witchcraft as an attribute of people is considered not unnatural. As an attribute of unrestrained human nature, virtually anybody can succumb to witchcraft leanings and access the powers of witchcraft through medicine. Accusation is thus always a possibility. So is deactivating the powers of witches equally through rituals of purification and powerful antiwitchcraft medicines.

Until the mid-twentieth century, deactivating the powers of witches was mostly in the hands of diviners of territorial shrines (*wambui*), but it was gradually assumed by peripatetic witchcraft suppression specialists, some of whom, such as Chikanga (Redmayne 1970) and Nguvumali (Swantz 1990) became very famous across large parts of the country (Willis 1968). These kinds of specialists were frequently called into villages by headmen and colonial authorities to address popular demands for witchcraft suppression services (Larson 1976a, 1976b), and not only in Tanzania (Richards 1935). Villagization in the 1970s put an end to mobile antiwitchcraft specialists who were prevented by the authorities from visiting newly established villages. Villagers now went in search of antiwitchcraft services, provided by Kalembwana and others, at single points, often in response to instructions from village authorities (Green 1994, 1997). This relationship between a single specialist and the party hierarchy in the 1980s, which advocated that those suspected of witchcraft were taken by their captors for shaving, led to the consolidation of Kalembwana's monopoly across much of Ulanga and neighboring Kilombero. The move toward dealing with witches as the work of antiwitchcraft practitioners rather than shrine diviners was significant in reorganizing the region's vibrant economy of the occult. It imposed a break between the attribution of responsibility for witchcraft through identification of the witch and what was sanctioned as public actions against them.[6] Individuals and wider groups of kin could ask healers with divination skills and diviners of territorial shrines to identify the witch or confirm their suspicions of witchcraft. The outcome of divination had no immediate impact on whether the witch would be formally accused and taken for shaving. Then, as now, people often sought the opinions of several diviners, not all of whom were in agreement.

Political liberalization during the 1990s had significant impacts on the management of witchcraft. The formal end of the single party system, democratization, and new roles of civil society introduced human rights discourses and market liberalization, innovations that provided the vehicles through which the ruling party retained its hold on power. An important effect of liberalization was an ending of the political role of villages as units of production to be managed by the state. Political and economic liberal trends legitimized a greater freedom for villagers, including freedom of movement, and the decreased role of political cadres in the administration of justice. Village authorities no longer sent people for shaving, although they could and did, encourage individuals to be shaved as a means to end a dispute. Those who resisted being sent for shaving now found themselves supported by the police and courts. Consequently, those willing to go for shaving found their decision reconfigured as an act of consent or even choice. Perhaps the majority of individuals involved in witchcraft disputes in Ulanga's villages do consent to go for shaving. Consenting to shaving is an indication that one is a good neighbor and that one wishes to be perceived as such. Being shaved is not an admission of guilt, and only a witch has anything to lose from the process.

This contextual restructuring of shaving as choice was matched by a reorganization of the delivery of antiwitchcraft services associated with Bibi Kalembwana under her grandson, Shaibu Magungu, from around 2002. In the years after Kalembwana's death, Magungu continued to shave witchcraft, using the same techniques and ritual structure, but he shifted the location of his practice from what was then the remote village of Ihowanja, previously only accessible on foot, to Mkasu, near Kiberege, a station on the TAZARA railway line and some forty miles from the national Tanzam highway.[7] Aware that his business now depended on people coming voluntarily for shaving, Magungu transformed his practice in other ways. By ending the requirement that those coming for shaving had to work on his fields as they had for Kalembwana, he radically cut the time clients had to stay at his homestead for shaving, from around a week to two or three days. Finally, he encouraged his son to open a branch at Mwaya, in the far south side of Ulanga District, so as to provide convenient, easy-to-reach services for those living in the immediate locality (Green and Mesaki 2005). This break between action against witchcraft and action against witches was consolidated through the effective monopolization of antiwitchcraft services by Bibi Kalembwana. Once these were effectively liberalized through contingent changes in the organization of antiwitchcraft services and new forms of state regulation, the architecture supporting the institutionalization of witchcraft was altered. Of these, by far the most significant was the recasting of dealing with witches as an act of individual choice, through protecting those refusing shaving, on the one hand, and by the local level state's disengagement from officially sanctioning antiwitchcraft practices, on the other. Witchcraft as cosmology can be sustained through experience of victimhood confirmed by divination, but action against witches becomes dissociated from formal institutions and thus requires greater public support.

Establishing credibility for any accusation is extremely important. As a result, the performative strategies of alleged victims and those they seek to accuse come under intense scrutiny.

CATCHING WITCHES IN RELATIONS

In present-day Ulanga District, imagined witchcraft remains an important agent of suffering and individuals continue to be suspected of witchcraft. Despite continuities in the constitution of evil, the institutional matrix through which it becomes actionable is changing. A flourishing network of diviners and healers work to identify witches and provide medicines to address the harm caused by a supposed witchcraft attack. While witchcraft remains central to the constitution of personal relations, its relation to wider political orders has been rendered peripheral through changes in the relation between state authority and antiwitchcraft specialists and in the role of village authorities in witchcraft disputes. Political liberalization has altered the relations through which village authorities engage with village residents and with state structures. Economic liberalization has provided a new model for the organization of antiwitchcraft services, recourse to which are represented, within the new discourse about rights and citizenship, as ultimately a matter of individual choice. In practice, although disputes about witchcraft have become increasingly personalized as a matter for individuals and their immediate families, acting against supposed witches involves making this experience of being a victim of witchcraft public. In the absence of supporting institutional sanctions for the public identification and capture of alleged witches, those acting for victims can no longer rely on the intervention of public authorities but must strive to capture those they suspect within particular relations that increase the possibility that they will consent to shaving. Relational capture depends on the web of popular opinion giving credence to an accusation and on the suspected witch's own perception that the quality of their relationships will be further compromised should they resist dealing publicly with their alleged witchcraft. Agentive performative strategies of victimhood and moral integrity come to have increasing prominence as part of the new ways in which witchcraft as an assault on the private person is made into a matter if not of public action then of public concern.

NOTES

1. Favret Sadaa (1980) speaks of witchcraft as existing in discourse in which interlocutors, witch and bewitched alike, become caught.

2. For accounts of practices against witches elsewhere in Tanzania, see Bryceson et al. (2010) and Mesaki (1994).

3. See Willis for a related argument regarding the "fuzziness" of social categories in Fipa society (1985).

4. I visited Magungu's practice at Mkasu several times between February and July 2012 and his son, Sadat's, practice at Mwaya in May. The low numbers of shaving clients could also be explained by the season. Most clients seek shaving, which involves a stay of two or three days, during the dry season after the harvest. Magungu claims that his client numbers increase substantially in August and September.

5. Until recently the funeral would have taken place perhaps a day or at the most two days after a death. The introduction in 2011 of a modern mortuary with refrigeration at the district hospital enables families to defer burials until they are ready.

6. This break is always potentially present, thus Parkin argues that dealing with the pollution of witchcraft is logically and often institutionally separable from dealing with the relationships requiring reordering after witchcraft through sanctions, compensation, or restitution (1985b, 240).

7. In 2010, a road was constructed from Malinyi, a trading center, and Ihowanja is now accessible by bus from Ifakara.

REFERENCES

Ashforth, Adam. 2005. *Witchcraft, Violence and Democracy in South Africa.* Chicago: University of Chicago Press.

Bryceson, Deborah, Jesper Jønsson, and Richard Sherrington. 2010. "Miners' Magic: Artisanal Mining, the Albino Fetish and Murder in Tanzania." *Journal of Modern African Studies* 48, no. 3:353–382.

Ciekawy, Diane. 1998. "Witchcraft and Statecraft: Five Technologies of Power in Colonial and Postcolonial Kenya." *African Studies Review* 41, no. 3:119–141.

Comaroff, John, and Comaroff Jean. L. 1999. "Occult Economies and the Violence of Abstraction: Notes from the South African Postcolony." *American Ethnologist* 26, no. 2:279–301.

Douglas, Mary. 1963. "Techniques of Sorcery Control in Central Africa." In *Witchcraft and Sorcery in East Africa,* edited by John Middleton and Edward Winter, 123–142. London: Routledge and Kegan Paul.

———. 1991. "Witchcraft and Leprosy: Two Strategies of Exclusion." *Man* (NS) 26, no. 4: 723–736.

Evans-Pritchard, Edward E. 1937. *Witchcraft Oracles and Magic among the Azande.* Oxford: Clarendon Press.

Favret Saada, Jeanne. 1980. *Deadly Words. Witchcraft in the Bocage.* Cambridge, Cambridge University Press.

Fisiyi, Cyprian. 1998. "Containing Occult Practices: Witchcraft Trails in Cameroon." *African Studies Review* 41, no. 3:143–165.

Fisiyi, Cyprian, and Peter Geschiere. 1990. "Judges and Witches, or How Is the State to Deal with Witchcraft." *Cahiers d' Etudes Africaines* 118, no. 30:135–156.

Green, Maia. 1994. "Shaving Witchcraft in Ulanga, *Kunyolewa* and the Catholic Church." In *Witchcraft in Contemporary Tanzania,* edited by Ray G. Abrahams, 23–45. Cambridge: African Studies Centre.

———. 1996. "Medicines and the Embodiment of Substances among Pogoro Catholics, Southern Tanzania." *Journal of the Royal Anthropological Institute* (NS) 2, no. 3:485–498.

———. 1997. "Witchcraft Suppression Practices and Movements: Public Politics and the Logic of Purification." *Comparative Studies in Society and History* 39, no. 3: 319–345.

———. 1999. "Overcoming the Absent Father: Procreation Theories and Practical Kinship in Southern Tanzania." In *Conceiving Persons: Ethnographies of Procreation, Fertility and Growth,* edited by Peter Loizos and Patrick Heady, 47–67. London: Athlone.

———. 2003. *Priests, Witches and Power.* Cambridge: Cambridge University Press.

———. 2005. "A Discourse on Inequality: Poverty, Public Bads and Entrenching Witchcraft in Post Adjustment Tanzania." *Anthropological Theory* 5, no. 3:247–266.

Green, Maia, and Simeon Mesaki. 2005. "'The Birth of the Salon': Poverty, Modernisation and Dealing with Witchcraft in Southern Tanzania." *American Ethnologist* 32, no. 3:371–388.

Kapferer, Bruno. 1997. *The Feast of the Sorcerer. Practices of Consciousness and Power.* Chicago: University of Chicago Press.

Larson, Lorne E. 1976a. "A History of the Mahenge (Ulanga) District." PhD thesis, University of Dar es Salaam.

———. 1976b. "Problems in the Study of Witchcraft Eradication Movements in Southern Tanzania." *Ufahamu* 6, no. 3:88–100.

Latour, Bruno. 1987. *Science in Action: How to Follow Scientists and Engineers through Society.* Cambridge: Harvard University Press.

Marwick, Maxwell G. 1950. "Another Modern Anti-Witchcraft Movement in East Central Africa." *Africa* 20, no. 2:100–113.

Mesaki, Simeon. 1994. "Witch Killing in Sukumaland." In *Witchcraft in Contemporary Tanzania,* edited by Ray G. Abrahams, 47–60. Cambridge: African Studies Centre.

———. 2009. "Witchcraft and the Law in Tanzania." *International Journal of Sociology and Anthropology* 1, no. 8:132–138.

Moore, Henrietta L. and Todd Sanders. 2002. *Magical Interpretations, Material Realities: Modernity, Witchcraft and the Occult in Postcolonial Africa.* London: Routledge.

Parkin, David, ed. 1985a. *The Anthropology of Evil.* Oxford: Blackwell.

———. 1985b. "Entitling Evil: Muslims and Non-Muslims in Coastal Kenya." In *The Anthropology of Evil,* 224–243. Oxford: Blackwell.

———. 1985c. Introduction to *The Anthropology of Evil,* 1–26. Oxford: Blackwell.

Redmayne, Alison. 1970. "Chikanga: An African Diviner with an International Reputation." In *Witchcraft Confessions and Accusations,* edited by Mary Douglas, 103–128. London: Tavistock.

Richards, Audrey. 1935. "A Modern Movement of Witchfinders." *Africa: Journal of the International African Institute* 8, no. 4:448–461.

Shaw, Rosalind. 1997. "The Production of Witchcraft, Witchcraft as Production: Memory, Modernity and the Slave Trade in Sierra Leone." *American Ethnologist* 24, no. 4:856–876.

Strathern, Marilyn. 1985. "Discovering 'Social Control.'" *Journal of Law and Society* 12, no. 2:111–134.

Swantz, Marja-Liisa. 1990. *The Medicine Man among the Zaramo of Dar es Salaam*. Uppsala, Sweden: Nordic Africa Institute.

Van Beek, Walter E. A. 2007. "The Escalation of Witchcraft Accusations." In *Imagining Evil: Witchcraft Beliefs and Accusations in Contemporary Africa*, edited by Gerrie ter Haar, 293–316. Trenton, NJ: Africa World Press.

Willis, Roy G. 1968. "Kamcape: An Anti-sorcery Movement in South West Tanzania." *Africa* 38, no. 1:1–15.

———. 1985. "Do the Fipa Have a Word For It?" In *The Anthropology of Evil*, 209–223. Oxford: Blackwell.

18 TRANSATLANTIC PENTECOSTAL DEMONS IN MAPUTO

LINDA VAN DE KAMP

Regularly, Pentecostals summoned me to pray when we were on the street in Maputo, the capital of Mozambique.[1] They stressed that we needed to be aware of and protect ourselves against negative spiritual influences that were hiding everywhere. We had to keep our distance from what was happening around us as we first had to judge the intentions of people who approached us. Pentecostals could often tell me the exact moment when someone had approached them on the street or in a building and how afterward they had lost their job or their partner had disappeared because the person they had met had evil intentions. They tried to anticipate potential harm as far as possible. Brazilian Pentecostal pastors warned women of the men who turned up with an impressive car and nice presents and advised them to investigate the men's intentions first. At the same time, Pentecostals needed to be conscious of any prospective chances. Meeting people, be they potential partners or employers, could be the start of a successful project or life path. Thus praying and "walking in the Holy Spirit" was vital when considering these situations and challenging blockades.

A particular relationship has emerged between transnational Brazilian Pentecostalism and Maputo. In an edited volume by Glick Schiller and Çağlar (2010), the authors demonstrate the variation in how transnational activities restructure, (re)shape, and (re)imagine urban life. The role and influence of transnational connections depend on the mutual constitution of the national, local, and global and have a different impact in different cities within one country. Through Brazilian Pentecostalism, Mozambican Pentecostals are developing a new vision of Maputo's history and particularly the role of "evil" in it, in contrast to or reelaborating the views and positions of their grand/parents in this city in the past. The new ways in which they perceive and experience the urban space follows from their engagement in the Afro-Brazilian Pentecostal battle against evil.

A central entry point into to the activities of Brazilian Pentecostals in Africa is the relevance of Afro-Brazilian spiritual images and concepts, such as *macumba* (van de Kamp 2013). *Macumba,* which is a foreign word in Mozambique,[2] is a pejorative term in Brazilian Pentecostal jargon and is used to denounce Afro-Brazilian religions in Brazil as witchcraft or black magic.[3] In Africa, the Brazilian Pentecostal pastors label the work of traditional healers and people's connections with ancestor spirits as *macumba* too. Despite the differences with Afro-Brazilian religions and the variety of religious practices in Africa, the Brazilian pastors claim that in all these cases they are dealing with the same demonic powers. The Brazilian Pentecostals bridge the distance between both sides of the Atlantic by linking their histories within a particular spiritual framework as it evolved in the Lusophone transatlantic history (see also Sarró and Blanes 2009). In their perspective, Africa is the original home of "evil spirits" that still exist there, and they came to Brazil via the transatlantic slave trade. In the Pentecostal framework, Afro-Brazilian and African spirits are understood to be demons operating under the auspices of the Christian devil (see also Meyer 1999). In this chapter, I aim to examine how this Afro-Brazilian Pentecostal view of evil and accompanying practices appeal to followers of Brazilian Pentecostalism in the context of Maputo, by focusing on one particular transatlantic Afro-Brazilian spirit, the so-called spirit of *pombagira* or "spirit spouse."

TRANSATLANTIC PENTECOSTALISM IN MAPUTO

Brazilian Pentecostal churches have been established in Mozambique since the beginning of the 1990s, when Christianity started to boom immensely in this former Portuguese colony in Southern Africa after the end of a civil war and of a socialist era, and the start of the liberalization of the economic, political, and religious domains (Cruz e Silva 2003; Freston 2005).[4] The Brazilian churches can be placed in what has been referred to as a global "third wave" of Pentecostalism or neo-Pentecostalism that started in the 1970s and, despite encompassing a large variety of Pentecostals, can be identified by a strong focus on the spiritual battle (Anderson 2004, 144–165; Freston 1995). The neo-Pentecostal view of the world is one of a spiritual battlefield between demonic and heavenly forces meaning that religious traditions in Africa are despised as belonging to the dominion of the powers of darkness (Meyer 1998).

Today, Brazilian Pentecostal churches are integrated and prominent in the (semi)urban landscapes of Mozambique, particularly in Maputo, despite the critique they have been receiving on their aggressive approach toward "African culture" and on the centrality of tithes and large financial offerings.[5] The most significant Brazilian Pentecostal church in Mozambique is the Igreja Universal do Reino de Deus (Universal Church of the Kingdom of God, known as Universal Church). Currently, the Igreja Mundial do Poder de Deus (the World Church of the Power of God), which is led by a former bishop of the Universal Church, is expanding rapidly. Another prominent, albeit smaller, Brazilian neo-Pentecostal church in Mozambique is the Igreja Pentecostal Deus é Amor (The Pentecostal Church God is Love, known as God is Love) that was at the start of the neo-Pentecostal era in Brazil (Chesnut 1997). Several Pentecostal churches set up by Mozambicans maintain close ties with Brazil, such as the fast-growing Evangelho em Acção (Gospel in Action). These churches share the demonic discourse about "African traditions" and the use of concepts like *macumba*.

Non-Brazilian transnational Pentecostal churches mostly originate from South Africa or Zimbabwe and sometimes also from Malawi or Tanzania. Other churches come from outside the Southern African region, such as the Redeemed Christian Church of God that has its roots in Nigeria and the Ghanaian Lighthouse Chapel. Many of these non-Brazilian churches attracted expatriates, but few Mozambicans as English used to be the prevailing language. More importantly, these non-Brazilian Pentecostal churches lack the cultural and spiritual imagery that has developed in the transnational setting of the Brazilian churches. During my first fieldwork period of 2005–2007 in Mozambique, the Brazilian Pentecostal churches were almost all led by Brazilians and the assistant pastors were mostly Mozambican and a few were Angolan.[6] The Portuguese language and the countries' shared history as a result of Portuguese colonialism have facilitated the connection between Brazilians, Angolans, and Mozambicans. Consequently, the international network these churches in Mozambique enjoy is primarily Lusophone, with a key role being played by Brazil.

The circulation of cultural and spiritual imagery between Brazilian pastors and Mozambican converts is grounded in the Lusophone Atlantic. This is a particular space of historical, cultural, and religious production between Portugal, Brazil, and Africa that has been shaped by diverse colonial encounters (Naro, Sansi-Roca, and Treece 2007).[7] Whereas in the past, Christian missionaries embarked in Portuguese ports and crossed the oceans to evangelize the peoples in Africa and America, today missionaries from these former mission areas share the gospel in Portugal and other places in the world. The Brazilian

Pentecostal activities in Mozambique are an example of a new chapter in the history of the Lusophone Atlantic space of interaction and exchange (see also Sarró and Blanes 2009).

A clear example of the Pentecostal Lusophone Atlantic exchange is the understanding of *feitiçaria*, a synonym for *macumba* or witchcraft for Pentecostals. The Portuguese used the word *feitiço* to refer to amulets and all kinds of devotional objects. When Portuguese explorers arrived in West Africa, they called the amulets Africans used *feitiços* (Pollak-Eltz 1970, 37–38). Other explorers, such as the Dutch, English, and French, misinterpreted the origins of the word *feitiço* and saw it as an African thing, applying the word to everything related to African religions. For them, *fetissos* were not only magic charms but also African gods and their priests were the *fetisseros* (Sansi-Roca 2007, 27). The Portuguese *feitiço* became synonymous with African religion, which increasingly became framed as devilish and evil in the colonial encounter (see, e.g., Pietz: 1985, 1987, 1988). In Brazil, at the end of the nineteenth century, the word *feitiçaria* started to appear in relation to criminal acts. Policemen and judges persecuted people involved in magical and spiritual practices that were used for evil purposes and were called *feitiços.* Moreover, this use of *feitiço* referred to the supposed evils in Brazilian culture, namely the presence of "inferior" civilizations, essentially African cultures and Afro-Brazilian religions such as Candomblé and Macumba (Sansi-Roca 2007, 30).[8] Pentecostals still connect Afro-Brazilian cults to this "fetishism." Pentecostal pastors in Brazil preach against *feiticeiros,* the priests of the Afro-Brazilian religious cults. Likewise, they preach against *feitiçaria* in Mozambique, where they regard the traditional healers, the *curandeiros,* as *feiticeiros* and call their practices *macumba.* The use of *feitiçaria* by Pentecostal pastors resonates with a particular history of evil in Maputo, the subject to which I now turn.

A SHORT HISTORY OF PERCEPTIONS OF EVIL IN MAPUTO

In the early twentieth century, when the authorities of Portugal's New State tried to restore their influence in the colonies, the system of *Indigenato* was implemented in Mozambique, introducing a distinction between citizen and subject (Mamdani 1996) with two classes of people: the "native" (*indígena*) and the "nonnative" or "assimilated" (*não-indígena* or *assimilado*). The native was positioned under customary law and had to do forced labor (*chibalo*). The nonnative (Portuguese, Afro-Portuguese, Asians, and those of mixed race) had Portuguese citizenship rights, lived under civil law, and was not subjected to forced labor. A group of natives could obtain the status of *assimilado,* depending on their position and behavior, by applying for a certificate of assimilation but were accused of being "pocket whites," dark-skinned people who carried a document in their pocket that said they were white (Penvenne 1995, 9). The *Indigenato* created a bifurcated world where Africans were inferior to whites (Harris 1966), but at the same time these marked oppositions were conditional and were experienced differently by rural and urban residents, by men and women, depending on which group and class they belonged to (O'Laughlin 2000; Penvenne 1995) and the degree of Portuguese influence in their region.

The Portuguese founded their first settlements in northern Mozambique. But, when gold was discovered in South Africa, it led to fast-developing trade through the port of Lourenço Marques in the south. Lourenço Marques, which Maputo was called until independence in 1975, became the country's capital in 1896. The colonial authorities transformed the place into a city of whites and *assimilados*, a city for the "civilized" (Jenkins 2006; Lachartre 2000) and were subsequently unprepared for the growth of the city's population, especially from the 1950s onward when growing economic relations with South Africa and foreign industrial investment resulted in the city expanding rapidly. Increasing numbers of indigenous people came to the city to engage in wage labor, but they were ignored by the Portuguese settlers who denied them the right to reside there. From the start, Lourenço Marques was made up of two distinct parts: the Portuguese *cidade de cimento* (cement city) and the indigenous *cidade de caniço* (reed city) that surrounded the southern European-styled inner city.

Many Pentecostals belonged to or were connected to former *assimilado* families in Lourenço Marques. In order to get a recognized position in the colonial economy and society, the *assimilados* had to break with or had to act as if they had broken with *feitiçaria*, with "uncivilized" or evil practices such as customary marriage and rituals dedicated to the ancestors (see, e.g., Honwana 2002). In many cases, the great-grandparents or grandparents of these Pentecostals became also part of the Catholic and Protestant mission churches or started their own church (see also Cruz e Silva 2001; Helgesson 1994). For example, Dona Lucia,[9] aged sixty-three, and a member of the God is Love Church, narrated how her grandfather worked in the mines in South Africa and when he returned he started a church that he had got to know there.[10] Her grandfather agreed with her grandmother about raising their children as they wanted. "The customs my grandmother had lived with, she would do away with them," Dona Lucia said, "but, my father had several wives who brought along their traditions."[11] When I asked her about her grandparents wanting to break with local customs she only said: "There is a lot of *macumba*. There is so much *ma-*

cumba, and God saved me from it." Although it could be dangerous to speak about evil and there could exist a reluctance to speak about it with a European like me, more generally, secrecy and silence surrounded issues related to "the tradition" (*a tradição*).[12] Lundin (2007, 168–173), who writes about how people have negotiated transformations in Maputo, speaks about "social schizophrenia" because in one person there could be a denial and openness toward tradition, especially with regard to spiritual livelihoods. This gained particular features after independence.

Dona Lucia's children or the following generation were raised and educated during the socialist FRELIMO government that came into power after independence in 1975. As part of FRELIMO's modernizing project, traditional practices had to be discontinued. Polygamous relations, initiation rites, religious rituals, and the like were forbidden. Even if certain practices would still take place and people did not suddenly stop their cultural practices, they worked in the FRELIMO administration, engaged in the socialist modernizing ideals, and assumed new identities (Sumich 2010; Macamo 2005). For example, I met Pentecostals who could not speak a local language because their parents had not allowed their children to speak it when growing up, which was in line with the socialist project, and wanted them to learn the official language well. Now these children cannot communicate or do so poorly with the elders who are not used to speaking Portuguese and who always played a crucial role in educating younger generations about cultural traditions.[13]

The 1989 FRELIMO Party Congress officially decided to break with the party's Marxist-Leninist ideology and implement multiparty democracy. This happened after several years of a centrally planned economy and civil war that resulted in Mozambique's economy becoming bankrupt. From 1987 onward and under the auspices of the World Bank and the International Monetary Fund, the government implemented various structural adjustment programs and privatized government-financed industries and its social services. With the end of its socialist policies, FRELIMO also abandoned the rules against local culture and started a strategy of rehabilitating presocialist cultural elements. Today, government officials communicate that Mozambicans have to value their culture as a force for developing a prosperous nation. *Curandeiros* (traditional healers) receive more support, government officials use authentic Mozambican clothes, and traditional rituals take place at official state ceremonies. There is a revival of Mozambican identity and discussions about what it actually is.

There seems to be a "seemingly arbitrary circulation of the unknown" for many in African cities (Simone 2001, 17) in relation to traditional culture. During the colonial era, Mozambican *assimilados* had to break with *feitiçaria* and under the subsequent Marxist-Leninist FRELIMO regime, *feiticeiros* (traditional healers) were persecuted. Today, these healers have become part of the nation-state project but the current revitalization of *curandeiros'* power over good and evil spirits keeps the imagery of *feitiçaria* alive. Although members of the upper and middle classes rarely speak openly about their visits to *curandeiros,* they warn each other of the disastrous influences of *feiticeiros* everywhere, fearing that their material well-being will be the subject of *feitiçaria* practices. Numerous stories circulate of suspicious medicines put under people's chairs at work, in newly purchased cars, or at the doors of luxury houses. Women share their anxieties about the *feitiços* used by other women to win over the hearts of their husbands.

In this myriad of meanings of fetish, the city becomes the central arena. De Boeck and Plissart (2004) have shown how there is a visible and an invisible city in Kinshasa where, in addition to the physical and visible urban reality, there is an invisible immaterial architecture and infrastructure that contains people's desires, imaginations, actions, and spiritual realities. A city such as Kinshasa is thus difficult to domesticate and impossible to capture in one master narrative. De Boeck and Plissart (2004, 19) compare it with fetishes because it is a "constant border-crossing phenomenon, resisting fixture, refusing capture." The same is true for Maputo. People's imagery does not consist of a corpus of fixed representations, and a variety of imageries is continuously being mediated by television, Pentecostal pastors, traditional healers, and state officials. The extent to which one of these bodies is able to capture the city is central in the cultural contestation about what should be considered *feitiçaria* or evil, with the nation's capital being the crucial place for the development of a specific cultural identity. In the case of Pentecostals, their efforts to build the most prestigious buildings at central locations in Maputo have gained media attention, and the loud decibels produced during church services that can be heard across a vast area are all part of their attempt to incorporate the urban space (see van Dijk 2001; de Witte 2008). Meanwhile, new influences are constantly entering the urban space via migrants, television, the Internet, and tourists. As a result, no one specific body, such as the state or the church, controls the whole urban space and a web of plural meanings and social imagery is boosted.

Converts are a part of these processes. Like Dona Lucia, many Pentecostals grew up in an environment where *feitiçaria* was something one was not supposed to talk about because it was only "the uncivilized other" who dealt with such matters. However, because different forms and interpretations of *feitiçaria* are less silenced and more present in the public sphere, *feitiçaria* has come to play a new role in people's lives. I met converts who were confused about family members who started by saying that something that happened long ago had consequences for their lives. For the first time, they were hearing that certain incidents with spirits in the family may have been behind their failure to marry. To find out about the influence of the past in the present, they had to participate with their kin in sessions with a local healer. But often, these healing sessions had not helped them and they misunderstood what happened during a ritual they had to carry out. A young Pentecostal woman, Patricia (twenty-nine years old) explained how the *curandeiro* started to put something on her feet and that when she asked what it was all about, her family told her she should not ask questions. *Curandeiros* explained that sometimes they are incapable of helping their urban clients because they are too detached from the worldview and practices of the healers, which complicated their participation in the healing process.[14] In addition, modern, urban people find the rituals of local healers disgusting because the blood of animals is used and they find the circumstances unhygienic, preferring the clean white spaces of Pentecostal churches. In contrast to their families and local healers, Pentecostal pastors explained openly to Patricia and others what the practices in their family mean according to the Pentecostal view in a way that connects with their aspirations.

THE AFRO-BRAZILIAN PENTECOSTAL BATTLE
AGAINST THE SPIRIT OF *POMBAGIRA*

At the services I attended in the God is Love Church in Maputo, there was no permanent pastor and Brazilian pastors who were traveling around Africa came for a few days or weeks. At one Friday afternoon service,[15] a Brazilian pastor, who had just arrived from Nigeria, preached about Revelations 12, focusing on how God kicked the devil out of heaven and conquered all demons. He gave examples of how as a consequence various types of demons were wreaking havoc in the lives of persons in Brazil. He particularly elaborated the spirit of *pombagira* who "destroys marriages." He told the audience about how, just after his arrival in Maputo the previous day, he and his wife had received several women in the church office: "When I said Paz do Senhor [Peace of the Lord], they fell down on the doorstep and some vomited all sorts of things, it's all *macumba*. The spirits themselves say who they are, so I immediately knew what kind of spirit I was dealing with. . . . This spirit [of *pombagira*] blocks women's possibilities for marrying or they don't conceive or the husband leaves after a few years of marriage. Because this spirit is jealous and doesn't want you to have another man."

The term *pombagira* was principally used in the God is Love Church. In the Universal Church and the other churches, the term *marido da noite* (husband of the night) or *marido espiritual* (spiritual husband) was mainly used but the pastors there normally talked about cases related to Afro-Brazilian religions. In Afro-Brazilian imagery, *pombagira* is a spirit that personifies the ambiguities of femininity and female sexuality (Hayes 2008) and is known as the Mistress of the Night or the Lady of the Cemetery. The spirit is attractive and dangerous and can also be the spirit of a prostitute. Even though experiences of Mozambican Pentecostal women are not usually linked to prostitution, various women said that a related problem is that they are not able to control their own bodies or marry because they are involved with evil spiritual forces.

Rumors were circulating in Maputo about women who are being "eaten" by spirits. When I talked about marriage, people often asked: "Why is it that so many girls in one family who are beautiful and well-educated are not marrying?" To them, it was clear that spiritual issues were involved. Lowering their voices, as this was a dangerous and serious matter, they said that (grand)parents were selling their (grand)children to evil spirits through a *feiticeiro* to become rich. Pentecostal and non-Pentecostal women told me how their sexual and marital relations were frustrated by so-called spirit spouses. According to these women or their kin they were related to a spirit—with whom they could experience sexual intercourse—who would not allow the women to engage in another relationship. I encountered various explanations for this phenomenon.

One claimed that the spirit was a war spirit created from the spirit of a murdered person who seeks revenge and attacks the murderer's family with illness and misfortune. To calm the spirit, compensation for his death and his reintegration into society is needed, which could happen through marriage to a girl in the murderer's family. In this way, the spirit becomes the girl's spouse but the girl can later only marry another man if special procedures are being followed. *Curandeiros* identified these spirits as belonging to persons who were murdered during wars in the colonial era.[16] In addition to the ongoing impact of these historical spirits, worries about a new wave of spirits seeking vengeance as a result of the latest postindependence civil war (until 1992) have increased (see Igreja, Dias-Lambranca, and Richters 2008; Marlin 2001; Schuetze 2010, 126–152). The spirits of persons killed in the civil war are expected to seek revenge in the coming years. Now that soldiers who underwent cleansing rituals (Granjo 2007) are getting old and dying, spirits that were temporarily calmed by these rituals are expected to become active again because they are still seeking revenge. According to both *curandeiros* and Pentecostal pastors, there are active avenging spirits in every (extended) family.

Another account about the spirit spouse explains how, in the current neo-liberal economic order, (grand)parents are selling their children to spirits to become rich. The (grand)parents consult a *feiticeiro* (sorcerer) who, in return, is given a girl (because the spirit is male) to "feed" the strong spiritual powers the sorcerer uses to produce luck and wealth. In the Southern African region, this spirit spouse that "eats" human flesh refers to the spirit of persons who have been appropriated or killed for the benefit of another person. This generally involves accumulating wealth at the cost of others, which points to witchcraft (e.g., Bähre 2002; Fry 2000, 79, 80; Niehaus 1997; West 2005, 35–39).

The Brazilian pastor, who was not aware of all these specificities, but would have received some information about the circulating rumors through his Mozambican assistants, announced at the end of his sermon, during a special moment for revelations about the demons who were operating in the lives of the Mozambican persons in the audience: "There are several women who are not able to marry." Some women raised their hands and the pastor pointed to a few women to come forward and asked them if the problem was the spirit of *pombagira*. They nodded. He turned to the audience again and said to everyone to direct their hands toward the women and scream "*queima, queima, queima*" (burn, burn, burn) to drive the demon away.

APPROPRIATING A "FOREIGN" SPIRIT

While men could also be related to a spirit spouse, most cases involved women. Elsewhere I dealt with the gendered dimensions of this spiritual relationship (van de Kamp 2011) and here I principally focus on the attraction for these women of the Afro-Brazilian Pentecostal framing of the spirit. The majority of the Mozambican women who frequented Brazilian Pentecostal churches could be defined as being upwardly mobile. They were advancing or busy attempting to advance in economic and social standing as a consequence of the neoliberal economic reforms that were implemented at the end of the 1980s. These women were seeking and accessing resources that put them in new sociocultural domains. They were exploring new lifestyles and cultural positions. Many of them questioned traditions in their extended families, such as prevailing gender roles, as well as the links their kin could maintain with ancestor spirits and how these spirits were influencing their own lives. One group of women that attended Pentecostal church services knew or suspected that they were involved in a spiritual relationship. Others, however, were hearing from Brazilian pastors that certain incidents with spirits in their family may have been behind their failure to stay with their partner or marry. These mostly younger women had grown up with no clear notion of possible relations with ancestral spirits and learned about spiritual influences in their lives for the first time through the Brazilian Pentecostal churches (van de Kamp 2012). Often, these young women were the daughters of parents who had been part of *assimilado* families.

One of them is Yvon (aged twenty-three) who came forward during the service when the spirits of *pombagira* were expelled. Yvon was attending classes at a school for higher vocational education. She turned to the Universal Church when the father of her child had sent her back to her family's home. As her participation in this church had had no effect, she had changed to the God is Love Church where the pastors informed her about her relation with a spirit of *pombagira*. Yvon told me about nightly visits from the spirit, which was an important reason why her partner had separated from her as he had witnessed his wife behaving as if she was having sexual intercourse with the spirit. Since Yvon had started participating in the God is Love Church, the spirit had calmed down but had not completely left her. She had to train her body into a new mode by learning to stay filled with the Holy Spirit for which she followed the advice given by the pastor's assistants about praying and modes of behavior. She stressed that she was not afraid anymore of *feitiçaria* like she was in the past. Now she knew how to fight against it. Yvon learned from the pastors that she had become related to her spirit spouse because her parents and grandparents had offered her to the devil. When I was talking to Yvon about her spirit spouse, she asked me anxiously whether I thought that her grandmother or her father would have indeed done such a thing. I suggested talking to her father about these issues but she shook her head. This was not an option as her father was against spiritual practices and would be angry. While the Afro-Brazilian Pentecostal spirit of *pombagira* offered Yvon a framework for understanding her difficult situation, a framework to talk about it and for working on changing her life, Patricia is an example of a visitor of Pentecostal services who did not necessarily adopt the Afro-Brazilian Pentecostal spiritual discourse but found it interesting to explore.

Patricia and her friends initially just attended the services of the Universal Church out of curiosity, having heard that the Brazilians were entertaining, exorcized spirits, cured diseases, presented solutions for problems, and could make one rich. During the first years in Mozambique, the church held services in empty cinemas and the pastors' performances rapidly gained popularity. Services used to be a good option for an evening out as hardly any film was screened at cinemas in the early 1990s. After the long period of civil war when everything, including entertainment, had been scarce, new activities and diversions were welcomed and embraced. When I met Patricia in early 2006, she took the work of the Brazilian pastors more seriously than before as strange things were happening to her. She dreamed strangely and was often sick. Patricia was afraid that she would have to follow up her grandmother's work; her grandmother was a *curandeira*. Since her grandmother had died, nobody had yet been appointed to live and work with her grandmother's spirits. As all Patricia's sisters and most of her cousins were married, she thought she probably had to follow up her grandmother's work. "Does that mean that all my studying and working has been for nothing?" she asked me with fear.[17] Patricia hoped that her prayers in church would protect her from becoming part of the spiritual history of her family.

Patricia's kin considered her unmarried status at the age of twenty-nine as abnormal. To end suspicion about her and therefore her family, her kin organized sessions with a *curandeiro* to find out about the family spirits' wishes. But Patricia was not tuned into the views of her family. As was said earlier, Patricia asked the *curandeiro* who started to put something on her feet what it was all about, but her family told her she should not ask questions. The stories Patricia heard about women married to spirits and her own participation in a Pentecostal church put her kin's activities in a different light. Moreover, she wanted to stay in control of her own life. She studied, had a job, and was constructing her own house. She could be independent of her kin. At the same time, she did not want to disassociate from her relatives and was also worried about the fact that she wanted to find the appropriate life partner and have children. She questioned why she was not succeeding in doing so. Patricia did not immediately take a pro or contra position with regard to the spirit she could probably be related to. Her relatedness to as well as independence from her kin and her interest in the history of the spirits in her family next to the challenging views the pastors provided her with, offered a space from where she could reflect on her situation. Patricia continued to attend her family's sessions with the *curandeiro* and the services in church.

FINAL CONSIDERATIONS: BECOMING
A PENTECOSTAL "STRANGER"

The Afro-Brazilian Pentecostal discourse of *macumba* effectuated both a closeness toward and a distance from realities in Maputo in the lives of Pentecostals that seems to be crucial in creating and promising an alternative life. *Macumba* and *pombagira* connect to local realities, but by using these foreign terms in Mozambique, they also disconnect from that reality. The accounts of Yvon and Patricia offer insights into how this works in different ways in the lives of those who engage in Afro-Brazilian Pentecostalism. By being diagnosed as having a relationship with *pombagira,* the young woman Yvon in the God is Love Church found a new framework to address her situation that related to her experiences with the spirit spouse and her partner. The analysis by the Brazilian pastor offered her the means to perceive her situation from a new perspective and by "burning" the spirit through the power of the Holy Spirit she could foresee a new life to take shape. While she stressed that her eyes were opened to her family's spiritual bondages that were influencing her life negatively, this also forced her to rethink her relationship with her kin, particularly with her father and grandmother who were accused of *feitiçaria* by the Brazilian pastors, which is considered a grave allegation. For Patricia, these Afro-Brazilian Pentecostal claims went too far. She kept different explanations about her condition open and used the Afro-Brazilian Pentecostal spiritual alternative to reflect on her life as she also participated in family sessions with a *curandeiro.*

The Pentecostal transnational connection between Africa and Brazil that includes a shared history of "African spirits" is a medium for discovering and reflecting on the "dark powers" at work in Mozambique. Particularly fascinating is the fact that no precise translation of the (Afro-)Brazilian cosmology to the Mozambican one seems to be necessary. The Brazilian pastors are unfamiliar with the history of spirits in Mozambique, such as of the spirit spouse, and Mozambicans are unfamiliar with the meaning and role of the spirit of *pombagira* in Brazil. The power of the Afro-Brazilian transnational translation is based on a superficial knowledge of the kind of spirits at work. To establish a connection between Brazilian pastors and Mozambican converts, it is important that pastors show that they know the tricks of the devil who uses local beliefs and relations to do his work. At the same time, it is necessary to have a distant position to evil. The less one knows, the more foreign one can be(come), and one can thus break more easily with devilish ties. While the pastor in the God is Love Church was not familiar with the histories and realities of the spirit spouse in Mozambique, he demonstrated that he is able to discern the real nature of these spirits anyway. Wherever he was, demons revealed themselves. He discovered the work of the devil in Mozambique within a day of arriving and to further demonstrate his transnational power over demons, he used examples from Nigeria, where he had just been: "I was in Nigeria. I have never seen so many *macumba*!, more than in Mozambique. They perform rituals where mothers give their children away to a demon in return for money! But, after driving a big car for some months, they become *louca* [crazy]."[18]

More generally, healers in Mozambican society stressed in their advertisements their experiences in other countries: using foreign knowledge seemed to prove the efficacy of their healing techniques and medicines. Popular healers, pastors, and prophets often appear to come from the other side of a border (Luedke and West 2006). Healers are frequently ambivalent beings at the cutting edge of societal structures. Healers can cross socially accepted boundaries as this gives them the power to heal. They possess spiritual powers that allow them to cross dangerous boundaries, boundaries that are too perilous for others to cross, but who they can guide to transform their lives.[19]

Brazilian pastors, coming from far away, are perceived as particularly powerful healers by Pentecostal followers. Yet here the transformation the Brazilian Pentecostals effectuate primarily results in a person becoming a stranger in the local environment rather than an "insider" in a strange reality (Werbner 1989, 223; van Dijk 1997). The latter was the case for the regional cults that have emerged in a context of labor migration in Southern Africa. They have had an important function in reorganizing sociocultural and spiritual lives and in providing a home for migrants who were strangers far away from home (see, e.g., van Binsbergen 1981). Instead, in the transnational movement of Afro-Brazilian Pentecostalism in Mozambique, the call for a break with evil forces shows religion as a producer of an alternative place (van de Kamp and van Dijk 2010). The pastors continuously demonstrate that they operate from a distinctive Pentecostal space and it is from that alternative and also superior position that they are able to discover the work of the devil everywhere: in Brazil, in Nigeria, and in Mozambique within a day of arriving. Brazilian pastors claim that in all these cases and wherever they are, they deal with the same *macumba* powers.

Upwardly mobile women, in particular, appropriate the Afro-Brazilian Pentecostal discourse and practices in their attempts to reshape their relationships, albeit in different ways. Through their development of new sociocultural lifestyles, including studying at university or schools of higher vocational education, they question the "secret" role of spiritual relationships in a city where spiritual livelihoods used to be silenced and have been contested. Where some people welcome the new national focus on tradition, others continue to stress its evil features that they see as the root of all problems in Mozambican society. The clearest expression of this latter standpoint is heard in Pentecostal churches where members forcefully reject national cultural politics. Both the Mozambican government (and related civil-society organizations) and the Pentecostal churches are thus engaged in a process of restyling aspects of Mozambican culture, but in different and even opposing ways: the Mozambican government is "civilizing" local healing, while Pentecostals stress its "uncivilized," evil features. People engaging in the Afro-Brazilian Pentecostal discourses are searching and creating alternative spaces in the city that provide opportunities to explore new possibilities and cultural positions, although they may generate new contestations, such as in the case of the relationship between Yvon and her kin. Through Afro-Brazilian Pentecostalism, various citizens of Maputo are interacting with the current possibilities in the visible and invisible city, shaping new meanings of fetish.

NOTES

I gratefully acknowledge the financial support of the Netherlands Organisation for Scientific Research, the Free University University in Amsterdam, and the African Studies Centre, Leiden, which enabled me to carry out the research on which this chapter is based.

 1. I did ethnographic research about the growth of Brazilian Pentecostalism in Mozambique between August 2005 and August 2007, and I returned to the field in July and August 2008 and July and August 2011. My main fieldwork location was Maputo where most of the Brazilian Pentecostal churches are based.

 2. Although a similar word in the Tsonga languages in southern Mozambique refers to the spirits (thanks to Elísio Macamo for this information), Pentecostals considered it as a Brazilian Pentecostal term and appropriated it in that way.

 3. There is no agreement in the literature on the linguistic origins of the term *macumba* and what it exactly denotes. Hayes (2007, 287) explained, "Some scholars linked 'macumba' to a Bantu language and a certain type of percussive musical instrument. Given the centrality of percussion in African and African-derived religions, this may account for the use of the term in reference to the ritual practices of Bantu-speaking slaves and their descendants, who were especially prominent in Rio de Janeiro from the late eighteenth to the mid-nineteenth century. Others associated the term with communities of runaway slaves" (2007, 286). According to the Brazilian Houaiss dictionary, *macumba* is a designation by laymen of Afro-Brazilian cults in general.

 4. In the last census of 2007, for the first time, Evangelicals and Pentecostals were counted together as one separate category, showing their growing importance. According to this census, 11 percent of the total population is Pentecostal (INE 2010) and 21 percent of the population is in Maputo City (INE 2009).

 5. Over the years, critical articles have been published in Mozambican journals: "*Multinacional, Comerciante da Fé, Parasite de Deus ou Profeta de Espírito?*" (*Savana*, October 7, 1994); "*Acção da IURD em Moçambique*" (*Notícias*, April 8, 1997); "*Desactivada Rede Criminosa na Igreja Universal*" (*Magazine Independente*, May 9, 2007); and see also "*Igreja Brasileira Multada por Violação da Lei Laboral*" (*Diário de Notícias*, June 6, 2011).

 6. This seems to be changing, among other things under the pressure of the Mozambican government who wants foreign churches to employ local pastors.

 7. Naro, Sansi-Roca, and Treece (2007, 8) criticize the idea of a "Lusotropicalism" as proposed by Gilberto Freyre, as an idea of an "all-encompassing, culturally specific and transhistorical Portuguese colonial project." They propose the Lusophone Black Atlantic as a space of historical and cultural production to demonstrate how the historical continuities across this historical space are composed of a myriad of local and specific

discontinuities, local cultures and "perspectival refractions" (ibid.) that extend their influence well beyond the Lusophone context.

8. For more on the current ambiguous presence of Afro-Brazilian religion in Brazil and issues of multicultural heritage see, for example, van de Port (2007).

9. *Dona* is Portuguese for "madam." The names I use are fictive.

10. Since the second half of the nineteenth century, labor migration to South Africa became an attractive option for young men in southern Mozambique (Harries 1994).

11. Conversation, November 21, 2006. The conversations and interviews used in this contribution were carried out in Portuguese and the translations are mine.

12. People often use the word *tradição* when referring to local customs, including beliefs and rituals related to (ancestral) spirits.

13. For more on this complex history of cultural identity, see among others Bertelsen (2003), Honwana (2002), Meneses (2006), O'Laughlin (2000), Sousa Santos and Trindade (2003), and West (2005).

14. Interviews with *curandeiros* on November 15, 2006, and February 8 and 28, 2007.

15. The service was held on March 2, 2007.

16. The *curandeiros* I spoke to in southern Mozambique date this as a practice from the nineteenth century when major social changes were taking place in Southern Africa as a result of the migration of Nguni groups (*Mfecane*). A special role was played by King Ngungunyane, who was from one of the Nguni groups that established the Gaza Empire in southern Mozambique. King Ngungunyane (1884–1895) was known for the violent wars he fought against Portuguese colonial oppression and his attempts to incorporate groups from other parts of the country, like the Ndau of central Mozambique, into his kingdom (Liesegang 1986). Since the Ndau were murdered and enslaved against their will and some of the dead Ndau bodies were not properly buried, they came to get revenge in Nguni and Tsonga families by *mupfuka;* the spirit of the dead person could resuscitate and seek rehabilitation and reintegration (see also Honwana 2003, 71–74; Langa 1992, 29–32, 43–46).

17. Conversation, October 29, 2006.

18. Up to this point, he did not seem to realize that these practices were also happening in Mozambique.

19. Various healing rituals, such as cleansing rituals after the civil war in Mozambique, are about crossing boundaries and moving from a polluted position to a pure one, see, for example, Granjo (2007). The insights on healing and crossing boundaries relate to the longer anthropological tradition of studying liminality (Turner 1967; van Gennep 1980 [1960]).

REFERENCES

Anderson, Allan. 2004. *An Introduction to Pentecostalism: Global Charismatic Christianity.* Cambridge: Cambridge University Press.

Bähre, Erik. 2002. "Witchcraft and the Exchange of Sex, Blood, and Money among Africans in Cape Town, South Africa." *Journal of Religion in Africa* 32:300–334.

Bertelsen, Bjørn Enge. 2003. "'The Traditional Lion Is Dead': The Ambivalent Presence of Tradition and the Relation between Politics and Violence in Mozambique." *Lusotopie* 2003:263–281.

Chesnut, Andrew. 1997. *Born Again in Brazil: The Pentecostal Boom and the Pathogens of Poverty.* New Brunswick, NJ: Rutgers University Press.

Cruz e Silva, Teresa. 2001. *Protestant Churches and the Formation of Political Consciousness in Southern Mozambique (1930–1974).* Basel, Switzerland: Schlettwein Publishing.

———. 2003. "Mozambique." In *Les Nouveaux Conquérants de la Foi. L'Église Universelle du Royaume de Dieu (Brésil),* edited by André Corten, Jean-Pierre Dozon, and Ari Pedro Oro, 109–117. Paris: Karthala.

De Boeck, Philip, and Marie-Frangoise Plissart. 2004. *Kinshasa: Tales of the Invisible City.* Amsterdam: Royal Museum for Central Africa, Ludion and Vlaams Architectuurinstituut.

De Witte, Marleen. 2008. "Accra's Sounds and Sacred Spaces." *International Journal of Urban and Regional Research* 32:690–709.

Freston, Paul. 1995. "Pentecostalism in Brazil: A Brief History." *Religion* 25:119–133.

———. 2005. "The Universal Church of the Kingdom of God: A Brazilian Church Finds Success in Southern Africa." *Journal of Religion in Africa* 35:33–65.

Fry, Peter. 2000. "O Espírito Santo contra o Feitiço e os Espíritos Revoltados: 'Civilização' e 'Tradição' em Moçambique." *Mana* 6:65–95.

Glick Schiller, Nina, and Ayse Çağlar, eds. 2010. *Locating Migration: Rescaling Cities and Migrants.* Ithaca: Cornell University Press.

Granjo, Paulo. 2007. "The Homecomer: Postwar Cleansing Rituals in Mozambique." *Armed Forces and Society* 33:382–395.

Harries, Patrick. 1994. *Work, Culture, and Identity: Migrant Laborers in Mozambique and South Africa, c. 1860–1910.* Portsmouth, NH: Heinemann.

Harris, Marvin. 1966. "Race, Conflict and Reform in Mozambique." In *The Transformation of East Africa: Studies in Political Anthropology,* edited by Stanley Diamond and Fred G. Burke, 157–183. New York: Basic Books.

Hayes, Kelly E. 2007. "Black Magic and the Academy: Macumba and Afro-Brazilian 'Orthodoxies.'" *History of Religions* 47:283–315.

———. 2008. "Wicked Women and Femmes Fatales; Gender, Power and Pomba Gira in Brazil." *History of Religions* 48:1–21.

Helgesson, Alf. 1994. *Church, State, and People in Mozambique: An Historical Study with Special Emphasis on Methodist Developments in the Inhambane Region.* Uppsala, Sweden: Swedish Institute of Missionary Research.

Honwana, Alcinda M. 2002. *Espíritos Vivos, Tradições Modernas. Possessão de Espíritos e Reintegração Social Pós-Guerra no Sul de Moçambique.* Maputo, Mozambique: Promédia.

———. 2003. "Undying Past: Spirit Possession and the Memory of War in Southern Mozambique." *Magic and Modernity: Interfaces of Revelation and Concealment,* edited by Birgit Meyer and Peter Pels, 60–80. Stanford, CA: Stanford University Press.

Igreja, Victor, Béatrice Dias-Lambranca, and Annemiek Richters. 2008. "Gamba Spirits, Gender Relations and Healing in Post-Civil War Gorongosa, Mozambique." *Journal of the Royal Anthropological Institute* 14:353–371.

Instituto Nacional de Estatística (INE). 2009. *Sinopse dos Resultados Definitivos do 3o Recenseamento Geral da População e Habitação—Cidade de Maputo.* Maputo, Mozambique: Instituto Nacional de Estatística.

————. 2010. *III Recenseamento Geral da População e Habitação 2007, Resultados Definitivos, Moçambique.* Maputo, Mozambique: Instituto Nacional de Estatística.

Jenkins, Paul. 2006. "Image of the City in Mozambique: Civilization, Parasite, Engine of Growth or Place of Opportunity?" In *African Urban Economies: Viability, Vitality or Vitiation?,* edited by Deborah Fahy Bryceson and Deborah Potts, 107–130. New York: Palgrave Macmillan.

Lachartre, Brigitte. 2000. *Enjeux Urbains au Mozambique: De Lourenço Marquès à Maputo.* Paris: Karthala.

Langa, Adriano. 1992. *Questões Cristãs à Religião Tradicional Africana, Moçambique.* Braga, Portugal: Editorial Franciscana.

Liesegang, Gerhard J. 1986. *Ngungunyane: A Figura de Ngungunyane Nqumayo, Rei de Gaza 1884–1895 e o Desaparecimento do seu Estado.* Colecção Embondeiro 8. Maputo, Mozambique: ARPAC.

Luedke, Tracy, and Harry West, eds. 2006. *Borders and Healers: Brokering Therapeutic Resources in Southeast Africa.* Bloomington: Indiana University Press.

Lundin, Iraê Baptista. 2007. *Negotiating Transformation: Urban Livelihoods in Maputo Adapting to Thirty Years of Political and Economic Changes.* Gothenburg, Sweden: Department of Human and Economic Geography, School of Business, Economics and Law, University of Gothenburg.

Macamo, Elísio S. 2005. "Denying Modernity: The Regulation of Native Labour in Colonial Mozambique and its Postcolonial Aftermath." In *Negotiating Modernity: Africa's Ambivalent Experience,* edited by Elísio Salvado Macamo, 67–97. London: Zed Books; Dakar, Senegal: Codesria Books; Pretoria: University of South Africa Press.

Mamdani, Mahmood. 1996. *Citizen and Subject: Contemporary Africa and the Legacy of Late Colonialism.* Princeton, NJ: Princeton University Press; Oxford: James Currey.

Marlin, Robert P. 2001. "Possessing the Past: Legacies of Violence and Reproductive Illness in Central Mozambique." PhD diss., Rudgers University.

Meneses, Maria Paula. 2006. "Traditional Authorities in Mozambique: Between Legitimisation and Legitimacy." In *The Shade of New Leaves: Governance in Traditional Authority: A Southern African Perspective,* edited by Manfred Hinz and Helgard K. Patemann, 93–120. Berlin: Lit Verlag.

Meyer, Birgit. 1998. "'Make a Complete Break with the Past': Memory and Postcolonial Modernity in Ghanaian Pentecostal Discourse." *Journal of Religion in Africa* 28:316–349.

————. 1999. *Translating the Devil. Religion and Modernity among the Ewe in Ghana.* Edinburgh: Edinburgh University Press for the International African Institute.

Naro, Nancy Priscilla, Roger Sansi-Roca, and David H. Treece, eds. 2007. *Cultures of the Lusophone Black Atlantic.* New York: Palgrave Macmillan.

Niehaus, Isak. 1997. "'A Witch Has No Horn': The Subjective Reality of Witchcraft in the South African Lowveld." *African Studies* 56:251–278.

O'Laughlin, M. Bridget. 2000. "Class and the Customary: the Ambiguous Legacy of the 'Indigenato' in Mozambique." *African Affairs* 99:5–42.

Penvenne, Jeanne Marie. 1995. *African Workers and Colonial Racism: Mozambican Strategies and Struggles in Lourenço Marques, 1877–1962.* Portsmouth, NH: Heinemann; London: James Currey; Johannesburg: Witwatersrand University Press.

Pietz, William. 1985. "The Problem of the Fetish, Part I." *Res: Anthropology and Aesthetics* 9:5–17.

———. 1987. "The Problem of the Fetish, Part II." *Res: Anthropology and Aesthetics* 13:23–45.

———. 1988. "The Problem of the Fetish, Part IIIa." *Res: Anthropology and Aesthetics* 16:105–123.

Pollak-Eltz, Angelina. 1970. *Afro-Amerikaanse Godsdiensten en Culten*. Roermond, The Netherlands: Romen.

Sansi-Roca, Roger. 2007. "The Fetish in the Lusophone Atlantic." In *Cultures of the Lusophone Black Atlantic*, edited by Nancy Priscilla Naro, Roger Sansi-Roca, and David H. Treece, 19–39. New York: Palgrave Macmillan.

Sarró, Ramon, and Ruy Blanes. 2009. "Prophetic Diasporas: Moving Religion across the Lusophone Atlantic." *African Diaspora: A Journal of Transnational Africa in a Global World* 2:52–72.

Schuetze, Christy. 2010. "The World is Upside Down: Women's Participation in Religious Movements and the Search for Social Healing in Central Mozambique." PhD diss., University of Pennsylvania.

Simone, AbdouMaliq. 2001. "On the Worlding of African Cities." *African Studies Review* 44:15–41.

Sousa Santos, Boaventura de, and João Carlos Trindade, eds. 2003. *Conflito e Transformação Social: Uma Paisagem das Justiças em Moçambique*. 2 vols. Porto, Portugal: Edições Afrontamento..

Sumich, Jason. 2010. *Nationalism, Urban Poverty and Identity in Maputo, Mozambique*. Working Paper 68. London: London School of Economics: Crises States Research Centre.

Turner, Victor. 1967. *The Forest of Symbols: Aspects of Ndembu Ritual*. Ithaca, NY: Cornell University Press.

Van Binsbergen, Wim. 1981. *Religious Change in Zambia: Exploratory Studies*. London: Kegan Paul International.

Van de Kamp, Linda. 2011. "Converting the Spirit Spouse: The Violent Transformation of the Pentecostal Female Body in Maputo, Mozambique." *Ethnos* 76:510–533.

———. 2012. "Afro-Brazilian Pentecostal Re-formations of Relationships across Two Generations of Mozambican Women." *Journal of Religion in Africa* 42:433–542.

———. 2013. "South-South Transnational Spaces of Conquest: Afro-Brazilian Pentecostalism, *Feitiçaria* and the Reproductive Domain in Urban Mozambique." *Exchange: A Journal of Missiological and Ecumenical Research* 42:343–365.

Van de Kamp, Linda, and Rijk van Dijk. 2010. "Pentecostals Moving South-South: Brazilian and Ghanaian Transnationalism in Southern Africa." In *Religion Crossing Boundaries: Transnational Dynamics in Africa and the New African Diasporic Religions*, edited by Afe Adogame and James Spickard, 123–142. Leiden, the Netherlands: Brill.

Van de Port, Mattijs. 2007. "Bahian White: the Dispersion of Candomblé Imagery in the Public Sphere of Bahia." *Material Religion* 3:242–273.

Van Dijk, Rijk. 2001. "Contesting Silence: the Ban on Drumming and the Musical Politics of Pentecostalism in Ghana." *Ghana Studies* 4:31–64.

———. 1997. "From Camp to Encompassment: Discourses of Transsubjectivity in the Ghanaian Pentecostal Diaspora." *Journal of Religion in Africa* 27:135–159.

Van Gennep, Anton. 1980 [1960]. *The Rites of Passage*. London: Routledge and Kegan Paul.

Werbner, Richard. 1989. *Ritual Passage, Sacred Journey: The Process and Organization of Religious Movement*. Washington, DC: Smithsonian Institution Press; Manchester: Manchester University Press.

West, Harry G. 2005. *Kupilikula. Governance and the Invisible Realm in Mozambique*. Chicago: Chicago University Press.

19 THE MEANING OF "APARTHEID" AND THE EPISTEMOLOGY OF EVIL

ADAM ASHFORTH

RAW NERVES

In May 2012, the former president of South Africa was interviewed on CNN by Christiane Amanpour and asked to repudiate apartheid as "morally indefensible." Despite having played the central role in dismantling apartheid, he could only do this, he replied, in a "qualified" way: "I don't apologize for saying that what drove me as a young man, before I decided we need to embrace a new vision, was a quest to bring justice for black South Africans in a way which would not—that's what I believed then—destroy the justice to which my people were entitled," de Klerk said the previous week on CNN. "My people, whose self-determination (was) taken away by colonial power in the Anglo-Boer War" (Burke 2012). South Africa's new ruling elite greeted de Klerk's reflections on the ideals of his youth with outrage. The former state president was quickly forced to retreat into claims his comments had been taken out of context. More than two decades after its demise, evidently, anything less than a full-throated condemnation of apartheid as evil is still taboo in South Africa.

De Klerk's 2012 interview contained nothing new. In his 1996 submission to South Africa's Truth and Reconciliation Commission (TRC) on behalf of the former ruling National Party (NP), he also presented apartheid as a well-intentioned policy that, perhaps unfortunately, failed. Of the men who devised the policy he testified: "Within the context of their time, circumstances and convictions they were good and honourable men—although history has subsequently shown that, as far as the policy of apartheid was concerned, they were deeply mistaken in the course upon which they embarked" (de Klerk 1996, 2). In de Klerk's official submission to the TRC, the harm that was done by the apartheid regime was portrayed as largely inadvertent—the unforeseen consequences of honorable individuals acting on laudable motives, or the work of a few "bad apples" for which the leadership could not be held responsible other than in a general sort of way. For these failings, the former state president apologized. And while he acknowledged that "abuses" became more widespread in the later years of NP rule, as resistance to apartheid intensified, he presented these as the product of a failure of command rather than the expression of a deliberate and evil—"morally reprehensible"—program.

The African National Congress (ANC), on the other hand has always presented a radically different interpretation of the past that stresses malicious racist motivations for apartheid. In their submission to the TRC in 1996, for example, the ANC stated: "Apartheid oppression and repression were therefore not an aberration of a well-intentioned undertaking that went horribly wrong. Neither were they, as we were later told, an attempt to stave off the 'evil of communism.' The ideological underpinning and the programme of apartheid constituted a deliberate and systematic mission of a ruling clique that saw itself as the champion of a 'super-race'" (African National Congress 1996,4). Apartheid, in short, was a crime—deliberate and systematic. Because of its institutionalizing of racial oppression, moreover, apartheid was a crime against humanity, as the United Nations decreed in 1966 (Dugard n.d.). Indeed, by the 1980s, during what we now know to have been the waning days of apartheid, critics of apartheid were unanimous in denouncing the evil inherent in the "system." In his speech at his investiture as chancellor of the University of the Western Cape in May 1988, for example, Archbishop Desmond Tutu preached: "apartheid is 'so utterly evil, immoral, unbiblical and unchristian that it can only be compared with that equally evil system—Nazism'" (Crary 1988). Judging by their response to the TRC report, it seems the vast majority of black South Africans still agree (van der Merwe and Chapman 2008,209).

This essay examines various ways of construing the meaning of "apartheid" and judging the ethical content of the term. It also explores some aspects of the interpretation of the evil nature of apartheid state power from the perspective of everyday life in Soweto in the early 1990s, drawing on several years of fieldwork in the township at that time (See Ashforth 2000, 2005). Understanding how the attribution of evil to the apartheid state operated in the dying days of apartheid might help us better understand why maintaining the sanctity of that label remains so important to so many people in the present.

APARTHEID: THE BIOGRAPHY OF A WORD

The word *apartheid* was first used to express the desire of Afrikaner national-ists in the 1930s, still smarting from their defeat by the armies of the British Empire at the turn of the century, to imagine a world in which their nation could survive and thrive (Giliomee 2009; Moodie 1975). Most of the early na-tionalist dreamers were clerics and scholars—sober, earnest, and no doubt, to quote de Klerk, "honourable." Some, as J. M. Coetzee has pointed out of Geof-frey Cronje, were more than a little crazy (Coetzee 1991). Their cogitations were for a long time marginal to the central political debates of the time concerning what was called the "Native Question," or the modes, means, and justifications for governing Africans (Ashforth 1990). Two decades were to pass before the term became part of Afrikaner nationalist political orthodoxy and the ruling ideology of a governing party.

One of the most difficult things to appreciate about *apartheid* as a doctrine, given the history of NP rule in South Africa after 1948, is that it was not—in essence, or, at least, not entirely—a species of *racial* thought. This is not to say that the founding fathers of the doctrine were not racists personally, or that the effects of the doctrine involved racial oppression, or, indeed, that the final purpose of the apartheid ideology as implemented by the NP was to ensure the continuation of a political structure of racial domination within the South African state. Rather, it is to emphasize that the core principles of the doctrine were not premised on concepts of race, but rather precepts of cultural nation-alism with Christian roots in Calvinist theology, "scientific" foundations in German anthropology, and political links to European nationalisms (Giliomee 2003; Greenfeld 1995; Penny and Bunzl 2003).

The basic underpinning of the apartheid idea is a version of a broader nineteenth- and twentieth-century narrative of the origin of nations. It went something like this: following an unfortunate incident on a building site in Babel (reported in the Bible in Genesis 11:5–8), God decided to scatter His peo-ple across the world and divide them into separate groups speaking different languages. These groups, as anthropological science of *volkekunde* teaches, are known as "cultures," or "*volk.*" Being creations of God, these separate and dis-tinct cultures are each entitled to exist and to flourish in their God-given forms according to their God-given designs. In order to do so, each culture must of necessity have its own homeland, a place where the members of the culture can live together without outside interference and express themselves in the full-ness of their being. Over time, as the history of Europe shows, distinct cultures develop to a point where they become self-aware, conscious of their existence as

distinct "nations." At this point, they become entitled to the right of self-determination; they have earned the right to their own state. All cultures, given time
and propitious circumstances, should be able to develop in a similar fashion.
Until all cultures reach the point of national self-determination, however, it is
incumbent upon the stronger and more developed cultures, nations, to guide
and protect the weaker and less developed, to assist them in their God-given
paths so as to allow them to develop along their own lines according to God's
divine plan. Amen.

Embraced by Afrikaner intellectuals, this nationalist narrative was expressed in the language of apartheid. It is not difficult to imagine how it might
have seemed attractive to idealistic young Afrikaners such as de Klerk—or, for
that matter, the later critic of apartheid Frederick van zyl Slabbert (van zyl Slabbert 1985, 85). Indeed, framed in this way, I have yet to find an American under-
graduate who can object to this divine scheme—no doubt from reluctance to
challenge biblical verities. In the South African context, anyone imbued with a
sense of the destiny of the Afrikaner nation—forged as it was in the crucible of
resistance to imperialist domination—could not help but notice that within the
territory of the Union of South Africa, created by that war against the Boers,
there seemed to be a number of African populations that could be deemed distinct "cultures," each with its own language and customs, which, given access
to a secure homeland, could one day develop into self-governing nations. In
English, the idea was translated as "separate development." Seeing the world in
this way, to be sure, was helped enormously by the influence of a thoroughly
misleading historiography purveyed by Afrikaner nationalists that taught that
the region was settled by "Bantu tribes" moving down from the north into un-
occupied lands at more or less the same time as white settlers arriving from the
south (Thompson 1962).

The elaboration of the principles of apartheid, in theory and practice, took
several decades. From the currency of a small group of intellectuals in the
1930s, the idea of apartheid by the late 1940s became the electoral slogan of the
NP (Herenigde Nasionale Party), articulated at length in the 1948 Sauer Report
(Herenigde Nasionale Party 1948). When the NP, unexpectedly and narrowly,
won election to office in that year, they proclaimed this strange new word as
their guiding principle, though in fact it contained only a vague outline of a
policy of radical segregation. Shortly after winning office, the NP government
commissioned a major study, the Tomlinson Commission (Commission for the
Socio-Economic Development of the Bantu Areas Within the Union of South
1955), to flesh out the details of their policy of separate development with a view
to creating the impression of a grand plan for government (Ashforth 1990).

From the start of NP rule, however, it was clear that the commitment to the "development" part of separate development was half-hearted at best.[1] The key recommendations of the Tomlinson Commission, fanciful as they were, were ignored.

Though the practical effect of the apartheid ideology on NP governance resulted more in an intensification of existing practices of racial domination than in a grand vision of separate development in the region, there were radical differences between the principles of apartheid and those enshrined in the original scheme for governing "Natives" within the state created under the auspices of the British Empire in the first decade of the twentieth century as the Union of South Africa. These differences hinged on the conception of the relation between African polities, their subjects, and the territories still occupied by them at the end of the nineteenth century. Whereas the apartheid scheme conceived of African polities and their associated territories, remnants as they were of the long history of conquest, as deriving from the nature of cultures, the British framed the relation in the language of empire, with a quasi-imperial regional state (the Union) recognizing the rights of "Native Tribes" with political sovereignty over distinct territories whose inhabitants had been ruled by "chiefs" since "time immemorial" (Ashforth 1990, chap. 2).

The imperial scheme established under British auspices, however, contained a central contradiction. For, according to the precepts of nineteenth-century British imperialism, citizenship was to be open, in principle, to all "civilized" men. In theory, then, over time as Africans attained the levels of education and property ownership deemed indicative of "civilization"—as many were—citizenship would have had to have been opened to the growing urban African population in South African cities. Various fixes for this contradiction were proffered in the second quarter of the century, notably those enshrined in the Stallard Commission's formulation that towns were the "white man's creation" wherein natives belonged only insofar, and for so long, as they "ministered unto the needs of the white man"—the rest being "surplus" and thus liable to removal to their putative rural homes (Ashforth 1990; Davenport 1976; Province of the Transvaal 1921). By the middle of the century, the absurdity of this conception was becoming all too evident in the face of massive urbanization of African workers and the steady growth of an educated, property-owning African middle class. The commitment of white voters to a political order enshrining their sense of racial superiority, however, remained unshakable. Various ad hoc solutions to what was termed "influx" were proposed, notably that of the Fagan Commission in 1947, but none provided the simplicity and elegance of the apartheid formula's resolution of the African citizenship conundrum, to wit: remove the possibility of Africans attaining full citizenship and relegate their political communities to remote "Homelands" in the name of national self-determination and separate development. That urban African elites and middle-class aspirants to full citizenship did not embrace this formulation with the same ardor as young Afrikaner idealists such as de Klerk is not surprising. That black South Africans did not universally share their dissatisfaction until several decades after the apartheid era began is a fact not generally heralded in the current era of African nationalist triumph.

By the late 1950s, the NP government began to look like it was getting serious about separate development, promulgating as it did legislation such as the Promotion of Bantu Self-Government Act (1959), which laid out a putative scheme to transform "native reserves" into self-governing homelands. Critics at the time, however, were quick to point out that these so-called homelands were being provided with nowhere near the resources necessary to turn the nationalist dream into reality. Nonetheless, substantial investments in physical and administrative infrastructure were made in the former reserves in the following decades, leaving a significant legacy in the present regional configuration of the postapartheid constitution with the provinces, such as Eastern Cape, having the largest territories of former homelands remaining significantly poorer and less developed than the more metropolitan and formerly "white" demarcated areas of the country.

Apartheid, then, was conceived in the language of postwar anti-imperial nationalism. By the time African nationalists across the continent began securing places at the helm of independent states, however, the term had become identified with racial domination in the manner of colonial regimes. In the international arena, independent India led the way in vilifying the apartheid regime in South Africa. In time, the antiapartheid movement became a global social movement, perhaps the first in world history (Skinner 2010; Thörn 2006). In tandem with the civil rights movement in the United States, campaigns against apartheid in the 1960s and 1970s succeeded in making "racial discrimination" (a deeply flawed description of the situation in South Africa) and "white supremacy" a uniquely illegitimate business, cementing a commitment to antiracism into the foundation of what it means to be a civilized human being. When apartheid officially ended, with the first fully inclusive election in the country's history, many saw the moment as the symbolic end of five hundred years of European imperialism in Africa.

Today, the term *apartheid* has come to stand for any and all forms of social separation and exclusion. Even where race is not at issue, to call something apartheid is to label it as a form of evil. The word has acquired a semantic solid-ity that carries a guaranteed weight of opprobrium. It simplifies and focuses moral judgment, clarifies political battle lines, and precludes dispassionate analysis of the issue at hand. Link the word *apartheid* with the word *Israel* or *Zionism,* for example, as former president Jimmy Carter has done, and observe the reaction (Carter 2006).

MORALITY AND APARTHEID

How should the ethical complexion of apartheid be judged in relation to the history of the south of Africa?

The answer to this question hinges on what the term *apartheid* is applied to. This is not always obvious and is worth clarifying. If we consider the wide range of discourse on the subject of apartheid over what is now almost a century of usage, five general referents of the term emerge: First, it has been used to describe a political ideal, a vision of a possible future in which different cultures can flourish in their own territories while coexisting with each other as independent entities. Second, it describes a doctrine, a set of principles guiding, or proposing to guide, the actions of government with a view to achieving the ideal outlined in the previous section. Third, it has been used to describe a policy, or set of policies, intended—or, at least, prescribed—to achieve in practice the ends specified by the idea. Fourth, it is the name of an ideology, a more or less consistent set of ideas and principles used to justify state policy and motivate political action in line with the specified ideals. Finally, it has been used to name a "system" and a "regime," both of which were said to be "evil." Needless to say, the term can also be applied to a whole era of South African history—in which case, ethics need not apply. Given these various points of reference, judgments about the morality of apartheid will involve different factors depending on the particular matter the term is applied to.

In the first instance, stated as an ideal, there is surely nothing inherently immoral about the idea of apartheid. As we have seen, it can be articulated as a vision of national freedom and human flourishing—a vision divinely ordained, for that matter—to which few in the postimperial age could object. In the past half-century or so, where the term *apartheid* stands for the arbitrary separation, by virtue of race or ethnicity, of populations that would otherwise be united in a singular national entity, the ideal stands for a uniquely illegitimate form of political order.

Questions about morality, however, inevitably creep into view when the matter at hand concerns apartheid as a political doctrine. For the apartheid vision of cultural and national separation could only have been legitimate if it were to have been embraced by all who were to become subject to it—or, at least, a solid majority of those people. Yet, as elaborated in the years prior to 1948 and subsequently, the doctrine of apartheid gave little weight to the obligation of its advocates to secure the consent of those whom they governed. The oft-repeated claims of regime leaders that they were not in fact governing the homelands and that the homelands were not, properly considered, part of the South African state (and, therefore, that their "citizens" were not really South Africans), obviating thereby the need to secure consent of the governed, were always more than a little disingenuous. Moreover, as the subsequent practice of the NP in government made clear, the doctrine of apartheid was designed to be imposed on all subject to it, regardless of their views about how they wished to be governed or, for that matter, to govern themselves.

A common defense of the policy of apartheid of the sort de Klerk was alluding to in his CNN interview was that it was more about carving out a space of self-determination for the Afrikaner nation than imposing a vision of a political future on Africans. (After all, their destiny was to "develop along their own lines" into self-governing nations.) Another common assertion on the part of apartheid's defenders prior to 1990, though rendered increasingly implausible in the years following the Soweto Uprising of 1976 as antiapartheid resistance grew, was that the cooperation of African leaders in the homelands was tantamount to consent. Neither of these assertions was plausible. The first failed because English-speaking white South Africans were from the start admitted to the nation as full citizens simply because of their race, while "coloreds" and "Indians" were later admitted to the political fold, albeit on a second- and third-tier basis. The second argument failed, too, because by no means all of the leaders who were constrained to govern homelands during the time of apartheid, notably Mangosuthu Buthelezi in Kwa-Zulu, acceded to the policy—at least according to them.

Viewed retrospectively, then, ethical judgment of apartheid as a policy, or set of policies, requires assessment of the consequences of efforts to implement it. At the start of the apartheid era, these ethical and political judgments were made prospectively in terms of future possibilities. As the mounting toll of human suffering became increasingly evident, however, both as a result of what might be called "positive" efforts by the state to implement the policy by means of programs such as "Group Areas," "Separate Amenities," and "Black Spot" removals (population relocation), as well as "negative" efforts to repress dissent, doubts about its morality grew even among the former true believers. In the final decade of the apartheid era, few defenders of the regime invoked the original vision of national separation, resorting rather to the putative imperative of resisting the spread of Communism in Africa. By the end of the era, in fact, even staunch former believers in the vision, such as de Klerk, sought to distance themselves from responsibility for its effects.

Ultimately, judgment of the morality of the policy of apartheid depends on an assessment of motives. If the policy, as de Klerk argued, had in fact been a well-intentioned mistake, it would surely be legitimate to leaven the accounting of suffering caused with references to benefits bestowed. Similarly, if the putative benefits turned out to be substantial and lasting, there might be reason to diminish the reckoning of pain suffered. However, if the intentions behind the policy are adjudged malicious—such as the promotion of white supremacy—no amount of benefit enjoyed could outweigh the harm inflicted. Not surprisingly, people who still remember the suffering and struggles of the apartheid era tend to find the insistence of people like de Klerk that apartheid was not all bad somewhat galling.

This brings us to the fourth dimension of the term *apartheid*: ideology. Here the key question is whether or not the noble vision, with its high ideals, was genuinely motivating the people involved in implementing the policy—from those at the highest realms of the state administration to the lowly voter who supported them. If the ideology was merely a mask for ulterior motives resulting in widespread suffering, the whole enterprise can only be judged immoral. Judgment of the morality of an ideology, however, cannot be divorced from assessment of its impact in practice—which, after all, distinguishes it from a mere vision or set of ideals. Four broad possible interpretations of apartheid ideology present themselves, which I shall rank here in ascending order of opprobrium: it was a noble vision that was inadequately implemented; it was a noble vision that turned out to be mistaken by virtue of the unwarranted suffering imposed in its implementation and, later, continuation after the noble goal was lost; it was, from the start, a cynical exercise in political legitimation for a system of racial domination serving a variety of vested interests; it was a deliberate program to exploit and oppress the black masses in the interests of white supremacy. None of these points of view can be sustained merely by reference to historical evidence. They all derive from prior political commitments.

Finally, when *apartheid* is used as a term describing a "system," how might its ethical character be evaluated? The word *system* refers to a set of components integrated into a single whole for the purpose of processing inputs into outputs. Outputs on systems created by humans are spoken of as "purposes." To refer to apartheid as a system, then, is to have made a decision—either explicitly or implicitly—about the purpose, or purposes, of the system. In practice, people who referred, and still refer, to the "apartheid system" were critics who argued that the fundamental purpose of the system was racial domination involving the oppression of blacks by whites, usually said to be connected with the related purpose of creating and sustaining economic power and wealth for whites. Proponents of apartheid in the years of NP rule, on the other hand, did not refer to a system, preferring instead the anodyne term *policy*. Talk of the apartheid system, then, particularly in the waning decades of NP rule and since, was not merely a dispassionate assessment of the cumulative impact of policies and ideologies. Rather, it was a mode of invoking a class of moral judgments to inform political practice.

Description of apartheid as a system of racial oppression, however, does not obviate all ethical considerations for it leaves the question: who was responsible for the system? For which, the obvious answer is: the whites. But such an answer would not only ignore the obvious fact that not all whites were actively supportive of, or responsible for, apartheid policies, but the reasoning of such an answer embodies the same sort of racial logic that was the grounds for opposing apartheid in the first place. Most leaders, activists, and ordinary opponents of apartheid were thus careful to distinguish between the moralities, or rather immorality, of the system and that of whites in general as a social category. No one doubted the system was evil; few insisted that all white people were. Even when the category "white" was disaggregated, as it commonly was, into "Afrikaner" (or, more commonly, and unflatteringly, in popular discourse, "Boer") and "English," each of which manifesting stereotypical racist tendencies of their own, a categorical denunciation was typically avoided. As a white man living in the black township of Soweto during the last years of the apartheid era, albeit one belonging to that other social category "white-from-overseas," I can testify not only to the importance of this distinction about moral responsibility in practice but also its rootedness in everyday life.

While the meaning of the term *apartheid* can be anatomized in clinical fashion, as in the preceding discussion, in everyday political discourse during the years known as those of "the Struggle," the nature of the evil that was the system was generally construed as a rather more complex phenomenon. For to name evil is to identify power, the power to cause harm, and the attribution of evil to a political system is not independent of the modes of attributing evil to the other powers that shape the fortunes of everyday existence. When these powers are also invisible, epistemological problems proliferate.

ON THE EVERYDAY EPISTEMOLOGY OF EVIL:
A VIEW FROM SOWETO

In my book *Witchcraft, Violence, and Democracy in South Africa* (2005), I argue that everyday "habits of interpreting power . . . put a premium on divining the true agencies behind the appearance of misfortune" in ways that contributed to the creation of a sense that the "apartheid system" was the source of virtually every kind of misfortune that could afflict black people (Ashforth 2005) The "evil" of the apartheid system, in this sense, was more than just an ethical judgment about the consequences of policies, but the naming of a source of power. Here, drawing on a further decade of fieldwork experience in South Africa and elsewhere in Africa, I want to explore again the question of how evil is construed in the context of everyday relations among human persons where life is lived in a world with witches. For, in such places evil cannot be understood independently of the putative capacities of persons to cause harm to others by mysterious means named, generically, "witchcraft."

Witchcraft, as we have been reminded countless times since Evans-Pritchard's famous formulation, is a way of making sense of "misfortune" that is a "function of personal relations" (1937). Use of the term *misfortune* in this context, however, is unfortunate for the term in English is redolent of mishap, chance, and bad luck. Yet, as Evans-Pritchard makes clear in his ethnographic discussions, it is precisely because people do *not* accept an element of fortune, chance, or luck in their sufferings that they readily attribute their suffering to malicious actions by others. A better formulation, in my view, would emphasize a predisposition to experience suffering as a form of harm deliberately inflicted by another person, or persons, for malicious motives. I would also argue that once the possibility of malicious harmful action by mysterious means, such as those spoken of as witchcraft, is accepted, this predisposition to treat suffering as harm is not only rational, but inevitable.

At the heart of discourses on witchcraft is a distinction between being and action. Being a witch is one thing; performing witchcraft is another. Sometimes this distinction is rendered in terms of "witchcraft" vis-à-vis "sorcery," though this language can be misleading because it tends to imply a distinction based on modes of action (typically based on using material substances as opposed to inherent powers) rather than between being and action. It is better, in my view, to think of the witch as a distinct kind of person—both superhuman and subhuman—which is given over entirely to evil, relinquishing claims to the community of humankind. Witchcraft—malicious, violent, action involving mysterious invisible powers of a sort we might term "supernatural"—on the other hand, can be perpetrated by anyone with the means and the motive, not just the witch. The fundamental predicate of all narratives about witchcraft is that it is perpetrated in secret by means mysterious and invisible, at least to those uninitiated in the arts of witchcraft and antiwitchcraft.

For those who know themselves not to be witches (which is pretty much everyone I have met in Africa over the past three decades), but who nonetheless consider themselves to be living in a world with witches (which is pretty much everyone), the practice of everyday life poses distinct problems. Principal among these is what I call the *epistemological double bind:* because anyone can perpetrate witchcraft, and because the witch will always hide his or her real motives, you cannot know who is the witch; and, because only the witch knows of what he is capable, you cannot know what harm is *impossible* for them to cause, so you must protect against everything. From this follows the *presumption of malice:* because you know they can harm you by mysterious unknowable means, you must presume that they will—this despite appearances to the contrary or explicit denials.

How might this structure of interpretation have shaped modes of interpreting the nature of power in relation to the "apartheid system?"

WHEN A PEOPLE'S SUFFERING IS HARM: POLITICAL DISCOURSE AT APARTHEID'S END

Until the last decade of the twentieth century, black people in South Africa were subjected to a steadily increasing burden of oppressive unjust rule imposed by often arbitrary and corrupt officials. From 1952 to 1986, for example, when pass laws required all Africans over the age of sixteen to carry documentation of their legal status at all time, a whole population was presumed to be in breach of the law unless they could prove otherwise. For most black people in the apartheid era, their primary experience of state power came from negotiating the labyrinthine regulations of the pass laws and "influx control system" regulating where they could live and how they could move. In urban areas, particularly after the Second World War, the townships were similarly spaces of harsh policing, while also places called home. Being exposed to the pass laws and township regulations—not to mention the liquor laws, which also criminalized millions of Africans—was to know a power that was at once systematic and arbitrary, material and mysterious. Rights of residence in urban areas, moreover, were not in fact rights but categories of exemption from a blanket prohibition on African settlement in towns and cities. Proving your entitlement meant accumulating papers and permits, finding the right office where officials would process your claims, and carrying documentation at all times. At the end of the day, however, despite all the laws, rules, and regulations, your fate depended on the whims of an official who might be harsh and unbending, or friendly and understanding, or—more often than the literature on the pass system reflects—open to a little financial inducement to "make a plan."

Despite its oppressive and racist character and the often arbitrary or corrupt behavior of its officials, the South African state was always a lawful, if not legitimate, state. For the most part, those who acted in the name of the state were authorized to do so by laws passed in the legislature following public debate and their actions were subject to judicial scrutiny. Africans had little say in the shape of these laws. Indeed, for most of the century, the head of state had virtually unlimited legislative, administrative, and judicial power—granted by law (the Native Administration Act of 1927)—over those classified as "native," "Bantu," and, eventually, "black." African populations within South Africa, and it is important to stress the plural here because not all populations were subjugated in the same way, were subjected to extensive regulation by virtue of administrative fiat, whether by officials operating under the auspices of the erstwhile Native Affairs Department, local officials managing townships and hostels, and the police. From an African perspective, then, unknown officials in distant offices made rules, unseen by and unaccountable to those subject to them. African subjection by officials of the white-dominated state, moreover, was coordinated with private authorities in farms, mines, homes, factories, and other places of employment and residence—which were also mostly white. In the final decade and a half of white rule, furthermore, a number of secretive agencies were established to maintain state security in the face of mounting, and increasingly violent, African resistance. No wonder, then, that the whole seemed like a vast and oppressive system, the very name of suffering in general. It took time, however, before a conviction emerged in everyday contexts that would attribute the generalized suffering of African people to the harm inflicted by the apartheid system—a connection that insufficient time has elapsed to decouple.

When I arrived in Soweto in 1990, at the tail end of the apartheid era, young political activists spoke of the "system" or the "regime" as an all-encompassing field of suffering. But this suffering was not merely misfortune in the sense of a random mishap or accident of fate. No, suffering was harm—deliberately inflicted. An individual's pain and the nation's oppression both had the same cause: apartheid. When activists—and virtually everyone in those days was an activist—spoke in terms of agency, of the motive force behind the evil regime, they referred to "the Government." The government, however, was an entity distinct from its material manifestations in the figure of the president and his men (and they were mostly men). Certainly, the "Comrades" in Soweto, as they styled themselves, recognized there was a public face to this power they named the government. But the real source of the power encapsulated in the word was essentially invisible, hidden from view: secret. For example, the men who were the public face of the government ceaselessly proclaimed that they governed in the interests of all, that they knew what the best interests of the black majority were, and that they had the support of those whom they governed. Everyone knew this was a lie. When they said: "we must protect our country against Communism," most black people heard "Communists are for the people" and cheered. If an activist died, from whatever manifest cause, no one would doubt that the government was ultimately responsible. Or, as in the last years of NP rule when the threat of HIV and AIDS became apparent, and officials announced that condoms would be provided free of charge to protect against HIV, people heard a clear message: the government wants to keep the black birthrate down to ensure white supremacy. Given the presumption of malicious motives, then, and the self-evident fact of secrecy, it was hard to say of the government: this they cannot do.

Indeed, the entity "the Government" in some respects resembled an invisible being, with whom, when one entered the life of politics or the struggle, one became locked in a life-or-death contest. Knowledge of the nature of this entity was secret, inaccessible to all but those who had gone over to the other side— "sellouts"—and they were not telling what they knew. Its actions could only be discerned in retrospect, from an accounting of the harms inflicted. And suffering was interpreted as harm. The real power of the idea of "the Government," it seemed to me in those early days of the transition to democracy, derived from its being the name of the ultimate effective cause of suffering. That is to say, because whites—either as individuals or as a social category—could not be held to blame for the apartheid system, the government and, by extension, all who supported it, became the agent responsible.

POLITICS OF BLAME IN THE POST-ANTI-APARTHEID ERA

Although less than half of the current population of the country was alive when apartheid came to an end (Statistics South Africa 2011), much is still at stake in accounting for the evil that was apartheid. Even at the highest levels of government, passionate debates rage about the legacy of apartheid in the present. On April 2, 2013, for example, Trevor Manuel, minister in the presidency of South Africa, admonished a summit meeting of civil servants about the lack of service delivery and told them it was time for the ANC in government to take responsibility for its failings: "We [government] should no longer say it's apartheid's fault," he is reported as saying, referring particularly to failings in the education sector (SAPA 2013). President Zuma lost no time in slapping him down. A week later, addressing a commemoration of the assassination of Communist Party leader Chris Hani, Zuma announced: "To suggest we cannot blame apartheid for what is happening in our country now, I think is a mistake to say the least" (Dodds, Seale, and SAPA, 2013). President Zuma is right, to say the least. It would be a mistake for the ANC to relinquish the right to blame apartheid for the problems of the present. For if those who are still suffering began to ask *Why?* without being able to place the blame somewhere other than on the governments of the ANC—local, provincial, and national—the consequences for the ruling party would probably be disastrous.

Today, when the question of the meaning of apartheid arises, it frequently ignites a political firestorm over who is to blame for the continuing misery of the multitudes that were expected to thrive after its demise. The conflagration is intensified, moreover, by the contributions to the politics of blame by disaffected white people who seem increasingly inclined to voice their disapproval of the current regime in starkly racist terms, particularly in the relatively anonymous confines of the Internet.[2]

In the past, however, particularly in the later years of NP rule, identifying the nature of the evil that was apartheid was a matter not merely of vilifying a political opponent, but of analyzing power. Naming the "apartheid system" as "evil," such as in Tutu's speech quoted earlier, was to identify a fundamental feature of the power that oppressed the black majority of South Africa, with very real consequences both for everyday life as well as the struggle for freedom. To suggest that apartheid was not in fact a deliberate program of maliciously inspired racism is tantamount to saying it was not evil. To deny the evil would be tantamount to denying that the suffering caused was not maliciously inflicted harm. And to deny that suffering is harm is tantamount to denying that it is suffering. The meaning of *apartheid,* then, is far from academic.

NOTES

1. Although young idealists like de Klerk might not have noticed this at the time, it was not lost on the chairman of the commission charged with figuring out how to make apartheid work. I interviewed Professor F. R. Tomlinson in 1981, some quarter of a century after presenting his report, and he was still viscerally angry with Dr. Hendrik Verwoerd, the former minister of Native Affairs (later prime minister) who commissioned his report. Tomlinson told me how, after laboring for four years on their report, bringing the best scientific knowledge to bear on the problem, they presented their work

to Verwoerd. The *Report,* of which he was still evidently proud, consisted of seventeen volumes with detailed assessments of every "Bantu Area" in the Union. Verwoerd, however, dismissed the proud authors of the report with disdain, ordering them to produce a one-volume summary. At that point, Tomlinson told me, they knew the government was not serious about development but merely wanted a document they could use for political propaganda.

2. For examples, see the comment section of any online news article published in South Africa headlining the name "Zuma."

REFERENCES

African National Congress. 1996. *Statement to the Truth and Reconciliation Commission.* http://www.anc.org.za/ancdocs/misc/trctoc.html.

Ashforth, Adam. 1990. *The Politics of Official Discourse in Twentieth-Century South Africa* Oxford: Oxford University Press.

———. 2000. *Madumo, a Man Bewitched.* Chicago: University of Chicago Press.

———. 2005. *Witchcraft, Violence, and Democracy in South Africa.* Chicago: University of Chicago Press.

Burke, Samuel. 2012. "Under Fire, South Africa's Former President Repudiates Apartheid." Atlanta: Cable News Network. Text and video, May 17. http://www.cnn.com /2012/05/16/world/africa/south-africa-de-klerk/.

Carter, Jimmy. 2006. *Palestine: Peace Not Apartheid.* New York: Simon and Schuster.

Coetzee, John M. 1991. "The Mind of Apartheid—Cronje, Geoffrey, (1907–)." *Social Dynamics—A Journal of the Centre for African Studies University of Cape Town* 17, no. 1:1–35.

Commission for the Socio-Economic Development of the Bantu Areas within the Union of South Africa. 1955. *Summary of the Report of the Commission for the Socio-Economic Development of the Bantu Areas within the Union of South Africa.* Pretoria, South Africa: Union of South Africa. (Also known as *Tomlinson Report.*)

Crary, David. 1988. "Tutu Says Evil of Apartheid Can Only Be Likened to Nazism." Associated Press newspaper report. http://www.apnewsarchive.com/1988/Tutu -Says-Evil-of-Apartheid-Can-Only-Be-Likened-To-Nazism/id-a00b2040d437a27 b872be86a69d4d5cc.

Davenport, Thomas R. H. 1976. "The Triumph of Colonel Stallard: The Transformation of the Natives (Urban Areas) Act between 1923 and 1937." *South African Historical Journal* 16, no. 2:77–89.

De Klerk, Frederik W. 1996. "Submission to the Truth and Reconciliation Commission by Mr F. W. de Klerk, Leader of the National Party." http://www.justice.gov.za/trc /hrvtrans/submit/np_truth.htm.

Dodds, C., L. Seale, and South African Press Association. 2013. "We CAN Blame Apartheid, Says Zuma." *The Star,* April 11. http://www.iol.co.za/news/politics/we-can -blame-apartheid-says-zuma-1.1498541#.VN5fAsaATVt.

Dugard, John. n.d. "Convention on the Suppression and Punishment of the Crime of Apartheid." Retrieved April 18, 2012. United Nations. http://legal.un.org/avl/ha /cspca/cspca.html.

Evans-Pritchard, Edward E. 1937. *Witchcraft Oracles and Magic among the Azande.* Oxford: Clarendon Press.

Giliomee, Hermann. 2003. "The Making of the Apartheid Plan, 1929–1948." *Journal of Southern African Studies* 29, no. 2:373–392.

———. 2009. *The Afrikaners: Biography of a People.* Charlottesville: University of Virginia Press; Cape Town, South Africa: Tafelberg.

Greenfeld, Liah. 1995. *Nationalism: Five Roads to Modernity.* Cambridge: Harvard University Press.

Herenigde Nasionale Party. 1948. *Verslag van die Kleurvraagstuk-Kommissie van die Herenigde Nasionale Party.* Pretoria, South Africa: Herenigde Nasionale Party. (Also known as *Sauer Report.*)

Moodie, T. D. 1975. *The Rise of Afrikanerdom: Power, Apartheid, and the Afrikaner Civil Religion.* Berkeley: University of California Press.

Penny, H. Glen, and Matti Bunzl. 2003. *Worldly Provincialism: German Anthropology in the Age of Empire.* Ann Arbor: University of Michigan Press.

Province of the Transvaal. Local Government Commission. 1921. *Report of the Local Government Commission 1921.* Pretoria, South Africa: Province of the Transvaal. (Also known as the Stallard Commission.)

Skinner, Rob. 2010. *The Foundations of Anti-apartheid: Liberal Humanitarians and Transnational Activists in Britain and the United States, c. 1919–64.* Houndmills, UK: Palgrave Macmillan.

South African Press Association. 2013. "Stop Blaming Apartheid says Manuel." *The Star*, April 3. http://www.iol.co.za/news/politics/stop-blaming-apartheid-says-manuel -1.1495041—.UWbrFYIzLfY.

Statistics South Africa. 2011. *Mid-Year Population Estimates 2011 Statistical Release.* Pretoria, South Africa: Statistics South Africa.

Thompson, Leonard M. 1962. "Afrikaner Nationalist Historiography and the Policy of Apartheid." *Journal of African History* 3, no. 1:125–141.

Thörn, Håkan. 2006. "Solidarity across Borders: The Transnational Anti-Apartheid Movement." *Voluntas: International Journal of Voluntary and Nonprofit Organizations* 17, no. 4:285–301.

Van der Merwe, Hugo, and Audrey R. Chapman. 2008. *Truth and Reconciliation in South Africa: Did the TRC Deliver.* Philadelphia: University of Pennsylvania Press.

Van zyl Slabbert, Frederick. 1985. *The Last White Parliament.* London: Sidgwick and Jackson.

LIST OF CONTRIBUTORS
AND AFFILIATIONS

Adam Ashforth	University of Michigan
Jennie E. Burnet	University of Louisville
Diane Ciekawy	Ohio University
René Devisch	Leuven University
Roy Dilley	University of St. Andrews
Léocadie Ekoué	Association Ahuefa, Pantin, France
Maia Green	University of Manchester
Dorothy L. Hodgson	Rutgers University
Jok Madut Jok	Loyola Marymount University
Kjersti Larsen	University of Oslo
Wyatt MacGaffey	Haverford College
Lotte Meinert	Aarhus University, Denmark
Julaina Obika	Gulu University, Uganda
William C. Olsen	Georgetown University
David Parkin	School of Oriental and African Studies, London
Susan J. Rasmussen	University of Houston
Judy Rosenthal	University of Michigan–Flint
Nancy Scheper-Hughes	University of California–Berkeley
Sónia Silva	Skidmore College
Ulrika Trovalla	Nordiska Afrikainstitutet
Walter E. A. van Beek	Tilburg University
Linda van de Kamp	University of Amsterdam
Susan Reynolds Whyte	University of Copenhagen

INDEX

CPSIA information can be obtained at www.ICGtesting.com
Printed in the USA
LVOW06s2122040116

469073LV00002B/106/P